Navigating Intellectual Property Challenges in Tourism

Ahmad Albattat
Management and Science University, Malaysia

Marco Valeri
Niccolò Cusano University, Italy

Norhidayah Azman
Management and Science University, Malaysia

Zunirah Mohd Talib
Management and Science University, Malaysia

Pankaj Kumar Tyagi
Chandigarh University, India

IGI Global
Publishing Tomorrow's Research Today

Vice President of Editorial	Melissa Wagner
Managing Editor of Acquisitions	Mikaela Felty
Managing Editor of Book Development	Jocelynn Hessler
Production Manager	Mike Brehm
Cover Design	Phillip Shickler

Published in the United States of America by
IGI Global Scientific Publishing
701 East Chocolate Avenue
Hershey, PA, 17033, USA
Tel: 717-533-8845
Fax: 717-533-8661
Website: https://www.igi-global.com E-mail: cust@igi-global.com

Library of Congress Cataloging-in-Publication Data

Names: Albattat, Ahmad, 1973- editor. | Norhidayah, Azman, 1987- editor. | Valeri, Marco, editor. | Talib, Zunirah Mohd, 1966- editor. | Tyagi, Pankaj Kumar, 1979- editor.
Title: Navigating intellectual property challenges in tourism / edited by Ahmad Albattat, Azman Norhidayah, Marco Valeri, Zunirah Mohd Talib, Pankaj Tyagi.
Description: Hershey, PA : IGI Global Scientific Publishing, [2025] | Includes bibliographical references and index. | Summary: "The insights offered in this book are not just theoretical but are grounded in practical applications that can significantly enhance the effectiveness and competitiveness of tourism enterprises. As the industry navigates its recovery and growth, the strategic use of intellectual property will be crucial in shaping its future"-- Provided by publisher.
Identifiers: LCCN 2024053069 (print) | LCCN 2024053070 (ebook) | ISBN 9798369341711 (h/c) | ISBN 9798369351796 (s/c) | ISBN 9798369341728 (ebook)
Subjects: LCSH: Tourism--Law and legislation. | Hospitality industry--Law and legislation. | Intellectual property--Law and legislation. | Patent laws and legislation. | Trademarks--Law and elgislation. | Intellectual property--Data processing. | Copyright--Electronic information resources. | Patents--Electronic information resources. | Entrepreneurship.
Classification: LCC K3974.T6 N38 2025 (print) | LCC K3974.T6 (ebook) | DDC 346.04/8--dc23/eng/20250123
LC record available at https://lccn.loc.gov/2024053069
LC ebook record available at https://lccn.loc.gov/2024053070

British Cataloguing in Publication Data
A Cataloguing in Publication record for this book is available from the British Library.

Table of Contents

Detailed Table of Contents

Tourism marketing relies more on licensing and collaboration for brand expansion and market penetration. In this chapter, licensing and collaboration in the tourism industry are shown to boost growth and innovation. Tourism brands can expand their reach by licensing their intellectual property to third parties, increasing revenue and brand visibility. Collaboration between businesses, governments, and local communities promotes resource sharing and innovation, improving marketing campaigns and visitor experiences. It discusses the pros and cons of these strategies, including the need for clear agreements, risk management, and partner goal alignment. It also discusses digital licensing, sustainability, and how technology will shape future strategies. Tourism brands can use licensing and collaboration to complement their strengths, create unique offerings, and gain a competitive edge. The chapter explains how these strategies can be used to navigate the changing tourism landscape through case studies and practical insights.

This chapter's purpose is to perform an analysis of the importance of these approaches in order to study the relevance of collaborative marketing strategies in the process of increasing tea tourism through the usage of both local and extended networks. This will be accomplished by conducting an investigation into the significance of these techniques. Because of this, it will be feasible to analyze the relevance of the several solutions that are offered. Integrated marketing programs that connect local tea farmers, tourism boards, and foreign partners are growing increasingly in demand as the need for initiatives of this sort continues to rise. foreign partners are also becoming increasingly important. The level of competition among these programs is gradually growing. In particular, this necessity is becoming an increasingly significant phenomena, particularly in light of the fact that tea tourism is continuing to acquire extra appeal from time to time.

Trademarks are vital elements of tourism that empower the industry by enabling destination differentiation, branding, and identification. This chapter evaluates trademarks' influence on tourism while focusing on the current non-traditional trademarks trend. In the tourism context, non-traditional trademarks comprise sensory features that create emotions, memories, and sensory experiences. This chapter examines how trademarks shape tourists' perceptions and decisions and improve their experiences. This research also studies how traditional trademarks, such as logos and slogans, have diversified to incorporate non-traditional features as sensory experiences and marketing gain popularity. This chapter will further investigate the legal and organizational implications of non-traditional trademarks. This chapter concludes by discussing the possibilities and risks associated with non-traditional trademarks in promoting or maintaining sustainable destination development and cultural signifiers.

The tourist industry of the twenty-first century has been shaped by significant trends that are affected by advancements in technology and innovative marketing strategies. Gastronomy tourism is one among them. The objective of this research is to discover the factors that impact the expansion of astronomy tourism, with the goal of predicting the factors that determine the availability of resources for global marketing efforts. An effective approach to categorizing food items can be achieved by considering the geographic sources of a particular gourmet cuisine. Consequently, the increasing reliance and utilization of "geographical indicators" (GIs) may encompass unique characteristics associated with a particular location or differentiating attributes derived from the history, culture, and folklore of a given geographic region. This study examines the economic significance and impact of geographical indication (GI) indicators on gourmet tourism, as well as the utilization of GI as a novel branding technique.

This chapter explores the pivotal role of Geographical Indications (GIs) in advancing tourism development and enhancing destination branding. This review aims to investigate how GIs can be strategically utilized to boost tourism and create distinctive brand identities for destinations. It also examines how GIs contribute to destination branding by defining branding concepts, exploring branding strategies that incorporate GIs, and reviewing successful campaigns. Challenges and considerations related to authenticity, commercialization, and maintaining the integrity of GIs are also discussed. Additionally, the chapter evaluates the economic, social, and cultural impacts of GIs on local communities. Leveraging GIs offers a powerful approach to enriching tourism experiences and strengthening regional identities, with significant implications for both local economies and cultural heritage.

Geographical indicators (GIs) promote tourism by highlighting regional characteristics and local product cultural significance. This chapter looks at Indian tourism marketing with GIs. Indian GIs like Darjeeling Tea, Kanjeevaram Silk, and Basmati Rice are defined, important, and statused. The chapter discusses how GIs promote regional identity and attract tourists seeking authentic, place-based experiences. It examines how GIs can boost destination branding, product differentiation, and sustainable tourism. This chapter discusses successful tourism GI applications and marketing campaigns using case studies. It addresses GI marketing issues like misuse, brand dilution, and quality control and offers solutions. The chapter discusses innovative trends like digital marketing, virtual tours, and regional collaboration. These opportunities help destinations increase appeal, attract niche markets, and promote sustainable tourism. The chapter illustrates how GIs boost tourism and regional development.

policy structure must evolve and require watermarking to protect digital content. In the digital era, copyright laws are ineffective and inapplicable.

Preface

In the vibrant and ever-evolving field of tourism, intellectual property (IP) is an indispensable yet often overlooked ally. As editors of *Navigating Intellectual Property Challenges in Tourism*, we invite you to explore the profound impact that IP can have on this dynamic sector. This book aims to shed light on how intellectual property, often associated with patents and trademarks, extends far beyond these traditional boundaries to become a transformative force in tourism.

The tourism industry, a cornerstone of global commerce and a crucial revenue source for many nations, has faced unprecedented challenges in the wake of the COVID-19 pandemic. As the sector embarks on a path to recovery, it is not merely about returning to pre-pandemic conditions but about seizing the opportunity to innovate and distinguish itself. Herein lies the power of intellectual property. IP is more than just a legal concept; it is a strategic asset that can enhance brand identity, safeguard cultural heritage, and drive innovation in a highly competitive market.

This edited book brings together a rich array of perspectives from leading scholars and practitioners across the globe. Our collection of papers is meticulously curated to address both conventional and contemporary issues surrounding IP in tourism. We delve into critical areas such as protecting cultural heritage through trademarks, leveraging copyright for effective tourism promotion, and the role of patents in fostering technological advancements. Each chapter is designed to offer fresh insights and practical guidance on navigating the complex IP landscape.

Our examination extends to the challenges posed by emerging technologies, the intersection of IP with eco-tourism and sustainability, and the impact of digital platforms on IP management. We also address pressing issues such as crisis management, cross-border IP challenges, and the engagement of local communities in IP rights. Through these discussions, we aim to provide valuable tools and strategies for anyone involved in the tourism industry—whether you are an academic, a researcher, a student, or a practitioner.

The insights offered in this book are not just theoretical but are grounded in practical applications that can significantly enhance the effectiveness and competitiveness of tourism enterprises. As the industry navigates its recovery and growth, the strategic use of intellectual property will be crucial in shaping its future.

We believe that *Navigating Intellectual Property Challenges in Tourism* will be an essential resource for understanding how IP can be leveraged to create value, protect assets, and drive innovation. We extend our deepest thanks to all contributors for their invaluable expertise and to our readers for their engagement with this vital topic.

Chapter 1: Navigating the IP Maze: A Guide for Tourism Entrepreneurs and Startups

In this chapter, we explore the vital role of intellectual property (IP) in the tourism industry, particularly for entrepreneurs and startups. The chapter offers practical insights into how trademarks, copyrights, patents, and geographical indications (GIs) can be leveraged to create and protect distinctive tourism products and services. By addressing the challenges of IP theft and infringement and examining the impact of emerging technologies like blockchain and AI, the chapter provides a roadmap for tourism businesses to effectively manage their IP assets. It serves as a comprehensive guide for navigating the complex IP landscape to enhance brand differentiation and competitive positioning in the tourism sector.

Chapter 2: Reconnoitering Potential of Intellectual Property in Tourism and Hospitality Industry: Historic and Legal Challenges

This chapter delves into the transformative potential of intellectual property within the hospitality and tourism sectors. It discusses how IP can enhance various operational aspects, from marketing and design to strategic management and customer relations. By examining historical and legal challenges, the chapter highlights the ethical and legal considerations associated with integrating IP into hospitality practices. It also explores the impact of Generative Artificial Intelligence (GAI) on the industry, providing a forward-looking perspective on how IP can be harnessed to deliver superior visitor experiences and improve industry standards.

Chapter 3: Intellectual Property Considerations in the Preservation and Revival of Folklore through Tourism: Strategies for Sustainable Cultural Heritage Management in India

Focusing on the intersection of folklore and tourism in India, this chapter addresses the challenges of commodifying cultural heritage while protecting indigenous intellectual property rights. It proposes strategies for sustainable cultural heritage management that align economic incentives with the ethical preservation of folklore. The chapter advocates for tailored IPR guidelines to ensure that local communities benefit from tourism without compromising the authenticity and respect for their cultural expressions, ultimately supporting a balanced approach to cultural heritage management.

Chapter 4: Cultural Heritage Tourism in Bangladesh: Balancing Preservation and Visitor Experience

This chapter presents a thorough evaluation of cultural heritage conservation practices in Bangladesh amidst growing tourism pressures. It investigates visitor perceptions and experiences to identify ways to improve site management and enhance visitor satisfaction. The chapter aims to propose actionable strategies for integrating conservation efforts with tourism development, ensuring that heritage sites are preserved while maximizing the socio-economic benefits for local communities. It contributes to the broader discourse on sustainable tourism by advocating for a balanced approach to heritage preservation and tourism growth.

Chapter 5: Leveraging Intellectual Property for Sustainable Tourism Growth

In this chapter, the role of intellectual property (IP) in promoting sustainable tourism growth is explored. It examines how various IP rights, including patents, trademarks, copyrights, and geographical indications, can be utilized to support eco-friendly innovations, protect cultural assets, and enhance sustainable branding efforts. Through a review of literature, case studies, and global practices, the chapter highlights the challenges and opportunities of managing IP within the context of sustainable tourism, providing valuable insights into how IP can drive environmentally and culturally responsible tourism development.

Chapter 6: Leveraging Intellectual Property for Destination Branding and Marketing in the Tourism Sector

This chapter investigates the critical role of intellectual property in the branding and marketing of tourism destinations. It explores how IP assets such as trademarks, copyrights, and geographical indications (GIs) are instrumental in creating and promoting distinctive tourism experiences. The chapter emphasizes the impact of IP on destination recognition and differentiation, examining how IP supports authentic marketing efforts and contributes to sustainable tourism by integrating cultural heritage. It also addresses challenges related to IP enforcement and explores innovative trends like digital marketing and AI in enhancing IP management.

Chapter 7: Synergising Brands: Licensing and Collaboration Strategies in Tourism

Focusing on licensing and collaboration, this chapter reveals how these strategies can enhance tourism brand expansion and market penetration. It discusses the benefits of licensing IP to third parties and the role of collaborative efforts between businesses, governments, and communities in driving innovation and improving visitor experiences. The chapter also covers the practical aspects of licensing agreements, risk management, and future trends, including digital licensing and sustainability. It provides insights into how strategic partnerships can create unique tourism offerings and strengthen brand presence.

Chapter 8: Collaborative Marketing Strategies for Tea Tourism: Leveraging Local and Global Networks

This chapter analyzes the importance of collaborative marketing strategies in promoting tea tourism. By investigating the role of local and global networks, the chapter highlights how integrated marketing programs can connect tea farmers, tourism boards, and international partners. It explores the rising demand for such strategies and their potential to enhance tea tourism through cooperative efforts, offering insights into how collaborative marketing can address competitive pressures and leverage local and global resources effectively.

Chapter 9: The Role of Trademarks in Tourism: A Study with Special Reference to Non-traditional Marks

In this chapter, the significance of trademarks in tourism is examined, with a focus on non-traditional trademarks that include sensory features. The chapter explores how these trademarks shape tourists' perceptions and experiences, enhancing destination branding and differentiation. It also discusses the evolution of traditional trademarks and the legal and organizational implications of incorporating non-traditional elements. The chapter concludes by evaluating the potential and risks associated with non-traditional trademarks in promoting sustainable destination development and preserving cultural signifiers.

Chapter 10: Savoring Safeguards: Intellectual Property Protection in Gastronomy Tourism

This chapter explores the role of intellectual property in gastronomy tourism, focusing on the protection of culinary traditions and innovations. It examines how geographical indications (GIs) can enhance the branding and marketing of gourmet cuisines by emphasizing their unique geographic and cultural attributes. The chapter also discusses the economic significance of GIs and their impact on the global marketing of gastronomic tourism. By analyzing the use of GIs as a branding tool, the chapter highlights their potential in fostering sustainable growth in gastronomy tourism.

Chapter 11: Leveraging Geographical Indications for Tourism Development and Destination Branding

This chapter examines how geographical indications (GIs) can be strategically used to boost tourism development and enhance destination branding. It reviews successful branding campaigns that incorporate GIs, discusses challenges related to authenticity and commercialization, and evaluates the economic, social, and cultural impacts of GIs on local communities. The chapter emphasizes the potential of GIs to enrich tourism experiences and strengthen regional identities, offering valuable insights into leveraging GIs for effective destination branding.

Chapter 12: The Power of Place: Geographical Indicators as a Marketing Tool in Indian Tourism

This chapter explores the role of geographical indicators (GIs) in Indian tourism marketing, focusing on iconic products like Darjeeling Tea and Kanjeevaram Silk. It discusses how GIs promote regional identity, attract tourists seeking authentic experiences, and contribute to destination branding. The chapter also addresses challenges related to GI marketing, such as misuse and quality control, and highlights innovative trends like digital marketing and virtual tours. It illustrates how GIs can enhance tourism appeal and support sustainable regional development.

Chapter 13: An Empirical Study on Intellectual Property Challenges in Eco-Tourism & Sustainable Human Resource Practices

This chapter presents an empirical study on the intellectual property challenges within eco-tourism and their impact on sustainable human resource practices. It analyzes issues related to IP violations, including the protection of indigenous knowledge and branding rights, using qualitative and quantitative data. The research emphasizes the need for integrating IP management with sustainable HR practices to foster innovation, ensure compliance, and promote ethical tourism. The study provides insights into overcoming challenges and advancing sustainability in eco-tourism enterprises.

Chapter 14: Addressing Copyright Challenges in the Travel and Tourism Sector - Implications for Digital Media and Intellectual Property

This final chapter addresses the complexities of copyright in the digital media landscape of travel and tourism. It explores issues such as unlicensed use of images, celebrity likenesses, and architectural copyrights, highlighting the impact of copyright violations on tourism businesses. The chapter examines the effectiveness of current copyright laws and suggests improvements, including watermarking and updated policies, to better protect digital content. It provides a critical analysis of how copyright challenges affect tourism marketing and offers recommendations for enhancing IP protection in the digital era.

As we conclude this exploration of intellectual property in tourism, it is evident that IP plays a transformative role in shaping the industry's landscape. Navigating Intellectual Property Challenges in Tourism has illuminated the multifaceted ways in which IP impacts this vibrant sector, offering both challenges and opportunities for stakeholders at all levels.

The chapters within this book reflect a diverse range of perspectives and expertise, underscoring how IP can be a powerful tool for innovation, sustainability, and cultural preservation in tourism. From the detailed analysis of India's growing engagement with intellectual property to practical guides for tourism entrepreneurs and startups, each contribution offers valuable insights into harnessing IP to enhance brand identity, protect cultural assets, and drive sector growth.

We have explored how intellectual property rights intersect with various facets of tourism—from safeguarding cultural heritage in India and Bangladesh to leveraging geographical indications for destination branding and sustainable tourism. The importance of IP in enhancing visitor experiences, promoting regional identities, and fostering economic growth has been thoroughly examined, revealing how strategic IP management can be pivotal in navigating the evolving tourism landscape.

The book also addresses pressing issues such as the impact of digital media on copyright, the role of non-traditional trademarks in destination branding, and the integration of IP with sustainable practices in eco-tourism. Each chapter provides practical tools and strategies to overcome these challenges, offering a comprehensive guide for academics, researchers, practitioners, and policymakers alike.

As the tourism industry continues to recover and evolve, the insights offered in this book will be invaluable in shaping its future. Intellectual property, far from being a mere legal construct, emerges as a critical asset for driving innovation, protecting cultural heritage, and ensuring sustainable growth. We extend our gratitude to all contributors for their expertise and to our readers for their engagement with this vital topic. It is our hope that this book will serve as a cornerstone for understanding and leveraging intellectual property to navigate the complexities of the tourism sector and build a more resilient and dynamic industry.

Ahmad Albattat
Management and Science University, Malaysia

Norhidayah Azman
Management and Science University, Malaysia

Marco Valeri
Niccolò Cusano University, Italy

Zunirah Mohd Talib
Management and Science University, Malaysia

Pankaj Kumar Tyagi
Chandigarh University, India

Chapter 1
Navigating the IP Maze: A Guide for Tourism Entrepreneurs and Startups

Bassam Samir Al-Romeedy
Faculty of Tourism and Hotels, University of Sadat City, Egypt

ABSTRACT

In the dynamic tourism industry, intellectual property (IP) has emerged as a crucial resource for entrepreneurs and startups, offering key benefits in brand differentiation, competitive positioning, and revenue enhancement. This chapter investigates the essential role of IP in tourism, focusing on the significance of trademarks, copyrights, patents, and geographical indications (GIs) in the creation and protection of distinctive tourism products and services. The research examines the processes involved in identifying, registering, and capitalizing on IP assets, offering practical guidance for tourism businesses to develop effective IP strategies. Furthermore, the study highlights the common challenges faced by tourism entrepreneurs, such as IP theft, infringement, and the complexities of managing IP in a global and digital environment. It also explores the potential of emerging technologies like blockchain and AI in strengthening IP protection and management.

INTRODUCTION

In the constantly changing tourism industry, IP has become a vital asset that can significantly boost the value and competitiveness of businesses. IP refers to the legal rights derived from the creative and innovative efforts of individuals and organizations, encompassing protections such as trademarks, copyrights, patents, and GIs. These rights are essential for safeguarding the unique aspects of a tourism business, from brand identity to proprietary technologies and local products, making

DOI: 10.4018/979-8-3693-4171-1.ch001

IP a fundamental element in the modern tourism landscape (Al-Romeedy, 2024e; Merges, 2011; Spinello, 2009). Tourism is a dynamic sector where standing out from the competition is crucial for attracting and retaining customers. This differentiation is often achieved through the strategic use of IP, which allows businesses to protect their brands, market unique experiences, and offer products that competitors cannot easily replicate. For example, trademarks act as the visual and symbolic representation of a destination's brand, while GIs protect the names of products tied to specific regions, ensuring their reputation for quality remains intact. Copyrights and patents safeguard creative content and technological innovations, which are increasingly vital in a digital-first tourism market (Drahos, 2016; Saint-Amour, 2011).

For tourism entrepreneurs and startups, effectively managing IP is a strategic necessity that offers a competitive edge in a crowded market. Properly identifying, protecting, and leveraging IP assets, such as brand names, logos, and proprietary technologies, is essential for establishing a business, securing investment, and expanding operations. This process begins with conducting an IP audit to assess the value of potential IP assets, followed by registering these assets with the appropriate authorities to ensure legal protection and enforcement. Navigating the complex IP landscape requires a deep understanding of the different types of IP relevant to the tourism industry and the specific challenges faced by tourism businesses (Pandey & Dharni, 2014; Aplin et al., 2013; Parr, 2018; Matulionyte et al., 2017; Palfrey, 2011; Auralita, 2023).

In the highly competitive tourism industry, IP serves as a crucial tool for differentiating a brand and establishing a unique market presence. Trademarks and branding, in particular, are vital for creating a strong identity for a destination. A well-crafted trademark can encapsulate the essence of a destination, fostering an emotional connection with potential visitors and distinguishing the destination from its competitors (Rodriguez-Sanchez et al., 2019; Alford & Jones, 2020). By effectively utilizing their IP assets, tourism businesses can build a strong, recognizable brand that resonates with their target audience. This not only helps to attract more visitors but also fosters long-term loyalty, as customers associate the brand with positive experiences and exclusive offerings.

Despite the clear advantages of IP, managing these assets can be challenging, especially for startups and entrepreneurs in the tourism sector. One of the most significant challenges is IP theft and infringement, where competitors or other entities use a business's IP without authorization. This issue is particularly problematic in the digital age, where content can be easily copied and distributed without permission (Figueroa-Domecq et al., 2023; Page & Connell, 2020). Globalization and digitalization have introduced additional layers of complexity to IP management. Tourism businesses often operate across multiple jurisdictions, each with its own set of IP laws and enforcement mechanisms. This makes it difficult to protect IP rights internationally, particularly for small businesses with limited resources. Additionally, the costs associated with IP registration and enforcement can be prohibitive for startups, making it crucial for them to adopt a strategic approach to IP management (Bassey, 2015; Tresiana & Duadji, 2018). The legal intricacies and the need for constant vigilance against infringement can impose a significant burden on tourism entrepreneurs, who must balance these demands with the growth and sustainability of their businesses. Understanding these challenges and developing proactive strategies to address them is essential for the long-term success of any tourism venture.

Emerging technologies are providing innovative solutions for IP management in the tourism industry. Blockchain offers a secure and transparent way to record and verify IP rights, especially for geographical indications (GIs) and trademarks. AI-powered tools help monitor online platforms for IP infringement, enabling quick responses to unauthorized use. Additionally, digital tools like smart contracts and licensing platforms simplify IP management, particularly in licensing and partnerships. These technologies not only enhance IP protection but also create new revenue opportunities for tourism businesses. Startups can benefit by streamlining IP management, reducing infringement risks, and unlocking new revenue streams (Moyle et al., 2020; Williams et al., 2021).

For tourism startups, developing a comprehensive IP strategy is vital for long-term success. This strategy should align with the business model and overall objectives of the company, taking into account the specific IP assets that require protection and the resources available for IP management. Early registration of IP assets is a key element of this strategy, as it establishes the legal foundation for enforcing rights and preventing infringement. Proactive protection measures, such as regularly monitoring the market for potential infringement and keeping IP records up-to-date, are also crucial (Aulet, 2024; Dana, 2021). Collaborating with IP professionals, such as attorneys and consultants, can provide valuable expertise and support in navigating the complexities of IP management. These professionals can assist startups in identifying their most valuable IP assets, developing a comprehensive IP strategy, and ensuring that all necessary protections are in place. IP assets can also be a significant source of revenue for tourism businesses. Licensing, franchising, and partnerships are just a few ways that companies can monetize their IP. For example, a tourism business with a strong brand identity might license its trademark to other companies, allowing them to use the brand in exchange for royalties. Moreover, IP plays a critical role in mergers, acquisitions, and investments. A well-protected IP portfolio can greatly enhance a business's value, making it more attractive to potential investors or buyers. Understanding the value of IP and how to leverage it in financial transactions is crucial for maximizing returns. IP is a vital asset for tourism entrepreneurs and startups, offering numerous benefits from brand differentiation to revenue generation. However, navigating the IP landscape requires a strategic approach, including the identification and protection of IP assets, the development of a robust IP strategy, and the use of emerging technologies to enhance IP management. By recognizing the importance of IP and taking proactive measures to protect and leverage these assets, tourism startups can position themselves for long-term success in a competitive market (Neck et al., 2023; Kickul & Lyons, 2020; Tomkowicz, 2013; Dutfield, 2017).

INTELLECTUAL PROPERTY (IP) IN TOURISM

IP refers to a set of legal protections that cover the creations of the human intellect, including inventions, literary and artistic works, designs, symbols, names, and images utilized in commerce. In the tourism sector, IP is vital for safeguarding the unique features that distinguish a destination, service, or product. This industry is marked by intense competition, with destinations, hotels, tour operators, and other stakeholders striving to distinguish themselves in a saturated market. In this scenario, IP rights are crucial for establishing and maintaining a distinct identity, promoting innovation, and preserving the brand value that businesses strive to develop.

IP holds critical importance in the tourism sector as it provides the legal foundation necessary to protect and monetize the unique assets that characterize a destination, service, or product. In an industry driven by creativity, cultural heritage, and the necessity for differentiation in a highly competitive environment, IP acts as an essential tool for protecting innovation, building brand identity, and promoting economic growth (Dias, 2024; Solvoll et al., 2015; Ateljevic & Page, 2017; Figueroa-Domecq et al., 2020).

One of the key functions of IP in tourism is the protection of unique assets central to the identity of a destination or business. This includes trademarks that represent the brand, GIs that verify the authenticity of local products, copyrights that safeguard creative works, and patents that protect technological innovations. By securing these assets through IP rights, tourism businesses and destinations can prevent unauthorized use, counterfeiting, and infringement, thereby maintaining the integrity and value of their offerings. For instance, a trademarked logo or slogan becomes a strong symbol of quality and authenticity, making it easier for consumers to identify and trust the brand (Tajeddini et al., 2017; Ratten et al., 2019).

In the tourism industry, brand identity is essential for attracting visitors and building long-term loyalty. IP is fundamental in this regard, enabling businesses and destinations to create and protect a distinctive brand that resonates with their target audience. Trademarks, for example, help establish a recognizable and consistent brand image across various marketing platforms, facilitating the communication of a destination or service's unique attributes. GIs further strengthen brand identity by connecting products to their geographical origins, adding cultural and historical significance that appeals to travelers seeking authentic experiences (Soltanifar et al., 2021; Burns, 2022).

The economic significance of IP in tourism is immense. A robust IP portfolio not only increases a business's market value but also opens up new revenue opportunities. For example, tourism businesses can license their trademarks or patented technologies to other companies, generating additional income. Likewise, the use of GIs can enhance the economic prospects of local communities by promoting products uniquely tied to a region's cultural heritage, thereby attracting more tourists and boosting sales. Additionally, IP rights can be a crucial factor in attracting investment, as investors are more inclined to support businesses that have secured their intellectual assets (Kolb, 2020; Lerner & Leamon, 2023; Masunah et al., 2022).

IP also drives innovation in the tourism industry. By offering legal protection for new ideas, processes, and technologies, IP motivates businesses to invest in research and development. Patents, in particular, encourage innovation by granting inventors exclusive rights, allowing them to benefit financially from their inventions without the immediate threat of competition. This is especially significant in the tourism industry, where technological advancements—such as booking platforms, virtual reality experiences, and mobile apps—can greatly enhance customer experiences and create competitive advantages.

GIs hold a distinct role in the tourism industry by promoting and preserving the cultural and natural heritage of specific regions. GIs protect the names of products that are deeply connected to particular areas, such as "Champagne" from France or "Darjeeling tea" from India. By safeguarding these products, GIs help maintain the authenticity and reputation of local goods, attracting tourists who wish to experience the unique culture and traditions of a region. This not only boosts the appeal of the destination but also supports the local economy, preserves cultural practices, and protects biodiversity (Chung et al., 2024; Crammond, 2024).

In the globalized and digitalized tourism market, protecting intellectual property (IP) is essential for addressing challenges like IP theft and counterfeiting. IP rights allow tourism businesses to enforce legal protection across multiple jurisdictions, particularly for those operating internationally or relying on digital platforms. Securing IP rights helps these businesses protect their assets, reduce infringement risks, and maintain a competitive edge. For entrepreneurs and startups, effective IP management is crucial for establishing a strong market presence, attracting investment, and ensuring long-term success in the competitive tourism industry (Redford, 2020; Wiśniewski, 2020; Crupi et al., 2021).

Securing investment is crucial for tourism startups aiming to scale, and a strong IP portfolio can significantly enhance their attractiveness to investors. A well-protected IP demonstrates stability and lowers legal risks, boosting investor confidence and potentially leading to better funding terms. IP also plays a key role in determining a startup's valuation during funding rounds or acquisitions, as it provides exclusive rights to innovative products, services, or brands, increasing revenue potential and market share. Additionally, IP facilitates expansion through new markets and business models like franchising, allowing startups to scale quickly while monetizing their assets (Grimaldi et al., 2021; Chirico et al., 2020; Yeganegi et al., 2021; Carayannis, 2020; Hernández-Chea et al., 2020; Kwon, 2020).

For startups, particularly in the digital space, IP-related legal risks can be significant. Without proper IP protection, they are vulnerable to infringement, where competitors may copy their innovations, branding, or content, leading to costly legal disputes that can drain resources. Securing IP rights proactively reduces these risks, deters potential infringers, and provides a legal foundation for enforcing rights if disputes arise. For tourism startups, IP is a crucial asset that helps build a strong brand, secure competitive advantages, and attract investment, positioning them for long-term success in a competitive industry (Power & Reid, 2021; Febriany et al., 2022; Zhao et al., 2020).

IDENTIFYING AND PROTECTING IP ASSETS

Identifying potential IP assets within a tourism business is a critical initial step in developing a robust IP portfolio that can safeguard and enhance the business's value. In the tourism sector, IP assets can manifest in various forms, including brand elements like logos and slogans, creative content, technological innovations, and traditional products tied to specific regions. To uncover these assets, tourism businesses should conduct a comprehensive review of their operations, marketing materials, services, and products to identify elements that are unique, valuable, and eligible for legal protection. One of the most prominent IP assets in a tourism business is its brand identity, which encompasses the business name, logo, and any associated trademarks. These components are vital for distinguishing the business in a competitive market and for creating a recognizable image that resonates with customers. For example, a distinctive logo or memorable slogan that captures the essence of a tourism service—such as "adventure tours" or "luxury escapes"—can be trademarked to prevent other businesses from using similar marks that could confuse consumers (Spinello, 2009; Matulionyte et al., 2017; Parr, 2018; Merges, 2011).

Beyond trademarks, tourism businesses should recognize their creative content as potential IP assets. This includes promotional materials such as videos, brochures, website content, and photography. These materials often result from considerable creative effort and investment, making them worthy of protection under copyright law. By identifying which content is original and valuable, businesses can secure their rights and prevent others from copying or using their materials without authorization.

Technological innovations, such as new booking systems, mobile applications, or virtual reality experiences, are also significant IP assets within the tourism industry. These innovations can be protected through patents, granting the business exclusive rights to use and commercialize the technology. It is crucial to identify these innovations early, as patents must be filed before the technology is publicly disclosed (Drahos, 2016; Auralita, 2023; Panda & Joy, 2021). Finally, businesses that promote local products or cultural experiences should consider GIs as a form of IP protection. GIs safeguard the names of products linked to specific regions, which possess qualities or a reputation tied to that location. For instance, a tourism business that markets local food products like "Parma Ham" or "Darjeeling Tea" can benefit from GI protection, enhancing the product's authenticity and appeal to tourists seeking genuine experiences (Pandey & Dharni, 2014; Dutfield, 2017).

THE ROLE OF IP AUDITS IN ASSESSING AND VALUING IP ASSETS

IP audits are essential for tourism businesses to evaluate, manage, and enhance the value of their IP assets. An IP audit involves a comprehensive review of all IP assets owned or used by a business, including trademarks, copyrights, patents, GIs, trade secrets, and other IP forms. The purpose of the audit is to identify these assets, assess their current protection status, evaluate their commercial value, and ensure effective management and utilization. An IP audit can help a business uncover unregistered or underutilized IP assets that could be used to gain a competitive edge. For instance, a business might find that it has developed unique branding elements that are not yet trademarked or that it possesses copyrighted materials being used without proper licensing. The audit also identifies potential IP risks, such as expired patents or trademarks needing renewal, and areas where IP rights might be susceptible to infringement (Kolb, 2020; Neck et al., 2023; Crammond, 2024).

Beyond identifying and managing existing IP assets, an IP audit lays the groundwork for valuing these assets. Understanding the value of IP is vital for strategic decisions such as licensing, franchising, mergers, and acquisitions. For example, a well-protected and valuable trademark portfolio can boost a business's market value, attract investors, and provide leverage in negotiations. Additionally, IP audits can uncover opportunities to create new IP assets or enhance the protection of existing ones. For example, a business might opt to file patents for new technologies, register copyrights for previously unprotected content, or seek GI status for local products. Regular IP audits are particularly beneficial for startups and growing businesses, offering ongoing insights into the business's IP portfolio and ensuring that all potential IP assets are fully protected and utilized (Redford, 2020; Soltanifar et al., 2021; Dana, 2021).

LEVERAGING IP FOR COMPETITIVE ADVANTAGE

In the fiercely competitive tourism industry, where numerous destinations and businesses compete for travelers' attention, utilizing IP is crucial for standing out and achieving long-term success. IP assets such as trademarks, copyrights, patents, and GIs can be strategically employed to build a unique identity, protect innovative offerings, and establish a robust market presence that distinguishes a business from its rivals. One effective strategy for differentiating a tourism brand through IP is to develop and safeguard a distinctive brand identity. This involves creating a unique mix of elements like logos, slogans, design features, and even distinctive sounds that embody the brand's essence. For example, a boutique hotel might design a unique logo that captures its luxurious yet intimate atmosphere and pair it with a memorable slogan emphasizing its commitment to personalized service. Registering these elements as trademarks ensures that no other business can legally use similar branding, thus avoiding consumer confusion and reinforcing its unique market position (Aulet, 2024; Grimaldi et al., 2021; Wiśniewski, 2020; Tresiana & Duadji, 2018).

GIs provide another powerful method for differentiation, especially for businesses that focus on local products or cultural experiences. A GI links a product to its specific region of origin, showcasing the unique qualities and heritage of that location. For instance, a wine tour operator in Tuscany might leverage the GI status of "Chianti" to set its offerings apart from other wine regions. By highlighting the authenticity and exclusivity of Chianti wines, the operator can attract tourists seeking genuine experiences that cannot be found elsewhere. This not only enhances the brand's appeal but also aids in preserving local traditions and boosting the regional economy (Rodriguez-Sanchez et al., 2019; Tajeddini et al., 2017).

Innovation is another area where IP can be used to gain a competitive edge. Patents protect technological advancements that can improve the travel experience, such as advanced booking systems, virtual reality tours, or eco-friendly accommodations. A tourism business that holds a patent for a new technology can offer unique services not available from competitors, attracting tech-savvy travelers and positioning itself as an innovator. Additionally, the exclusivity provided by patents enables the business to capitalize on its innovations without immediate competition, offering a significant market advantage (Power & Reid, 2021; Yeganegi et al., 2021).

Copyrights are crucial for distinguishing a tourism brand by protecting unique creative content associated with the business. This includes high-quality marketing materials, original photography, promotional videos, and engaging website content. By securing copyrights, a business ensures that its creative assets are protected from unauthorized use. For instance, a travel agency that creates a series of original, high-definition videos showcasing exclusive travel experiences can copyright these videos to prevent competitors from using them. This protection helps maintain the agency's competitive edge by keeping its content unique and compelling (Panda & Joy, 2021; Zhao et al., 2020; Merges, 2011).

Additionally, licensing IP assets can strategically expand a brand's reach while maintaining quality control. A tourism brand with a valuable trademark or patented technology can license its IP to other businesses in different regions, facilitating growth without the need for direct investment in new locations. For example, a successful tour operator with a patented booking system might license this technology to operators in other countries, generating revenue and enhancing its global presence. This approach not only boosts the brand's visibility but also strengthens its reputation as an industry leader (Spinello, 2009; Drahos, 2016; Carayannis, 2020).

Trademarks are particularly powerful for developing and safeguarding a destination's brand identity. In tourism, where brand recognition and loyalty are essential, trademarks help establish a consistent and memorable image that appeals to travelers. A well-designed trademark can encapsulate a destination's essence, highlighting its unique attractions, cultural heritage, and the experiences it offers. Creating a strong trademark for a destination starts with identifying what makes it unique and appealing. This could include natural beauty, cultural significance, historical landmarks, or culinary traditions. Once these attributes are pinpointed, they can be translated into a visual and verbal identity, such as a logo and slogan. For example, a tropical island might design a logo featuring a palm tree and a setting sun, accompanied by a slogan like "Your Paradise Awaits." This trademarked branding not only captures the destination's charm but also makes it instantly recognizable to potential visitors (Saint-Amour, 2011; Pandey & Dharni, 2014; Auralita, 2023; Figueroa-Domecq et al., 2020).

Trademarks are crucial for maintaining consistent branding across various marketing platforms, which is essential for building a strong and memorable brand identity in the tourism sector. A consistent trademark reinforces a destination's image, making it more appealing to both new and returning visitors by ensuring a commitment to quality and authenticity. This consistency in branding enhances customer trust and encourages repeat business. Additionally, the strategic use of GIs further strengthens a destination's brand by linking its reputation to the authenticity of local products or cultural practices, thereby attracting tourists seeking genuine experiences (Aplin et al., 2013; Parr, 2018; Matulionyte et al., 2017; Dutfield, 2017; Solvoll et al., 2015; Tomkowicz, 2013).

CHALLENGES IN IP MANAGEMENT FOR TOURISM ENTREPRENEURS

Common IP challenges faced by tourism startups and entrepreneurs

Tourism startups and entrepreneurs frequently face significant challenges in managing their IP, which can impact their business's success and sustainability. A major issue is IP theft, where competitors or unauthorized parties use a business's protected trademarks, copyrights, or patents without permission. This can undermine the brand's value, create consumer confusion, and erode competitive advantage. For instance, a startup with a distinctive logo or slogan might discover that others are using similar branding, potentially misleading customers and harming the original brand's reputation (Ateljevic & Page, 2017; Bassey, 2015; Alford & Jones, 2020).

Infringement is another prevalent issue, especially in the tourism sector, where creative content is often shared and reproduced across multiple platforms. Copyright infringement can occur if a competitor uses a business's promotional videos, photos, or written materials without authorization, diminishing the original creator's revenue and undermining their efforts. Trademark infringement can also happen if other businesses use logos, names, or symbols that closely resemble those of an established brand, resulting in a loss of brand exclusivity and customer trust (Rodriguez-Sanchez et al., 2019; Page & Connell, 2020).

Enforcing IP rights presents additional challenges, particularly for startups with limited resources. Even when a tourism business identifies instances of IP theft or infringement, enforcing their rights can be a protracted, complex, and costly process. Legal action may be necessary to halt unauthorized use of IP, but this often involves navigating diverse legal systems across different jurisdictions. For startups, the time and financial costs associated with such legal proceedings can be prohibitive, diverting focus and resources away from core business operations (Tresiana & Duadji, 2018; Figueroa-Domecq et al., 2023; Tajeddini et al., 2017).

Legal complexities and costs associated with IP management

Managing IP in the tourism sector involves navigating a complex landscape of legal requirements, which can be particularly challenging for startups and entrepreneurs. The process for registering IP rights—whether for trademarks, copyrights, patents, or GIs—varies greatly depending on the type of IP and the jurisdiction. Each type has its own criteria, application procedures, and legal standards. For example, registering a trademark involves conducting a thorough search to confirm its uniqueness and then undergoing a detailed application process that may include multiple stages of examination and publication. Similarly, patent applications require a comprehensive technical description of the invention and proof of its novelty and utility. GIs necessitate demonstrating the link between a product's quality and its place of origin, which often requires extensive documentation and evidence (Ratten et al., 2019; Soltanifar et al., 2021; Burns, 2022; Dana, 2021).

The costs associated with these processes can be significant, especially for startups with limited budgets. Expenses include legal fees, application costs, and the costs of conducting IP searches and preparing necessary documentation. Furthermore, maintaining IP protection involves ongoing costs such as renewal fees and monitoring for potential infringements. For businesses operating in multiple countries, these costs are compounded, as IP protection must often be secured and maintained in each jurisdiction separately (Neck et al., 2023; Kickul & Lyons, 2020).

Moreover, in the event of IP disputes, the legal complexities can escalate quickly. Enforcing IP rights typically involves litigation or alternative dispute resolution, both of which require specialized legal expertise and can be time-consuming and costly. Even if legal action is successful, it may not fully offset the losses incurred due to infringement (Kolb, 2020; Lerner & Leamon, 2023). For tourism entrepreneurs and startups, these challenges highlight the need for a strategic approach to IP management. This involves not only securing the necessary legal protections but also implementing proactive measures to monitor and enforce IP rights. Engaging with IP professionals, such as attorneys and consultants, can assist businesses in navigating the complexities of IP law, optimizing their IP strategies, and mitigating the risks associated with IP management (Masunah et al., 2022; Redford, 2020).

THE ROLE OF TECHNOLOGY IN IP MANAGEMENT

How emerging technologies can enhance IP protection

The rapid advancement of technology has introduced innovative methods and tools that significantly improve the management and protection of IP in the tourism sector. Two of the most influential emerging technologies in this area are blockchain and AI. These technologies offer novel solutions to IP protection challenges, enhancing security, efficiency, and transparency in managing IP assets (Chung et al., 2024; Crammond, 2024).

Blockchain technology is particularly effective for enhancing IP protection due to its decentralized, immutable, and transparent characteristics. A blockchain is a distributed ledger that records transactions across multiple computers, ensuring that the data is secure, tamper-proof, and accessible to all network participants. In IP management, blockchain can establish a secure and transparent record of IP ownership, transactions, and licensing agreements. For instance, registering a trademark or copyright on a blockchain creates a permanent, unalterable record of ownership. This facilitates proof of ownership and tracking of IP history, reducing the risk of disputes and infringement (Crupi et al., 2021; Grimaldi et al., 2021; Chirico et al., 2020; Yeganegi et al., 2021). Blockchain also aids in enforcing IP rights by providing a clear, time-stamped record of the creation or transfer of IP assets. This is particularly valuable in cases where multiple parties may claim ownership. Using blockchain, tourism businesses can establish an indisputable chain of custody for their IP assets, which is crucial in legal disputes. Furthermore, blockchain's transparency supports efficient licensing and royalty payments, as all transactions are recorded and can be executed automatically through smart contracts (Carayannis, 2020; Hernández-Chea et al., 2020; Al-Romeedy, 2024a, b).

AI is transforming IP management by automating and enhancing various protective measures. AI algorithms can conduct extensive searches of existing trademarks, copyrights, and patents to ensure that new applications are original and do not infringe on existing rights. This process saves tourism businesses time and resources, as traditional IP searches can be labor-intensive and prone to errors. AI can also monitor digital platforms, social media, and online marketplaces for potential IP infringement, quickly identifying unauthorized use of trademarks, copyrighted materials, or patented technologies. AI's capability to process large volumes of data rapidly allows it to detect patterns and anomalies indicative of infringement. For example, AI-powered image recognition software can scan the internet for unauthorized use of a business's logos or images, flagging instances of misuse. This enables businesses to take prompt action to protect their IP, such as issuing takedown notices, pursuing legal actions, or negotiating licensing agreements. Additionally, AI can forecast potential IP risks and trends, helping businesses make more informed decisions about their IP strategies (Kwon, 2020; Power & Reid, 2021; Al-Romeedy, c, d).

The use of digital tools for monitoring and enforcing IP rights

The digital age has markedly transformed how IP rights are monitored and enforced, with digital tools becoming increasingly pivotal in this process. These tools offer tourism businesses innovative ways to safeguard their IP assets from infringement, particularly in the online environment where the risk of unauthorized use is heightened. Web crawling and scraping software are essential digital tools for IP monitoring. These tools automatically scan the internet, including websites, social media platforms, and online marketplaces, to detect instances of IP infringement. For instance, web crawlers can be programmed to search for specific keywords, images, or brand names, identifying any unauthorized usage. This enables businesses to promptly detect and address potential infringements, such as counterfeit products sold under a trademarked name or copyrighted content distributed without permission (Febriany et al., 2022; Panda & Joy, 2021; Zhao et al., 2020; Wiśniewski, 2020).

Automated takedown services are another critical digital tool, simplifying the process of removing infringing content from the internet. These services utilize algorithms to detect unauthorized IP usage and automatically generate and dispatch takedown notices to the relevant platforms or websites. This automation accelerates the enforcement process and alleviates the burden on businesses, particularly startups and small enterprises that may lack the resources for manual monitoring (Al-Romeedy & Hashem, 2024).

Digital Rights Management (DRM) systems are also vital for protecting copyrighted materials in the tourism sector, where assets like images, videos, and written content are crucial. DRM systems regulate how digital content is used, distributed, and accessed, preventing unauthorized copying, sharing, or modification. For example, a tourism business producing promotional videos can employ DRM to ensure that these videos are only accessible to authorized users and cannot be downloaded or redistributed without consent. DRM also tracks content usage, providing insights into its reach and alerting businesses to any potential infringements.

Additionally, AI-powered analytics tools play a significant role in monitoring IP usage and identifying infringement trends. These tools analyze large volumes of data from various sources, helping businesses detect patterns of infringement or emerging threats, such as new counterfeit products entering the market. By utilizing these insights, businesses can adjust their IP strategies to effectively address current challenges and enhance their asset protection (Aplin et al., 2013; Parr, 2018; Gaafar & Al-Romeedy, 2024a; Dutfield, 2017; Ateljevic & Page, 2017).

Potential of smart contracts and digital licensing in tourism

The rise of smart contracts and digital licensing has opened up new avenues for managing IP in the tourism sector. Smart contracts are self-executing agreements with terms directly encoded into software. Operating on blockchain technology, they automatically enforce contract conditions once predefined criteria are met. In IP management, smart contracts can streamline licensing processes, ensuring that IP rights are upheld and royalties are efficiently collected (Figueroa-Domecq et al., 2020; Bassey, 2015; Solvoll et al., 2015; Dias, 2024). For example, a tourism business that licenses its brand to franchisees in various regions can utilize a smart contract to automatically process royalty payments based on sales or usage metrics. The contract activates once conditions—such as achieving a specific sales threshold—are fulfilled, reducing the need for manual oversight and mitigating dispute risks. Additionally, smart contracts can enforce usage restrictions, ensuring that licensees adhere to agreed terms, such as using the trademark only in designated regions or for certain products.

Digital licensing platforms are becoming increasingly vital for the tourism industry, offering a centralized, secure method for managing and distributing IP rights. These platforms leverage blockchain and other digital technologies to provide transparent, automated solutions for IP licensing, simplifying the process of granting, tracking, and enforcing licenses. For instance, a digital licensing platform could enable a tourism business to license its copyrighted content—such as photos or travel itineraries—to multiple clients, with each transaction recorded on the blockchain. This ensures a clear, immutable record of each agreement, reducing the likelihood of misunderstandings or breaches.

The integration of digital licensing and smart contracts also enhances the scalability of IP management, especially for startups and small businesses aiming to broaden their reach. By automating critical aspects of the licensing process, these technologies minimize administrative burdens and enable businesses to handle a greater volume of licenses with less effort. This is particularly advantageous in the global tourism market, where businesses often need to manage IP across various jurisdictions and navigate differing legal requirements (Rodriguez-Sanchez et al., 2019; Figueroa-Domecq et al., 2023; Gaafar & Al-Romeedy, 2024b).

IP STRATEGY AND PLANNING FOR STARTUPS

Developing an IP strategy aligned with the business model and long-term goals

For tourism startups, establishing a solid IP strategy is essential for laying a strong groundwork for both growth and enduring success. A well-crafted IP strategy must align closely with the startup's business model and long-term objectives to ensure that IP assets effectively support the company's overall vision. This alignment is critical because IP impacts various business facets, including branding, marketing, product development, and competitive positioning. To develop an IP strategy, startups should start by identifying the key elements of their business that need protection. This might involve securing trademarks for brand identity, copyrights for unique content such as marketing materials or digital assets, patents for innovative technologies or processes, and GIs if the business is linked to specific regional products or services. By pinpointing which IP assets are most valuable, startups can prioritize their protection efforts and allocate resources efficiently (Kickul & Lyons, 2020; Kolb, 2020; Lerner & Leamon, 2023; Masunah et al., 2022).

The IP strategy should also outline how these assets can contribute to achieving the startup's long-term goals. For instance, if the startup plans to expand internationally, it should focus on securing trademarks in significant foreign markets. Likewise, if the business depends on proprietary technology, obtaining patents early can safeguard against competitors copying or duplicating the innovation. Essentially, the IP strategy should act as a guide through various growth stages, ensuring that IP protection evolves with the company's needs. Furthermore, the IP strategy must be flexible and responsive, considering the fast-evolving nature of the tourism industry. As new technologies and market dynamics emerge, startups may need to reassess their IP portfolio and adjust their strategy to leverage new opportunities or address potential risks. Continuous monitoring and evaluation of IP assets are necessary to ensure they remain aligned with the startup's evolving business model and goals (Burns, 2022; Neck et al., 2023).

Integrating IP management into overall business planning

IP management should be seamlessly integrated into the overall business strategy rather than treated as a separate task. For startups, this involves incorporating IP considerations into every facet of their operations, including product development, marketing, partnerships, and expansion plans. By weaving IP management into their business planning, startups can ensure that their IP assets are effectively leveraged to drive growth, enhance competitiveness, and create value. A crucial method for integrating IP management into business planning is through regular IP audits and evaluations. These assessments enable startups to identify their current IP assets, review their protection status, and determine if additional safeguards are necessary. For instance, an IP audit might reveal whether a startup's trademarks are registered in all relevant markets or if its digital content is sufficiently covered by copyrights. Routine IP audits help startups proactively address potential protection gaps and prevent costly legal disputes in the future (Redford, 2020; Chung et al., 2024; Dana, 2021; Soltanifar et al., 2021).

Aligning IP decisions with the company's market strategy is another key aspect of integrating IP management into business planning. When planning to introduce a new product or service, startups should consider the IP implications early in the development phase. This could involve conducting trademark searches to ensure the product name is available for registration or filing for patents to protect new technologies before they are publicly disclosed. By factoring IP into product development and market entry strategies, startups can reduce the risk of IP conflicts and enhance the value of their innovations. Additionally, IP management should be synchronized with financial planning. This includes budgeting for costs related to IP registration and enforcement, as well as evaluating potential revenue streams from IP assets through licensing or partnerships. For example, a startup with a valuable patent portfolio might seek opportunities to license its technology to other firms, generating additional revenue with minimal capital investment. By incorporating IP considerations into financial planning, startups can make informed decisions that align with their broader business objectives (Crammond, 2024; Wiśniewski, 2020; Aulet, 2024).

The importance of early IP registration and proactive protection strategies

For startups, securing IP assets through early registration is crucial for obtaining legal protection and establishing a robust market presence. Postponing IP registration can expose a startup to risks such as infringement, brand dilution, and the loss of competitive advantage. Hence, startups should implement proactive protection strategies that emphasize early registration and ongoing monitoring of their IP assets (Ratten et al., 2019; Moyle et al., 2020; Power & Reid, 2021; Febriany et al., 2022). Early IP registration offers significant advantages, including the establishment of legal ownership, which grants exclusive rights to use, license, or sell the IP. For instance, registering a trademark early ensures that competitors cannot use a similar mark in the same industry, thereby protecting the startup's brand identity. Likewise, promptly filing a patent application for new technologies prevents competitors from replicating the innovation, allowing the startup to benefit from its invention without the threat of imitation.

Proactive protection also includes vigilant market monitoring for potential IP infringements and prompt action when violations occur. This can involve setting up alerts for unauthorized use of trademarks or copyrighted materials, conducting regular patent searches, or monitoring online platforms for counterfeit goods. By actively monitoring and addressing potential infringements, startups can safeguard their IP assets and maintain their competitive position (Panda & Joy, 2021; Zhao et al., 2020; Grimaldi et al., 2021; Chirico et al., 2020). Furthermore, startups should consider obtaining IP protection in multiple jurisdictions, especially if they intend to expand globally. IP rights are typically territorial, meaning that protection in one country does not automatically extend to others. Therefore, startups aiming for international growth should prioritize registering their trademarks, patents, and copyrights in key foreign markets to ensure comprehensive protection. This strategy not only protects the startup's assets but also facilitates successful expansion into new regions (Alford & Jones, 2020; Figueroa-Domecq et al., 2023).

Collaborating with IP professionals for effective IP management

Managing IP can be particularly challenging for startups, especially those with limited resources and expertise in IP law. Engaging with IP professionals such as attorneys, consultants, and patent agents can offer crucial guidance and support, helping startups effectively manage their IP assets and avoid expensive errors. IP professionals provide specialized knowledge and experience, aiding startups in the complexities of IP registration, enforcement, and commercialization. For example, an IP attorney can help with comprehensive trademark searches, preparation of patent applications, and drafting of licensing agreements. They can also offer strategic advice on structuring an IP portfolio, prioritizing protection measures, and handling risks related to IP litigation.

Furthermore, IP professionals keep startups informed about the latest trends in IP law and technology, ensuring that their IP strategies are up-to-date and effective. For instance, a startup might collaborate with an IP consultant to explore how emerging technologies like blockchain or AI can enhance their IP protection strategies. By leveraging the expertise of IP professionals, startups can gain a competitive edge and ensure their IP assets are well-protected and optimized for growth (Tresiana & Duadji, 2018; Rodriguez-Sanchez et al., 2019; Solvoll et al., 2015; Ateljevic & Page, 2017; Auralita, 2023). In addition to legal advice, working with IP professionals can also provide startups with valuable connections and resources. Many IP experts have extensive networks within the industry, including potential investors, partners, and other key stakeholders. Accessing these networks can open up new opportunities for collaboration, funding, and market expansion, thereby reinforcing the startup's IP strategy and overall business success (Al-Romeedy, 2024a; Dias, 2024).

MONETIZING IP IN THE TOURISM INDUSTRY

Methods for monetizing IP assets

Monetizing IP in the tourism sector involves utilizing IP assets to create revenue streams through various mechanisms such as licensing, franchising, and strategic alliances. These strategies enable tourism businesses to capitalize on their IP without necessarily expanding their operations or assuming additional risks, thereby generating new income and increasing the overall value of the business. Licensing is a prevalent method for monetizing IP. Through licensing agreements, tourism businesses can permit other parties to use their trademarks, copyrighted materials, patented technologies, or GIs in exchange for royalties or licensing fees. For instance, a prominent hotel chain might license its trademark to another company, allowing them to operate a hotel under the same brand in a different location. This approach not only generates revenue for the original business but also extends the brand's reach without requiring direct investment in new properties. Similarly, a tourism company with a patented reservation system could license the technology to other travel agencies, earning royalties while enabling the technology's wider use (Figueroa-Domecq et al., 2020; Bassey, 2015; Gaafar & Al-Romeedy, 2024a).

Franchising is another effective strategy for IP monetization, especially for businesses with a well-established brand. In a franchise model, the franchisor allows the franchisee to operate a business using its trademarks, business model, and other proprietary assets. In return, the franchisee pays an initial franchise fee and ongoing royalties. For example, a renowned tour operator could franchise its brand to local operators in various regions, permitting them to offer tours under the same name while adhering to the franchisor's standards. This method not only generates continuous revenue through franchise fees and royalties but also supports global brand expansion. Franchising is particularly advantageous in tourism, where brand recognition and consistency are crucial for customer trust and satisfaction.

Strategic partnerships provide another method for monetizing IP. By collaborating with other businesses, tourism companies can form joint ventures that leverage each partner's IP assets to create new products or services. For instance, a luxury resort might partner with a high-end fashion brand to offer exclusive travel experiences, such as fashion-themed vacation packages. The resort's trademark adds value to the partnership, while the fashion brand's IP enhances the overall offering. This collaboration allows both parties to tap into new customer segments and generate additional revenue. Partnerships can also include co-branding efforts, where multiple brands combine their IP to create unique products or experiences, thereby broadening market reach and enhancing profitability (Page & Connell, 2020; Tajeddini et al., 2017; Al-Romeedy & Hashem, 2024).

The role of IP in creating revenue streams beyond the core business

IP significantly contributes to revenue generation beyond a tourism business's core activities. By leveraging IP assets, businesses can diversify their income streams, reduce reliance on a single revenue source, and enhance overall financial stability. For example, a tourism company with valuable copyrights—such as high-quality photography or video content—can license these assets to other entities like travel agencies, hotels, or media firms. This approach enables the company to earn revenue from its creative assets without the need for constant production of new material. Additionally, the company might consider publishing opportunities, such as creating and selling coffee table books or digital guides featuring its copyrighted content. This not only generates direct sales revenue but also boosts the company's brand visibility and reputation.

Tourism businesses holding patents for innovative technologies can also explore licensing opportunities. For instance, a patented eco-friendly hotel design or energy-efficient technology could be licensed to other hospitality providers, construction companies, or governmental bodies interested in sustainable tourism. By licensing these technologies, the original patent holder earns royalties while promoting the broader adoption of sustainable practices within the industry (Tomkowicz, 2013; Dutfield, 2017; Parr, 2018; Matulionyte et al., 2017).

GIs present additional avenues for revenue generation. A tourism company associated with a GI can extend its brand to include merchandise like food products, apparel, or souvenirs. For example, a company organizing wine tours in the Champagne region of France could sell branded Champagne glasses, historical books about the region, or other related items. These merchandise sales provide extra revenue while reinforcing the company's connection to the region and its cultural heritage.

Franchising is another effective method for creating revenue streams beyond the core business. By franchising its brand, a tourism company can earn ongoing income from franchise fees and royalties, even in regions where it does not directly operate. This strategy allows the business to expand its market presence and profitability with minimal capital investment and operational management (Pandey & Dharni, 2014; Aplin et al., 2013; Hernández-Chea et al., 2020).

The value of IP in mergers, acquisitions, and investments

In mergers, acquisitions, and investments, IP often represents a crucial and highly valuable asset for tourism businesses. Effectively understanding and leveraging IP can significantly influence these transactions, affecting the business's market valuation, negotiating leverage, and appeal to potential buyers or investors. During mergers and acquisitions (M&A), the value of a company's IP portfolio plays a vital role in assessing its overall worth. Businesses with strong IP assets, such as trademarks, patents, and copyrights, are generally perceived as more valuable due to the competitive advantage, brand recognition, and future revenue potential these assets provide. For instance, a hotel chain with a well-known brand and registered trademarks across various markets is likely to command a higher acquisition price compared to a competitor with less established IP assets. Similarly, a technology-focused travel startup with patented innovations may attract higher offers from buyers interested in integrating advanced technology into their operations (Yeganegi et al., 2021; Carayannis, 2020; Kwon, 2020).

Investors also highly value IP when considering investments in tourism businesses. A strong IP portfolio indicates that the company has protected its unique offerings, thereby reducing the risk of imitation and enhancing the likelihood of sustained profitability. For startups, having registered trademarks, patents, or copyrights can be a decisive factor in securing funding, as investors prefer businesses that have secured their competitive edges. Furthermore, IP can be used as collateral in financing arrangements, providing additional financial leverage for the business.

In M&A deals, the strategic value of IP can drive synergies between the acquiring and target companies. For example, a large tourism conglomerate might acquire a smaller company to gain access to its patented technology or capitalize on its strong brand presence in a specific market. The acquired IP can then be integrated into the conglomerate's operations, boosting overall competitiveness and market share. Conversely, a company with underutilized IP assets might choose to sell or license them as part of a divestiture strategy, unlocking value and generating cash flow for reinvestment in other business areas.

To maximize the value of IP in M&A and investment scenarios, tourism businesses should conduct comprehensive IP audits and valuations as part of their due diligence process. This involves evaluating the scope, validity, and enforceability of the IP assets and assessing their potential to generate future revenue. By presenting a detailed and convincing case for their IP value, businesses can negotiate better terms and achieve higher valuations in these transactions (Merges, 2011; Drahos, 2016; Spinello, 2009; Saint-Amour, 2011; Al-Romeedy, 2024b, c, d).

CONCLUSION AND RECOMMENDATIONS

This study has emphasized the pivotal role of IP in the tourism industry, especially for entrepreneurs and startups aiming to build sustainable and competitive enterprises. IP assets—including trademarks, copyrights, patents, and GIs—are crucial for safeguarding the distinctive elements of a tourism brand, boosting its market presence, and creating new revenue opportunities. The research highlights the necessity of crafting a comprehensive IP strategy that aligns with the business's overall model and long-term objectives, seamlessly integrating IP management into all facets of business planning, and proactively securing early registration and ongoing protection of IP assets. Additionally, the study examined various strategies for monetizing IP, such as licensing, franchising, and strategic partnerships, which enable businesses to capitalize on their IP assets and generate income beyond their core operations. The impact of IP on mergers, acquisitions, and investments was also explored, illustrating how a strong IP portfolio can significantly increase a business's valuation and appeal to potential investors or buyers. Finally, the study addressed the role of emerging technologies like blockchain and AI in enhancing IP protection, showing how these advancements can help tourism businesses better secure their IP assets in an increasingly globalized and digital market.

Based on the study's findings, tourism entrepreneurs and startups can follow several practical recommendations to effectively manage the complexities of IP. First, they should focus on creating a detailed IP strategy that aligns with their business goals and model. This strategy should identify essential IP assets, such as trademarks, copyrights, and patents, and outline the necessary steps for their protection and maintenance. It should also include how these assets can be utilized to promote growth, market expansion, and revenue generation. A crucial step in IP protection is to register assets as early as possible. Startups need to perform comprehensive searches to confirm that their trademarks, copyrights, or patents are unique and not in use by others. Early registration not only secures legal ownership but also prevents competitors from using similar assets that might weaken the brand's value. For those planning international expansion, securing IP protection in key foreign markets is also advisable. Moreover, integrating IP management into the broader business planning process is essential. This involves conducting regular IP audits to evaluate the status of existing assets, identify potential risks, and determine if additional protection is required. Entrepreneurs should also align their IP decisions with their market strategy, incorporating IP considerations into product development, branding, and expansion efforts.

Tourism businesses should also explore ways to monetize their IP assets through licensing, franchising, and strategic partnerships. Licensing agreements can generate royalties from trademarks, copyrighted materials, or patented technologies.

Franchising can broaden the brand's reach and provide ongoing revenue streams, while strategic partnerships can enhance market presence and offer new products or services by combining IP assets with those of other businesses. Furthermore, staying informed about emerging technologies like blockchain and AI is crucial. Blockchain can offer a secure, transparent record of IP ownership and transactions, while AI can automate the monitoring of digital platforms for potential infringements. Utilizing these technologies can enhance the effectiveness and efficiency of IP protection.

Given the complexities of IP law, startups should consider working with IP professionals, such as attorneys, consultants, and patent agents. These experts can assist in navigating the IP registration process, drafting licensing agreements, and managing IP disputes. They can also keep businesses updated on legal changes and emerging trends that might affect their IP strategy.

Lastly, entrepreneurs should understand the strategic value of their IP in mergers, acquisitions, and investments. A strong IP portfolio can increase a business's market valuation and provide leverage in negotiations. Conducting thorough IP audits and valuations during due diligence can help ensure that the full value of IP assets is recognized in these transactions.

REFERENCES

Al-Romeedy, B. (2024a). Sustainable Bytes: The Digital Literacy and Skills Revolution in Tourism. In *Dimensions of Regenerative Practices in Tourism and Hospitality* (pp. 206-221). IGI Global.

Al-Romeedy, B. (2024b). Web of Wonders: Sustainable Digital Marketing Strategies for Unforgettable African Tourism Destinations. In *Promoting Responsible Tourism With Digital Platforms* (pp. 168–188). IGI Global. DOI: 10.4018/979-8-3693-3286-3.ch010

Al-Romeedy, B. (2024c). Breaking Chains, Building Futures: Blockchain's Impact on Sustainable Tourism. In *Promoting Responsible Tourism With Digital Platforms* (pp. 90-107). IGI Global.

Al-Romeedy, B. (2024d). Tomorrow's Travel Companion: The Role of Artificial Intelligence in Shaping the Future of Tourism. In *Marketing and Big Data Analytics in Tourism and Events* (pp. 162-182). IGI Global.

Al-Romeedy, B. (2024e). Unlocking the Power of Data: Exploring the Dynamic Role of MKIS in Revolutionizing Tourism Marketing. In *Marketing and Big Data Analytics in Tourism and Events* (pp. 183-204). IGI Global.

Al-Romeedy, B., & Hashem, T. (2024). From Insight to Advantage: Harnessing the Potential of Marketing Intelligence Systems in Tourism. In *Marketing and Big Data Analytics in Tourism and Events* (pp. 80-98). IGI Global.

Alford, P., & Jones, R. (2020). The lone digital tourism entrepreneur: Knowledge acquisition and collaborative transfer. *Tourism Management*, 81, 104139. DOI: 10.1016/j.tourman.2020.104139

Aplin, T., Aplin, T., & Davis, J. (2013). *Intellectual property law: text, cases, and materials*. Oxford University Press. DOI: 10.1093/he/9780199643301.001.0001

Ateljevic, J., & Page, S. (2017). *Tourism and entrepreneurship*. Routledge. DOI: 10.4324/9780080942728

Aulet, B. (2024). *Disciplined Entrepreneurship: 24 Steps to a Successful Startup, Expanded & Updated*. John Wiley & Sons.

Auralita, L. (2023). Unlocking the Power of Intellectual Property: Safeguarding Books Against Piracy. *Journal of Judicial Review*, 25(1), 1–16. DOI: 10.37253/jjr.v25i1.7743

Bassey, B. (2015). Transforming the Nigeria tourism industry through tourism entrepreneurial development. *African Journal of Business Management*, 9(15), 569–580. DOI: 10.5897/AJBM2015.7844

Burns, P. (2022). *Entrepreneurship and small business*. Bloomsbury Publishing.

Carayannis, E. (2020). *Encyclopedia of creativity, invention, innovation and entrepreneurship*. Springer International Publishing. DOI: 10.1007/978-3-319-15347-6

Chirico, F., Criaco, G., Baù, M., Naldi, L., Gomez-Mejia, L., & Kotlar, J. (2020). To patent or not to patent: That is the question. Intellectual property protection in family firms. *Entrepreneurship Theory and Practice*, 44(2), 339–367. DOI: 10.1177/1042258718806251

Chung, D., Yang, S., & Marhold, K. (2024). Investigating the Relationship between Technological Entrepreneurship and National Innovativeness: Moderating Effects of Intellectual Property Protection and R&D Transfer Environment. *Entrepreneurship Research Journal*, 14(3), 1341–1371. DOI: 10.1515/erj-2020-0530

Crammond, R. (2024). Developing intellectual property management skills and the entrepreneurial university element: An educator perspective. *International Journal of Intellectual Property Management*, 14(4), 389–409. DOI: 10.1504/IJIPM.2024.139664

Crupi, A., Cesaroni, F., & Di Minin, A. (2021). Understanding the impact of intellectual capital on entrepreneurship: A literature review. *Journal of Intellectual Capital*, 22(3), 528–559. DOI: 10.1108/JIC-02-2020-0054

Dana, L. (2021). *World encyclopedia of entrepreneurship*. Edward Elgar Publishing. DOI: 10.4337/9781839104145

Dias, Á. (2024). Tourism business startup: recognizing opportunities and barriers to entry. In *Handbook of Tourism Entrepreneurship* (pp. 188–200). Edward Elgar Publishing. DOI: 10.4337/9781803920023.00022

Drahos, P. (2016). *A philosophy of intellectual property*. Routledge.

Dutfield, G. (2017). *Intellectual property rights and the life science industries: A twentieth century history*. Routledge. DOI: 10.4324/9781315252131

Febriany, T., Kurniawan, H., & Setiyawan, D. (2022). The Implementation of Intellectual Property Registration for Startups in the Industrial Revolution Era 4.0 in Pontianak. *Indonesia Law Reform Journal*, 2(3), 382–388. DOI: 10.22219/ilrej.v2i3.23309

Figueroa-Domecq, C., De Jong, A., & Williams, A. (2020). Gender, tourism & entrepreneurship: A critical review. *Annals of Tourism Research*, 84, 102980. DOI: 10.1016/j.annals.2020.102980

Figueroa-Domecq, C., Kimbu, A., de Jong, A., & Williams, A. (2023). Sustainability through the tourism entrepreneurship journey: A gender perspective. In *Gender and Tourism Sustainability* (pp. 107–130). Routledge. DOI: 10.4324/9781003329541-7

Gaafar, H., & Al-Romeedy, B. (2024a). Bridging the Digital Divide: Unleashing the Power of Big Data Analytics for Touristic Destination Promotion. In *Marketing and Big Data Analytics in Tourism and Events* (pp. 17-37). IGI Global.

Gaafar, H., & Al-Romeedy, B. (2024b). Data Fusion for Destination Success: Exploring the Integration of MKIS and BDA in Marketing Touristic Destinations. In *Marketing and Big Data Analytics in Tourism and Events* (pp. 38-60). IGI Global.

Grimaldi, M., Greco, M., & Cricelli, L. (2021). A framework of intellectual property protection strategies and open innovation. *Journal of Business Research*, 123, 156–164. DOI: 10.1016/j.jbusres.2020.09.043

Hernández-Chea, R., Vimalnath, P., Bocken, N., Tietze, F., & Eppinger, E. (2020). Integrating intellectual property and sustainable business models: The SBM-IP canvas. *Sustainability (Basel)*, 12(21), 8871. DOI: 10.3390/su12218871

Kickul, J., & Lyons, T. (2020). *Understanding social entrepreneurship: The relentless pursuit of mission in an ever changing world.* Routledge. DOI: 10.4324/9780429270406

Kolb, B. (2020). *Entrepreneurship for the creative and cultural industries.* Routledge. DOI: 10.4324/9780367817046

Kwon, O. (2020). A study on how startups approach sustainable development through intellectual property. *Sustainable Development (Bradford)*, 28(4), 613–625. DOI: 10.1002/sd.2012

Lerner, J., & Leamon, A. (2023). *Venture capital, private equity, and the financing of entrepreneurship.* John Wiley & Sons.

Masunah, J., Dyani, P., Gaffar, V., & Sari, M. (2022). Production of shadow puppet performances in building artistic entrepreneurship. *Journal of Sustainable Tourism and Entrepreneurship*, 3(2), 104–116.

Matulionyte, R., Paton, E., McIntyre, P., & Gleadhill, D. (2017). The system of book creation: Intellectual property and the self-publishing sector of the creative industries. *Creative Industries Journal*, 10(3), 191–210. DOI: 10.1080/17510694.2017.1393193

Merges, R. (2011). *Justifying intellectual property*. Harvard University Press. DOI: 10.4159/harvard.9780674061125

Moyle, C., Moyle, B., & Burgers, H. (2020). Entrepreneurial strategies and tourism industry growth. *Tourism Management Perspectives*, 35, 100708. DOI: 10.1016/j.tmp.2020.100708

Neck, H., Neck, C., & Murray, E. (2023). *Entrepreneurship: The practice and mindset*. Sage publications.

Page, S., & Connell, J. (2020). Tourism and entrepreneurship. In *Tourism* (pp. 262–279). Routledge. DOI: 10.4324/9781003005520-15

Palfrey, J. (2011). *Intellectual property strategy*. Mit Press. DOI: 10.7551/mitpress/9066.001.0001

Panda, B., & Joy, S. (2021). Intellectual property rights-based debt financing to startups: Need for a changing role of Indian banks. *Vikalpa*, 46(3), 143–152. DOI: 10.1177/02560909211041817

Pandey, N., & Dharni, K. (2014). *Intellectual property rights*. PHI Learning Pvt. Ltd.

Parr, R. (2018). *Intellectual property: valuation, exploitation, and infringement damages*. John Wiley & Sons. DOI: 10.1002/9781119419235

Power, B., & Reid, G. (2021). The impact of intellectual property types on the performance of business start-ups in the United States. *International Small Business Journal*, 39(4), 372–400. DOI: 10.1177/0266242620967009

Ratten, V., Costa, C., & Bogers, M. (2019). Artisan, cultural and tourism entrepreneurship. *International Journal of Entrepreneurial Behaviour & Research*, 25(4), 582–591. DOI: 10.1108/IJEBR-05-2018-0319

Redford, A. (2020). Property rights, entrepreneurship, and economic development. *The Review of Austrian Economics*, 33(1), 139–161. DOI: 10.1007/s11138-019-00485-6

Rodriguez-Sanchez, I., Williams, A., & Brotons, M. (2019). The innovation journey of new-to-tourism entrepreneurs. *Current Issues in Tourism*, 22(8), 877–904. DOI: 10.1080/13683500.2017.1334763

Saint-Amour, P. (2011). *The copywrights: intellectual property and the literary imagination*. Cornell University Press.

Soltanifar, M., Hughes, M., & Göcke, L. (2021). *Digital entrepreneurship: Impact on business and society*. Springer Nature. DOI: 10.1007/978-3-030-53914-6

Solvoll, S., Alsos, G., & Bulanova, O. (2015). Tourism entrepreneurship–review and future directions. *Scandinavian Journal of Hospitality and Tourism, 15*(sup1), 120-137.

Spinello, R. (2009). *A defense of intellectual property rights*. Edward Elgar Publishing. DOI: 10.4337/9781848449428

Tajeddini, K., Ratten, V., & Denisa, M. (2017). Female tourism entrepreneurs in Bali, Indonesia. *Journal of Hospitality and Tourism Management*, 31, 52–58. DOI: 10.1016/j.jhtm.2016.10.004

Tomkowicz, R. (2013). *Intellectual Property Overlaps: Theory, Strategies, and Solutions*. Routledge. DOI: 10.4324/9780203804049

Tresiana, N., & Duadji, N. (2018). Social entrepreneur model for tourism development in Kiluan Bay. *MIMBAR, Jurnal Sosial dan Pembangunan, 34*(1), 83-92.

Williams, A., Rodríguez Sánchez, I., & Škokić, V. (2021). Innovation, risk, and uncertainty: A study of tourism entrepreneurs. *Journal of Travel Research*, 60(2), 293–311. DOI: 10.1177/0047287519896012

Wiśniewski, J. (2020). On the impossibility of intellectual property. *Quarterly Journal of Austrian Economics*, 23(1), 33–45. DOI: 10.35297/qjae.010051

Yeganegi, S., Laplume, A., & Dass, P. (2021). The role of information availability: A longitudinal analysis of technology entrepreneurship. *Technological Forecasting and Social Change*, 170, 120910. DOI: 10.1016/j.techfore.2021.120910

Zhao, R., Cao, Y., Zheng, X., & Wang, H. (2020). The innovation economy calls for proactive growth of intellectual property by various innovation carriers–A China case. *Global Transitions Proceedings*, 1(1), 23–31. DOI: 10.1016/j.gltp.2020.04.001

Chapter 2
Reconnoitering Potential of Intellectual Property in the Tourism and Hospitality Industry:
Historic and Legal Challenges

Bhupinder Singh
https://orcid.org/0009-0006-4779-2553
Sharda University, India

Kamalesh Ravesangar
https://orcid.org/0009-0004-2154-184X
Tunku Abdul Rahman University of Management and Technology, Malaysia

ABSTRACT

Intellectual property presents significant prospects for the hospitality and tourism sector, impacting various aspects such as operations, design, marketing, destination management, human resources, revenue management, accounting and finance, strategic management and more. IPR holds promise for enhancing the hospitality industry's visitor experience in a number of ways, including by providing tailored suggestions and strengthening security protocols. Staff members may learn at their own speed and in a way that suits their learning preferences when customized training experiences are provided, depending on individual strengths and limitations. However, the incorporation of GAI in hospitality and tourism sector raises ethical, legal, social and economic considerations that demand thoughtful examination by hospitality and tourism enterprises. This chapter explores the diverse arena of the applications of Intellectual property in Tourism and Hospitality Industry for

DOI: 10.4018/979-8-3693-4171-1.ch002

Strengthening Customer Relationships Delivering Better Experiences with futuristic approach.

1. INTRODUCTION

IPR integration may help boost hotel operations by automating regular chores like cleaning and room maintenance, especially when combined with robots. Staff can concentrate on more important tasks thanks to this automation, which improves overall service quality (Dwivedi et al., 2024). Artificial intelligence (AI)-powered chatbots and virtual assistants, for example, may provide visitors customized recommendations for nearby sites while also enhancing staff-guest engagement by opening up new channels of communication (Gupta, et al., 2024). This leads to a staff that is more skilled and knowledgeable overall, improving customer satisfaction and generating more income for the company (Khan et al., 2024). AI-driven systems may also optimize resource utilization, which lowers costs and improves sustainability. It is clear that this kind of technology is going to play a major role in the hotel industry's business plan in the future (Wang, 2024). Beyond benefits for the visitor, IPRmay enhance the working environment for employees in the hotel and tourist industries. In the tourist and hospitality sectors, making an impression on visitors is a top priority. Traditional methods, however, frequently fall short of individual tastes, producing a generic experience (Alyasiri et al., 2024). The use of IPR(GAI) presents a novel approach and it is capable of producing completely original literature, graphics, and even code. Businesses may create experiences that are tailored to each customer's requirements and preferences by utilizing GAI, which strengthens client connections and increases loyalty (Mogaji et al., 2024).

The enhancing of the guest experience is the hotel industry's primary objective, and it never changes (Gursoy & Cai, 2024). Advanced technologies like cloud computing, blockchain, and the Internet of Things have already improved consumer satisfaction and streamlined processes. IPRnow has the potential to take this a step further, opening the door to further efficiency and customisation in the hotel industry (Kannan, 2024). As a result, companies looking to meet high service standards now need to integrate technology. As evidence that IPRis more than simply a fleeting trend but rather a revolutionary force, 30% of professionals in the travel and hospitality industry are already being impacted by it (Singha & Singha, 2024). This astounding growth points to a future in which technology will be essential to improving travel experiences. Let's examine how artificial intelligence is expected to change the travel and hospitality sector (Abrokwah-Larbi, 2024).

Figure 1. Introduction Split Sections

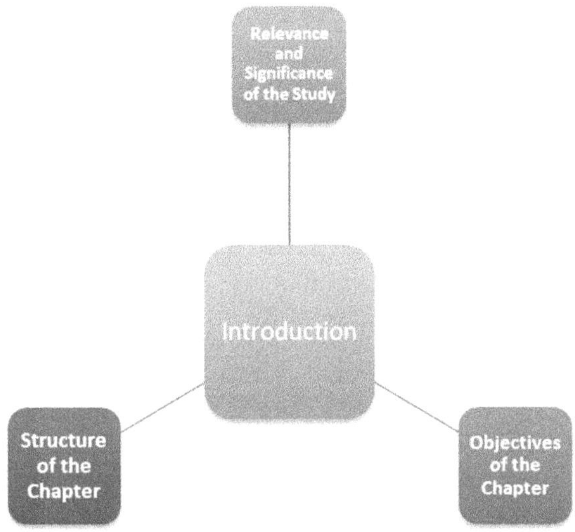

(Source- Original)

1.1 Relevance and Significance of the Study

Intellectual propertyhas taken center stage in transforming business processes, offering innovative solutions that meet growing customer demands (Caboni & Hagberg, 2019). In the tourism and hospitality industry, where customer satisfaction is paramount, GenAI provides a wealth of opportunities to create personalized experiences and foster deeper customer relationships (Yang et al., 2024). From the perspective of the customer, the travel business has greatly improved with the application of IPRfor language translation, which eliminates conventional hurdles associated with language barriers (Xue, 2022). With the help of technology, traveling abroad may be more pleasurable and accessible (Moorhouse et al., 2018). Visitors can converse and comprehend various languages with ease (Wang et al., 2024). The travelers feel more secure and independent when they can comfortably order meals, explore, and engage with locals. These kinds of technological advancements make traveling more relaxing and engaging (Baltierra, 2023).

The adoption of cutting-edge AI-driven translation solutions is a wise financial decision for hospitality organizations (Plotkina et al., 2022). They are able to efficiently service a larger, global clientele because to this innovation. It helps companies to reach a wider audience and be more inclusive, which facilitates more seamless interactions with customers (Peukert, 2019). With the help of these AI tools, businesses can provide smooth multilingual customer service and personalize experiences for each customer, strengthening relationships (Halid et al., 2024). These solutions also lessen the requirement for a workforce that speaks many languages, which saves money and increases operational effectiveness while upholding high service standards (Syed et al., 2021).

1.2 Objectives of the Chapter

The tourist and hospitality industry is one that has seen the most rapid transformation due to the quick rise of Intellectual property(GenAI). This chapter has the following objectives to:

- examines how GenAI might improve customer experiences and foster stronger customer connections in this sector.
- clarifies how tourist and hospitality firms may utilize GenAI to enhance customer engagement, tailor experiences, and maximize operational efficiency by utilizing AI capabilities including natural language processing, text creation, and automated customer care.
- talks about the difficulties and moral issues that come with using GenAI in the travel and hospitality industry.

Figure 2 .Objectives of the Chapter

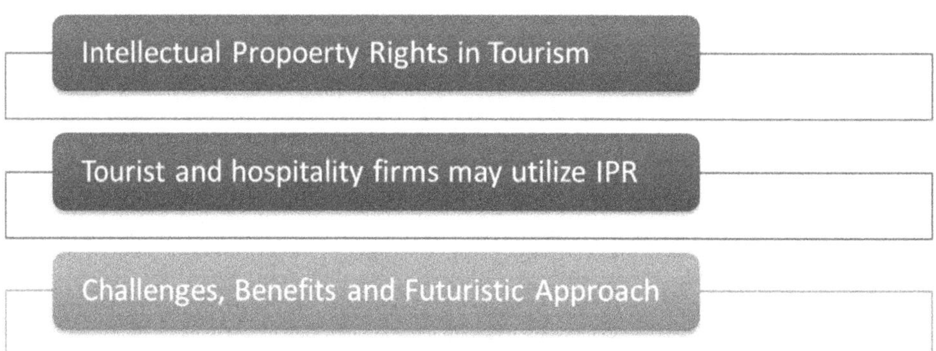

(Source- Original)

1.3 Structure of the Chapter

This chapter specifies the diverse arena of Reconnoitering Potential of Intellectual property in Tourism and Hospitality Industry: Strengthening Customer Relationships Delivering Better Experiences. Section 2 elaborates the Intellectual Property Rights in Tourism and Hospitality Industry. Section 3 explores the IPR in Travel and Hospitality: Applications. Section 4 discusses the Developing and Strengthening Customer Relationships in Hospitality and Tourism. Section 5 highlights the Challenges, Ethical Issues and Valuable Solutions. Finally, Section 6 Conclude the Chapter with Future Scope.

Figure 3. The Flow of this Chapter

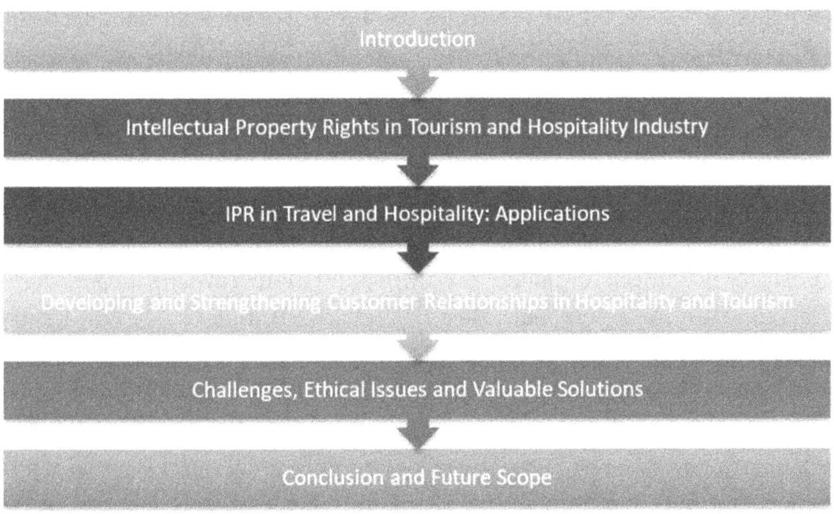

(Source- Original)

2. INTELLECTUAL PROPERTY RIGHTS IN TOURISM AND HOSPITALITY INDUSTRY

Businesses may create highly customized offerings and adverts thanks to IPR (Zhang, 2020). AI creates customized ads that are more pertinent to the consumer by examining their behavior and interests (Carton, 2019). This leads to personalized travel offers that pique customers' attention, increasing engagement and increasing the likelihood of conversion. Strategic use of technology in marketing results in more effective campaigns and happier customers (Soliman & Al Balushi, 2023). It also builds stronger bonds and deeper connections between brands and their patrons. Chatbots driven by IPRare transforming customer service in the travel and hospitality sectors (Mohamed, 2024). These bots use cutting-edge machine learning and natural language processing to comprehend and reply to consumer enquiries with remarkable precision. They are available around-the-clock and offer prompt assistance to passengers (Bhatnagar, 2022). This continuous accessibility, which does away with lengthy wait periods for human agents, is a significant advance over traditional customer support (Singh, 2023).

The wide range of travel-related inquiries may be handled by these chatbots, from straightforward ones like the status of flights to trickier ones like itinerary modifications or lodging suggestions (Henke & Jacques Bughin, 2016). Because of their ability to learn from encounters, they get more accurate and tailored over time (Kaushal & Yadav, 2023). It enables businesses to tailor services according to in-depth knowledge of client preferences, including eating selections and accommodation choices (Singh, 2023). This degree of customization boosts operational effectiveness in addition to visitor experiences (King, 2022). Hospitality businesses may obtain a competitive edge by utilizing artificial intelligence to provide visitors with one-of-a-kind experiences that make them want to come back (Savickaite, 2024). This leads to increased client satisfaction, more efficient operations, and lower costs for hospitality organizations. More and more travelers are searching for vacations that suit their personal tastes (Babet, 2020). Indeed, 74% of them give more weight to experiences that align with their particular interests than just price. This is addressed by generative AI, which makes vacation planning more interesting and customized (Sadowski, 2023). It does this by analyzing user preferences to recommend travel places and activities that suit individual interests, making travel experiences not only pleasurable but also highly personalized (Sharma & Singh, 2022). Because every vacation is customized to the individual likes and dislikes of the tourist, it fosters a sense of uniqueness and happiness (Gao & Liu, 2022). Thus, IPRgives hospitality companies a chance to better understand and serve their customers' demands (Rajamannar, 2021).

The predictive analytics capabilities of IPRare extended to trip planning, where it analyzes a variety of data, such as booking trends, weather patterns, and consumer comments (Singh, 2022). So identifying important patterns through in-depth analysis, hospitality organizations are better equipped to make judgments (Ancillai, 2019). Businesses may modify their offers, including price strategies and inventory management, by comprehending these tendencies (Singh, 2022). For instance, businesses might modify their pricing if AI detects periods of high booking. With matching services to traveler interests, this strategy not only increases income but also improves customer pleasure (George, 2023).

3. IPR IN TRAVEL AND HOSPITALITY: APPLICATIONS

Artificial intelligence that creates text, graphics, or other media in response to human input is known as IPR(Kuusinen, 2019). It generates material that is similar to what it was trained on by identifying patterns in the data and forecasting probable answers (Singh, 2022). Deep learning, which employs artificial neural networks to handle more complicated patterns than typical machine learning, includes IPR(Wheeler, 2023). IPRmodels may be divided into text-to-text, text-to-image, text-to-video, and text-to-task models based on their functions (Sedkaoui, 2018). Well-known public IPR tools are Dall-E, Google's Bard, and OpenAI's ChatGPT. Businesses may gain a competitive edge and change operations by implementing IPR(Neuwirth, 2023). Several uses for IPRin business include content curation, fraud detection through pattern recognition, improved customer interactions, and enhanced customization (Schaeffer, 2017). So, improving the client experience has always been the primary goal of the hotel sector (Singh, 2019). Over the past ten years, the industry has witnessed substantial technical breakthroughs and intense competition (Venkatesh, 2021). Regardless of location or time, clients may now use their mobile devices to complete a range of duties related to the hospitality business, including making bookings, scheduling events, checking in, or checking out (Reviglio della Venaria, 2020). These cutting-edge technologies like cloud computing, blockchain, and the Internet of Things have many uses, save money on operations, and eliminate the need for face-to-face contacts between staff and clients, all of which increase customer satisfaction (Maes, 2018). The requirement for internal IT infrastructure may be reduced by utilizing cloud services, and the Internet of Things has completely changed how electronic equipment is maintained (Berman & Pollack, 2021). The considering of these developments, it is imperative that businesses in the hotel sector adopt cutting-edge technology, such as generative artificial intelligence, to improve the quality of their services and enhance customization (Bug & Bernd, 2020).

Figure 4. Applications of the IPR in Travel and Hospitality

(Source- Original)

Assistance and Support for Customers: Chatbots and virtual assistants driven by GenAI are transforming customer service in the travel and hotel industry (Deshbhratar et al., 2023). These AI-powered solutions may handle client enquiries, handle reservations, and provide tailored suggestions in addition to round-the-clock assistance (Lycett et al., 2024). These technologies lower operating expenses and improve customer satisfaction by automating repetitive processes (Meibner et al., 2020). AI-driven customisation boosts conversion rates and streamlines operations from a commercial standpoint. Higher occupancy rates and more effective pricing strategies are the outcomes of hospitality operators' increased ability to precisely match their products with consumer wants (Semeradova, & Weinlich, 2022). Businesses may proactively modify their services by anticipating future booking trends with the use of Generative AI's predictive capabilities. This strategy guarantees continuously excellent levels of customer service and loyalty while optimizing income (Sengupta & Cao, 2022).

Customer Experience and Personalization: Because GenAI can evaluate large volumes of data, firms may provide clients with customized suggestions (Lombart et al., 2020). This is translated into individualized dining experiences, customized trip itineraries, and amenities for hotel rooms in the tourism sector (Santulli, 2019). This customized approach shows that it understands each client's preferences, which improves customer relationships. Customers can easily browse the wide range of trip possibilities thanks to IPR(Lavoye et al., 2023). This technique drastically reduces the bewildering number of alternatives by presenting the most relevant options based on prior actions and personal preferences (Thomas, 2021). This focused strategy ensures a more fulfilling experience by saving time and precisely matching personal travel preferences. As a result, clients have a less stressful and more efficient reservation procedure (Abdelmaged, 2021).

Improved Hotel Experience: Throughout a visitor's stay, GAI chatbots may communicate with them, offering advice, information, and immediate problem-solving (Akhtar, 2018). GAI may customize in-room amenities, change the temperature of the room according to the preferences of the visitor, and use virtual reality tours to create immersive experiences (Lavoye, 2023). Traveler categories may be targeted with customized and localized marketing content from GAI, which highlights attractions and activities that align with their interests (Yim & Park, 2019).

Promotion and Content Development: The generation of marketing content, such as advertisements, social media postings, and website content, is a growing use of GenAI (Zhu, 2024). Businesses in the travel and hospitality industries may generate vast amounts of content while keeping a consistent brand voice thanks to automated content generation (Marr, 2021). This skill is particularly helpful for drawing in and keeping people interested in the brand (Fan et al., 2022).

Personalized Trip Planning: With interacting with potential passengers and learning about their preferences, AI chatbots powered by IPRare able to develop personalized trip plans that recommend locations, things to do, and lodging options based on their interests (Collins, 2019). Using historical behavior and current data, GAI may create personalized marketing material for campaigns, restaurant and attraction suggestions, and travel brochures that are tailored to certain interests and demographics (Chen & Lin, 2022).

Effectiveness of Operations: Several operational facets of the travel and hospitality industries may be optimized with the help of IPR(Pietronudo & Leone, 2022). Artificial intelligence (AI) algorithms may automate cleaning schedules and dynamic pricing models, among other tasks, to save costs and increase efficiency (Pamuru et al., 2021). An improved overall client experience is a result of this operational efficiency (Machairidis & Mourmouras, 2020).

4. DEVELOPING AND STRENGTHENING CUSTOMER RELATIONSHIPS IN HOSPITALITY AND TOURISM

IPRis revolutionizing the tourism and hotel sector, particularly in terms of enhancing visitor experiences and boosting income (Raghavan & Pai, 2021). Its characteristics may be used to several facets of the business, increasing operational effectiveness and personalizing client relationships (Schwarz, 2022). Businesses in the tourist and hospitality industries may build more meaningful and profound connections with their visitors by utilizing IPR(GAI) (Lavuri & Akram, 2023). With fusing hotel-specific features such facilities, surrounds, location, and reviews with a potential guest's personal information like- hobbies, preferences, and household data, hospitality businesses can produce dynamic, personalized narratives that seem authentic and human (Caliskan et al., 2023). This individualized approach makes it more likely that a potential visitor will decide to make a reservation at a certain resort (Kacprzak & Hensel, 2023).

24/7 Personalized Support: GAI-enabled chatbots are able to provide round-the-clock assistance by quickly and effectively responding to visitor inquiries and this encourages a feeling of worth and support (Vinaykarthik, 2022).

Hyper-Personalization: GAI enables companies to speak to customers by name, make reference to past exchanges, and provide recommendations that are specifically catered to their interests (Kamal & Himel, 2023).

Proactive Customer Service: GAI-powered predictive analytics can foresee visitor requirements and proactively attend to them, building anticipation and going above and beyond (Ahmed, 2022).

Delivering Improved Experiences: GAI may improve visitor experiences by establishing a more customized and engaging setting (Vuong & Mai, 2023). Travel experiences are being revolutionized by IPRthrough virtual tour guides (Singh, 2024). With the help of these AI-powered guides, travelers may engage in interactive and immersive excursions of global destinations, giving them a virtual presence in places that suit their interests (Auttri et al., 2023). Every user's experience is customized by the AI, whether they are on a tour of historical sites or exploring contemporary architecture (Zaki, 2022). Also, it offers up-to-date information about news or events pertaining to the locations they are visiting (Soliman & Al Balushi, 2023). This technology facilitates the planning and enjoyment of virtual tours for users by expanding access to worldwide places and personalizing travel experiences (Bhatnagar, 2022).

Tailored Itineraries: GAI can create travel schedules that maximize time and resources by integrating lodging, activities, and transportation in a seamless manner (Singh, 2023) (Henke & Jacques Bughin, 2016). IPRtravel planners are a big step forward for hospitality companies in providing all-inclusive vacation experiences (Kaushal & Yadav, 2023). These planners create whole trips with day-by-day plans, going beyond just proposing locations (Singh, 2023). They take care of everything, including scheduling efficient transportation, purchasing tickets for local attractions, and suggesting the ideal times to visit well-known locations (King, 2022). Businesses may differentiate themselves in a crowded market and provide customers an exceptionally smooth and pleasurable travel experience by offering such comprehensive and well-thought-out travel packages (Babet, 2020).

Language-Free Communication: Via removing language barriers, GAI-powered translation technologies may promote inclusiveness and smooth communication (Sadowski, 2023).

Virtual and Augmented Reality: GAI can produce augmented reality experiences that improve exploration and discovery as well as immersive virtual tours of various locations (Sharma & Singh, 2022).

Figure 5. Key Genesis of Strengthening Customer Relationships in Hospitality and Tourism

(Source- Original)

In the hotel and tourism sector, IPRmay be applied in a number of ways to improve the visitor experience, from enhancing safety and security to providing tailored suggestions (Mashood et al., 2023). AI-driven chatbots and virtual assistants, for instance, may provide hotel visitors personalized recommendations for nearby sights and activities (Gao & Liu, 2022). Also, by creating additional avenues for contact, these technologies help improve communication between hotel employees and visitors (Rajamannar, 2021).

5. CHALLENGES, ETHICAL ISSUES AND VALUABLE SOLUTIONS

For years, travel businesses have benefited from artificial intelligence (AI) models that optimize timetables and hotel inventories, manage revenue, and generate look-alike audience models (Singh, 2022). Also, IPRgoes one step further by enabling dynamic content by means of swift content generation and dynamic display (Ancillai et al., 2019). Large language model (LLM)-based IPRtools such as ChatGPT and Google's Bard have sparked industry-specific investments and applications (Singh, 2022). This quick acceptance also presents new dangers for companies, including issues with copyright, consumer confidence, and factual errors (George, 2023). Although there are many advantages to GenAI in the travel and hospitality industries, there are also a number of difficulties and moral issues to be aware of like-

Security and Privacy of Data: Since GenAI mostly relies on data analysis, data security and privacy are important issues (Wind & Hays, 2016). Robust data protection methods are necessary for the travel and hospitality business to secure client information (Kuusinen, 2019). Keeping customers' confidence requires adhering to laws like the GDPR (Singh, 2022).

Fairness and Bias: Biases that exist in training data may unintentionally be reinforced by GenAI algorithms (Naji et al., 2024). To guarantee a just and equal client experience, tourism and hospitality organizations need to be especially watchful when it comes to managing prejudice (Wheeler, 2023).

Employment Concerns: GenAI automation may result in employment losses in the travel and hospitality industry (Sedkaoui, 2018). Businesses must strike a balance between the need to maintain jobs and offer possibilities for upskilling and reskilling and automation (Neuwirth, 2023).

Figure 6. Challenges and Ethical Issues

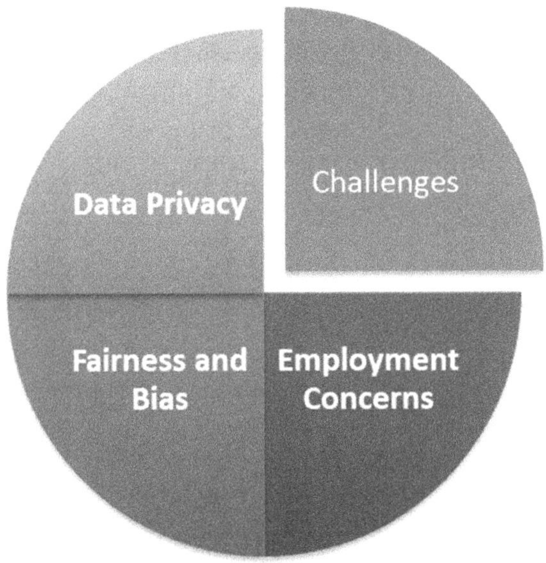

(Source- Original)

The efficiency of hotel operations may also be increased by combining IPR with robots (Schaeffer, 2017). Automated systems may handle repetitive jobs like maintenance and cleaning of rooms, freeing up humans to focus on more important duties like providing excellent guest services (Singh, 2019). AI-powered systems can maximize the use of resources, such as water and electricity, which reduces costs and improves sustainability (Venkatesh, 2021). It is conceivable that hotels will use this sort of technology in their business plans in the future (Reviglio della Venaria, 2020). In addition to these practical benefits, IPRmay enhance the working conditions for employees in the hotel and tourist sectors (Duan, et al., 2024). The providing of individualized training experiences based on each employee's skills and limitations, employers enable their workforce to learn at their own speed and in a way that best fits their preferences (Tzampazaki et al., 2024). With a workforce that is more skilled and well-trained, the company may see an increase in revenue growth and better client experiences as a result of this customized training method (Hanafiah et al., 2024).

It is important to consider the ethical implications of generative AI, just like with any new technology and thus examines the possibilities of this technology in great detail, taking into account both its advantages and potential drawbacks (Tembrevilla et al., 2024). To make sure that IPR is used in a responsible and transparent manner is crucial (Schmaltz et al., 2024). In addition to hotels and other hospitality businesses being transparent about their use of IPRto enhance the visitor experience, guests should be aware of when and how their data is being utilized (Bala & Gupta, 2024). Making sure IPR is applied in a fair and equitable manner is another crucial component (Hazarika & Rahmati, 2023) (Varela et al., 2024). This entails making sure that the advantages of the technology are dispersed equally across various groups, such as employees and visitors, and that it does not reinforce preexisting prejudices or disparities (Gupta, 2024) (Saragih et al., 2024).

Figure 7. Viable Solutions

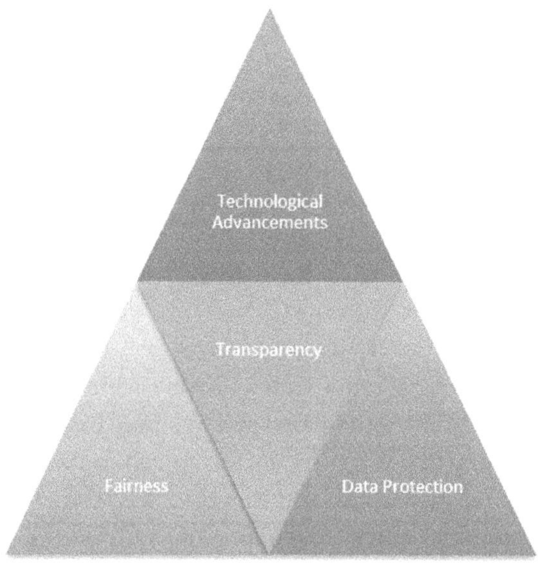

(Source- Original)

6. CONCLUSION AND FUTURE SCOPE

The hospitality and tourism industry's demand trend analysis is being revolutionized by generative AI. It performs expertly the processing of rival pricing, market trends, and historical data to enable dynamic service rate optimization as a crucial function in the highly competitive world of today. In order to identify minute trends in demand, the AI also scans social media. This data yields insightful information that can be used to control costs and allocate resources. This keeps prices competitive while also improving operational efficiency. IPR improves energy use by modifying lighting, heating, and cooling according to consumption patterns; this lowers expenses and encourages sustainability. In the travel and hospitality sector, Intellectual property has enormous potential for improving consumer connections and providing better experiences. GenAI can boost customer happiness and loyalty through applications in marketing, customization, customer service, and operational efficiency. When using GenAI, care must be taken to solve issues with prejudice, data privacy, and job displacement. With taking these things into account, companies in the travel and hospitality industries may fully utilize GenAI's potential to build a future where technology and human interaction coexist peacefully.

REFERENCES

Abdelmaged, M. A. M. (2021). Implementation of virtual reality in healthcare, entertainment, tourism, education, and retail sectors.

Abrokwah-Larbi, K. (2024). Transforming metaverse marketing into strategic agility in SMEs through mediating roles of IMT and CI: theoretical framework and research propositions. *Journal of Contemporary Marketing Science*.

Ahmed, A. (2022). Marketing 4.0: The Unseen Potential of AI in Consumer Relations. *International Journal of New Media Studies: International Peer Reviewed Scholarly Indexed Journal*, 9(1), 5–12.

Akhtar, O. M. A. R. (2018). Understanding use cases for augmented, mixed and virtual reality. *Altimeter. Online verfügbar unter*https://marketing. prophet. com/acton/ct/33865/p-00b2/Bct/l-00a9/l-00a9*: 17b/ct16_0/1*.

Alyasiri, O. M., Selvaraj, K., Younis, H. A., Sahib, T. M., Almasoodi, M. F., & Hayder, I. M. (2024). A Survey on the Potential of Artificial Intelligence Tools in Tourism Information Services. *Babylonian Journal of Artificial Intelligence*, 2024, 1–8. DOI: 10.58496/BJAI/2024/001

Ancillai, C., Terho, H., Cardinali, S., & Pascucci, F. (2019). Advancing social media driven sales research: Establishing conceptual foundations for B-to-B social selling. *Industrial Marketing Management*, 82, 293–308. DOI: 10.1016/j.indmarman.2019.01.002

Ancillai, C., Terho, H., Cardinali, S., & Pascucci, F. (2019). Advancing social media driven sales research: Establishing conceptual foundations for B-to-B social selling. *Industrial Marketing Management*, 82, 293–308. DOI: 10.1016/j.indmarman.2019.01.002

Auttri, B., Chaitanya, K., Daida, S., & Jain, S. K. (2023). Digital Transformation in Customer Relationship Management: Enhancing Engagement and Loyalty. [EEL]. *European Economic Letters*, 13(3), 1140–1149.

Babet, A. (2020). Utilization of personalization in marketing automation and email marketing.

Babet, A. (2020). Utilization of personalization in marketing automation and email marketing.

Bala, R., & Gupta, P. (2024). Virtual Reality in Education: Benefits, Applications and Challenges. *Transforming Education with Virtual Reality*, 165-180.

Baltierra, S. (2023, January). Virtual Reality and Augmented Reality Applied to E-Commerce: A Literature Review. In *Human-Computer Interaction: 8th Iberoamerican Workshop, HCI-COLLAB 2022, Havana, Cuba, October 13–15, 2022, Revised Selected Papers* (p. 201). Springer Nature.

Berman, B., & Pollack, D. (2021). Strategies for the successful implementation of augmented reality. *Business Horizons*, 64(5), 621–630. DOI: 10.1016/j.bushor.2021.02.027

Bhatnagar, S. (2022). Digital Disruptions and Transformation of Bank Marketing.

Bhatnagar, S. (2022). Digital Disruptions and Transformation of Bank Marketing.

Bug, P., & Bernd, M. (2020). The future of fashion films in augmented reality and virtual reality. *Fashion and film: moving images and consumer behavior*, 281-301.

Caboni, F., & Hagberg, J. (2019). Augmented reality in retailing: A review of features, applications and value. *International Journal of Retail & Distribution Management*, 47(11), 1125–1140. DOI: 10.1108/IJRDM-12-2018-0263

Çalışkan, G., Yayla, İ., & Pamukçu, H. (2023). The use of augmented reality technologies in tourism businesses from the perspective of UTAUT2. *European Journal of Innovation Management*.

Carton, S. (2019). *What impact will immersive technologies such as augmented and virtual reality have on the retail sector?* (Doctoral dissertation, Dublin, National College of Ireland).

Chen, Y., & Lin, C. A. (2022). Consumer behavior in an augmented reality environment: Exploring the effects of flow via augmented realism and technology fluidity. *Telematics and Informatics*, 71, 101833. DOI: 10.1016/j.tele.2022.101833

Collins, R. (2019). Marketing Implications of Utilizing Augmented Reality for In-Store Retailing.

Deshbhratar, S., Joshi, S., Alwaali, R. N., Saear, A. R., & Marhoon, H. A. (2023, September). Augmented reality of online and physical retailing: A study of applications and its value. In *AIP Conference Proceedings* (Vol. 2736, No. 1). AIP Publishing. DOI: 10.1063/5.0170917

Duan, W., Khurshid, A., Khan, K., & Calin, A. C. (2024). Transforming industry: Investigating 4.0 technologies for sustainable product evolution in china through a novel fuzzy three-way decision-making process. *Technological Forecasting and Social Change*, 200, 123125. DOI: 10.1016/j.techfore.2023.123125

Dwivedi, Y. K., Pandey, N., Currie, W., & Micu, A. (2024). Leveraging ChatGPT and other Intellectual property(AI)-based applications in the hospitality and tourism industry: Practices, challenges and research agenda. *International Journal of Contemporary Hospitality Management*, 36(1), 1–12. DOI: 10.1108/IJCHM-05-2023-0686

Fan, X., Jiang, X., & Deng, N. (2022). Immersive technology: A meta-analysis of augmented/virtual reality applications and their impact on tourism experience. *Tourism Management*, 91, 104534. DOI: 10.1016/j.tourman.2022.104534

Gao, Y., & Liu, H. (2022). Artificial intelligence-enabled personalization in interactive marketing: a customer journey perspective. *Journal of Research in Interactive Marketing*, (ahead-of-print), 1-18.

Gao, Y., & Liu, H. (2022). Artificial intelligence-enabled personalization in interactive marketing: a customer journey perspective. *Journal of Research in Interactive Marketing*, (ahead-of-print), 1-18.

George, A. S. (2023). Future Economic Implications of Artificial Intelligence. *Partners Universal International Research Journal*, 2(3), 20–39.

George, A. S. (2023). Future Economic Implications of Artificial Intelligence. *Partners Universal International Research Journal*, 2(3), 20–39.

Gupta, R., Nair, K., Mishra, M., Ibrahim, B., & Bhardwaj, S. (2024). Adoption and impacts of generative artificial intelligence: Theoretical underpinnings and research agenda. *International Journal of Information Management Data Insights*, 4(1), 100232. DOI: 10.1016/j.jjimei.2024.100232

Gupta, V. (2024). An Empirical Evaluation of a Intellectual propertyTechnology Adoption Model from Entrepreneurs' Perspectives. *Systems*, 12(3), 103. DOI: 10.3390/systems12030103

Gursoy, D., & Cai, R. (2024). Artificial intelligence: An overview of research trends and future directions. *International Journal of Contemporary Hospitality Management*. Advance online publication. DOI: 10.1108/IJCHM-03-2024-0322

Halid, H., Ravesangar, K., Mahadzir, S. L., & Halim, S. N. A. (2024). Artificial Intelligence (AI) in Human Resource Management (HRM). In *Building the Future with Human Resource Management* (pp. 37–70). Springer International Publishing. DOI: 10.1007/978-3-031-52811-8_2

Hanafiah, M. H., Asyraff, M. A., Ismail, M. N. I., & Sjukriana, J. (2024). Understanding the key drivers in using mobile payment (M-Payment) among Generation Z travellers. *Young Consumers*, 25(5), 645–664. DOI: 10.1108/YC-08-2023-1835

Hazarika, A., & Rahmati, M. (2023). Towards an evolved immersive experience: Exploring 5G-and beyond-enabled ultra-low-latency communications for augmented and virtual reality. *Sensors (Basel)*, 23(7), 3682. DOI: 10.3390/s23073682 PMID: 37050742

Henke, N., & Jacques Bughin, L. (2016). The age of analytics: Competing in a data-driven world.

Henke, N., & Jacques Bughin, L. (2016). The age of analytics: Competing in a data-driven world.

Kacprzak, A., & Hensel, P. (2023). Exploring online customer experience: A systematic literature review and research agenda. *International Journal of Consumer Studies*, 47(6), 2583–2608. DOI: 10.1111/ijcs.12966

Kamal, M., & Himel, A. S. (2023). Redefining Modern Marketing: An Analysis of AI and NLP's Influence on Consumer Engagement, Strategy, and Beyond. *Eigenpub Review of Science and Technology*, 7(1), 203–223.

Kannan, R. (2024). Revolutionizing the Tourism Industry through Artificial Intelligence: A Comprehensive Review of AI Integration, Impact on Customer Experience, Operational Efficiency, and Future Trends. *International Journal for Multidimensional Research Perspectives, 2*(2), 01-14.

Kaushal, V., & Yadav, R. (2023). Learning successful implementation of Chatbots in businesses from B2B customer experience perspective. *Concurrency and Computation*, 35(1), e7450. DOI: 10.1002/cpe.7450

Kaushal, V., & Yadav, R. (2023). Learning successful implementation of Chatbots in businesses from B2B customer experience perspective. *Concurrency and Computation*, 35(1), e7450. DOI: 10.1002/cpe.7450

Khan, U., & Khan, K. A. Intellectual property(GAI) in hospitality and tourism marketing: Perceptions, risks, benefits, and policy implications. *Journal of Global Hospitality and Tourism, 3*(1), 269-284.

King, K. (2022). *AI Strategy for Sales and Marketing: Connecting Marketing, Sales and Customer Experience*. Kogan Page Publishers.

King, K. (2022). *AI Strategy for Sales and Marketing: Connecting Marketing, Sales and Customer Experience*. Kogan Page Publishers.

Kuusinen, M. (2019). Scenarios for digital marketing: a Delphi-based analysis for 2028.

Kuusinen, M. (2019). Scenarios for digital marketing: a Delphi-based analysis for 2028.

Lauer-Schmaltz, M. W., Cash, P., Hansen, J. P., & Maier, A. (2024). Towards the Human Digital Twin: Definition and Design—A survey. *arXiv preprint arXiv:2402.07922*.

Lavoye, V. (2023). Augmented reality in consumer retail: a presence theory approach.

Lavoye, V., Tarkiainen, A., Sipilä, J., & Mero, J. (2023). More than skin-deep: The influence of presence dimensions on purchase intentions in augmented reality shopping. *Journal of Business Research*, 169, 114247. DOI: 10.1016/j.jbusres.2023.114247

Lavuri, R., & Akram, U. (2023). Role of virtual reality authentic experience on affective responses: Moderating role virtual reality attachment. *Journal of Ecotourism*, •••, 1–19.

Lombart, C., Millan, E., Normand, J. M., Verhulst, A., Labbé-Pinlon, B., & Moreau, G. (2020). Effects of physical, non-immersive virtual, and immersive virtual store environments on consumers' perceptions and purchase behavior. *Computers in Human Behavior*, 110, 106374. DOI: 10.1016/j.chb.2020.106374

Lycett, M., Meechao, K., & Reppel, A. (2024). *Materializing Design Fictions for Metaverse Services.*

Machairidis, E., & Mourmouras, N. (2020). The impact of augmented, virtual and mixed reality technologies on consumer purchase decision, in the Greek market.

Maes, P. (2018). *Disruptive Selling: A New Strategic Approach to Sales, Marketing and Customer Service*. Kogan Page Publishers.

Marr, B. (2021). *Extended reality in practice: 100+ amazing ways virtual, augmented and mixed reality are changing business and Society*. John Wiley & Sons.

Mashood, K., Kayani, H. U. R., Malik, A. A., & Tahir, A. (2023). ARTIFICIAL INTELLIGENCE RECENT TRENDS AND APPLICATIONS IN INDUSTRIES. *Pakistan Journal of Science*, 75(02). Advance online publication. DOI: 10.57041/pjs.v75i02.855

Meißner, M., Pfeiffer, J., Peukert, C., Dietrich, H., & Pfeiffer, T. (2020). How virtual reality affects consumer choice. *Journal of Business Research*, 117, 219–231. DOI: 10.1016/j.jbusres.2020.06.004

Mogaji, E., Viglia, G., Srivastava, P., & Dwivedi, Y. K. (2024). Is it the end of the technology acceptance model in the era of generative artificial intelligence? *International Journal of Contemporary Hospitality Management*, 36(10), 3324–3339. DOI: 10.1108/IJCHM-08-2023-1271

Mohamed, Ů. (2024). *Integrating Digital Techniques/Technologies in Developing Egyptian Museums (Case Study: Alexandria Library Museums-Alexandria City).* Sohag Engineering Journal.

Moorhouse, N., tom Dieck, M. C., & Jung, T. (2018). Technological innovations transforming the consumer retail experience: a review of literature. *Augmented Reality and Virtual Reality: Empowering Human, Place and Business*, 133-143.

Naji, K. K., Gunduz, M., Alhenzab, F., Al-Hababi, H., & Al-Qahtani, A. (2024). A Systematic Review of the Digital Transformation of the Building Construction Industry. *IEEE Access : Practical Innovations, Open Solutions*, 12, 31461–31487. DOI: 10.1109/ACCESS.2024.3365934

Neuwirth, R. J. (2023). Prohibited artificial intelligence practices in the proposed EU artificial intelligence act (AIA). *Computer Law & Security Report*, 48, 105798. DOI: 10.1016/j.clsr.2023.105798

Neuwirth, R. J. (2023). Prohibited artificial intelligence practices in the proposed EU artificial intelligence act (AIA). *Computer Law & Security Report*, 48, 105798. DOI: 10.1016/j.clsr.2023.105798

Pamuru, V., Khern-am-nuai, W., & Kannan, K. (2021). The impact of an augmented-reality game on local businesses: A study of Pokémon go on restaurants. *Information Systems Research*, 32(3), 950–966. DOI: 10.1287/isre.2021.1004

Peukert, C., Pfeiffer, J., Meißner, M., Pfeiffer, T., & Weinhardt, C. (2019). Shopping in virtual reality stores: The influence of immersion on system adoption. *Journal of Management Information Systems*, 36(3), 755–788. DOI: 10.1080/07421222.2019.1628889

Pietronudo, M. C., & Leone, D. (2022). The Power of Augmented Reality for Smart Environments: An Explorative Analysis of the Business Process Management. In *Machine Learning for Smart Environments/Cities: An IoT Approach* (pp. 73–91). Springer International Publishing. DOI: 10.1007/978-3-030-97516-6_4

Plotkina, D., Dinsmore, J., & Racat, M. (2022). Improving service brand personality with augmented reality marketing. *Journal of Services Marketing*, 36(6), 781–799. DOI: 10.1108/JSM-12-2020-0519

Raghavan, S., & Pai, R. (2021). Changing Paradigm of Consumer Experience Through Martech–A Case Study on Indian Online Retail Industry. *International Journal of Case Studies in Business* [IJCSBE]. *IT and Education*, 5(1), 186–199.

Rajamannar, R. (2021). *Quantum marketing: mastering the new marketing mindset for tomorrow's consumers*. HarperCollins Leadership.

Rajamannar, R. (2021). *Quantum marketing: mastering the new marketing mindset for tomorrow's consumers*. HarperCollins Leadership.

Reviglio della Venaria, U. (2020). Personalization in Social Media: Challenges and Opportunities for Democratic Societies.

Reviglio della Venaria, U. (2020). Personalization in Social Media: Challenges and Opportunities for Democratic Societies.

Sadowski, J. (2023). Total life insurance: Logics of anticipatory control and actuarial governance in insurance technology. *Social Studies of Science*, •••, 03063127231186437. PMID: 37427796

Sadowski, J. (2023). Total life insurance: Logics of anticipatory control and actuarial governance in insurance technology. *Social Studies of Science*, •••, 03063127231186437. PMID: 37427796

Santulli, M. (2019). *The influence of augmented reality on consumers' online purchase intention: the Sephora Virtual Artist case* (Doctoral dissertation).

Saragih, H. S., Saputra, M. R. U., & Dewantara, M. H. (2024). Exploring Topics and Trends in Service Robots, Artificial Intelligence, and Realities in Tourism: A Text-Mining Approach. *Emerging Technologies in Business: Innovation Strategies for Competitive Advantage*, 239.

Savickaite, S. (2024). *Using Virtual Reality to explore individual differences in perception due to neurodiversity* (Doctoral dissertation, University of Glasgow).

Schaeffer, E. (2017). *Industry X. 0: Realizing digital value in industrial sectors*. Kogan Page Publishers.

Schaeffer, E. (2017). *Industry X. 0: Realizing digital value in industrial sectors*. Kogan Page Publishers.

Schwarz, M. (2022). Augmented Reality in Online Retail: Generational Differences Between Millennials and Generation Z Using Virtual Try-On's.

Sedkaoui, S. (Ed.). (2018). *Big data analytics for entrepreneurial success*. IGI Global.

Sedkaoui, S. (Ed.). (2018). *Big data analytics for entrepreneurial success*. IGI Global.

Semerádová, T., & Weinlich, P. (2022). The place of virtual reality in e-retail: Viable shopping environment or just a game. In *Moving businesses online and embracing e-commerce: Impact and opportunities caused by COVID-19* (pp. 92–117). IGI Global. DOI: 10.4018/978-1-7998-8294-7.ch005

Sengupta, A., & Cao, L. (2022). Augmented reality's perceived immersion effect on the customer shopping process: Decision-making quality and privacy concerns. *International Journal of Retail & Distribution Management*, 50(8/9), 1039–1061. DOI: 10.1108/IJRDM-10-2021-0522

Sharma, A., & Singh, B. (2022). Measuring Impact of E-commerce on Small Scale Business: A Systematic Review. *Journal of Corporate Governance and International Business Law*, 5(1).

Sharma, A., & Singh, B. (2022). Measuring Impact of E-commerce on Small Scale Business: A Systematic Review. *Journal of Corporate Governance and International Business Law*, 5(1).

Singh, B. (2019). Profiling Public Healthcare: A Comparative Analysis Based on the Multidimensional Healthcare Management and Legal Approach. *Indian Journal of Health and Medical Law*, 2(2), 1–5.

Singh, B. (2019). Profiling Public Healthcare: A Comparative Analysis Based on the Multidimensional Healthcare Management and Legal Approach. *Indian Journal of Health and Medical Law*, 2(2), 1–5.

Singh, B. (2022). Understanding Legal Frameworks Concerning Transgender Healthcare in the Age of Dynamism. *ELECTRONIC JOURNAL OF SOCIAL AND STRATEGIC STUDIES*, 3(1), 56–65. DOI: 10.47362/EJSSS.2022.3104

Singh, B. (2022). Relevance of Agriculture-Nutrition Linkage for Human Healthcare: A Conceptual Legal Framework of Implication and Pathways. *Justice and Law Bulletin*, 1(1), 44–49.

Singh, B. (2022). COVID-19 Pandemic and Public Healthcare: Endless Downward Spiral or Solution via Rapid Legal and Health Services Implementation with Patient Monitoring Program. *Justice and Law Bulletin*, 1(1), 1–7.

Singh, B. (2022). Understanding Legal Frameworks Concerning Transgender Healthcare in the Age of Dynamism. *ELECTRONIC JOURNAL OF SOCIAL AND STRATEGIC STUDIES*, 3(1), 56–65. DOI: 10.47362/EJSSS.2022.3104

Singh, B. (2022). Relevance of Agriculture-Nutrition Linkage for Human Healthcare: A Conceptual Legal Framework of Implication and Pathways. *Justice and Law Bulletin*, 1(1), 44–49.

Singh, B. (2022). COVID-19 Pandemic and Public Healthcare: Endless Downward Spiral or Solution via Rapid Legal and Health Services Implementation with Patient Monitoring Program. *Justice and Law Bulletin*, 1(1), 1–7.

Singh, B. (2023). Blockchain Technology in Renovating Healthcare: Legal and Future Perspectives. In Revolutionizing Healthcare Through Artificial Intelligence and Internet of Things Applications (pp. 177-186). IGI Global.

Singh, B. (2023). Federated Learning for Envision Future Trajectory Smart Transport System for Climate Preservation and Smart Green Planet: Insights into Global Governance and SDG-9 (Industry, Innovation and Infrastructure). *National Journal of Environmental Law*, 6(2), 6–17.

Singh, B. (2023). Blockchain Technology in Renovating Healthcare: Legal and Future Perspectives. In Revolutionizing Healthcare Through Artificial Intelligence and Internet of Things Applications (pp. 177-186). IGI Global.

Singh, B. (2023). Federated Learning for Envision Future Trajectory Smart Transport System for Climate Preservation and Smart Green Planet: Insights into Global Governance and SDG-9 (Industry, Innovation and Infrastructure). *National Journal of Environmental Law*, 6(2), 6–17.

Singh, B. (2024). Legal Dynamics Lensing Metaverse Crafted for Videogame Industry and E-Sports: Phenomenological Exploration Catalyst Complexity and Future. *Journal of Intellectual Property Rights Law*, 7(1), 8–14.

Singha, R., & Singha, S. (2024). Building Capabilities and Workforce for Metaverse-Driven Retail Formats. In *Creator's Economy in Metaverse Platforms: Empowering Stakeholders Through Omnichannel Approach* (pp. 111-131). IGI Global. DOI: 10.4018/979-8-3693-3358-7.ch007

Soliman, M., & Al Balushi, M. K. (2023). Unveiling destination evangelism through IPRtools. *ROBONOMICS: The Journal of the Automated Economy*, 4(54), 1.

Soliman, M., & Al Balushi, M. K. (2023). Unveiling destination evangelism through IPRtools. *ROBONOMICS: The Journal of the Automated Economy*, 4(54), 1.

Syed, A. A., Gaol, F. L., Pradipto, Y. D., & Matsuo, T. (2021). Augmented and virtual reality in e-commerce—A survey. *ICIC Express Letters*, 15, 1227–1233.

Tembrevilla, G., Phillion, A., & Zeadin, M. (2024). Experiential learning in engineering education: A systematic literature review. *Journal of Engineering Education*, 113(1), 195–218. DOI: 10.1002/jee.20575

Thomas, S. (2021). Investigating interactive marketing technologies-adoption of augmented/virtual reality in the Indian context. *International Journal of Business Competition and Growth*, 7(3), 214–230. DOI: 10.1504/IJBCG.2021.116266

Tzampazaki, M., Zografos, C., Vrochidou, E., & Papakostas, G. A. (2024). Machine Vision—Moving from Industry 4.0 to Industry 5.0. *Applied Sciences (Basel, Switzerland)*, 14(4), 1471. DOI: 10.3390/app14041471

Varela, L., Putnik, G., & Romero, F. (2024). Collaborative manufacturing and management contextualization in the Industry 4.0 based on a systematic literature review. *International Journal of Management Science and Engineering Management*, 19(1), 78–95. DOI: 10.1080/17509653.2023.2174200

Venkatesh, D. N. (2021). *Winning with employees: Leveraging employee experience for a competitive edge*. SAGE Publishing India.

Venkatesh, D. N. (2021). *Winning with employees: Leveraging employee experience for a competitive edge*. SAGE Publishing India.

Vinaykarthik, B. C. (2022, October). Design of Artificial Intelligence (AI) based User Experience Websites for E-commerce Application and Future of Digital Marketing. In *2022 3rd International Conference on Smart Electronics and Communication (ICOSEC)* (pp. 1023-1029). IEEE.

Vuong, N. A., & Mai, T. T. (2023). Unveiling the Synergy: Exploring the Intersection of AI and NLP in Redefining Modern Marketing for Enhanced Consumer Engagement and Strategy Optimization. *Quarterly Journal of Emerging Technologies and Innovations*, 8(3), 103–118.

Wang, J., Sun, Y., Zhang, L., Zhang, S., Feng, L., & Morrison, A. M. (2024). Effect of display methods on intentions to use virtual reality in museum tourism. *Journal of Travel Research*, 63(2), 314–334. DOI: 10.1177/00472875231164987

Wang, P. Q. (2024). Personalizing guest experience with IPRin the hotel industry: There's more to it than meets a Kiwi's eye. *Current Issues in Tourism*, •••, 1–18.

Wheeler, J. (2023). *The Digital-First Customer Experience: Seven Design Strategies from the World's Leading Brands*. Kogan Page Publishers.

Wheeler, J. (2023). *The Digital-First Customer Experience: Seven Design Strategies from the World's Leading Brands*. Kogan Page Publishers.

Wind, Y. J., & Hays, C. F. (2016). *Beyond advertising: Creating value through all customer touchpoints*. John Wiley & Sons.

Xue, L. (2022). *Designing effective augmented reality platforms to enhance the consumer shopping experiences* (Doctoral dissertation, Loughborough University).

Yang, L., Kumar, R., Kaur, R., Babbar, A., Makhanshahi, G. S., Singh, A., Kumar, R., Bhowmik, A., & Alawadi, A. H. (2024). Exploring the role of computer vision in product design and development: A comprehensive review. [IJIDeM]. *International Journal on Interactive Design and Manufacturing*, 18(6), 1–48. DOI: 10.1007/s12008-024-01765-7

Yim, M. Y. C., & Park, S. Y. (2019). "I am not satisfied with my body, so I like augmented reality (AR)": Consumer responses to AR-based product presentations. *Journal of Business Research*, 100, 581–589. DOI: 10.1016/j.jbusres.2018.10.041

Zaki, H. O. (2022). The Impact Of Artificial Intelligence On Content Marketing. *Journal of Strategic Digital Transformation In Society*, 2(3).

Zhang, J. (2020). A systematic review of the use of augmented reality (AR) and virtual reality (VR) in online retailing.

Zhu, W., Owen, C. B., Li, H., & Lee, J. H. (2024). Personalized in-store e-commerce with the promopad: An augmented reality shopping assistant. *Electronic Journal for E-commerce Tools and Applications*, 1(3), 1–19.

Chapter 3

Intellectual Property Considerations in the Preservation and Revival of Folklore Through Tourism: Strategies for Sustainable Cultural Heritage Management in India

Anuttama Ghose
https://orcid.org/0000-0002-7210-4074
School of Law, Dr. Vishwanath Karad MIT-World Peace University, Pune, India

S. M. Aamir Ali
https://orcid.org/0000-0002-8686-0217
Symbiosis Law School, Symbiosis International University (Deemed), Pune, India

ABSTRACT

The commodification of folklore through tourism in India poses unique intellectual property challenges. This chapter explores strategies for sustainable cultural heritage management that respect both the economic and cultural value of these traditions. It contends that while tourism can drive economic growth and foster cultural exchange, it risks misappropriating and decontextualising folklore if not managed with consideration for indigenous intellectual property rights To address this, the chapter advocates for the development of tailored IPR guidelines to safeguard the interests of local communities that are the custodians of folklore. The chapter proposes a balanced approach that aligns the economic incentives of tourism with

DOI: 10.4018/979-8-3693-4171-1.ch003

the ethical preservation of folklore, ensuring that cultural expressions are not only maintained but also respected and understood, thereby contributing to the sustainable management of India's rich traditions.

1. INTRODUCTION

Various festivals around the world celebrate the diverse cultures of the globe, featuring a wide range of traditional practices and contemporary artistic expressions through mediums like dance, music, theatre, ceremonies, customs, rituals, cinema, photography, visual arts, crafts, and culinary traditions. The interconnection between tourism, heritage, intellectual property issues, and sustainable development is significant. Tourism is widely acknowledged as a vital catalyst for sustainable human development on a global scale, making a significant contribution to employment and income generation in numerous nations worldwide. India is a nation known for its diverse array of folk and ethnic cultures, encompassing various ethnicities, languages, and religions. These groups come from diverse backgrounds and have different ways of life. They have both blended and maintained their cultural practices for hundreds of years (Upadhyaya, 1954). The intricacies of folklore and its regulations are amplified by the presence of numerous ethnic groups, each with their unique languages, dialects, attire, and artistic expressions like paintings, myths, tales, songs, music, dance, and theatre, among other cultural aspects. To streamline these stories, they have certain common factors, such as the economy and the size of the community. To ensure the preservation of folk cultures and prevent their exploitation for commercial purposes, it is crucial to establish dedicated intellectual property regulations for folklore. The IP system has also become a vital aspect of the growth of the tourist industry. The legal framework aims to foster an environment that promotes the development of creativity and innovation. It also enables individuals and corporations to receive recognition and financial benefits for their inventions or creations (Upadhyaya, 1954). The IP system can be a valuable tool in promoting and protecting the growth of tourism, as well as preserving folklore and traditional cultural expressions.

The chapter serves a diverse range of purposes. Firstly, it seeks to delve into the complex relationship between folklore, tourism, and intellectual property in the Indian context. The author sought insights into the folk culture in India and its impact on tourism promotion in the country by consulting *Vandita's* work (Hajra, 2015). This involves an examination of how folklore, with its various stories, customs, and artistic expressions, intersects with tourism activities in the country. It also explores the intellectual property considerations related to this topic, as discussed by *Dorothy Yen*, particularly in relation to smaller destinations. Additionally, this research aims to understand the obstacles and potential benefits associated with the conservation and revitalisation of folklore in the tourism industry (Yen et al., 2023). The author cited the research conducted *by Pratheep P.S.* to explore the adverse cultural effects linked to tourism and propose potential remedies for these concerns (Pratheep, 2017). Through a thorough examination of case studies and examples provided by renowned experts in the field, such as *Vandita Hajra* (Hajra, 2015), *Kailash C. Baral* (Baral, 2023) and *Li Yang* (Yang, 2014), this study aims to shed light on the various challenges experienced by indigenous communities and cultural practitioners. Additionally, it aims to emphasise the potential advantages of tourism in preserving cultural heritage. Additionally, the study seeks to provide practical approaches for the sustainable management of cultural heritage. The author has cited various literature in this area, including the works of *Dian Yulie Reindrawati* (Reindrawati, 2023) and *Regina Scheyvens* (Scheyvens, 1999), to gain insights into the impact of tourism on local communities and their empowerment. Through a multidisciplinary approach, this research seeks to provide practical strategies that empower local communities, foster cultural authenticity, and promote responsible tourism practices that uphold intellectual property rights. Ultimately, the research aims to make a valuable contribution to scholarly discussions and the formulation of policies. The research aims to contribute to discussions on folklore preservation, tourism development, and cultural heritage protection by adopting an interdisciplinary approach. The importance of community participation and conservation programs is a crucial aspect of the research conducted by *S. Mostafa Rasoolimanesh, Mastura Jaafar* (Rasoolimanesh & Jaafar, 2016), and *Sandeep Kumar Walia* (Walia, 2020), as mentioned by the author. This chapter offers valuable insights to policymakers, practitioners, and scholars, with the goal of promoting sustainable cultural heritage management practices that respect the rights and aspirations of local communities while preserving India's diverse cultural heritage.

2. CONCEPTUALIZING FOLKLORE PRESERVATION AND IPR PROTECTION IN INDIA: BACKGROUND AND LEGAL UNDERSTANDING:

Folklore refers to the collective body of expressive culture that is shared by a certain group of people, culture, or subculture. This encompasses many forms of verbal traditions, such as narratives, folklore, fables, sayings, verses, humorous anecdotes, and other forms of spoken traditions. Folklore, comprising a rich tapestry of traditional knowledge, cultural expressions, and artistic creations passed down through generations, holds profound significance within communities worldwide. However, the preservation and protection of folklore present unique challenges, particularly concerning its intersection with intellectual property laws. Intellectual property laws, primarily designed to protect individual creativity and innovation, often struggle to accommodate the collective and dynamic nature of folklore (Stoianoff & Wright, 2018). As a result, folklore frequently exists in a legal grey area, lacking clear legal frameworks for its recognition, ownership, and exploitation.

2.1 Understanding Folklore through Traditional Knowledge and Traditional Cultural Expressions:

Traditional knowledge encompasses the vast array of knowledge, achievements, and practices of indigenous and local communities across the globe. Oral transmission is the method through which traditional knowledge is handed down from one generation to another. It encompasses the accumulated wisdom of the past and embodies the unique aspects of the local culture and environment. It is commonly shared and manifests as narratives, music, traditional tales, sayings, cultural norms, faiths, ceremonies, community rules, indigenous dialects, and farming practices, encompassing the cultivation of crops and breeding of animals (Johnsson & Tualima, 2018). The knowledge has been transmitted across generations through various forms of expression such as singing, dancing, painting, carving, chanting, and performance, which has led to its classification as an "oral tradition." Traditional knowledge is highly valuable in various domains such as agriculture, fishing, health, horticulture, forestry, and environmental management. In recent times, there has been a growing appreciation for the value of age-old knowledge. This information is valuable not only for everyday users but also for those involved in contemporary manufacturing and farming (Johnsson & Tualima, 2018). Products derived from plants, including medicinal and cosmetic goods, along with various health and beauty aids, exemplify the extensive utilisation of traditional knowledge. Other valued items that rely on traditional expertise include agricultural and non-wood forest goods and handicrafts (Ghose & Ali, 2023).

Traditional wisdom has the potential to benefit sustainable development greatly. A significant portion of the world's genetic resources are found in areas with a high concentration of indigenous and local populations. Many of these societies have long engaged in the practice of cultivating and utilising a diverse range of biological resources. Thanks to their dedication, the local biodiversity has flourished, and the ecosystem has remained in good health due to a range of activities they have undertaken. However, indigenous and local groups play a crucial role in preserving biodiversity and promoting sustainable resource management. The expertise and approach of these individuals are highly valuable to the global society, serving as a valuable source of data and a blueprint for biodiversity policy. In addition, indigenous members and local communities play a crucial role in conservation and sustainable usage due to their close proximity and extensive understanding of local habitats (Antons, 2013).

As per the definition provided by the World Intellectual Property Organization, Traditional Cultural Expressions encompass various forms of expression that hold significant importance to the social and cultural identity of local communities. These expressions are carefully preserved and nurtured by the individuals or groups who hold them while also being subject to continuous change and evolution (Antons, 2013). There are two categories of TCEs: visible and invisible. According to the interpretation, songs and instrumental music, regardless of whether they have been recorded, are considered TCEs. The community, instead of an individual, asserts ownership over TCEs, and this assertion of ownership is based on established precedent. It is often difficult to determine the original creator of a TCE, and over time, the TCE has entered the 'Public Domain' due to its frequent usage.

The concept of "Popular Antiquity" marked the initial phase of scholarly engagement with the study of folklore (Dominas et al., 2016). Essentially, it relied on the examination of historical precedents and other relevant factors. Greater emphasis was placed on the study of history. In the second part of the historical phase, the field of folklore experienced another significant development with the introduction of the German word Volkskunde (Stein, 1987). In 1846, Wiliam John Thomas introduced a new term, replacing the phrase Popular Antiquity, and established the field of folklore (Emrich, 1946). This field of study focuses on the analysis of individuals and societies. In 1965, Alan Dundes introduced folkloristics as a method for studying folk materials (Bronner, 2007). That was a significant achievement in the scientific study of folklore worldwide. Amidst the evolving socio-political and socio-environmental landscape, the field of folkloristics has also undergone transformation. One of the key areas of focus in the scientific study of folkloristics is the utilisation of folk materials (Bronner, 2007). In 1958, Peter Heintz coined the term "Folkiorismus" to describe the field of social science.

In the 1950s, there was a shift in the perception of folklore when it came to commercialisation. This change was referred to as "folklore." However, in light of the evolving environment, folklorists have revisited the issue and given it a new name: "folklorism" (Newall, 1987). This concept proves beneficial for various forms of folklore commercialisation, including its use in promoting tourism. In the 1960s, Bausinger made significant contributions to the development of a theoretical relationship between folklore and tourism through folklorism, with the involvement of folklorists (Newall, 1987). The contribution of folklorists has been crucial in introducing folklore to the public sphere.

2.2 Conceptualizing Heritage and Cultural Heritage:

Heritage is typically recognised as encompassing sites, objects, and traditions that are chosen and safeguarded for their distinctiveness, grandeur, aesthetic appeal, and/or historical and cultural importance. This version of the past is derived from objects, representations, memories, and commemorations, and it holds significant importance in shaping and defining the understanding of heritage in academic discussions and public policy. The concept of 'heritage' encompasses a wide range of natural and cultural resources, such as land, water, animals, plants, buildings, art, traditions, and practices that hold significant cultural and historical value (Herrera, 2013). Over time, the concept of heritage has broadened to encompass intangible elements like oral histories and traditions, acknowledging previously overlooked aspects of heritage. The notion of cultural heritage highlights the traditional nature of intangible cultural heritage and the assignment of social or cultural importance to specific forms of heritage.

The definition of world heritage, according to UNESCO, refers to places on Earth that possess exceptional universal value. Additionally, culture encompasses a range of unique spiritual, material, intellectual, and emotional characteristics that define a society or social group (Leimgruber, 2010). These aspects can be expressed through various forms such as art, literature, ways of living, traditions, and beliefs. The designation of world heritage sites originated from the Convention Concerning the Protection of the World Cultural and National Heritage, which was adopted by UNESCO in 1972 and officially took effect in 1975 after being ratified by 22 countries (Chacón, 2020). This convention established the existing framework for the protection and management of significant cultural heritage sites worldwide. It also offers a potential framework for examining the concept of "cultural heritage" in the initial stages. Monuments, town sites, archaeological sites, and works of art are classified as "cultural heritage sites" under the three types of designated sites outlined in the UNESCO convention. However, what distinguishes these types of websites as the platforms for the dissemination of "cultural heritage", and what precisely constitutes this heritage? Heritage can take on various manifestations, encompassing both tangible and intangible aspects, as it is passed down through generations. Intangible forms of heritage encompass oral traditions, community bonds, and language. On this page, we will delve into tangible forms of heritage – physical remnants that carry significant cultural and historical knowledge from one generation to another (Josefsson & Aronsson, 2016).

By examining tangible cultural heritage, we can gain insight into the cultural aspects of a society or group. This includes monuments, town sites, archaeological sites, and works of art that embody the spiritual, material, intellectual, and emotional characteristics of the society (Josefsson & Aronsson, 2016).

2.3 Understanding Intangible Cultural Heritage and its nexus with intellectual property rights:

Before we delve into the connection between these two fields, it's important first to understand the concept of "Culture Heritage." The essence of a society's cultural heritage lies in the collective knowledge and practical application of a specific domain, along with the intentional display of that expertise through enduring symbols. The definition of "intangible cultural heritage" according to UNESCO's Convention for Safeguarding of the Intangible Cultural Heritage, 2003, encompasses a wide range of elements, including practices, representations, expressions, knowledge, skills, instruments, objects, artefacts, and cultural spaces that are recognised by communities, groups, and sometimes individuals as part of their cultural heritage. It is worth noting that cultural heritage can encompass both tangible artefacts and intangible traditions. Examples of tangible heritage include historical texts, objects, structures, and similar items. On the other hand, intangible heritage encompasses folktales, songs, musical compositions, and cultural practices (Lotz, 2002).

There are two major types of intellectual property rights that hold great importance: economic property rights and copyright-derived rights. Given their conceptual origins, they cannot be physically touched or held. Industrial property rights cover patents, industrial designs, and trademarks, while copyright protects original creative works like books, sculptures, films, poetry, and more. Traditional Knowledge (TK) and Traditional Cultural Expression (TCE) are two widely used perspectives for analysing cultural heritage in the context of intellectual property (IP). One issue that arises is the lack of a universally agreed-upon definition for TK or TCE on a global level (Mgbeoji, 2001).

The concept of TCE covers a broad spectrum of historical and contemporary expressions of pre-existing materials, such as adaptations, imitations, revitalisations, and other forms. In order to be considered a TCE, it is necessary to possess the characteristics of being a defining feature of a tradition and having survived as a living tradition within a community. Many indigenous communities have long desired a legal safeguard that allows them to benefit from the transmission of their knowledge across generations, ensuring that it cannot be exploited without proper permission. On the other hand, the Traditional Knowledge (TK) of traditional communities includes their cultural traditions, customs, and the expertise associated with these aspects. Traditional knowledge extends beyond the realm of the arts and encompasses various fields, including agriculture, science, technology, ecology, biodiversity, and medicine. Based on the WIPO Draft Article on TK, it is stated that the transmission of this accumulated knowledge should occur over a span of at least five generations in order for it to be recognised as traditional knowledge (Poorna et al., 2014).

There is a strong argument for ensuring equal access to cultural heritage, as its benefits reach beyond the confines of any one nation. On the other hand, the concept of intellectual property (IP) is inherently tied to specific territories. Thus, granting certain individuals exclusive intellectual property rights may hinder others from obtaining the same knowledge and benefits. Unlike traditional knowledge or traditional cultural expressions, cultural heritage is not subject to legal time constraints, allowing for the uninterrupted enjoyment of the associated rights. Although the legal ownership of Leonardo da Vinci's Monalisa painting may have expired, it remains an invaluable cultural gem that should be cherished by everyone.

3. UNVEILING THE THEORETICAL SYNERGIES BETWEEN THE FOLKLORE AND TOURISM

Lately, there has been a growing emphasis on experiential travel, where travellers aim to truly immerse themselves in the essence of the destinations they visit. India's tourism sector is experiencing a gradual transformation due to the rise of cultural tourism, which has had a significant impact on the country's reputation. The concept of 'authenticity' is almost unstoppable in tourist research. Tourism is often defined as the coming together of individuals, locations, and items. Individuals travel to various destinations and engage with the items present in those locations. This process is facilitated by both the tourism sector and the larger local society (Bendix, 1989). Genuineness is naturally crucial to historical tourism. Therefore, it is imperative for destination administrators to safeguard the integrity of site architecture and present genuine representations to visitors. Effectively preserving a heritage site can help to enhance its authenticity. The preservation of the image and atmosphere of the historical period at the heritage destination is crucial for tourists to perceive authenticity. Therefore, it is important to convey site authenticity to tourists, which can be achieved through interactive traditional performances, interpreters wearing traditional costumes, or interactive mobile applications. Authenticity is a crucial idea when it comes to marketing cultural heritage sites. Authenticity should be regarded as a means of managing perception when used as a marketing tool (Folklore, 1916). The tourism consumer has a mental representation of the landscape and a strong inclination to acquire it. Authenticity should serve as a driving force that compels the tourism consumer to take action within this framework. Consumers base their purchasing decisions on the level of veracity of a product or service. Therefore, the demonstration of genuineness emerges as a decisive factor for prospective travellers when making their selection. With the advancement of the consumer economy, individuals are now looking for genuine experiences rather than artificial ones. This is why there has been a transition from theme parks to a quest for more authentic destinations (Upadhyaya, 1954).

It is becoming increasingly evident that the relationship between tourism and social change is more significant and intricate than policymakers acknowledge in their optimistic plans. Contrary to expectations, tourism often has negative effects on the well-being of local people. However, it is important for critics of the tourism policy to acknowledge that in a financially disadvantaged country like India, there is a pressing need for rapid economic growth by any means available. Given the significant financial limitations, tourism seems to be a feasible solution as it is expected to generate quick and substantial returns, particularly in the form of foreign currency, with relatively low investment. This method aligns well with affluent individuals' strong inclination to explore exotic destinations, which are many in India. If international tourism indeed promotes social interaction between countries, fostering improved understanding and goodwill across nations, then it becomes an appealing prospect for policymakers (Goldstein, 2015).

From a practical standpoint, policymakers often face a difficult decision; they must choose between two undesirable options. While tourism may not be the instant economic solution that its supporters suggest and may even lead to social issues, it is also impossible to stop the global trend of tourism in open societies. Additionally, it would be unwise to ignore the appealing qualities of tourism as a development strategy. Every decision regarding tourist growth, whether in favour or against it, carries significant implications. In areas where tourism was previously restricted, barriers have been removed, while in places where tourism is allowed without limitations, many areas have transformed into exclusive destinations for the wealthy. Attempting to separate itself from the forces of these events would be impractical and idealistic for any society, considering that tourism undeniably has worldwide implications. Nevertheless, it would be feasible to alleviate its consequences if tourism is seen from a more comprehensive standpoint of socio-economic progress and transformation (Goldstein, 2015).

India's rich folk music captures the essence of the nation, resonating with the hearts of its people. Like folk dances, the acquisition of folk music is typically a result of immersion rather than formal instruction due to the economic constraints of rural life. The musicians themselves craft the folk instruments used to accompany the music from commonly available materials like silk, peritoneum, bamboo, and coconut shells. In India, there is a song for every occasion. It's similar to having a soundtrack for every imaginable moment in life. Tourists from around the globe, including cultural enthusiasts, artists, and musicians, are drawn to the captivating elements of Indian folk music. The Rajasthan International Folk Festival, held against the majestic backdrop of Mehrangarh Fort in the historic city of Jodhpur, showcases a captivating blend of international and Indian folk music (Sruthijith, 2010). This enchanting event attracts numerous music enthusiasts from both India and abroad.

4. PROBING THE INTERPLAY OF TOURISM AND FOLKLORE THROUGH CASE STUDIES AND INITIATIVES IN INDIA

The integration of folklore and the tourism industry creates a harmonious relationship where both sides benefit. Folklore gains wider recognition, and tourism flourishes with the addition of genuine cultural experiences. Tourism in India has frequently intertwined with the diverse folklore that is deeply ingrained in the country's cultural heritage. Traditional folklore holds great significance as it carries the rich cultural heritage and identity of a community, encompassing beliefs, customs, rituals, and narratives that have been passed down through generations. When tourists explore different places, they frequently come across local traditions like storytelling, music, dance, rituals, and handicrafts. These cultural elements add depth and meaning to their travel experiences (Upadhyaya, 1954).

The diverse range of folk dances in India comprises a vast collection of non-classical dance forms. These dances are known for their spontaneous nature and their ability to provide cultural enrichment and relaxation. They are a direct expression of collective wisdom and profound ideas that have stood the test of time. The workshops on folk dances organised by state tourism boards are exceptional opportunities for tourists to immerse themselves in local culture. For example, the Chhau Dance workshop held in the Victoria Memorial grounds by the West Bengal Tourism Development Corporation on World Tourism Day 2014 was particularly noteworthy (Hajra, 2015). In India, experiencing a homestay, staying at a heritage hotel, or visiting a theme village like Chowki Dhani in Jaipur, Rajasthan is simply not the same without witnessing a captivating folk dance performance (Rongmei, 2022). The desert safaris of Rajasthan offer a captivating experience with the mesmerising Kalbelia dance and the fiery fire dance, accompanied by the enchanting music of local Manganiyar musicians (Rongmei, 2022).

The vibrant tapestry of Indian folk culture is occasionally showcased through its distinctive art of folk theatre, captivating a wide range of people across India. Nowadays, various socio-cultural institutions are actively involved in reviving, promoting, and appreciating Indian folk theatre. They organise workshops, seminars, fairs, and festivals to showcase the rich cultural heritage of India and attract tourists from around the world. Indian folk theatre encompasses a wide range of performances from different regions. Some notable examples include Bhavai and Akhyana from Gujarat, Jatra from West Bengal, Yakshagana from Karnataka, Swang from Haryana, Uttar Pradesh, Rajasthan, and Malwa regions of Madhya Pradesh, Naqal from

Punjab, Ramleela during the Dussehra festival in Northern India, Kalaripayattu – a martial dance-drama, Theyyam from Kerala, Terukkuttu – a Tamil street theatre, Tamasha from Maharashtra, and Bhand Pather from Kashmir, which pays tribute to the lives of reshis (Islamic rishis or seers) (Hajra, 2015). Puppetry holds significant cultural value in various regions of India, including Orissa, Rajasthan, Kerala, Andhra Pradesh, and Karnataka. The Bharat Kala Museum in Udaipur, Rajasthan, offers daily puppetry shows that are popular among tourists. Many accommodation establishments in India now include a visit to a local fair and witnessing Ramleela as part of their Diwali itineraries (Hajra, 2015).

In the rural areas of India, we have the privilege of observing a diverse array of gods and goddesses. These deities may not be part of the prominent pan-Indian Brahmanical Hinduism, but they hold great significance as regional deities closely tied to villages and towns. Occasionally, these supernatural entities may intersect with deities from tribal cultures as well. These rituals are not universally practised among all Indian communities. Instead, they are unique to particular tribal or caste groups, extended families, neighbourhoods, or villages. The purpose of these rituals is to attain specific goals, such as a bountiful harvest, safeguarding against illnesses, or promoting fertility. Whether it's the Manasa temple in Chandigarh, the Jalaram Bapa temple in Virpur, or the Karni Mata temple in Deshnoke, these sacred places attract numerous tourists and devout locals every day (Hajra, 2015). Similarly, the annual folk festival of Tirupati, known as 'Ganga Jatara', celebrates the powers of the deity Gangamma and draws crowds from all over Andhra Pradesh. The Pandharpur yatra, a pilgrimage that brings together people from across India, and the Khandoba Mahadev temple in Jejuri, Maharashtra, are also popular destinations. Lastly, the Vishnoi Village near Jodhpur, Rajasthan, is another noteworthy place associated with folk deities. The Vishnois of Rajasthan are a sect of the Hindu religion that is known for their strong commitment to protecting trees and wildlife, demonstrating their dedication to environmental preservation. The cult was founded by a highly knowledgeable individual who possessed great insight. This visionary saint, Guru Jambheshwar Ji, established the cult in the year 1485 AD. His teachings emphasised the significance of safeguarding plants and animals, recognising their crucial role in maintaining the delicate equilibrium of nature. The Vishnoi Village Safari was initiated by the Rajas and Maharajas of Jodhpur to provide visitors, both Indian and foreign, with an authentic experience of Rajasthan. It has now become an essential part of any tourist's itinerary in Jodhpur (Hajra, 2015).

Games have been an integral part of Indian culture for centuries. Examples can be found in the mythology of India, where the recurring theme of Lord Shiva and Goddess Parvati playing Pachisi, as well as the story in the Mahabharata where the Pandavas lost their common wife Draupadi over a game of dice, mark significant turning points in their journeys. Amidst the current trend of personal development courses, it is worth noting the value of Indian traditional folk games. These games not only impart skills such as basic mathematics, logical and lateral thinking, strategy building, aiming, and concentration, but they are also environmentally friendly and suitable for individuals of all ages. Additionally, they fostered interaction between different generations. India's outdoor and martial folk games have gained popularity as exciting adventure tourism options and are now being showcased in various tourism festivals. The Snake Boat Race Festivals, held in various locations such as Aranmulla, Kumarakom, and Alapuzza in Kerala, as well as the Canoe Race during Island Tourism Festivals in Andamans, are significant tourism attractions in India.

The rich folklore and folktales of India serve as a reflection of our diverse society, carrying with them timeless wisdom and the values that shape our community. These aspects attract a multitude of visitors to India for cultural studies. One fascinating storytelling tradition from India is "Kaavad Bachana" from Rajasthan. In this tradition, a storyteller uses a vibrant cupboard called a 'kaavad' to depict stories from ancient epics like Ramayana, Mahabharata, and the Puranas. Through this visual and sacred journey, the listener is transported to another world. A lecture and presentation took place during last year's Jodhpur RIFF. There is a resemblance to "Pater gaan" from West Bengal, where the singer unveils a scroll painting while singing songs that depict the events portrayed on the scroll. An organisation called Bangla Natak Dot Com hosts a festival called Pat Maya in West Bengal, highlighting the rich tradition of "Pater Gaan" (Hajra, 2015).

Making and selling handicrafts is second only to farming in terms of employment in countries like India, yet in the West, they are seen as a form of luxury and as unique works of art made by studio craftspeople and artists. At various tourism-oriented festivals around India, such as Agra's Taj Mahotsav, Maharashtra's Ajanta Ellora Festival, Himachal Pradesh's International Folk Festival, Jammu and Kashmir's Gurez Festival, Punjab's Pinjore Heritage Festival, Gujarat's Kutch Utsav, and Haryana's Surajkund Crafts Festival, Kerala's Ashtamudi Craft and Art Festival, Goa's Margao Crafts Festival, etc., local folk arts and crafts are also showcased during these festivals. Given the intertwined nature of culture, crafts, and tourism, these festivals have made a significant impact on the Indian tourism scene by helping to differentiate products. One of the main draws of travelling is the chance to immerse oneself in the local culture. Festivals, which usually have a distinct regional flavour, provide perfect opportunities for travellers to do just that. Tourists' purchases of folk handicrafts contribute significantly to the local economy, which in turn aids in the promotion of responsible tourism principles and diversifies the tourist experience by complementing homestays and cultural experiences (Hajra, 2015).

5. CONTEMPORARY ISSUES IN FOLKLORE PRESERVATION AND TOURISM IN INDIA:

The complex nature of contemporary issues surrounding folklore preservation and tourism in India reflects the intricate interplay between cultural heritage, economic development, and community identity. An important issue to consider is the exploitation and commercialisation of traditional stories and customs in the tourism sector. Although folklore can be a valuable asset for attracting visitors and enhancing the tourism experience, there are concerns about its appropriation for commercial purposes (Bunten, 2008). These concerns revolve around issues of authenticity, cultural misrepresentation, and exploitation. Communities with rich cultural heritage often face the unfortunate consequence of being left out or disadvantaged when it comes to reaping the economic rewards of tourism. This not only widens social disparities but also erodes the authenticity of their unique cultural traditions. In addition, the fast pace of globalisation and modernisation presents challenges to the conservation of traditional folklore practices and knowledge systems. As societies experience rapid socio-economic changes, traditional methods of sharing and cultural customs are being replaced by more mainstream or Westernized forms of entertainment and communication. This occurrence, along with the decline of communication channels between generations, puts at risk the ongoing existence and energy of cultural traditions. In addition, the digital era brings forth various possibilities and obstacles to the conservation of folklore. As we explore the possibilities of digital platforms for preserving and sharing folklore, we must also consider the complex issues surrounding ownership, control, and access to digital representations of cultural heritage (Jarvenpa, 1994).

5.1. Legal Dilemmas and Exploitation of Intellectual Property Rights

India's efforts to protect its folktales and traditional cultural expressions (TCEs) have not yet been met with effective legislative measures. India's copyright law is founded on the principle of original authorship. Traditional cultural expressions present a unique challenge as they are frequently performed by entire communities, and their original creators remain unidentified (Boateng, 2013).

The debate surrounding the Sambalpuri song was unique as the individuals responsible For its composition were actually known, which is not typically the case with other traditional melodies. Furthermore, the duration of copyright protection is limited, after which the work would become part of the public domain. However, when it comes to folklore and traditional cultural expressions (TCEs), it is argued that copyright protection should be perpetual (Springer, 2007). The current copyright laws do not foresee these issues. The Copyright Act does not specifically address the protection of TCEs. The Act may offer a certain level of indirect safeguard for the rights of TCE owners, although its provisions primarily focus on protecting modern TCEs.

The term "traditional cultural expressions" has been specifically defined by the World Intellectual Property Organization (WIPO) as "expressions of folklore." It has become a term used to refer to works that encompass and safeguard the unique elements of a community's rich artistic heritage (Springer, 2007). There are various instances of this, such as traditional tales passed down through generations and melodic tunes performed using musical instruments. For these individuals, the concept of "traditional" does not refer to something old-fashioned but rather to something that is connected to an indigenous or traditional society (whether based on location or shared beliefs) and is practised in the customary way of that particular group. However, the aspect that has been safeguarded is a specific representation of the cultural work in question, showcasing creativity or at least an adaptation that includes distinct elements and showcases the use of expertise and discernment (Springer, 2007).

Copyright law focuses on the individual responsible for creating a work, but it recognises that in certain cases, such as traditional expressions or those carried out in a traditional manner, there may not be a clear author in the traditional sense as defined by copyright law. Hence, these conventional elements of communication transform into a universal concept that cannot be exclusively controlled due to their ongoing usage and significance in cultural heritage. It is important to note that traditional song lyrics, being a part of the cultural fabric rather than an original work of art, cannot be claimed under copyright or exclusive rights for exploitation once they have been published. Copyright can be claimed for specific collections or expressions if they demonstrate enough evidence of originality. There is a compelling argument for safeguarding novel adaptations and derivative works (Montenyohl, 1996).

Although generic parts are not inherently copyrightable, an original compilation can still be protected by copyright. This is based on an analysis of the concept of originality in India and the prevailing standard in other jurisdictions. The case of *Eastern Book Company v. D. B. Modak* (2008), which draws inspiration from the Canadian case of *CCH Canadian v. Law Society of Upper Canada* (2004), has established a clear standard for copyright protection in India – the requirement of "Skill and Judgment" as the basis for originality. The copyright pertains to the compilation as a whole rather than its individual components. The facts of the case heard by the Delhi High Court can be compared to a similar situation in *Institute of Inner St–dies v. Charlotte Anderson and Ors*. (2011). In that case, it was determined that basic dance moves and social routines cannot be copyrighted as they are considered to be common aspects across cultures.

Nevertheless, renditions of folk songs that demonstrate notable originality and require a considerable level of artistic and/or intellectual judgment may potentially be subject to copyright protection. A legal expert with a deep understanding of English would likely argue that while a Rajasthani folk song such as "Kesariya Balam" may not be eligible for copyright protection on its own, a modified version of the song that deviates significantly from its original composition could potentially be subject to copyright. Thus, if a new rendition of the classic song is recorded and distributed without permission, it could potentially lead to a claim of copyright infringement. Nevertheless, a legal expert with a strong command of the English language would argue that relying solely on the lyrics, which are generic and typical in nature, would not hold up in a legal proceeding. According to the Copyright Act of India, Section 22 specifies that the copyright of an author persists for an additional 60 years after their demise once their work is published. Therefore, it is important to consider the duration of copyright protection for traditional songs, especially when recognising the creator's contribution, which may seem contradictory to the concept of tradition (Booth, 2015).

The term "Traditional" suggests the presence of a communal economy where authorship is not the primary focus. Whether it's newly written pieces or the rich musical heritage passed down over time, the concept of public domain, allowing unrestricted access for those who wish to participate in the communal economy, is so widely accepted that using the phrase seems unnecessary. Composers in traditional societies often agree to their work being incorporated into the very participatory processes that initially inspired them. Given the ever-changing landscape of musical practice across diverse societies, it can be quite difficult to establish ownership of musical works and ensure fair compensation for their creators (Booth, 2015).

5.2. Balancing Commercialization, Authenticity and Cultural Appropriations

Music has played a significant role in shaping individuals, communities, and cultures throughout history. Out of all the various genres of music, folk music holds immense importance to culture and civilisation. Folk music, true to its name, is a genre that exalts and honours the common people through its heartfelt lyrics and captivating rhythms. Preserving the people's cultural and historical identity serves as a link to the past. The commodification of folklore involves transforming traditional cultural expressions, such as music, dance, and storytelling, into marketable products. This process often commercializes and modernizes folk traditions for mass consumption, tourism, and media. While it can promote cultural heritage and provide economic benefits to local communities, it also risks distorting or diluting authentic practices. The commercialization may prioritize profit over cultural integrity, leading to the loss of original meanings and practices.

The recent big release from Dharma Productions, Jugg Jugg Jeeyo, has sparked controversy on Twitter due to its inclusion of two regional classics—Nach Punjaban by Pakistani artist Abrar-ul-Haq and Dupatta Tera Sat Rang Da by late Punjabi singer Surjit Bindrakhia (Hindustan Times, 2022). These examples are indicative of a broader pattern where local music is adapted and copied for wider appeal. For years, the field has been reimagining beloved melodies and traditional tunes from various regions of India, such as Tamil Nadu, Punjab, and Telangana. Badshah, a renowned artist and rapper, is currently facing allegations of plagiarism regarding his song Genda Phool. The song is said to have been inspired by Ratan Kahar, the true singer and writer of the song Boroloker Biti Lo. Genda Phool portrays the joyous celebration of Durga Puja and incorporates songs and music from Bangla popular culture (Ghosh, 2020). Badshah responded to the charges by stating that his team had conducted a comprehensive investigation of the song and discovered that previous versions of the song did not credit Ratan Kahar for the lines (Ghosh, 2020).

It is often disheartening to see the original intent and artistic value of music being disregarded when a popular song from a particular region is remade without the consent of the original creator, completely ignoring its cultural significance. It appears that the original artist or members of the local community were not consulted when the song was adapted, resulting in remakes that have been modernised to the extent that they are nearly unrecognisable. This action is indefensible as it eliminates our historical background and excludes us from the cultural tapestry of the entire nation. It doesn't function in other places due to variations in culture (Okumu, 2016).

For instance, folk music is considered to be "collectively owned" and, therefore, cannot be protected by copyright laws due to the challenges in determining its origins. However, there are a few noteworthy exceptions to this rule. Preserving a folk song becomes challenging when its original singer cannot be identified, making it difficult to apply copyright laws. It is not uncommon for folk songs to be frequently reproduced or reinterpreted in Bollywood without the formal acquisition of the copyright to the original songs. This is because folk music is not recognised as a genre in Bollywood. Nevertheless, the rights to original music can be held by one entity or distributed among multiple parties.

5.3. Evaluating the Threats to the Traditional Communities

India boasts a rich tapestry of indigenous groups and diverse cultural identities, each with its unique cuisine, clothing, language, and social organisation. India boasts a remarkably diverse population. The musical style of a community reflects its cultural heritage and traditions. In recent years, there has been a notable increase in the popularity of traditional melodies and musical instruments. This can be attributed to the wide availability of free content through social media as well as over-the-top (OTT) platforms. Due to this, more and more Indian pop performers, alongside music producers, started integrating native music forms into their work in response to the rising demand for Indian folk songs and styles among listeners. Due to this, the commercial Indian music industry has witnessed a significant rise in the incorporation of native musical instruments and techniques. This trend is evident in pop albums and the songs featured in movies (Manuel, 1988).

As a result, the rich musical heritage of traditional Indian music was revealed, leading to the rise of numerous renowned artists and musicians who achieved great success in the mainstream music industry. Another example can be found in Tamil folk music, specifically in the genre called gaana, which gained popularity through Tamil movies. Gaana is a form of city folk music that has its roots in Chennai, particularly among the marginalised communities. Many of the singers in gaana hail from communities of fishermen or slum dwellers, utilising lively and energetic beats to express their everyday experiences and the obstacles they encounter. This music is deeply intertwined with the lives of the people, inseparable from their daily existence. Music producers have taken these musical techniques and incorporated them into completely new genres, creating unique compositions. Consequently, the quality of the original work of art is diminished (Kumar, 2018).

In this scenario, traditional music forms are deconstructed and reimagined to the extent that they become unrecognisable and are often met with disapproval. Folk performers are frequently dismissed and not given the recognition they deserve in the music industry. Both Rajasthani and Punjabi folk music are often incorporated and reimagined in Bollywood tunes. There was a disagreement between Coke Studio and the song producer and lyricist of a Sambalpuri folk song called Rangabati (Mohanty, 2017). The song was mistakenly labelled as a remix of an Odiya number, even though it was originally written as a Sambalpuri song. This was the main cause of the disagreement.

Cultural identities face significant challenges when indigenous populations are exposed to acts of cultural appropriation and unauthorised remixing. While it is crucial to embrace innovative interpretations and variations, it is equally important to recognise the significance of folk music as a cherished cultural asset that is safeguarded by the community. This would align with a core principle of intellectual property law, which aims to achieve a just equilibrium between the creator and the general public. It is worth noting that India does not currently have specific rules in place to protect intellectual property related to Traditional Cultural Expressions (TCE).

An important concern revolves around the growing trend of mass tourism and the emphasis on quantity rather than quality in policies related to tourism development. This approach frequently results in the commercialisation and standardisation of cultural experiences, sidelining genuine folklore expressions in favour of tourist attractions driven by market demands. Consequently, local communities might experience a sense of obligation to adhere to commercialised portrayals of their cultural heritage, which could potentially undermine the genuineness and authenticity of their folklore traditions.

5.4. Tourism Development Policies and Practices

Despite tourism's promise of boosting economies, creating jobs, and fostering cross-cultural understanding, the policies and practices that aim to make it a reality frequently run into problems that threaten local traditions and their survival. Further complicating matters is the fact that tourism policies do not incorporate cultural sustainability concepts. Sustainable tourism development must prioritise the preservation and promotion of cultural heritage, even though economic expansion and infrastructure development are frequently at the centre of tourism policy. To preserve folklore and ensure that tourist destinations remain viable in the future, policies must address the social and cultural impacts of tourism. These impacts include but are not limited to, the displacement of local communities, the loss of cultural authenticity, and the erosion of traditional knowledge systems.

More community input and inclusion is also required when tourism policies are being developed. Many decisions about the growth of tourism do not include indigenous and underprivileged populations, even though their folklore traditions are essential to cultural tourism. Policymakers can guarantee that tourist development projects are in line with local communities' interests and goals by integrating participatory planning and community-based tourism into policy frameworks. This includes encouraging a fair distribution of tourism-related profits and advantages, establishing partnerships between government entities, tourism-related businesses, and community organisations, and acknowledging that communities have the right to control and benefit from their cultural heritage (Antons, 2013).

6. STRATEGIES FOR INTEGRATING LEGAL, ETHICAL AND COMMUNITY PERSPECTIVE IN CULTURAL HERITAGE MANAGEMENT AND TOURISM DEVELOPMENT

When it comes to tackling these challenges, policymakers have a crucial role to play in promoting a sustainable and culturally sensitive approach to tourism development in India. By emphasising the importance of preserving and promoting folklore, policymakers can make a significant impact on cultural diversity, empower local communities, and enhance visitor experiences in the realm of tourism (De Carlo & Dubini, 2010). There is a need for a fundamental change in approach, focusing on policies that emphasise quality rather than quantity. It is important to incorporate principles of cultural sustainability and prioritise community involvement and ownership in the decision-making processes related to tourism. By actively pursuing these initiatives, tourism policies can play a crucial role in promoting a deep connection with cultural traditions, while also safeguarding the future of tourism destinations in India.

6.1 Legal and Policy Intervention: Strengthening IPR and Folklore Policies

According to the Indian Constitution, Article 29 ensures the protection of cultural identity, and it is the responsibility of the government to facilitate the preservation of indigenous groups' cultural heritage. It is crucial to establish formal protection to deter theft of intangible TCEs and ensure the preservation of the art, recognition of rights, and economic empowerment of the community (Dodson & Barr, 2007). In addition, development and research in this sector are of utmost importance and need to be addressed urgently. Before offering protection, it is crucial first to identify TCEs and folklore. It would be beneficial to create an online library for TCEs and folk music, organising them by the regions or communities that practice and preserve them. This approach is similar to the "Traditional Knowledge Digital Library," which contains a vast collection of traditional pharmaceutical formulas. This requires extensive research on the TCEs and the societies that surround them. Having a register that acknowledges the TCE and its users would offer a form of protective measure.

The main driving force behind the protection of TCEs is to ensure that communities have economic and moral rights over their folklore and folk music. It suggests that communities should be entitled to receive recognition as the creators of the music whenever it is performed and also have the ability to safeguard their artistic work from any form of distortion. Experts have suggested that communities should establish organisations to act as central hubs for this purpose. However, there is currently no existing model for implementing this. Although this may seem like a challenging task, it is indeed feasible to identify communities and establish organisations or trusts to support and promote their traditional art and music through thorough research. These groups can help set up systems for distributing royalties and assigning credit. However, it is crucial for the government to actively support them by providing legal assistance and promoting awareness of intellectual property rights among folk music and folklore creators (Bratspies, 2006).

An effective approach to safeguarding traditional cultural expressions (TCEs) and preventing the inappropriate use of culturally significant folk lyrics and music in mainstream media could involve the establishment of a dedicated unit within the Government's IP Office. This unit would focus on promoting and protecting TCEs at both national and state levels. Additionally, the unit would play an active role in implementing specific rules and issuing notices to prevent the misuse of these cultural expressions in popular culture. Here are some broader concepts that could be examined as part of a larger initiative to protect indigenous intellectual property and empower local communities in the economy (Coombe, 1998).

6.2 Empowering Local Communities and Encouraging Collaborative Conservation Initiatives

An effective way to empower local communities is by implementing community-based tourism initiatives that emphasise the active participation and ownership of community members in tourism activities. These initiatives enable communities to highlight their cultural heritage, provide genuine folklore experiences to visitors, and gain economic advantages from tourism while maintaining control over their cultural resources. Through the provision of training, support for capacity-building, and access to resources, policymakers can empower communities to establish and oversee tourism ventures in a manner that is both sustainable and respectful of local culture. This approach ensures that tourism activities are in line with the values, aspirations, and priorities of the community (Jamieson, 1998).

In addition, it is crucial to have collaborative conservation initiatives that involve various stakeholders such as government agencies, non-governmental organisations, academia, and local communities. These initiatives play a vital role in protecting both folklore heritage and natural ecosystems. Through fostering partnerships and promoting dialogue among various stakeholders, collaborative conservation initiatives can harness collective expertise, resources, and perspectives to tackle intricate challenges like habitat degradation, cultural erosion, and unsustainable tourism practices. These initiatives may include participatory research, habitat restoration projects, cultural mapping exercises, and community-led conservation efforts to safeguard folklore traditions, natural landscapes, and biodiversity hotspots (Boyd, 2002).

6.3. Promoting ethical tourism practices

It is crucial to prioritise the promotion of ethical tourism practices in order to support the sustainable development of tourism in India and safeguard its rich folklore heritage. Responsible tourism practices place a strong emphasis on principles such as ethical travel, cultural awareness, and environmental preservation. These practices aim to ensure that tourism activities bring positive benefits to local communities, uphold cultural traditions, and minimise any harm to natural ecosystems. Through the incorporation of ethical principles into tourism policies and practices, policymakers and stakeholders have the opportunity to develop tourism experiences that enhance the well-being of both visitors and host communities while also preserving the genuine and cultural significance of folklore heritage (Springer, 2007).

Promoting ethical tourism practices involves nurturing cultural respect and sensitivity among tourists. It is important to increase awareness about the cultural importance of folklore traditions, educate visitors about local customs, beliefs, and taboos, and promote respectful behaviour towards cultural sites and practices. It is crucial for tourism operators, guides, and visitors to undergo cultural sensitivity training. This training can effectively address cultural misunderstandings, ensuring that folklore heritage is respected and protected and preventing any unintentional disrespect or exploitation. In addition, supporting genuine and immersive cultural experiences that enable tourists to interact with local communities and practitioners of folklore directly promotes mutual understanding and appreciation. This not only enhances the tourism experience but also helps preserve cultural authenticity. By advocating for responsible tourism practices like proper waste management, water conservation, and protection of wildlife, tourists can reduce their environmental footprint and help preserve culturally significant environments (Springer, 2007).

7. CONCLUSION

Despite the fact that India's folk culture has been instrumental in the expansion and diversification of the country's tourism industry, it is still a significant portion of the market that is mostly unexplored in many states. In addition to preserving intangible cultural assets, folk culture tourism helps communities become more self-sufficient in building their skills. Despite the fact that this particular sector of tourism is associated with the negative effects of commodification and trinketisation of culture, as well as the production of false culture, it is still possible to consider it to be one of the most environmentally friendly kinds of tourism if we take a responsible and pro-poor approach to the design of it. We must keep in mind that, in this modern age of tourism, folk culture is being used to meet consumption ends, and as a result, their inherent qualities are increasingly being lost as destinations serve as an answer to the expectations that tourists have regarding the experiences that they wish to live, we must keep this from happening.

A holistic and Inclusive strategy that acknowledges the interconnection of cultural, environmental, and socio-economic components is required in order to promote tourism and safeguard folkloric heritage through the empowerment of local communities and the encouragement of collaborative conservation activities. Policymakers have the ability to create enabling environments for sustainable tourism that benefit both local communities and visitors while simultaneously protecting the rich tapestry of folklore heritage in India. This can be accomplished by giving community participation, cultural authenticity, and environmental stewardship a higher priority in tourism development and conservation policies. India has the ability to harness the transformative potential of tourism as a force for positive change, thereby maintaining cultural variety, increasing livelihoods, and promoting mutual respect and understanding among varied people. This may be accomplished through concentrated efforts and partnerships..

REFERENCES

Antons, C. (2013). Asian Borderlands and the Legal Protection of Traditional Knowledge and Traditional Cultural Expressions. *Modern Asian Studies*, 47(4), 1403–1433. https://www.jstor.org/stable/24494202. DOI: 10.1017/S0026749X12000443

Baral, K. C. (Ed.). (2023). *Cultural forms and practices in northeast India*. Springer Nature Singapore., DOI: 10.1007/978-981-19-9292-6

Bendix, R. (1989). Tourism and Cultural Displays: Inventing Traditions for Whom? *Journal of American Folklore*, 102(404), 131–146. DOI: 10.2307/540676

Boateng, B. (2013). The Hand of the Ancestors: Time, Cultural Production, and Intellectual Property Law. *Law & Society Review*, 47(4), 943–973. https://www.jstor.org/stable/43670364. DOI: 10.1111/lasr.12053

Booth, G. (2015). Copyright Law and the Changing Economic Value of Popular Music in India. *Ethnomusicology*, 59(2), 262–287. DOI: 10.5406/ethnomusicology.59.2.0262

Boyd, S. (2002). Cultural and heritage tourism in Canada: Opportunities, principles and challenges. *Tourism and Hospitality Research*, 3(3), 211–233. https://www.jstor.org/stable/23747289. DOI: 10.1177/146735840200300303

Bratspies, R. M. (2006). The New Discovery Doctrine: Some Thoughts on Property Rights and Traditional Knowledge. *American Indian Law Review*, 31(2), 315–340. DOI: 10.2307/20070790

Bunten, A. C. (2008). Sharing Culture or Selling Out? Developing the Commodified Persona in the Heritage Industry. *American Ethnologist*, 35(3), 380–395. DOI: 10.1111/j.1548-1425.2008.00041.x

CCH Canadian v. Law Society of Upper Canada (2004) 236 DLR (4th) 395.

Chacón, G. E. (2020). Material Culture, Indigeneity, and Temporality: The Textile as Legal Subject. *Textual Cultures, 13*(2), 49–69. https://www.jstor.org/stable/26966965

Coombe, R. J. (1998). Intellectual Property, Human Rights & Sovereignty: New Dilemmas in International Law Posed by the Recognition of Indigenous Knowledge and the Conservation of Biodiversity. *Indiana Journal of Global Legal Studies*, 6(1), 59–115.

De Carlo, M., & Dubini, P. (2010). Integrating Heritage Management and Tourism at Italian Cultural Destinations. *International Journal of Arts Management*, 12(2), 30–43.

Dodson, M., & Barr, O. (2007). Breaking the Deadlock: Developing an Indigenous Response to Protecting Indigenous Traditional Knowledge. *Australian Indigenous Law Review*, 11(2), 19–32.

Dominas, K., Wesołowska, E., & Trocha, B. (Eds.). (2016). *Antiquity in Popular Literature and Culture* (1st ed.). Cambridge Scholars Publishing., https://www.cambridgescholars.com/resources/pdfs/978-1-4438-9024-3-sample.pdf

Eastern Book Company v. D. B. Modak (2008) (36) PTC 1 (SC).

Emrich, D. (1946). "Folk-Lore": William John Thoms. *California Folklore Quarterly*, 5(4), 355–374. DOI: 10.2307/1495929

Folklore from India. (1916). Folklore from India. *Folklore*, 27(4), 418–419. https://www.jstor.org/stable/1255595. DOI: 10.1080/0015587X.1916.9718944

Ghose, A., & Ali, S. M. A. (2023). Protection and preservation of traditional cultural expressions & traditional knowledge in handicraft trade: Advocating the need for a global cultural policy framework. *Revista de Direito Internacional*, 20(2). Advance online publication. DOI: 10.5102/rdi.v20i2.9109

Ghosh, S. (2020, March 31). Plagiarism! The curious case of Badshah's 'Genda Phool' and a Bengali folk singer in darkness! *The Times of India*. https://timesofindia.indiatimes.com/entertainment/bengali/music/plagiarism-the-curious-case-of-badshahs-genda-phool-and-a-bengali-folk-singer-in-darkness/articleshow/74914938.cms

Goldstein, D. (2015). Vernacular Turns: Narrative, Local Knowledge, and the Changed Context of Folklore. *Journal of American Folklore*, 128(508), 125–145. DOI: 10.5406/jamerfolk.128.508.0125

Hajra, V. (2015). Role of Indian Folk Culture in Promotion of Tourism in the Country. *Indian Journal of Research*, 4(2), 231–235. https://www.worldwidejournals.com/paripex/recent_issues_pdf/2015/February/February_2015_1425292942__76.pdf

Herrera, A. (2013). Heritage Tourism, Identity and Development in Peru. *International Journal of Historical Archaeology*, 17(2), 275–295. DOI: 10.1007/s10761-013-0221-6

Institute of Inner St–dies v. Charlotte Anderson and Ors. (2011) CS(OS) 2252/2011 & I.A. No.14617/2011.

(2007). Introduction: The Analytics of Alan Dundes. InBronner, S. J. (Ed.), *Meaning of Folklore: The Analytical Essays of Alan Dundes* (pp. 1–35). University Press of Colorado., DOI: 10.2307/j.ctt4cgrzn.4

Jamieson, W. (1998). Cultural Heritage Tourism Planning and Development: Defining the Field and Its Challenges. *APT Bulletin: The Journal of Preservation Technology*, 29(3/4), 65–67. DOI: 10.2307/1504616

Jarvenpa, R. (1994). Commoditization versus Cultural Integration: Tourism and Image Building in the Klondike. *Arctic Anthropology*, 31(1), 26–46.

Johnsson, D. Z., & Tualima, H. Y. (2017). Cultural Heritage, Traditional Knowledge and Intellectual Property. In Xanthaki, A., Valkonen, S., Heinämäki, L., & Nuorgam, P. (Eds.), *Indigenous Peoples' Cultural Heritage: Rights, Debates, Challenges* (pp. 218–228). Brill. DOI: 10.1163/9789004342194_011

Josefsson, J., & Aronsson, I. L. (2016). Heritage as life-values: A study of the cultural heritage concept. *Current Science*, 110(11), 2091–2098. DOI: 10.18520/cs/v110/i11/2091-2098

JugJugg Jeeyo. T-Series refutes Pakistani singer's claims over Nach Punjaban song, says 'legally acquired rights'. (2022, May 23). *Hindustan Times*. https://www.hindustantimes.com/entertainment/bollywood/jugjugg-jeeyo-t-series-refutes-pakistani-singer-s-claims-over-nach-punjaban-song-says-legally-acquired-rights-101653307639742.html

Kumar, V. R. (2018). The Influence of Sufism in Gaana Songs. *International Journal of Current Humanities and Social Science Researches*, 2(4), 22–26.

Leimgruber, W. (2010). Switzerland and the UNESCO Convention on Intangible Cultural Heritage. *Journal of Folklore Research*, 47(1–2), 161–196. DOI: 10.2979/jfr.2010.47.1-2.161

Lotz, M. (2002). Colliding Worlds: Indigenous Rights, Traditional Knowledge, and Plant Intellectual Property. *Business & Professional Ethics Journal*, 21(3/4), 71–94. DOI: 10.5840/bpej2002213/416

Manuel, P. (1988). Popular Music in India: 1901-86. *Popular Music*, 7(2), 157–176. https://www.jstor.org/stable/853534. DOI: 10.1017/S0261143000002737

Mgbeoji, I. (2001). Patents and Traditional Knowledge of the Uses of Plants: Is a Communal Patent Regime Part of the Solution to the Scourge of Bio Piracy? *Indiana Journal of Global Legal Studies*, 9(1), 163–186. https://www.jstor.org/stable/20643824

Mohanty, D. (2017, June 29). Odia folk song Rangabati controversy: District magistrate ends song and dance. *Hindustan Times*. https://www.hindustantimes.com/india-news/odia-folk-song-rangabati-controversy-district-magistrate-ends-song-and-dance/story-Kqw0YuqaAFDsPrfZDbOmgM.html

Montenyohl, E. (1996). Divergent Paths: On the Evolution of "Folklore" and "Folkloristics.". *Journal of Folklore Research*, 33(3), 232–235.

Newall, V. J. (1987). The Adaptation of Folklore and Tradition (Folklorismus). *Folklore*, 98(2), 131–151. https://www.jstor.org/stable/1259975. DOI: 10.1080/0015587X.1987.9716408

Okumu, O. S. (2016). The concept of intangible cultural heritage in Kenya. In Deisser, A.-M., & Njuguna, M. (Eds.), *Conservation of Natural and Cultural Heritage in Kenya: A Cross-Disciplinary Approach* (1st ed., pp. 45–58). UCL Press., DOI: 10.2307/j.ctt1gxxpc6.10

Poorna, R. L., Mymoon, M., & Hariharan, A. (2014). Preservation and protection of traditional knowledge – diverse documentation initiatives across the globe. *Current Science*, 107(8), 1240–1246.

Pratheep, P. S. (2017). The Impact of tourism on Indian culture. *KnE Social Sciences*, 429–437. https://doi.org/DOI: 10.18502/kss.v1i3.765

Rasoolimanesh, S. M., & Jaafar, M. (2016). Community participation toward tourism development and conservation programs in rural world heritage sites. In Butowski, L. (Ed.), *Tourism-From Empirical Research Towards Practical Application*. InTech., DOI: 10.5772/62293

Reindrawati, D. Y. (2023). Challenges of community participation in tourism planning in developing countries. *Cogent Social Sciences*, 9(1), 2164240. Advance online publication. DOI: 10.1080/23311886.2022.2164240

Rongmei, P. R. (2022, November 24). Experience the best of traditional Rajasthan at Chokhi Dhani. *The Times of India*. https://timesofindia.indiatimes.com/travel/destinations/experience-the-best-of-traditional-rajasthan-at-chokhi-dhani/articleshow/95735982.cms

Scheyvens, R. (1999). Ecotourism and the empowerment of local communities. *Tourism Management*, 20(2), 245–249. DOI: 10.1016/S0261-5177(98)00069-7

Springer, R. (2007). Folklore, Commercialism and Exploitation: Copyright in the Blues. *Popular Music*, 26(1), 33–45. https://www.jstor.org/stable/4500298. DOI: 10.1017/S0261143007001110

Sruthijith, K. K. (2010, November 16). Jodhpur: A faith in rhythms of Rajasthan. *The Economic Times*. https://economictimes.indiatimes.com/jodhpur-a-faith-in-rhythms-of-rajasthan/articleshow/6936423.cms?from=mdr

Stein, M. B. (1987). Coming to Terms with the Past: The Depiction of "Volkskunde" in the Third Reich since 1945. *Journal of Folklore Research*, 24(2), 157–185.

Stoianoff, N. P., & Wright, E. (2018). Fair Use and Traditional Cultural Expressions. In Corbett, S., & Lai, J. C. (Eds.), *Making Copyright Work for the Asian Pacific: Juxtaposing Harmonisation with Flexibility* (pp. 75–94). ANU Press. DOI: 10.22459/MCWAP.10.2018.03

Upadhyaya, K. D. (1954). A General Survey of Folklore Activities in India. *Midwestern Folklore*, 4(4), 201–212.

Walia, S. K. (Ed.). (2020). *The routledge handbook of community-based tourism management: Concepts, issues & implications* (1st ed.). Routledge., DOI: 10.4324/9780429274664

Yang, L. (2014). Ethnic tourism. In Jafari, J., & Xiao, H. (Eds.), *Encyclopedia of Tourism* (pp. 1–3). Springer International Publishing., DOI: 10.1007/978-3-319-01669-6_80-1

Yen, D., Jang, J., Wei, L., Morgan, N., & Pritchard, A. (2023). Leveraging folklore and fantasy to promote small destinations: The case of Visit Wales. *Journal of Policy Research in Tourism, Leisure & Events*, 1–15. DOI: 10.1080/19407963.2023.2263860

KEY TERMS AND DEFINITIONS

Cultural Heritage Management: Cultural heritage management refers to the profession and application of overseeing cultural heritage, which incorporates elements from cultural conservation, restoration, museology, archaeology, history, and architecture.

Cultural Tourism: Cultural tourism refers to the act of tourists engaging in the study, exploration, experience, and consumption of a destination's physical and intangible cultural attractions and goods, including arts, architecture, historical and cultural heritage, culinary heritage, literature, music, creative industries, and living cultures with their lifestyles, value systems, beliefs, and customs.

Ethical Tourism: Ethical tourism and responsible tourism include considering the repercussions of one's behaviour as a visitor on the environment, local residents, and the local economy.

Folklore: Folklore refers to the collective body of expressive culture that is shared by a certain group of people, culture, or subculture. This encompasses many forms of verbal traditions, such as narratives, folklore, fables, sayings, verses, humorous anecdotes, and other forms of spoken traditions

Chapter 4
Cultural Heritage Tourism in Bangladesh:
Balancing Preservation and Visitor Experience

Mohammad Badruddoza Talukder
https://orcid.org/0009-0008-1662-9221
International University of Business Agriculture and Technology, Bangladesh

Mushfika Hoque
https://orcid.org/0009-0000-4645-5105
Daffodil Institute of IT, Bangladesh

ABSTRACT

This study aims to comprehensively assess the state of cultural heritage conservation practices at sites across Bangladesh, considering both their effectiveness and sustainability amidst growing tourism pressures. The study explores visitor perceptions and experiences at these heritage sites to enhance tourism management strategies. By understanding visitors' perspectives, including their satisfaction levels, cultural learning experiences, and challenges encountered, the research seeks to inform targeted improvements in visitor services and site management practices. The research aims to propose actionable recommendations for mitigating negative impacts while maximizing the benefits of tourism to local communities and heritage preservation efforts. Ultimately, this study contributes to the broader discourse on sustainable tourism development by advocating for integrated conservation and management strategies that balance the preservation of cultural heritage with the socio-economic benefits derived from tourism activities in Bangladesh.

DOI: 10.4018/979-8-3693-4171-1.ch004

INTRODUCTION

Cultural heritage tourism holds immense potential to celebrate and promote Bangladesh's rich historical and cultural heritage (Ananya, 2021). With a legacy spanning millennia, Bangladesh boasts many archaeological sites, ancient monuments, traditional crafts, and vibrant cultural practices that attract tourists from around the globe (Amam, 2024). However, the challenge lies in maintaining a delicate equilibrium between conserving these invaluable assets and ensuring a fulfilling experience for visitors (Pande & Shi, 2023).

Bangladesh's cultural heritage encompasses diverse influences from ancient civilizations to colonial legacies, each contributing to the nation's unique identity (Talukder et al., 2024a). Sites like the ancient city of Mahasthangarh, the historic mosques of Bagerhat, and the natural landscapes of the Sundarbans Biosphere Reserve exemplify the country's cultural richness and natural beauty. These sites are history repositories and living testaments to Bangladesh's enduring artistic traditions.

Yet, the surge in tourism poses significant conservation challenges. Increased footfall, infrastructure development, and cultural commodification can threaten the very heritage that draws visitors. Preservation efforts must, therefore, be meticulous, integrating sustainable practices that safeguard monuments, protect ecosystems, and respect local communities (Firoj & Mohammad, 2024). Moreover, cultural heritage tourism in Bangladesh holds promise for economic growth and community development (Pasternak, 2024). When managed responsibly, tourism can foster local pride, generate employment opportunities, and support heritage conservation through revenue generation (Ahmed, 2024). However, achieving this balance requires thoughtful planning, stakeholder collaboration, and innovative strategies prioritizing preservation and visitor experience.

This study explores the complexities of cultural heritage tourism in Bangladesh by exploring strategies for sustainable management, community involvement, and visitor education (Das et al., 2024). By examining successful case studies and global best practices, it seeks to provide actionable insights that can guide policymakers, conservationists, and tourism stakeholders in preserving Bangladesh's cultural treasures while offering enriching experiences for visitors (Knežević, 2017). Through these efforts, Bangladesh can strive towards a future where cultural heritage tourism thrives in harmony with conservation, ensuring that its storied past continues to inspire and endure for generations to come (Salimullah & Nabi, 2022).

OBJECTIVES

- To assess current conservation practices at cultural heritage sites in Bangladesh
- To understand visitor perceptions and experiences to improve tourism management
- To identify challenges posed by tourism to cultural heritage sites

LITERATURE REVIEW

Cultural heritage tourism in Bangladesh plays a pivotal role in showcasing the nation's rich historical and cultural heritage to the world (Peng et al., 2023). The country's diverse cultural landscape, spanning ancient archaeological sites, architectural wonders, and vibrant traditional practices, forms the bedrock of its tourism appeal. Key sites such as Mahasthangarh, the ancient city dating back to the 3rd century BCE, and the UNESCO World Heritage-listed mosques of Bagerhat exemplify Bangladesh's cultural richness and historical significance (Vaz Serra et al., 2023a).

The intersection of tourism and cultural heritage preservation presents both opportunities and challenges. Tourism contributes significantly to the economy through revenue generation, job creation, and infrastructure development (Rahman, 2019). However, the rapid growth of tourism can also strain delicate heritage sites, leading to overcrowding, wear and tear of structures, and environmental degradation (Siddique, 2017). These challenges necessitate effective conservation strategies that balance tourism development with preserving cultural integrity and authenticity (Mitric et al., 2024).

Studies emphasize the importance of sustainable tourism practices in mitigating negative impacts on cultural heritage sites. Sustainable tourism aims to minimize environmental impact, preserve cultural authenticity, and provide socio-economic benefits to local communities. Strategies include visitor management techniques, such as limiting visitor numbers and implementing strict guidelines for site access and behavior (Noaime, 2023). Community involvement is also crucial, as local stakeholders often possess valuable traditional knowledge and are essential partners in heritage conservation efforts.

Visitor experiences and perceptions play a significant role in shaping cultural heritage tourism strategies. Understanding tourists' motivations, expectations, and behaviors helps design interpretive programs and educational initiatives that promote cultural understanding and respect (Adetola et al., 2024). Educational programs to raise awareness about the significance of cultural heritage sites can foster a sense of responsibility among visitors towards conservation efforts. Policy frameworks and governance structures guide sustainable tourism development (Zhao et al., 2024). Bangladesh's cultural heritage management policies balance preservation goals with tourism promotion, often incorporating international best practices while adapting to local contexts. Effective policies ensure that tourism development aligns with conservation imperatives, safeguarding heritage sites for future generations (Qi, 2023).

CULTURAL HERITAGE SITES OF BANGLADESH

Bangladesh has more cultural heritage sites spreading all over its area. A glimpse of these cultural heritage sites will provide readers with insight into the country's resources for cultural heritage sites. The cultural heritage sites for tourism in Bangladesh are presented below with the location and proper description:

Table 1. Different Cultural Heritage Tourism Sites in Bangladesh

Cultural Heritage Sites	Location	Description
Mahasthangarh	Bogura district	An ancient archaeological site dating back to the 3rd century BCE is believed to be the oldest city in Bangladesh and an important center of early urban civilization. Features include ancient city walls, citadels, and archaeological artifacts (Chabot et al., 2022).
Historic Mosque City of Bagerhat	Bagerhat district	A UNESCO World Heritage Site known for its collection of medieval Islamic monuments, including the Sixty Dome Mosque (Shat Gombuj Masjid) and the Nine-domed Mosque (Nau Gombuj Masjid). Represents a fusion of Turkic and Bengali architectural styles (Afroz, 2022).
Paharpur Vihara	Naogaon district	UNESCO World Heritage Site, the largest Buddhist monastery south of the Himalayas. Built during the Pala Empire (8th century), it was a center of Buddhist learning and pilgrimage, featuring a central stupa and extensive monastic complex (Islam & Sajib, 2021).
Sompur Mahavihara	Pabna district	Another UNESCO World Heritage Site is renowned for its archaeological remains from a significant Buddhist monastery dating back to the 8th century. Features include monastic cells, stupas, and terracotta plaques depicting Buddhist iconography (Rahaman et al., 2010).
Sundarbans	Khulna division	The world's largest mangrove forest, shared with India and a UNESCO World Heritage Site. It is known for its biodiversity, including the Royal Bengal tiger, saltwater crocodiles, and diverse bird species. It is also significant for traditional honey collection by local communities (Hossain et al., 2024).
Lalbagh Fort	Dhaka	A Mughal fort complex dating back to the 17th century showcasing Mughal architectural styles and historical significance. Features include the tomb of Pari Bibi, the Lalbagh Mosque, and the audience hall (Diwan-i-Aam).

continued on following page

Table 1. Continued

Cultural Heritage Sites	Location	Description
Sixty Dome Mosque (Shat Gombuj Masjid)	Bagerhat district	A prominent feature of the Historic Mosque City of Bagerhat, known for its impressive architecture with sixty pillars supporting its roof. A UNESCO World Heritage Site and a significant example of medieval Islamic architecture in Bengal (Rasheed et al., 2023).
Kantaji Temple	Dinajpur district	A terracotta Hindu temple dating back to the 18th century during the reign of Maharaja Pran Nath. Known for its intricate terracotta ornamentation depicting scenes from Hindu epics, it is a fine example of Bengal's late medieval architecture and craftsmanship (Rahman et al., 2024).
Sona Mosque	Chapai Nawabganj district	A 15th-century mosque known for its ornate terracotta decorations and unique architectural style, blending Indo-Islamic and Bengali motifs. It reflects the artistic and cultural fusion prevalent during the Bengal Sultanate period (Said, 2024).
Moinamati Archaeological Site	Comilla district	It is an important archaeological site with ruins of ancient Buddhist settlements dating from the 8th to 12th centuries. Features include stupas, viharas, and artifacts, providing insights into the region's historical and cultural evolution under different Buddhist dynasties.

Source: Authors Compilation.

THE CONTEXT OF CULTURAL HERITAGE TOURISM IN BANGLADESH

Cultural heritage tourism in Bangladesh unfolds a vibrant narrative of historical richness, architectural splendor, and natural wonders that collectively define the country's cultural identity (Talukder & Muhsina, 2024). Situated in South Asia, Bangladesh is adorned with a tapestry of ancient civilizations, Islamic legacies, and Buddhist traditions, each leaving an indelible mark on its landscape. This cultural tapestry is woven with many archaeological sites, religious monuments, traditional crafts, and ecological marvels, all contributing to Bangladesh's allure as a destination steeped in heritage (Talukder et al., 2024b).

At the heart of Bangladesh's cultural heritage are its iconic sites. Mahasthangarh, dating back over two millennia, stands as a testament to the early urban civilizations of the region, showcasing ancient city walls, citadels, and artifacts that offer a glimpse into the country's early history. The Historic Mosque City of Bagerhat, a UNESCO World Heritage Site, preserves the grandeur of medieval Islamic architecture through its mosques and tombs, notably the Sixty Dome Mosque, exemplifying the fusion of Turkic and Bengali architectural styles (Mohammad et al., 2024).

Further enriching Bangladesh's heritage are its Buddhist legacies. Paharpur Vihara, one of the largest Buddhist monastic complexes south of the Himalayas, and Sompur Mahavihara in the Pabna district reflect the country's pivotal role in ancient Buddhist scholarship and pilgrimage routes. These sites are adorned with stupas and monastic cells, echo Bangladesh's deep-rooted connection to Buddhism and its regional cultural influence. In addition to its archaeological and religious treasures, Bangladesh's natural heritage shines through the Sundarbans, the world's largest mangrove forest and a UNESCO World Heritage Site shared with India (Mohammad & Fahmida, 2023). This vast ecosystem supports diverse flora and fauna, including the iconic Royal Bengal tiger, and underscores the country's commitment to preserving its natural and cultural heritage in harmony.

Cultural heritage tourism in Bangladesh serves as a gateway to explore these treasures, offering visitors immersive experiences that blend historical exploration with cultural immersion. However, the sector faces challenges such as sustainable management of tourist flows, preservation of fragile sites, and equitable distribution of economic benefits among local communities (Nekmahmud & Hassan, 2021). Efforts to promote sustainable tourism practices emphasize conservation, community engagement, and the development of responsible tourism initiatives that preserve Bangladesh's rich cultural legacy for future generations to cherish and explore.

EXISTING STRATEGIES AND INITIATIVES IN THE CONTEXT OF EFFECTIVENESS AND SUSTAINABILITY

Preserving cultural heritage sites in Bangladesh involves various strategies and initiatives to address conservation challenges, promote sustainable tourism, and engage local communities. Evaluating these strategies reveals achievements and ongoing challenges in safeguarding the country's diverse cultural heritage.

1. **Conservation Strategies and Techniques**: Conservation efforts often focus on structural stabilization, restoration of architectural elements, and preservation of art and artifacts using traditional techniques and materials. These strategies have effectively mitigated immediate threats such as structural decay and environmental damage. However, the sustainability of these efforts depends on continuous monitoring and maintenance, which requires ongoing financial resources and skilled labor (Chauhan et al., 2024). Long-term funding commitments and capacity building are needed to sustain conservation outcomes.
2. **Community Engagement and Participation**: Involving local communities in conservation activities has fostered a sense of ownership and stewardship over heritage sites. Community participation has increased awareness, reduced vandalism, and improved site management practices. Sustainable community engagement requires ongoing support, capacity building, and empowerment to ensure lasting benefits. Challenges include balancing traditional practices with

modern conservation standards and ensuring equitable distribution of benefits among community members (Habimana, 2024).

3. **Educational and Awareness Programs**: Educational initiatives, including workshops, interpretive signage, and guided tours, have enhanced visitor understanding and appreciation of cultural heritage. These programs contribute to responsible tourism behavior and support conservation efforts. Continuous education and awareness are crucial for sustaining public interest and support for heritage conservation. Integration with school curricula and digital outreach can broaden the impact of these programs beyond site visitors(Foluke Eyitayo Adediran et al., 2024).
4. **Policy and Legal Frameworks**: Government policies and legal frameworks provide essential guidelines and protections for cultural heritage sites. These include heritage legislation, zoning regulations, and incentives for heritage conservation projects. Implementation and enforcement of policies can be challenging due to resource constraints, bureaucratic inefficiencies, and competing development interests. Strengthening institutional capacity and collaboration between government agencies, NGOs, and private sectors is essential for effective governance.
5. **International Collaboration and Support**: Bangladesh benefits from international collaborations with UNESCO, bilateral partners, and NGOs, which provide technical expertise, funding, and capacity-building opportunities. The long-term sustainability of international collaborations depends on fostering local ownership, building local expertise, and ensuring projects align with national priorities and cultural contexts (Filho et al., 2024).

CURRENT CONSERVATION PRACTICES AT CULTURAL HERITAGE SITES IN BANGLADESH

Current conservation practices at cultural heritage sites in Bangladesh reflect a blend of traditional methods and modern approaches to safeguard these valuable assets for future generations (Zhang, 2023). The country faces unique challenges, such as environmental factors, urbanization pressures, and the need for sustainable tourism management. Here are some essential conservation practices currently employed:

1. **Documentation and Research**: Conservation efforts begin with comprehensive documentation and research to understand heritage sites' historical significance, architectural features, and condition. Archaeological surveys, mapping, and

documentation of artifacts help formulate conservation plans (Salimullah & Nabi, 2022).

2. **Structural Conservation**: Many conservation projects focus on stabilizing and restoring the structural integrity of monuments and buildings. This involves techniques such as masonry consolidation, reinforcement of foundations, and restoration of damaged elements using traditional materials and methods.
3. **Conservation of Art and Artefacts**: Preserving sculptures, murals, inscriptions, and other artistic elements is crucial. Conservationists employ cleaning, consolidation, and protection techniques to prevent deterioration and ensure the longevity of these cultural treasures (Rusho & Hassan, 2024).
4. **Environmental Management**: Environmental factors like climate change, pollution, and natural disasters threaten cultural heritage sites. Conservation efforts include mitigating environmental impacts, such as drainage improvements, vegetation management, and climate-responsive conservation planning (Afroz, 2022).
5. **Community Engagement**: Involving local communities in conservation efforts fosters a sense of ownership and ensures sustainable management practices. Community participation may include training in heritage conservation techniques, cultural education programs, and involvement in site management committees.
6. **Visitor Management**: Sustainable tourism practices are essential to minimize the impact of visitor activities on heritage sites. Strategies include limiting visitor numbers, establishing visitor guidelines, and promoting responsible behavior through visitor education and interpretation programs (Zhang et al., 2023).
7. **Capacity Building and Training**: Training programs for conservation professionals, archaeologists, and site managers enhance expertise in heritage conservation techniques and management practices. Capacity-building initiatives also empower local stakeholders to actively participate in conservation efforts (Mohammad & Fahmida, 2023).
8. **Policy and Legal Frameworks**: Effective conservation is supported by robust policies, regulations, and legal frameworks. These frameworks guide heritage site management, conservation practices, funding allocation, and collaboration between government agencies, NGOs, and international partners.
9. **Technology and Innovation**: Adopting modern technologies such as 3D scanning, remote sensing, and digital documentation aids in conservation planning, monitoring, and research. Innovations in materials science also contribute to sustainable conservation practices.

10. **Monitoring and Evaluation**: Continuous monitoring and evaluation are essential to assess the effectiveness of conservation interventions. Regular inspections, condition assessments, and impact assessments help identify emerging threats and adapt conservation strategies accordingly (Hossain et al., 2024).

Conservation practices at cultural heritage sites in Bangladesh are evolving to address contemporary challenges while respecting the country's rich artistic legacy by integrating scientific research, community involvement, sustainable tourism practices, and innovative technologies—Bangladesh endeavors to preserve and promote its cultural heritage for future generations to appreciate and cherish.

IMPACT OF CULTURAL HERITAGE TOURISM IN BANGLADESH

Cultural heritage tourism has emerged as a significant sector within Bangladesh's broader tourism industry, reflecting the nation's rich historical, cultural, and architectural legacy. As visitors from around the world flock to explore ancient sites such as Mahasthangarh, the Historic Mosque City of Bagerhat, and the Paharpur Vihara, the impact of this influx is multifaceted, affecting economic development, cultural preservation, community empowerment, education, infrastructure, and the environment. This examination delves into the various dimensions of cultural heritage tourism in Bangladesh, highlighting its contributions to the local economy, cultural sustainability, community well-being, and the broader societal and environmental landscape (Rahman et al., 2024).

Economic Benefits: Cultural heritage tourism creates jobs in various sectors, including tour guiding, hospitality, transportation, and retail. Local artisans and craftsmen also benefit from increased demand for traditional crafts and souvenirs. Increased tourist footfall leads to the growth of local businesses such as restaurants, hotels, and shops (Islam et al., 2023). This economic activity generates income for local entrepreneurs and helps stimulate regional economies. Tourism revenue can attract public and private investment in infrastructure projects such as roads, airports, and public facilities, benefiting tourists and residents.

Cultural Preservation: Revenue from tourism can be allocated to the conservation and restoration of heritage sites. This funding is crucial for maintaining historical monuments' structural integrity and aesthetic value. The presence of tourists and the global attention they bring can raise awareness about the importance of preserving cultural heritage (Karim, 2022a). This can lead to more assertive advocacy and support for heritage conservation initiatives. Tourism often encourages the organization of cultural festivals and events that celebrate and preserve traditional music, dance, and art forms.

Community Empowerment: Local communities can generate income and improve their livelihood by engaging in tourism-related activities. This economic participation fosters a sense of ownership and responsibility towards heritage conservation. Tourism can lead to skill development in hospitality, language proficiency, and business management. Training programs and workshops enhance residents' capabilities to engage in and benefit from tourism. Community involvement in showcasing their heritage to tourists enhances cultural pride and strengthens local identities (Islam & Akter, 2021).

Educational Opportunities: Tourists gain insights into the history, culture, and traditions of Bangladesh through guided tours, museums, and interpretive signage at heritage sites. Exposure to tourists and international perspectives can enhance the knowledge and skills of residents, promoting cultural exchange and understanding. Increased interest in heritage sites can lead to more research and documentation efforts, preserving historical knowledge for future generations (Nowreen & Moran, 2022).

Environmental Impact: Tourism can fund environmental conservation projects, such as reforestation, waste management, and wildlife protection, especially in natural heritage sites like the Sundarbans. Without proper management, tourism can lead to environmental degradation, including littering, pollution, and habitat destruction (Nabi & Salimullah, 2022). Over-tourism can strain local resources and disrupt ecosystems. Implementing eco-friendly tourism practices, such as using renewable energy, reducing waste, and promoting sustainable transport, can mitigate adverse environmental impacts.

Infrastructure Development: Improved roads, bridges, and public transport systems make heritage sites more accessible to tourists and locals. Enhanced visitor amenities such as restrooms, information centers, and medical facilities improve the tourist experience and benefit local communities. Infrastructure investments can lead to the development of both urban and rural areas, promoting balanced regional development.

Social and Cultural Exchange: Tourists and locals engage in cultural exchange, sharing traditions, stories, and experiences. This fosters mutual understanding and respect. Tourism helps build global connections and networks, promoting Bangladesh as a destination on the world stage and encouraging international collaboration in various fields. Positive interactions with tourists can enhance Bangladesh's cultural diplomacy efforts, projecting a positive image of the country abroad (Sayeda et al., 2020).

Challenges of Over-Tourism: Over-tourism can lead to the overuse of local resources such as water, electricity, and food, affecting the quality of life for residents. High visitor numbers can cause physical wear and tear on heritage sites, leading to structural damage and loss of historical value (Sharma & Sharma, 2021). The influx of tourists can disrupt local communities, leading to noise pollution, traffic congestion, and changes in local culture and traditions. Effective management strategies, such as visitor quotas, timed entry, and the development of alternative tourism sites, are essential to balance tourism growth with preservation efforts.

PERCEPTIONS AND EXPERIENCES OF VISITORS TOWARD CULTURAL HERITAGE TOURISM IN BANGLADESH

The perceptions and experiences of visitors toward cultural heritage tourism are crucial for ensuring the sustainability and success of tourism initiatives in Bangladesh. Visitor perceptions shape satisfaction levels, revisit intentions, and word-of-mouth recommendations, directly influencing tourism revenues and destination image. Positive experiences foster emotional connections and cultural appreciation, encouraging responsible tourism behaviors and support for conservation efforts. Conversely, negative perceptions, such as concerns over authenticity or infrastructure shortcomings, can deter future visitors and impact local communities' economic opportunities (Tiberghien et al., 2017). Some of the perceptions and experiences of visitors toward cultural heritage tourism in Bangladesh are provided below:

Cultural Fascination: Visitors often express a deep interest in Bangladesh's rich cultural heritage, encompassing historical landmarks, ancient ruins, religious sites, and traditional arts. Many visitors are drawn to these cultural treasures' unique architecture, intricate craftsmanship, and spiritual significance.

Educational and Learning Opportunities: Cultural heritage tourism in Bangladesh offers visitors educational opportunities to learn about the country's history, traditions, and cultural practices. Visitors engage in guided tours, museum visits, and interactive exhibitions that provide insights into the cultural significance of heritage sites (Basheer et al., 2023).

Emotional Connections: Visitors often describe emotional connections to heritage sites, experiencing awe, reverence, and a sense of wonder when exploring ancient temples, archaeological sites, and historical monuments. These sites' spiritual and historical narratives evoke powerful emotions among visitors.

Challenges in Accessibility and Infrastructure: Many visitors encounter challenges related to accessibility and infrastructure at heritage sites in Bangladesh. Poor road conditions, inadequate signage, and limited visitor facilities such as restrooms and information centers can detract from the overall visitor experience (Amam, 2024).

Impact of Overcrowding: Overcrowding at popular heritage sites can diminish the visitor experience, making it difficult for visitors to appreciate the tranquility and historical ambiance of the sites. Tourists may feel rushed or unable to fully explore and absorb the cultural significance of the surroundings.

Cultural Authenticity and Commercialization: Visitors are sometimes concerned about the authenticity of cultural experiences, fearing that commercialization and tourist-driven adaptations may dilute the genuine cultural heritage of Bangladesh. They seek authentic encounters with local traditions and customs, free from commercial exploitation.

Interaction with Local Communities: Positive interactions with local communities enhance visitors' experiences of cultural heritage tourism in Bangladesh. Visitors value opportunities to engage with residents, artisans, and cultural experts who share insights into traditional practices, folklore, and daily life (Boukas & Ioannou, 2020).

Environmental and Conservation Concerns: Conscious visitors express concerns about environmental sustainability and conservation efforts at heritage sites. They advocate for responsible tourism practices that minimize environmental impact, promote biodiversity conservation, and preserve natural landscapes surrounding cultural landmarks.

Safety and Security: Ensuring the safety and security of visitors is paramount. Visitors expect well-maintained facilities, effective crowd management, and adequate security measures to protect the cultural heritage sites and tourists (Jaskari, 2023).

Recommendations and Feedback: Visitors often provide suggestions and feedback aimed at improving the visitor experience and enhancing the preservation of cultural heritage in Bangladesh. They advocate for better infrastructure, enhanced interpretation services, sustainable tourism practices, and community involvement in heritage conservation efforts.

MEASURES TO BALANCE PRESERVATION AND VISITOR EXPERIENCE FOR CULTURAL HERITAGE TOURISM

Balancing preservation and visitor experience for cultural heritage tourism requires a multifaceted approach that ensures the protection of heritage sites while providing an enriching and sustainable tourist experience.

Sustainable Visitor Management: Sustainable visitor management is essential, with strategies like implementing visitor quotas and timed entry systems to control the number of tourists at any given time, thereby reducing overcrowding and minimizing site wear and tear. Booking systems can also help regulate visitor flow and ensure a steady stream of tourists without overwhelming the heritage sites (Amam, 2024).

Infrastructure Development: Infrastructure development enhances visitor experience while preserving site integrity. Providing adequate visitor facilities such as restrooms, information centers, seating areas, and waste disposal systems ensures visitor comfort. Simultaneously, improving accessibility with well-maintained access routes can cater to tourists of all abilities without causing environmental damage (Ahmed, 2024).

Conservation Practices: To preserve heritage sites' structural integrity and aesthetic value, conservation practices must be prioritized, involving regular maintenance and restoration activities. Using traditional conservation techniques and materials appropriate to the historical context of the sites ensures authenticity and sustainability.

Educational Programs: Educating visitors through interpretive signage, brochures, and digital guides can foster respect and appreciation for the sites, while guided tours led by knowledgeable guides enhance the visitor experience and ensure adherence to site rules (Ananya, 2021).

Community Engagement: Engaging local communities in tourism activities is crucial for fostering a sense of ownership and responsibility towards heritage sites. Local involvement allows communities to share their knowledge, traditions, and crafts with visitors and ensures that they benefit economically through employment opportunities and revenue-sharing mechanisms.

Environmental Management: Sustainable tourism practices, such as waste reduction, recycling, and using renewable energy sources, help minimize the environmental impact of tourism while protecting surrounding natural habitats from damage caused by construction and visitor activities (Sayeda et al., 2020).

Technological Integration: Technological integration, such as virtual tours and augmented reality experiences, can reduce physical strain on heritage sites while providing access to those who cannot visit in person. Implementing visitor feedback systems helps continuously improve visitor management strategies and experiences.

Policy and Regulation: Strengthening heritage legislation and developing comprehensive tourism management plans are vital for balancing preservation with tourism development, providing guidelines for infrastructure development, visitor behavior, and conservation practices(Pasternak, 2024).

Monitoring and Evaluation: Regular environmental and social impact assessments and visitor analytics enable better planning and timely interventions to address tourism's effects on heritage sites and local communities.

Awareness Campaigns: Awareness campaigns promoting responsible tourism behavior, coupled with cultural sensitivity training for tour operators, guides, and hospitality staff, ensure that preservation is conveyed to visitors (Basheer et al., 2023).

OPPORTUNITIES FOR CULTURAL HERITAGE TOURISM IN BANGLADESH

Cultural heritage tourism in Bangladesh presents significant opportunities for economic growth, cultural preservation, and community development. Bangladesh can attract global tourists by showcasing its diverse historical sites, traditional arts, and spiritual landmarks, fostering cultural exchange and international diplomacy (Karim, 2022a). This tourism sector generates revenue through entrance fees, and local crafts stimulate local economies, create jobs, and promote entrepreneurial ventures. The opportunities for cultural heritage tourism in Bangladesh are provided here:

Economic Growth: Cultural heritage tourism can significantly boost the economy by attracting domestic and international tourists. The revenue generated through entrance fees to heritage sites, guided tours, and related tourism services can provide a substantial income stream. The demand for local crafts, souvenirs, and traditional goods can also invigorate local markets and artisanal industries. This influx of money stimulates local economies by creating direct and indirect employment opportunities. Job creation spans various sectors, including hospitality, transportation, retail, and crafts. Furthermore, tourism promotes entrepreneurship as residents seize opportunities to start businesses catering to tourists, such as guesthouses, restaurants, and craft shops, fostering economic diversification and resilience (Nowreen & Moran, 2022).

Cultural Preservation: The increased attention and revenue from tourists often lead to more significant efforts to preserve and restore cultural heritage sites. These efforts are essential for maintaining sites' historical and cultural integrity for future generations. Preservation initiatives include regular maintenance, restoration projects, and the implementation of protective measures to prevent degradation. Furthermore, the pride and recognition that come with tourism can enhance local communities' sense of identity and heritage. As tourists express interest in Bangladesh's culture and history, it encourages the government and local communities to invest more in safeguarding their cultural assets. This mutual reinforcement between tourism and preservation ensures that cultural heritage remains vibrant and intact.

Community Development: Tourism can catalyze significant improvements in local infrastructure. The revenue generated from tourism activities often funds the development of better roads, improved water supply systems, and enhanced health-care facilities. These improvements benefit tourists and significantly improve the quality of life for residents. Furthermore, tourism offers a platform for local people to engage in various entrepreneurial activities, providing them with new sources of income and economic independence. Local businesses such as guesthouses, restaurants, and artisan shops can thrive with the influx of tourists, creating a more dynamic and prosperous community environment (Rahman et al., 2024). The revenue from tourism can also be reinvested in community development projects, ensuring sustainable growth and development.

Global Exposure: Promoting cultural heritage sites can elevate Bangladesh's status on the global tourism map. Attracting international tourists creates opportunities for cultural exchange and diplomacy, fostering better understanding and relationships between Bangladesh and other countries (Sharma & Sharma, 2021). This global exposure enhances the country's image, showcasing its rich cultural and historical heritage to a broader audience. Additionally, increased international interest can attract foreign investment in tourism and related industries, further boosting economic growth. Global recognition can lead to international partnerships, collaborative conservation efforts, and participation in worldwide heritage and tourism forums, positioning Bangladesh as a critical player in the global cultural tourism market.

Educational Opportunities: Heritage tourism promotes academic activities that benefit locals and visitors. Historical research and archaeological studies can be spurred by the interest generated through tourism, leading to discoveries and a deeper understanding of Bangladesh's cultural history. Educational tours and programs can provide valuable learning experiences, helping visitors gain insights into the country's rich heritage. These programs can include workshops, lectures, and interactive exhibits that engage tourists and enhance their knowledge (Dong et al., 2020). For residents, increased interaction with tourists can provide opportunities to learn new languages, acquire hospitality skills, and gain broader cultural perspectives. This educational exchange fosters a greater appreciation of their heritage and the importance of preserving it.

Sustainable Tourism: When appropriately managed, cultural heritage tourism can promote sustainable practices that balance economic development with preserving cultural and natural resources. Sustainable tourism initiatives include promoting eco-friendly practices, such as reducing waste, using renewable energy sources, and encouraging sustainable transportation options. These practices help minimize the environmental impact of tourism activities. Additionally, sustainable tourism involves developing strategies to manage visitor numbers and behaviors to prevent over-tourism and its associated problems, such as site degradation and resource depletion (Paulino & Cruz, 2024). By integrating sustainability principles into tourism planning and management, Bangladesh can ensure that future generations preserve and enjoy its cultural heritage sites while contributing to long-term economic stability and environmental health.

CHALLENGES OF CULTURAL HERITAGE TOURISM IN BANGLADESH

Overcrowding and Wear: High numbers of tourists can lead to overcrowding at cultural heritage sites, resulting in physical damage to the structures and surrounding areas (Karim, 2022b). The constant foot traffic can cause wear and tear on ancient pathways, buildings, and artifacts, leading to accelerated degradation (Bhargava, 2022). Additionally, overcrowding diminishes the quality of the visitor experience, making it difficult for tourists to fully appreciate the site's historical and cultural significance. This overcrowding can also strain local infrastructure, leading to issues such as traffic congestion and inadequate facilities, further reducing the overall visitor experience and potentially causing long-term damage to the site (Karim, 2022a).

Environmental Degradation: Increased tourism activities can significantly impact the environment surrounding heritage sites. Problems like vehicle pollution, littering, and inadequate waste management can degrade these sites' natural beauty and integrity (Zhang, 2023). Tourism can also lead to the depletion of local resources, such as water and energy, which can negatively affect both the site and the local community. Furthermore, if not managed sustainably, the construction of tourism-related infrastructure can disrupt local ecosystems, leading to loss of biodiversity and habitat destruction (Sharma & Sharma, 2021). These environmental issues can ultimately harm the sites that attract tourists, undermining efforts to promote sustainable tourism.

Inadequate Infrastructure: Many cultural heritage sites in Bangladesh lack the necessary infrastructure to accommodate large numbers of tourists (Yang, 2023). Poor transportation links, such as inadequate roads and public transport options, can make it difficult for tourists to access these sites. Additionally, the absence of proper facilities, such as restrooms, visitor centers, and accommodations, can deter tourists and negatively impact their experience (Kulindwa, 2024). Insufficient visitor services, including signage, guides, and information, can leave tourists feeling lost and uninformed. Without significant investment in infrastructure, these sites may struggle to attract and retain visitors, limiting their potential economic benefits.

Cultural Dilution: The influx of tourists can sometimes lead to commercializing and diluting local culture and traditions. Communities may alter their cultural practices and crafts to cater to tourist expectations, leading to a loss of authenticity and cultural integrity (Jaskari, 2023). Traditional festivals, rituals, and crafts may be adapted or simplified to appeal to a broader audience, diminishing their original meaning and significance. This can result in a homogenized cultural experience that lacks depth and fails to accurately represent the rich diversity of Bangladesh's cultural heritage. Additionally, many tourists can disrupt local communities' daily lives and cultural practices, leading to tensions and a sense of loss among residents (Nabi & Salimullah, 2022).

Economic Disparities: While tourism can bring significant financial benefits, these are not always evenly distributed. In some cases, the profits generated from tourism may not reach the local communities, leading to economic disparities and social tension (Stojanović, 2024). Large tourism operators and investors often capture a significant share of the revenue, leaving local businesses and residents with limited financial gains. This economic imbalance can exacerbate existing inequalities and create social divisions (Vaz Serra et al., 2023b). Furthermore, the reliance on tourism revenue can make local economies vulnerable to fluctuations in tourist numbers, leading to economic instability and insecurity for those who depend on tourism for their livelihoods (Nowreen & Moran, 2022).

Conservation Costs: The cost of maintaining and conserving heritage sites can be high, requiring substantial financial and human resources (Luekveerawattana, 2024). Without adequate funding and management, these sites may suffer from neglect and deterioration, counteracting the benefits of tourism. Conservation efforts often require specialized skills and materials, which can be expensive and difficult to source. Additionally, ongoing maintenance is essential to address the wear and tear caused by tourist activities (Ahmed, 2024). Ensuring sufficient resources are allocated for conservation can be challenging, particularly in regions with limited financial resources. Without proper investment, heritage sites risk losing their cultural and historical value, undermining the long-term sustainability of cultural heritage tourism (Meng et al., 2024).

Security Concerns: Ensuring the safety and security of tourists is essential for maintaining a positive reputation and attracting visitors (Agwi & J, 2024). Any crime, violence, or natural disasters can deter tourists and negatively impact the tourism sector. Perceptions of insecurity, even if not based on actual events, can significantly influence tourists' decisions to visit a destination (Escudeiro et al., 2023). Ensuring robust security measures, such as effective law enforcement, emergency response systems, and public safety initiatives, is crucial for creating a safe tourist environment. Additionally, providing accurate information and guidance to tourists can help mitigate potential risks and enhance their sense of security while visiting cultural heritage sites (Islam et al., 2023).

Balancing Modernization and Preservation: Striking a balance between modern development and the preservation of heritage sites is a significant challenge (Ramires et al., 2024). Urbanization and infrastructure development may sometimes threaten the integrity of cultural sites, as modern construction can encroach upon or damage historical areas (Talukder & Muhsina, 2024). Integrating modern amenities and facilities without compromising heritage sites' historical and cultural value requires careful planning and regulation (Chen & Arus, 2024). Preservation efforts must consider the needs of local communities and the potential impact of development on their cultural heritage. Implementing sustainable development practices and engaging stakeholders in decision-making can help achieve modernization and preservation goals (Amam, 2024).

CONCEPTUAL FRAMEWORK

Figure 1 shows how the responsible authorities of cultural heritage tourism can balance the preservation and visitor experience in cultural heritage sites in Bangladesh.

Figure 1. Techniques to balance preservation and visitor experience in cultural heritage sites in Bangladesh

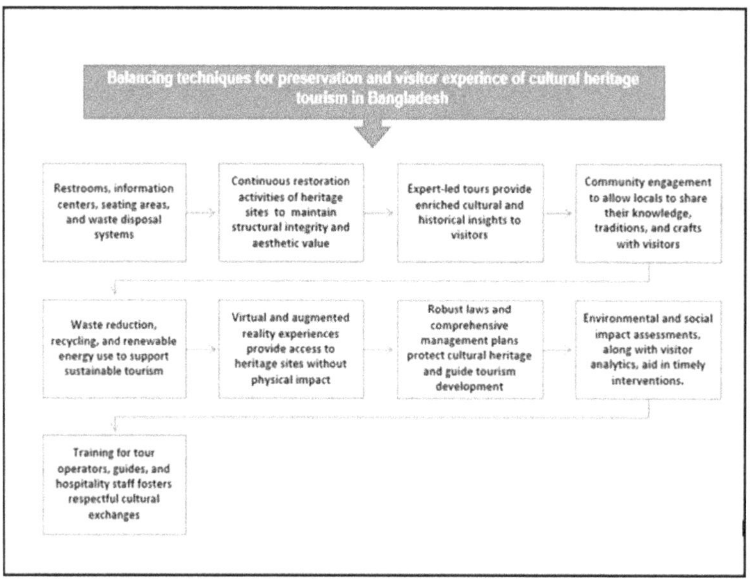

Source: Author's Compilation

RECOMMENDATIONS

- The responsible authority of cultural heritage sites in Bangladesh should implement sustainable visitor management strategies, including capacity limits, timed entry systems, and educational programs on responsible tourism practices.

- Bangladesh should strengthen partnerships with local communities to ensure their involvement in tourism planning, benefit-sharing, and conservation efforts.
- The authority needs to develop and implement visitor management plans to control tourist flow, minimize overcrowding at sensitive heritage sites, and improve transportation infrastructure, including roads, parking facilities, and public transport options to enhance accessibility to heritage sites.
- We should implement strict environmental regulations and guidelines to mitigate pollution from tourism activities, including vehicle emissions and waste management, by promoting sustainable tourism practices among tourists and local communities to reduce environmental impact and preserve natural resources.
- Develop programs to educate tourists about local cultures, traditions, and customs to foster respect and appreciation for Bangladesh's cultural heritage by encouraging community participation in tourism planning and management to ensure that local perspectives and interests are considered.
- Foster partnerships between tourism operators and local communities to ensure equitable distribution of economic benefits from tourism and encourage entrepreneurship among residents through training programs and support for small-scale tourism enterprises.
- Allocate sufficient financial resources for the conservation and maintenance of heritage sites, including regular monitoring and upkeep of structures and artifacts through implementing sustainable funding mechanisms, such as entrance fees and heritage conservation funds, to ensure ongoing financial support for conservation projects.
- Enhance security measures at heritage sites to ensure the safety and well-being of visitors, including effective law enforcement and emergency response systems through collaboration with local authorities and communities to address security concerns and promote a safe environment for tourists and residents.
- Adopt integrated planning approaches that balance tourism development with heritage preservation and community well-being by incorporating sustainable development principles into tourism policies and strategies to minimize negative impacts on cultural and natural resources.
- Engage stakeholders, including government agencies, NGOs, local communities, and tourism operators, in collaborative decision-making to ensure holistic and sustainable tourism development.

FUTURE DIRECTIONS

Looking ahead, the future direction for cultural heritage tourism in Bangladesh must prioritize a balanced approach that harmonizes preservation efforts with enhancing visitor experiences. This entails adopting innovative conservation practices that leverage technology and sustainable management strategies to mitigate the impacts of tourism on heritage sites. Emphasizing community engagement and capacity building will ensure local participation and ownership in tourism initiatives, fostering a sense of responsibility towards heritage conservation. Moreover, integrating cultural authenticity into tourism offerings and promoting responsible tourism behaviors among visitors will help preserve Bangladesh's rich cultural heritage. Strengthening infrastructure, including improved accessibility and visitor facilities, will enhance the visitor experience while minimizing negative impacts on heritage sites. Strategic partnerships between government agencies, local communities, and private sectors will be essential in mobilizing resources and expertise towards sustainable tourism development. This collaborative approach can facilitate effective policy frameworks, investment in conservation efforts, and developing diversified tourism products that showcase Bangladesh's cultural diversity. By focusing on these future directions, Bangladesh can position itself as a leading cultural heritage destination while safeguarding its heritage for future generations, ensuring sustainable socio-economic benefits, and promoting global appreciation of its cultural legacy.

CONCLUSION

In conclusion, Bangladesh's cultural heritage tourism presents opportunities and challenges that require careful consideration and strategic management. The country's rich cultural heritage, encompassing ancient sites, traditional arts, and spiritual landmarks, holds immense potential to attract tourists, foster economic growth, and promote cultural exchange. However, effective conservation practices, sustainable tourism strategies, and community involvement are essential to mitigate the challenges posed by tourism. Overcrowding, environmental degradation, inadequate infrastructure, and cultural dilution are significant concerns that must be addressed through integrated planning and investment. By prioritizing conservation efforts, improving visitor management, and promoting responsible tourism practices, Bangladesh can enhance visitor experiences while preserving its cultural authenticity and natural environment.

Moreover, ensuring equitable economic benefits, supporting local entrepreneurship, and engaging communities in tourism development are critical for fostering inclusive growth and reducing economic disparities. Sustainable funding mechanisms and stakeholder partnerships will support conservation initiatives and maintain heritage site integrity. A holistic approach that balances preservation with enhancing visitor experiences is paramount. By leveraging technological advancements, community participation, and strategic partnerships, Bangladesh can sustainably develop its cultural heritage tourism sector, positioning itself as a global cultural destination while safeguarding its heritage for future generations.

REFERENCES

Adediran, F. E., Okunade, B. A., Daraojimba, R. E., Adewusi, O. E., Bukola, A., & Igbokwe, J. C. (2024). Blockchain for social good: A review of applications in humanitarian aid and social initiatives. *International Journal of Science and Research Archive*, 11(1), 1203–1216.

Adetola, B. O., Akinola, O., & Aina, A. D. (2024). Tourism Policies and Performance of Nigerian Heritage Sites. *Advances in Research*, 25(3), 227–240. DOI: 10.9734/air/2024/v25i31067

Afroz, D. (2022). Impacts of non-climatic factors on heritage sites- a case study on khalifataabad, bangladesh. *Khulna University Studies*, 271–280. DOI: 10.53808/KUS.2022.ICSTEM4IR.0016-se

Agwi, C., & J, A. (2024). *An Exploratory Study of Fintech Security Concerns among its Users in Nigeria*. DOI: 10.22541/au.170664227.79688144/v1

Ahmed, N. (2024). Tourism Impact on the Cultural Heritage of Countries in the Middle East. *Journal of Applied Geographical Studies*, 3(1), 41–53. DOI: 10.47941/jags.1623

Amam, M. (2024). Influence of Cultural Heritage Preservation on Tourism Development in Egypt. *American Journal of Arts. Social and Humanity Studies*, 4(1), 22–32. DOI: 10.47672/ajashs.2063

Ananya, S. A. (2021). Sustainable Tourism Principles and Practices in Bangladesh. In Hassan, A. (Ed.), *Tourism Products and Services in Bangladesh* (pp. 101–113). Springer Singapore., DOI: 10.1007/978-981-33-4279-8_5

Basheer, S., Farooq, S., Hassan, V., Malik, Y. M., & Reshi, M. A. (2023). Augmented Reality and Virtual Reality in Cultural Heritage Tourism Enhancing Visitor Experiences. In Rawal, Y. S., Sinha, R., Mukherjee, S. K., & Batabyal, D. (Eds.), *Advances in Hospitality, Tourism, and the Services Industry* (pp. 13–34). IGI Global., DOI: 10.4018/978-1-6684-9957-3.ch002

Boukas, N., & Ioannou, M. (2020). Co-creating visitor experiences in cultural heritage museums: The avenue towards sustainable tourism development. *International Journal of Tourism Policy*, 10(2), 101. DOI: 10.1504/IJTP.2020.110862

Chabot, Y., Lefevre, V., & Lefrancq, C. (2022, June 20). The paleoenvironment of Mahasthangarh (Bangladesh) during the Pre-Modern Period. DOI: 10.5194/icg2022-75

Chauhan, S., Bansal, O., & Puriya, A. (2024). Innovating Urbanity: The Synergy of Smart Cities and Circular Economy in India. In Majumdar, S., Kandpal, V., & Anthopoulos, L. G. (Eds.), *Smart Cities* (pp. 249–278). Springer Nature Switzerland., DOI: 10.1007/978-3-031-59846-3_11

Chen, C., & Arus, B. B. M. (2024). Chinese Cultural and Opera Stage Architectural Design for Urbanization Henan, China. *South Asian Journal of Social Sciences and Humanities*, 5(3), 114–134. DOI: 10.48165/sajssh.2024.5307

Das, I. R., Talukder, M. B., & Kumar, S. (2024). Implication of Artificial Intelligence in Hospitality Marketing. In Kumar, S., Talukder, M. B., & Pego, A. (Eds.), *Advances in Hospitality, Tourism, and the Services Industry* (pp. 291–310). IGI Global., DOI: 10.4018/979-8-3693-1978-9.ch014

Dong, J. D., Peng, M., & Uddin, M. G. (2020). Mapping The Linguistic Landscape of the Cultural Heritage Sites and Tourist Spots in Bangladesh. *Randwick International of Education and Linguistics Science Journal*, 1(2), 226–241. DOI: 10.47175/rielsj.v1i2.89

Dr. S.K. Bhargava. (2022). Sustainable Development of Cultural-Heritage Tourism Planning with Issues and Challenges. *Social Science Journal for Advanced Research, 2*(3), 1–5. DOI: 10.54741/ssjar.2.3.1

Escudeiro, N., Escudeiro, P., Cunha, B., & Gouveia, M. C. (2023). Inclusive Cultural Heritage Tourism. In Abreu, A., Carvalho, J. V., Liberato, D., & Galdames, I. S. (Eds.), *Advances in Tourism, Technology and Systems* (Vol. 340, pp. 207–217). Springer Nature Singapore., DOI: 10.1007/978-981-19-9960-4_19

Firoj, K., & Mohammad, B. T. (2024). Measuring sustainability in the broadcasting media industry in Bangladesh. *I-Manager's. Journal of Management*, 18(3), 51. DOI: 10.26634/jmgt.18.3.20234

Habimana, J. (2024). Rural Development Strategies through Livestock Policy. *International Journal of Livestock Policy*, 3(1), 1–15. DOI: 10.47941/ijlp.1747

Hossain, M., Saha, C., Saha, S., Islam, H. M. N., Ahmed, M., Ahmed, T., Sikder, A. H. F., & Billah, M. (2024). Is the Sundarbans of Bangladesh in a State of Pollution? *Open Journal of Forestry*, 14(01), 19–41. DOI: 10.4236/ojf.2024.141002

Islam, M., Farjana, F., Nasrin, N., & Ahmed, M. S. (2023). The economic, social and environmental implications of heritage tourism: Evidence from Bangladesh. *SN Business & Economics*, 3(2), 42. DOI: 10.1007/s43546-022-00411-2

Islam, S. A. M. Z., & Al Sajib, S. M. S. (2021). Technology Supported Tourism: A Study on the Buddhist Vihara at Paharpur in Bangladesh. In Hassan, A. (Ed.), *Technology Application in the Tourism and Hospitality Industry of Bangladesh* (pp. 157–173). Springer Singapore., DOI: 10.1007/978-981-16-2434-6_10

Islam, S. M. N., & Akter, Sk. R. (2021). Problems and Prospects of Tourism Industry in Bangladesh: A Study on Cumilla District. *South Asian Journal of Social Studies and Economics*, 27–35. DOI: 10.9734/sajsse/2021/v10i430271

Jaskari, M.-M. E. (2023). Rhythms of Living Cultural Heritage: Co-Creating Memorable Tourism Experiences. In Rawal, Y. S., Sinha, R., Mukherjee, S. K., & Batabyal, D. (Eds.), *Advances in Hospitality, Tourism, and the Services Industry* (pp. 180–195). IGI Global., DOI: 10.4018/978-1-6684-9957-3.ch014

Karim, K. M. R. (2022a). Opportunities and the Challenges of Tourism Industry in Bangladesh. In Jana, N. C., Singh, A., & Singh, R. B. (Eds.), *Livelihood Enhancement Through Agriculture, Tourism and Health* (pp. 223–236). Springer Nature Singapore., DOI: 10.1007/978-981-16-7310-8_11

Knežević, Ž. (2017). Cultural heritage and tourism – an introduction. *Liburna*, 2(1). Advance online publication. DOI: 10.15291/lib.992

Kulindwa, Y. J. (2024). Community Involvement in Cultural Heritage Tourism: The Case of Ngorongoro Conservation Area, Tanzania. In Sigala, M., Fang, M., Yeark, A., Albrecht, J. N., & Vorobjovas-Pinta, O. (Eds.), *Case Based Research in Tourism, Travel, and Hospitality* (pp. 213–230). Springer Nature Singapore., DOI: 10.1007/978-981-97-1891-7_12

Kumar, S., Talukder, M. B., Kabir, F., & Kaiser, F. (2024). Challenges and Sustainability of Green Finance in the Tourism Industry: Evidence from Bangladesh. In Taneja, S., Kumar, P., Grima, S., Ozen, E., & Sood, K. (Eds.), (pp. 97–111). Advances in Finance, Accounting, and Economics. IGI Global., DOI: 10.4018/979-8-3693-1388-6.ch006

Kumar, S., Talukder, M. B., & Pego, A. (Eds.). (2024). *Utilizing Smart Technology and AI in Hybrid Tourism and Hospitality*. IGI Global., DOI: 10.4018/979-8-3693-1978-9

Leal Filho, W., Dibbern, T., Pimenta Dinis, M. A., Coggo Cristofoletti, E., Mbah, M. F., Mishra, A., Clarke, A., Samuel, N., Castillo Apraiz, J., Rimi Abubakar, I., & Aina, Y. A. (2024). The added value of partnerships in implementing the UN sustainable development goals. *Journal of Cleaner Production*, 438, 140794. DOI: 10.1016/j.jclepro.2024.140794

Luekveerawattana, R. (2024). Enhancing innovation in cultural heritage tourism: Navigating external factors. *Cogent Social Sciences*, 10(1), 2301813. DOI: 10.1080/23311886.2024.2301813

Meng, L., Yan, F., Fang, Q., & Si, W. (2024). Research on the Educational Tourism Development of Intangible Cultural Heritage: Suitability, Spatial Pattern, and Obstacle Factor. *Sustainability (Basel)*, 16(11), 4647. DOI: 10.3390/su16114647

Mitric, J., Radulovic, I., Popovic, T., Scekic, Z., & Tinaj, S. (2024). AI and Computer Vision in Cultural Heritage Preservation. *2024 28th International Conference on Information Technology (IT)*, 1–4. DOI: 10.1109/IT61232.2024.10475738

Mohammad, B. T., & Fahmida, K. (2023). Economic impact of river tourism: Evidence of Bangladesh. *I-Manager's. Journal of Management*, 18(2), 47. DOI: 10.26634/jmgt.18.2.20235

Mohammad, B. T., Mushfika, H., & Iva, R. D. (2024). Opportunities of tourism and hospitality education in bangladesh: Career perspectives. *I-Manager's. Journal of Management*, 18(3), 21. DOI: 10.26634/jmgt.18.3.20385

Nabi, R., & Salimullah, A. H. M. (2022). Promoting Catamaran Tourism in Bangladesh: The Challenges of Blue Economy. In Hassan, A. (Ed.), *Technology Application in Tourism Fairs, Festivals and Events in Asia* (pp. 181–208). Springer Singapore., DOI: 10.1007/978-981-16-8070-0_11

Nekmahmud, Md., & Hassan, A. (2021). Tourism Products and Services in Bangladesh: In Search of Policy and Development Frameworks. In Hassan, A. (Ed.), *Tourism Products and Services in Bangladesh* (pp. 3–24). Springer Singapore., DOI: 10.1007/978-981-33-4279-8_1

Noaime, E. (2023). *Historic Syrian Cities in the Post-War Period: Balancing Cultural Preservation and Tourism Investment*. DOI: 10.20944/preprints202303.0457.v1

Nowreen, S., & Moran, S. (2022). Broadening Tourism and Cultivating Sustainability: Exploring Opportunities in Bangladesh. *Journal of Sustainable Development*, 16(1), 93. DOI: 10.5539/jsd.v16n1p93

Pande, K., & Shi, F. (2023). Managing visitor experience at religious heritage sites. *Journal of Destination Marketing & Management*, 29, 100800. DOI: 10.1016/j.jdmm.2023.100800

Pasternak, K. (2024). Manor tourism as an indicator of the promotion of the cultural and historical heritage of small towns and rural settlements. *moscow economic journal*, 366–390. DOI: 10.55186/2413046X_2024_9_3_154

Paulino, F. F., & Cruz, T. (2024). Cultural Heritage, Tourism and Sustainable Development. The Model of the Cultural Heritage Digital Media Lab. In Chica-Olmo, J., Vujičić, M., Castanho, R. A., Stankov, U., & Martinelli, E. (Eds.), *Sustainable Tourism, Culture and Heritage Promotion* (pp. 139–149). Springer Nature Switzerland., DOI: 10.1007/978-3-031-49536-6_15

Peng, K., Tao, X., Jiang, J., & Zhai, J. (2023). The Experience Design of Cultural Heritage Tourism in the Perspective of Gamification. In Marcus, A., Rosenzweig, E., & Soares, M. M. (Eds.), *Design, User Experience, and Usability* (Vol. 14034, pp. 127–146). Springer Nature Switzerland., DOI: 10.1007/978-3-031-35705-3_10

Qi, F. (2023). Balancing Cultural Heritage Preservation and Cultural Industry Development: The Role and Challenges of Museums. *Highlights in Business. Economics and Management*, 21, 1071–1073. DOI: 10.54097/hbem.v21i.14961

Rahaman, H., Rashid, M. M., & Rahman, M. (2010). Heritage interpretation: Collective reconstruction of Sompur Mahavihara, Bangladesh. *2010 16th International Conference on Virtual Systems and Multimedia*, 163–170. DOI: 10.1109/VSMM.2010.5665990

Rahman, K., Prayogo, E., Fiyana, B. S., & Ardianti, R. (2024). Cultural landscape management and environmental protection at plaosan temple. *Journal of Law and Sustainable Development*, 12(6), e03424. DOI: 10.55908/sdgs.v12i6.3424

Rahman, M., Tanchangya, T., Rahman, J., Aktar, M. A., & Majumder, S. C. (2024). Corporate social responsibility and green financing behavior in Bangladesh: Towards sustainable tourism. *Innovation and Green Development*, 3(3), 100133. DOI: 10.1016/j.igd.2024.100133

Ramires, K. S., López, G. A., & Suárez, A. (2024). Revitalizing Colonial Architecture in Havana, Cuba: Balancing Preservation and Modernization. *Studies in Art and Architecture*, 3(1), 10–20. DOI: 10.56397/SAA.2024.03.02

Rasheed, S., Iqbal, M. M. J. I., & Sharmin, F. (2023). A Walk Through the History and Exploring the Conservation Project of Lalbagh Kella, an Incomplete Mughal Fort of Dhaka, Bangladesh. *American Journal of Interdisciplinary Research and Innovation*, 2(1), 42–53. DOI: 10.54536/ajiri.v2i1.1214

Rusho, M. A., & Nazmul Hassan. (2024). *Pioneering The Field Of Digital Archeology In Bangladesh*. https://doi.org/DOI: 10.17605/OSF.IO/GM9JP

Said, B. (2024). Architectural Influence of the Islamic University Mosque on New Mosques in Constantine: A Comparative Study. *Journal of Islamic Architecture*, 8(1), 152–160. DOI: 10.18860/jia.v8i1.23040

Salimullah, A. H. M., & Nabi, R. (2022). Protection of Sacred Tourism Sites, Festivals and Events in Bangladesh over Augmented Reality: An Experience of Cultural Heritage Based Tourism. In Hassan, A. (Ed.), *Technology Application in Tourism Fairs, Festivals and Events in Asia* (pp. 99–118). Springer Singapore., DOI: 10.1007/978-981-16-8070-0_6

Sayeda, T., Shetu, S. A., & Rahman, M. S.-U. -. (2020). Policy Overview for Bangladesh Tourism. In M. S.-U.- Rahman & A. Hassan (Eds.), *Tourism Policy and Planning in Bangladesh* (pp. 3–17). Springer Singapore. DOI: 10.1007/978-981-15-7014-8_1

Sharma, E., & Sharma, S. (2021). Talent Management Challenges for Heritage Tourism and Rural Sustainability: A Case Study of Surajgarh Fort Heritage Hotel, India. In Srivastava, S. (Ed.), *Capacity Building Through Heritage Tourism* (1st ed., pp. 157–169). Apple Academic Press., DOI: 10.1201/9781003034391-8

Stojanović, M. (2024). Intangible Cultural Heritage and Tourism—Sketches on Identity. *Etnoantropološki Problemi / Issues in Ethnology and Anthropology, 19*(1). DOI: 10.21301/eap.v19i1.9

Talukder, M. B., & Hossain, M. M. (2021). Prospects of Future Tourism in Bangladesh: An Evaluative Study. I-Manager's. *Journal of Management*, 15(4), 1–8. DOI: 10.26634/jmgt.15.4.17495

Talukder, M. B., Kumar, S., Kaiser, F., & Mia, Md. N. (2024a). Pilgrimage Creative Tourism: A Gateway to Sustainable Development Goals in Bangladesh. In M. Hamdan, M. Anshari, N. Ahmad, & E. Ali (Eds.), *Advances in Public Policy and Administration* (pp. 285–300). IGI Global. DOI: 10.4018/979-8-3693-1742-6.ch016

Talukder, M. B., Kumar, S., Kaiser, F., & Mia, Md. N. (2024b). Pilgrimage Creative Tourism: A Gateway to Sustainable Development Goals in Bangladesh. In M. Hamdan, M. Anshari, N. Ahmad, & E. Ali (Eds.), *Advances in Public Policy and Administration* (pp. 285–300). IGI Global. DOI: 10.4018/979-8-3693-1742-6.ch016

Talukder, M. B., & Muhsina, K. (2024). Prospect of Smart Tourism Destination in Bangladesh. In Correia, R., Martins, M., & Fontes, R. (Eds.), *Advances in Hospitality, Tourism, and the Services Industry* (pp. 163–179). IGI Global., DOI: 10.4018/979-8-3693-2137-9.ch009

Tiberghien, G., Bremner, H., & Milne, S. (2017). Performance and visitors' perception of authenticity in eco-cultural tourism. *Tourism Geographies*, 19(2), 287–300. DOI: 10.1080/14616688.2017.1285958

Vaz Serra, P., Seabra, C., & Caldeira, A. (2023). From Cultural Heritage to Cultural Tourism: A Historical-Conceptual Approach. In Carvalho, J. V., Abreu, A., Liberato, P., & Peña, A. (Eds.), *Advances in Tourism, Technology and Systems* (Vol. 345, pp. 91–101). Springer Nature Singapore., DOI: 10.1007/978-981-99-0337-5_8

Yang, H. (2023). Research on the Application of Interaction Design in the Digital Education of Traditional Crafts. In Marcus, A., Rosenzweig, E., & Soares, M. M. (Eds.), *Design, User Experience, and Usability* (Vol. 14033, pp. 221–238). Springer Nature Switzerland., DOI: 10.1007/978-3-031-35708-4_17

Zhang, M., Liu, Z., & Lai, K. (2023). The Meta-universe Platform Roblox for the Conservation of the Globally Important Agricultural Heritage Systems (GIAHS): The Case of the Floating Garden Agricultural Practices. In Marcus, A., Rosenzweig, E., & Soares, M. M. (Eds.), *Design, User Experience, and Usability* (Vol. 14034, pp. 215–226). Springer Nature Switzerland., DOI: 10.1007/978-3-031-35705-3_16

Zhang, Z. (2023). Digital Operational Strategies in The Post-Pandemic Era for Travel Companies: A Case Study of Ctrip. *Highlights in Business. Economics and Management*, 23, 521–525. DOI: 10.54097/h0w3ar97

Zhao, X., Elahi, E., Wang, F., Xing, H., & Khalid, Z. (2024). Sustainable tourism development for traditional Chinese drama's intangible cultural heritage. *Heliyon*, 10(3), e25483. DOI: 10.1016/j.heliyon.2024.e25483 PMID: 38333833

Chapter 5
Leveraging Intellectual Property for Sustainable Tourism Growth

Asha John
https://orcid.org/0000-0002-8237-1918
Chandigarh University, India

Pankaj Kumar Tyagi
Chandigarh University, India

Vipin Nadda
https://orcid.org/0009-0002-1041-2941
University of Sunderland, London, UK

ABSTRACT

The tourism industry is at a crossroads, facing the dual challenge of promoting growth while ensuring sustainability. Intellectual property (IP) offers vital tools for balancing these objectives by protecting innovations, cultural heritage, and sustainable practices within the tourism sector. This chapter explores the role of various IP rights, such as patents, trademarks, copyrights, and geographical indications, in driving sustainable tourism development. By analyzing existing literature, case studies, and global practices, the chapter highlights how IP can be leveraged to promote eco-friendly innovations, protect cultural assets, and support sustainable branding efforts in tourism. The research draws on secondary data to provide a comprehensive overview of the challenges and opportunities associated with managing IP in the context of sustainable tourism.

DOI: 10.4018/979-8-3693-4171-1.ch005

1. INTRODUCTION

The tourism industry is considered one of the most rapidly developing industries, playing a significant role in the formation of the economy. However, this growth has been associated with development impacts that have had negative consequences on the physical environment, indigenous cultures, and standards of living (Choi & Sirakaya-Turk, 2005). As awareness of these issues increases globally, there is a growing demand for more responsible tourism. Sustainability implementation is facilitated through changes in innovation and branding, requiring IP to offer the legal support needed to enable innovations, brands, and cultures related to sustainability (World Intellectual Property Organisation, 2020). This chapter explores how IP rights can be leveraged for the development of sustainable tourism. It also provides insights into patents, trademarks, copyrights, geographical indications, and their contributions to sustainable innovations, cultural heritage protection, and the sensible branding of tourist attractions (Timothy & Nyaupane, 2009). The chapter also discusses the risks and opportunities related to IP management in the context of globalisation in the tourism industry (World Intellectual Property Organisation, 2019).

Objectives:

1. To explore the role of intellectual property in promoting sustainable tourism practices.
2. To analyse the impact of intellectual property on the protection of cultural heritage within the tourism sector.
3. To identify the challenges and opportunities in managing intellectual property for sustainable tourism development.

Research Methodology:

The data for this chapter has been collected from secondary sources, including articles published in peer-reviewed journals, industry reports, case studies, and laws. The methodology involves:

- **Literature Review:** This paper synthesises current literature on intellectual property and sustainable tourism and their relation (Richards & Hall, 2003). Precedent literature includes international journal articles, books, and industry research papers on the subject of IP application in tourism (World Intellectual Property Organisation, 2020).

- **Case Study Analysis:** Exploration of case studies that present different ways IP has been used in the travel sector towards sustainability. This paper includes case studies from different areas of the world to provide a global focus on the discussed topics and areas within the tourism industry (Bramley & Bienabe, 2013).
- **Legal and Policy Analysis:** A synthesis of IP regulation systems in international and national tourism, including international agreements that may influence sustainable tourism growth, as well as national and international legislation and other regulations applicable to this sphere (United Nations World Tourism Organisation, 2019).

1.2. Overview of Intellectual Property in the Tourism Industry

The main functions of IP in tourism are to provide the legal framework for the protection and development of innovations, brands, and cultural identity items (World Intellectual Property Organisation, 2016). This becomes increasingly important as tourism expands globally, necessitating the protection of ideas, inventions, innovations, and cultures (Forsyth, 2013). By protecting the rights over the use of these assets, owners and creators gain an economic advantage by exploiting such assets in offering sustainable and authentic tourism services (Smith, 2003).

Definitions and Application of the Concept of IP

Intellectual property refers to the fundamental aspects of human creativity, including inventions, literary and artistic works, symbols, names, and images used in commerce (World Intellectual Property Organisation, 2017). These rights are essential in the tourism industry for several reasons:

1. **Protection of Innovations:** Legal shields, such as patents, are useful in improving the sustainability of different forms of tourism. For example, patents can protect renewable energy technologies for resorts or waste management technologies, ensuring innovators are rewarded for their inventions (Popp, 2019).
2. **Brand differentiation:** Trademarks cover brand identities, guaranteeing that slogans and logos help businesses involved in tourism distinguish themselves in the market. A strong brand image can draw consumers and develop credibility, particularly when linked to sustainability or cultural relevance (World Intellectual Property Organisation, 2013).
3. **Cultural Heritage Preservation:** Protection of cultural heritage cannot be complete without copyrights and geographical indications (GIs). Copyrights strengthen ownership of cultural items, such as music, art, and literature, while

GIs protect tangible and intangible products associated with particular regions, ensuring the local population benefits from tourism-generated revenue (Kuruk, 2007; Barham, 2003).

4. **Economic Growth and Sustainability:** Innovations and cultural assets safeguarded through IP rights promote the economic development of tourism. These protections allow businesses and communities to capitalise on their strengths, achieving competitive advantage and contributing to growth while encouraging responsible consumption and production (Choi & Sirakaya-Turk, 2005).

1.3. Types of IP Rights Relevant to Tourism: Patents, Trademarks, Copyrights, and GIs

Several types of IP rights are particularly relevant to the tourism industry, each serving a specific function in protecting and promoting tourism-related assets:

a. **Patents:** A patent confers exclusive rights to an invention, allowing the inventor to control the commercial application of the invention for a limited period, usually 20 years (World Intellectual Property Organisation, 2016). In tourism, patents protect innovations that improve operational efficiency, positively impact the environment, or enhance the tourist experience, such as environmentally friendly materials and products for hotel construction (Popp, 2019).

Case Example: A hotel chain can patent a water conservation system for hotel services, reducing costs while being environmentally friendly, thereby improving the brand's reputation (Anderson, 2012).

b. **Trademarks:** A trademark is any visible feature capable of distinguishing goods or services provided by one trader from similar goods or services provided by others (World Intellectual Property Organisation, 2013). Trademarks are vital in the tourism sector to uniquely identify products or services, creating brand awareness and consumer loyalty (Gretzel et al., 2006).

Case Example: An eco-tourism firm may create an identity symbol that raises awareness of its environmentally friendly activities, acting as a quality and reliability seal that distinguishes it from competing firms (D'Souza et al., 2007).

c. **Copyrights:** Copyrights pertain to literary, dramatic, musical, and artistic works, as well as other authorial creations (U.S. Copyright Office, 2021). In tourism, copyrights protect creative works used to advertise destinations, such as videos, songs, magazines, and electronic informational products, ensuring authors and local communities' profit from the tourism sector (Cohen, 1988).

Case Example: A tourism board may employ copyrighted images and videos in promoting a place, ensuring that these assets are not exploited without authorisation, preserving the credibility of the promotional process and the destination's image (Richards, 1996).

d. **Geographical Indications (GIs):** GIs are signs used on products with a geographical reference and characteristics intrinsically linked to that reference (Vandecandelaere et al., 2009). GIs are important in tourism as they protect and market special products of a region, many of which are tourist attractions. By doing so, they maintain the integrity and worth of the region's heritage and artistry (Rangnekar, 2004).

Case Example: The registration of "Champagne" as a GI helps maintain the quality and standards of the beverage, supporting the economic growth of the Champagne region in France (Barham, 2003).

A clear understanding of the significance of IPRs is that they form the basic building block of sustainable tourism development. IPRs protect innovations, cultural heritage, and brands, making it easier for tourism enterprises and local communities to capitalise on their unique qualities while embracing sustainability (Gervais, 2005).

2. THE ROLE OF IP IN DRIVING SUSTAINABLE TOURISM INNOVATION

While the protection of specific knowledge and ideas ensures increased innovation in tourism, it also promotes the conservation of the environment, sustainable branding, and cultural commodities. Through this paper, we discover that IP plays a very critical role in enhancing innovation in the tourism industry. In the context of sustainable tourism, IP drives innovation in several ways:

i. **Incentivizing Eco-Friendly Innovations**: IPR, especially patent law, offers inventors and companies legal monopoly over their innovations, such as environmentally friendly technology or processes. This exclusivity encourages manufacturers to invest in research and development of environmentally friendly products because they know that those products are shielded by law (Popp, 2019).

ii. **Facilitating Knowledge Transfer**: By engaging in licensing, companies and inventors can transfer their IP to others, who in turn can provide the broader context of tourism sustainability (Gervais, 2005; Vandecandelaere, Arfini, Belletti, & Marescotti, 2009).
iii. **Encouraging Collaboration**: By developing IP rights, cooperation with numerous stakeholders such as the government, non-governmental organizations, and private entities is enhanced. This way, innovative cooperation in the context of clear regulations of IP can create avenues for effective partnerships among the identified groups tasked with developing and maintaining a sustainable tourism outline (Forsyth, 2013b; United Nations World Tourism Organization, 2019).

A type of IP is patents, which shield inventions, including environment conservation technologies that may be vital for sustainable tourism. Here's how patents promote eco-innovations:

i. **Protection and Commercialization**: Patents protect inventions and give inventors the sole right to use and exploit their environmental innovations. This legal protection helps stimulate a company's investment in the development of new technologies that minimize the negative impact of tourist activity on the environment, such as energy-efficient transportation, waste disposal, and environmentally friendly construction materials (Thakur, 2018; Popp, 2019).
ii. **Encouraging R&D:** The potential to receive a patent creates conditions for more intensive innovation in producing environmentally friendly products. Sustainably focused R&D investment is instrumental in developing sustainable strategies that address the impact of tourism on carbon footprints, resource efficiency, and biodiversity (Gervais, 2005; Richards & Hall, 2003).
iii. **Spurring Market Growth**: Patent ownership and licensing can create new markets for eco-innovations. It not only allows the patent holder to benefit but also encourages other market players to incorporate these sustainable technologies (Giovannucci, Barham, & Pirog, 2010; United Nations World Tourism Organization, 2019).

2.2. Supporting Sustainable Branding through Trademarks

Trademarks are another critical component of IP that supports sustainable tourism by enabling companies to build and protect their brands around eco-friendly practices:

i. **Building Trust and Recognition**: Trademarks enable organizations to differentiate their sustainable products or services from those of other organizations. A well-established trademark associated with sustainability can foster consumer trust in eco-friendly tourism offerings, encouraging them to choose ecological products (D'Souza, Taghian, Lamb, & Peretiatko, 2007; Smith, 2003).
ii. **Promoting Sustainable Practices**: Trademarks can help companies that value sustainability by making the public aware of their environmentally friendly practices. For instance, eco-labels and certification marks—both of which fall under the category of trademarks—can inform customers that the firm adheres to specific environmental standards (World Intellectual Property Organization [WIPO], 2013; Richards & Hall, 2003).
iii. **Combating Greenwashing**: Trademarks protect buyers from false sustainability claims. When properly managed, trademarks prevent firms that are not genuinely committed to sustainable development from using certain eco-labels or marks, thereby reducing greenwashing (United Nations World Tourism Organization, 2019; Kuruk, 2007).

2.3. Introduction to Copyrights and the Protection of Cultural Narratives

Collective rights include creations of people and cultures in copyrights, which cover stories, arts, books, music, and other related works. In the context of sustainable tourism, copyrights play a vital role in preserving and promoting cultural heritage:

- **Safeguarding Cultural Heritage**: Copyrights ensure that indigenous and local peoples' cultural assets are safeguarded against unauthorized use or exploitation. This protection helps preserve the authenticity of cultural tourism experiences offered to tourists (Forsyth, 2013a; Kuruk, 2007).
- **Enabling Cultural Innovation**: When original cultural content is safeguarded through copyrights, it allows for the development of new cultural artifacts that reflect current and changing societal demographics. This can lead to the creation of unique and sustainable tourism products, such as cultural tours, shows, and materials that are both culturally significant and environmentally conscious (Forsyth, 2013b; Timothy & Nyaupane, 2009).
- **Promoting Ethical Tourism**: Copyrights play an ethical role in ensuring that the creators of cultural products are properly compensated. This enhances the economic viability of cultures that depend on tourism for support while also protecting their cultural heritage (Smith, 2003; World Intellectual Property Organization [WIPO], 2017).

3. PATENTING AS A PILLAR OF SUSTAINABLE TOURISM INNOVATION

The patenting operationalization of Intellectual Property is an important element of the advancement of sustainable tourism innovation due to its triple function of protecting, developing, and branding eco-innovations, as well as safeguarding cultural assets. This way, the benefits the tourism industry has experienced through the application of IP can sustain further advancements in positive environmental impacts, help empower communities worldwide, and produce 'real,' memorable, and 'immersive' touring experiences for tourists (Gervais, 2005; Forsyth, 2013).

3.1. Geographical Indications and the Preservation of Local Cultures

Geographical Indications (GIs) are intellectual property rights which seeks to point at a product that is originated from a given region where the quality, reputation or other characteristic associated with the good is owed mainly to the place of origin. GIs has a significant function in portraying culture bearers and promoting sustainable tourism and economic growth in areas originally associated with unique products (Barham, 2003; Bienabe, Kirsten, & Bramley, 2013). Geographical Indications or GI refers to a marking placed on a product that has, for one or many reasons, a link to a particular place and is unique and associated with that place in some way. Some of the well-known examples are Champagne, which is produced in the wine-making areas of France and Darjeeling tea which is produced in Darjeeling, India.

i. **Cultural Significance:** GIs contribute to the maintenance of generational traditions, skills, practices and in promoting the culture of the people. GIs guarantee that the cultural value linked to a given product is not eroded through imitation of the name of the product in question (D'Souza, Taghian, Lamb, & Peretiatko, 2007).
ii. **Economic Benefits:** GIs can also deliver economic benefits in terms of enabling the producers of the goods to have higher prices in the market since they are deemed to be of better quality because of the place they originate from. Consequently, this may assist in the support of the local communities that generate such produce (Bramley & Bienabe, 2013; Rangnekar, 2004).

3. 2. GIs as a Tool in Sustainable Tourism

GIs can therefore be a strong instrument in establishing sustainable tourism since it boosts the quality of the local products and therefore attracts the right kind of tourists who will use them in a way that the community will benefit from.

i. **Promotion of Local Products:** GIs are useful in marketing locally identifiable products that are so keen to the region's cultural palate. For instance, if a country organisation a GI label on a specific kind of cheese or wine, then tourists who are interested in tasting, and learning more about the said products will be automatically drawn towards the country (WIPO, 2019).
ii. **Sustainable Economic Development:** Since GI promotes a link between the products and their origin, it makes it possible to aid the rural populace and come up with sustainable measures (WIPO, 2016). In this case, tourists consume food and other produce, get their accommodation and partake in activities in GI regions, without inciting the need for massive infrastructure projects that harm the environment, hence may positively impact the economy without harm to the environment (WIPO, 2020a; WIPO, 2020b).
iii. **Preservation of Traditional Practices:** GIs contribute to the sustenance of traditional ways of farming, processing and producing food and non-food products. Besides, it keeps cultural records, as well as preserves land and other resources to be used and produced sustainably.

3. 3. Challenges in Managing GIs

However, like any other formal commitments they also come accompanied with a few challenges most of which pertain to management of these GIs, their enforcement and the aspect of sharing of the gains thereby ensuring that all stakeholders benefit from the exercise (WIPO,2020b).

i. **Enforcement Issues:** It may be rather complex to make certain that the GI label is used accurately, to prevent misuse or counterfeit of the own GI label within the international markets. County implementation entails legal drugs in place and international collaboration (WIPO, 2020a).
ii. **Balancing Modernization and Tradition:** Of course, GIs serve to protect the non-industrialized practices, but often they create a conflict of interest in the agricultural industry between the non-industrialized practices and the contemporary fully mechanized practices. This is where moderation and negotiation

of the two comes in as a contingency factor that will enhance the sustainability of GIs (WIPO, 2017; WIPO, 2019).

iii. **Benefit Sharing:** Another challenge is the protection of the benefits that are to accrue from the GIs in fair distribution in the community; especially to the small holder producers. Larger producers can over power the market if it is not well regulated and this will pose a problem to the smaller traditional producers (United Nations World Tourism Organization, 2019).

4. INTELLECTUAL PROPERTY AND THE DIGITALISATION OF SUSTAINABLE TOURISM

With the rise of tourism into the digital sphere, the Intellectual Property (IP) has a significant function of protecting the innovation, encouraging sustainability and grappling with issues of digital tourism. Digital technologies in the tourism sector create many prospects for sustainability, however new risk related to IP have emerged and must be treated (U.S. Copyright Office, 2021).

4. 1. Digital Tourism

Digital tourism is a new chapter and a step forward in the way tourists introduce themselves to destinations, make their decisions and contributions to the tourism value chain. Thus, applying websites and other info technologies, including mobile applications, social networks, and others, the tourism industry has developed and improved the provision of services and experiences (Tussyadiah & Wang, 2016). It is not a shift for the sake of shifting to the digital age, it is the shift that constructs the travel experiences to be more geared toward customization, realism, and sustainability. Technologies and practices that are associated with Virtual tourism include; The advanced methods of booking have enhanced the traveling services through enabling the travellers to book suites and select the most appropriate service providers within the shortest time (Timothy & Nyaupane, 2009). Thanks to virtual tours and effective digital marketing, places have an opportunity to engage with the audience in an effective manner and give the people an idea of what they might expect when they finally decide to visit the place. These tools are also useful in the development of a sustainable tourism agenda because they effectively point out sustainable choices and behaviours. In this digital environment, IP law steps in and serves as the safe guard to the innovated technology and the content that fuels digital tourism. The enhanced technologies such as Virtual reality (VR) and augmented reality (AR) through which tourists can virtually visit different tourist attractions are protected by patents and copyrights to prevent copying of the underlaying software and/or content (Thakur, 2018). In the same way, integrated marketing communication, which incorporate images, videos and other marketing components depend on the IP laws to safeguard the value and content of the materials. In addition, through the modern technology the use of big data and analytics in monitoring and in decision making of the actors in the tourism industry has made tourism more sustainable (Smith, 2003). If visitor behaviors are studied, tourism resources can be used more effectively, visitor concentrations and impacts, can be controlled and managed effectively and efficiently. The various technologies, algorithms and computer programs that are applied and generated from big-data spectrums are shielded by legal cognizable patents as well as trade secrets so as to guarantee that the innovation of such technologies are safeguarded and that the advantages accrued to the utilization of these technologies can be optimally harnessed.

i. **Virtual Tourism:** Second, it creates tourism without mobility through virtual reality (VR) and augmented reality (AR) that enable people to 'visit' places they actually do not have to be physically present in them, hence minimizing the negative impacts normally related to tourism. These are under IP law especially the patents and the copyrights that protect the software and the content used in the experiences in the virtual world (United Nations World Tourism Organization, 2019).
ii. **Digital Marketing:** It also comprises the utilisation of intellectual property protected materials for instance, pictures, clips and branding for marketing purposes during the digitalised tourism advancement. This content is essential for supporting the sustainable tourist offerings, for example, the sustainable accommodation and tourist activities, due to the access to the international audience (Bienabe, Kirsten, & Bramley, 2013).
iii. **Data-Driven Tourism:** Advanced technologies such as big data and analytics are continuing their use for the observation of the tourists, controlling visitors' streams, and resource allocation for tourism to become more sustainable. The dynamic algorithms and other software tools that are incorporated into the data-driven tourism are some of the most protected assets by patents and trade secrets (Bienabe, Kirsten, & Bramley, 2013).

4. 2. E-Commerce and Sustainable Tourism

The global access in the selling and marketing of tourism-related products and services has significantly been revolutionized by the e-commerce. Consumption has been made easier through the procurement of sustainable tourism primarily ant eco-friendly hotels (Barham, 2003), locally sourced products etc through a click on a button. Sites make direct relations with consumers and providers of sustainable tourism possible, and this kills the middleman to avoid fake representation of providers. Intellectual Property (IP) has the following purposes in this digital ecosystem: It protects distinctive features of sustainable tourism products. For example, trademarks leave sure that eco-certifications besides as acknowledged brand identities remain protected and trusted by the populace. Copyrights apply on the creative materials in the digital marketing while patents cover innovative novelties that improve on the sustainability of the tourism services. Moreover, it is necessary to address issues related to IP enforcement regarding e-commerce platforms and, namely, prevent rogue sellers from engaging in selling counterfeit products, using others' branding without permission, etc, which may negatively contribute to the development of consumer distrust and, therefore – the failure of implemented sustainable tourism activities. Online markets have had a positive impact on the promotion and sale of tourism services and product since they provide a direct connection between the buyer and sustainable tourism products (Anderson, 2012). IP has a critical task of providing the required assurance and guarantee of the success of these platforms.

i. **Sustainable Product Certification:** Some of the products which can be promoted through e-commerce include green souvenirs (Richards & Hall, 2003), locally produced souvenirs or other products that possess GI or certification marks. Through these IP tools, there is a guarantee that the products in the market are original and conform to stringent sustainable standards.
ii. **Fair Trade and Ethical Branding:** That is the reason trademarks and certification marks have a primary role in supporting and developing several fair trade and ethical tourism products. For instance, labels such as Fair Trade or Rainforest Alliance can be used on e-commerce website to segregate goods that are from environmentally friendly and are sourced through ethical labour means (Bienabe, Kirsten, & Bramley, 2013).
iii. **IP Protection in Online Marketplaces:** As is the case with any emergent market, the need to protect IP which may be in the form of trademarks, copyrights, and other forms of intellectual property becomes extremely important due to the high levels of imitation and subsequent counterfeiting of branded products that may emerge in the new market (Cohen, 1988). For instance, unauthorised use of company/brand images, videos or names in the online selling platforms that deal in second hand goods or counterfeit products is damaging to genuine sustainable tourism products and services (Choi & Sirakaya-Turk, 2005).

4. 3. IP threats in the Digital Tourism

Digital tourism refers to the application of information technology in the development, marketing and delivering of tourism products and services. This shift has brought about new improved but special Intellectual Property (IP) issues which needs to be treated so as to protect new inventions for growth in the future. With most tourism businesses shifting online, questions of piracy, brand protection, piracy, and security of data have emerged or escalated. All these require strong legal frameworks of IP protection and innovative measures to protect the interest of the creatives and companies while encouraging ethical and fair tourisms in cyberspace.

i. **Copyright Infringement:** Again, the tourism industry faces a major challenge of protecting its IP since it is very easy to make multiple copies and distribute the content such as; picture, clips, and a written description among the fans (D'Souza, Taghian, Lamb, & Peretiatko, 2007). Paid digital content needs to be protected so that people who create content as well as organizations involved in running sustainable travel activities are paid fairly in order to encourage growth of the business.
ii. **Brand Protection:** Where the internet has become the core source of contact for many tourism businesses, trademark and domain name protection becomes even necessary. Cybersquatting in which third parties with intent to create a reputation for themselves invade domain names similar to the already existing brands, is a major problem that threatens to weaken the foundations of sustainable tourism brands (Dwyer & Kim, 2003).
iii. **Digital Piracy:** Unauthorised distribution of VR (Virtual Reality) experiences or Virtual Tours results in serious losses of revenue and loss of reputation. Substantial procedures have to be put in place in order to address the problem of digital piracy in tourism (Thakur, 2018).
iv. **Data Privacy and Ownership**: The generation and usage of big data in digital tourism have the challenges arising from data collection and management as well as data privacy and ownership (Thakur, 2018). As is well known, data management is not typically considered a field of IP law however aspects of IP do arise where algorithms or resulting data insights are involved.

5. THE ROLE OF IP IN PROTECTING AND PROMOTING CULTURAL HERITAGE

Culture includes the, monuments, artefacts and other features borne by a people and other characteristics or features of places that catalyse tourist traffic globally (U.S. Copyright Office, 2021). From the rise of tourism, the emphasis is placed on the culture and hence the need to guard against the abuses and misrepresentation of culture. IP instruments provide advanced measures for protecting and for promoting cultural values while at the same time helping to ensure that the positive impacts of tourism are felt by owners of the underlying cultural resources (Timothy & Nyaupane, 2009).

5.1. Cultural Heritage in the Context of Tourism

Cultural assets therefore include historical sites and structures, arts and handcrafts, music, dance, theatre, languages, and beliefs, and so on that are part of cultural lore and tradition. These elements constitute the very fabric of community existence and thus form part of the essence of every community that's associated with tourism. Aside from the physical appeal of a place, visitors go to places for opportunities for cultural interactions that include, festivals, arts, and food (Timothy & Nyaupane, 2009).

The process of establishing tourism related to cultural values could bring economic advantages to local communities, it will preserve the cultural values and create jobs. But if not controlled it results in cultural Particularly, the importance and originality of cultural practices are erased for the sake of material gains (Smith, 2003). This is where IP comes in handy, where legal instruments are given to communities and their artifacts to avoid exploitation and misuse of their culture vis-à-vis tourism by vested interests (United Nations World Tourism Organization, 2019).

5.2. IP Mechanisms for Cultural Heritage Protection

Several IP mechanisms can be leveraged to protect and promote cultural heritage in the tourism context

i. **Copyright:** Copyright law protects the expressions of ideas in literary and artistic works, that are part of cultural identity such as literature, music, art among others. For instance, where traditional music and dances have been recorded, they can be copyrighted and; to use them commercially one has to obtain permission and may be may have to pay royalties to the creators or their groups (Vandecandelaere, Arfini, Belletti, & Marescotti, 2009). However, free from the protection of conventional copyrights are traditional cultural ones that are not embodied in a material thing or product. To this end, work has been done to introduce changes and adaptations to the copyright legislative regimes that will provide the indigenous and local communities with a convenient settlement framework.

ii. **Trademarks and Certification Marks:** Trademarks aim at providing protection to symbols, names and slogans employed in business and are extendable to cultural goods in tourism Trademarks cover symbols, names and slogans that are utilized in commerce and business and thus can be applied on cultural goods in the tourist industry. Certification marks are useful especially in Cultural heritage where they may give an indication that a product complies with particular cultural standards or is of origin of a specific culture. For instance, a certification mark could denote the Original Indigenous Handicrafts (Tussyadiah & Wang, 2016) and prevent imitation products (World Intellectual Property Organization [WIPO], 2013) from the market to ensure that the consumers pay for original cultural artefacts and the subsequent profits go back to the indigenous community.

iii. **Geographical Indications (GIs):** GIs cover items that have a unique association with a particular territory and have characteristics or a reputation associated therewith. GFs are typically employed to safeguard foodstuffs and drinks, such as Champagne wines of France or Darjeeling tea of India; however, the paradigm does not stop with such products. Speaking of tourism, GIs make it possible to protect and strengthen cultural individuality of the region and market it as the destination that offers genuinely original products (Choi & Sirakaya-Turk, 2005). It is not only assists in maintaining craft-based production techniques but also ensures that the incidence of tourism revenues are returned back to the local people.

iv. **Protection of Traditional Knowledge (TK) and Cultural Expressions (TCEs):** It refers to knowledge, innovations, practices and experiences in the field acquired by indigenous and local communities over generations. They may cover such areas as agriculture, pharmacology, mythology, proverbs, riddles, songs, stories, sustenance, and techniques. TK and TCEs are generally not well protected by the current conventional IP systems (Choi & Sirakaya-Turk, 2005; Forsyth, 2013a) but there are legal frameworks and actions that cater for the protection of TK and TCEs. For instance, the national legislation or the international treaties, including the Convention on Biological Diversity, protect indigenous peoples' means and their cultural assets. The same protocols are used at the community level to safeguard these assets from exploitation together with documentation to guarantee any commercial usage is proper or justified (Gervais, 2005).

5. 3. Difficulties in the Conservation of Cultural Property

While IP mechanisms provide valuable tools for protecting cultural heritage, several challenges complicate their effective implementation in the tourism context.

i. **Misappropriation and Exploitation:** This implies that the misappropriation and commercialization of cultural assets is a very crucial issue (Forsyth, 2013b). Some forms of cultural heritage include traditional designs, music or dance, and rituals; such factional forms can be exploited by third parties who relay them without the authorization of the originating communities, which results in cultural degradation. This not only removes opportunities for boosting the communities' revenues but may well lead to misrepresentation of cultural practices (Kuruk, 2007).
ii. **Lack of Awareness and Access to IP Tools:** Some culture related assets in many cultures and particularly in the rural and indigenous population, may not be aware of, or lack the resources to protect their IP rights. Sometimes even, when there is awareness, there are trade laws, licensing fees, attorney and patent examiners' fees, and other legal procedures which hinder one from getting a protection for the IP. This may leave the communities open to be exploited by other key commercial forces in the society (Popp, 2019).
iii. **Balancing Commercialization and Preservation:** Tourism potential of the cultural heritage as well as the protection of cultural sites for the future generations is another important factor. Advertisement of culture can cause culture and, in the process, dilute it until it loses its worth and real value. For instance, the dance, ethnic music, or art works such as jewellery might be changed to meet the tastes of the tourist thus the very essence of the cultural products is reduced (Gretzel & Jamal, 2009).
iv. **International Legal Frameworks and Enforcement:** It is a well-known fact that cultural heritage may be profaned across national borders and therefore its protection may involve cooperation that transcends national boundaries (Giovannucci, Barham, & Pirog, 2010). Despite the global conventions like that of UNESCO on the Convention for the Safeguarding of the Intangible Cultural Heritage there is always a question of implementation. National laws may differ significantly, and international co-ordination and support for exercising these measures may be inadequate at the international level.

6. POLICY, REGULATION, AND THE FUTURE OF IP IN SUSTAINABLE TOURISM

As the sustainable tourism becomes more prominent, the concept of Intellectual Property (IP) to protect innovation, cultural heritage, and brand easily grows in significance. As the coordinated efforts of governments and international organizations, policies and regulations make an important role in the sustainable development of tourism industry by guiding the industry's application of IP. Developing new and future trends and challenges in this area suggest it is high time that adaptive, innovative and preventive measures are undertaken in order to continue with a facilitative role of IP in sustainable tourism.

6.1. The Role of Governments and International Organizations

Governments and international organizations play a pivotal role in shaping the policy and regulatory frameworks that govern IP in the context of sustainable tourism (Dwyer & Kim, 2003). These entities are responsible for creating and enforcing laws that protect IP rights, promoting fair competition, and ensuring that the benefits of tourism are equitably distributed.

- **National Governments:** At the national level, governments are tasked with implementing IP laws that protect innovations related to sustainable tourism. This includes granting patents for eco-friendly technologies, registering trademarks for sustainable tourism brands, and enforcing copyrights for digital content. Governments also play a key role in raising awareness about the importance of IP among tourism businesses, particularly small and medium-sized enterprises (SMEs) that may lack the resources to navigate complex IP systems (Rangnekar, 2004).
- **International Organizations:** International organizations, such as the World Intellectual Property Organization (WIPO) and the United Nations World Tourism Organization (UNWTO), are instrumental in promoting the harmonization of IP laws across borders and providing guidance on best practices for IP management in tourism. WIPO, for example, has developed resources and initiatives aimed at helping countries integrate IP into their sustainable tourism strategies. The UNWTO advocates for policies that balance tourism development with the preservation of cultural and natural resources, often highlighting the role of IP in achieving these goals (Tussyadiah & Wang, 2016).
- **Regional Bodies:** Regional organizations, such as the European Union (EU), also contribute to the development of IP policy in tourism by establishing

regulations that protect geographical indications (GIs) and other forms of IP across member states. The EU's GI system, for instance, ensures that products like Champagne or Parmigiano-Reggiano are protected within the EU and recognized globally, thereby supporting local economies and promoting sustainable practices (Tussyadiah & Wang, 2016).

6. 3. Future Challenges and Opportunities

Several issues and prospects will define the future of IP in the context of sustainable tourism and innovative policy adaptive strategies and foresight.

i. **Balancing Commercialization and Preservation:** Another view of the portfolio of tasks will be in the conflict between the requirements for developing culture and natural resources and ensuring their availability to future generations (Tussyadiah & Wang, 2016; U.S. Copyright Office, 2021). When there is an over-commercialization, this results in watering down of culture and more so destruction of the natural environment thus defeat of the very value of tourism. Policy-makers will have to design policies that support the proper commercialisation, where IP is employed as a shield and asset for cultural and natural heritage without detriment of this latter (Thakur, 2018).
ii. **Globalization and IP Enforcement:** With more internationalisation of tourism the enforcement of IP rights is likely to become more difficult. This is especially applicable for the digital assets' protection issue (Dwyer & Kim, 2003), as the content posted in the internet can be rapidly reproduced and shared across the jurisdictions. The challenges in the area of IP enforcement will remain and be closely connected with the necessity of establishing the universal mechanisms of international cooperation (Cohen, 1988).
iii. **Climate Change and IP:** By now global climate change is anticipated to modulate tourism significantly especially in the sensitive areas. This will generate new questions for IP in sustainable tourism, as well as open up new possibilities (Bienabe, Kirsten, & Bramley, 2013). On one hand, there will be a rising demand for new advancements in environmentally friendly tourism industry solutions which include technologies and structures that for instance adapt to the changing climate and protection and control over which will need robust IP rights. On the other hand, climate change consequences may undermine cultural and natural heritage and therefore there may be a higher level of difficulty to protect the asset through IP mechanisms (Anderson, 2012).
iv. **Inclusive Growth and IP Accessibility:** Harmonizing the accessibility of the benefits of IP protections to all the stakeholders especially the indigenous communities, SMEs, and developing countries will be a big challenge. Policy

makers will have to emerge with innovative and enabling IP systems that would enable the disenfranchised to engage in tourism, Systems that would meet the needs of persons with disabilities or the elderly for instance. This also involves giving knowledge and materials that will enable these groups to deal with the IP systems and safeguard their cultural resources against exploitation (WIPO, 2017).

7.CONCLUSION

Sustainable tourism has emerged and is expanding over the years and in this, Intellectual Property or IP is a key factor to support and spur on this sector. Sustainable tourism is the application of innovations with tourism and protection of cultural assets in areas of mutual impact of IP. This conclusion shall provide a brief of the studies made highlighting the implications of the findings, recommendations regarding the utilisation of the IP and prospects of the future IP in relation to sustainable tourism.

Key Findings

i. **IP Mechanisms and Sustainable Practices:** Patents, trademarks, copyrights and GIs are some tools known as IP mechanisms that are vital in stimulating sustainable tourist innovation. Patents have the aim of protecting inventions in the field of environmental protection; trademarks allow the branding of sustainable tourism activities; GIs are used to protect traditional products and practices linked to certain geographical areas (Popp, 2019; Bramley & Bienabe, 2013). They also help promote the adoption of sustainable solutions and preserve cultural and environmental resources as well as their proper utilisation.
ii. **Challenges in Cultural and Environmental Protection:** Some of the impacts that the process of commercialisation of culture/nature through tourism brings include; violation of indigenous people's rights, over exploitation and poor rights protection of indigenous people's knowledge systems (Gretzel, Fesenmaier, Formica, & O'Leary, 2006; Gretzel & Jamal, 2009). These challenges must be met by the existing or future IP frameworks to avoid squatting and commercial misappropriation of cultural assets at the same time demand for cultural tourism maintains the fairness of the stake generated from the industries in the originating indigenous communities.

iii. **The Role of Policy and Regulation:** Another core domain in the management of IP in the tourism sector is the policies and regulations at national and international levels. International nongovernmental organisations and governments need to align IP laws (WIPO, 2020a), protect cultural materials, and propagate sustainable tourism. Notably the changes in the current marketplace such as digitalization and changes in policy and emergence of sustainability certifications suggest the need for dynamic policies to address the complexities in the tourism business.
iv. **Future Opportunities and Challenges:** The future trends of IP in sustainable tourism shall be influenced by a few factors such as the question of growth to inclusiveness, climate change, and international IP protection (World Intellectual Property Organization [WIPO], 2013). It is however, possible to cultivate IP for the purposes of innovation, cultural heritage protection and conservation, and the realization of responsible tourism. However, the above difficulties will need strategic policies and the stakeholders to take proactive approaches.

Recommendations for Leveraging IP in Sustainable Tourism

i. **Strengthen IP Protections for Sustainable Innovations:** The governments and stakeholders in the industries should improve the IP rights that support green innovation and solutions. This encompasses backing the activities that contribute to the filing of green technology patents, promoting research to sustainable tourism options and offering the necessary enticements to organizations to embrace new approaches on decreased adverse environmental effects (World Intellectual Property Organization [WIPO], 2013).
ii. **Promote IP Education and Awareness:** Promoting the use of IP within the Tourism sector especially amongst SMEs as well as indigenous people is therefore necessary. Awareness raising initiatives in relation to the rights and the systems should be established to provide training materials that can be used to educate the stakeholders on the use of the tools in protection of the innovation and cultural products.
iii. **Enhance Protection of Cultural Heritage:** IP frameworks should be extended to afford more protection to traditional knowledge and cultural expressions. This involves establishing sui generis protection regimes that capture the essential features of cultural heritage and entailing that IP systems are compatible with indigenous and local communities' rights (WIPO, 2016).

iv. **Foster International Cooperation:** Interdisciplinary cooperation will provide the opportunity to resolve the international IP disputes affecting sustainable tourism. WIPO and UNWTO should engage in sharing of achievements, encouragement of formulation of standard IP policies as well as promotion of policies on sustainable tourism (WIPO, 2017).
v. **Support Sustainable Tourism Certifications:** Promoting the rights of IP tools as intellectual property rights protection to ownership of sustainability certifications and eco-labels will educate the consumers on which practices to support in tourism. In order to safeguard the authenticity of the certification marks and to prevent abuse, it is necessary that such marks are strictly controlled.

Future of IP and Sustainable Tourism

the future of IP in sustainable tourism can be viewed as having potential as well as threats. As a result, the develop of the IP will emerge to a more significant factor in the development of the tourism industry by encouraging innovation, preserving the cultural identity and the preservation of the environment (Vandecandelaere, Arfini, Belletti, & Marescotti, 2009).

Key trends to watch include:

i. **Technological Advancements:** Further VR/AR and data analytical growth: witnessing new trends in the struggle for and generation of IPs. Preserving and regulating the use of these technologies shall be the key to a successful implementation of sustainable tourism.
ii. **Climate Change Adaptation:** Climate change effects will thus create the need to search for better sustainable tourism options and coping mechanisms. Specifically, IP will feature in the safeguarding of creations that tackle climate change issues affecting the tourism sector, and the general bolstering of the industry (WIPO, 2020b).
iii. **Inclusive IP Systems:** The future will demand better IP systems that will allow marginalized groups to engage in intellectual property protection and make certain benefits a result of IP protection is distributed fairly. This includes issues to do with indigenous peoples and small businesses in the tourism sector (Vandecandelaere, Arfini, Belletti, & Marescotti, 2009).
iv. **Global Collaboration:** Coping with global IP issues and advocating for sustainable tourism is going to remain an international matter. In the future, efforts to legal harmonization of IP, sharing and learning of best practices as well as support of SDG will be critical in shaping the destiny of IP in tourism (WIPO, 2019).

REFERENCES:

Anderson, C. K. (2012). The impact of social media on lodging performance. *Cornell Hospitality Quarterly*, 53(3), 232–244. DOI: 10.1177/1938965512459194

Barham, E. (2003). Translating terroir: The global challenge of French AOC labeling. *Journal of Rural Studies*, 19(1), 127–138. DOI: 10.1016/S0743-0167(02)00052-9

Bienabe, E., Kirsten, J., & Bramley, C. (2013). *Developing geographical indications in the South*. Springer.

Bramley, C., & Bienabe, E. (2013). Why do geographical indications matter? In Gangjee, D. (Ed.), *Research handbook on intellectual property and geographical indications* (pp. 15–30). Edward Elgar Publishing., DOI: 10.4337/9781783472608.00007

Choi, H., & Sirakaya-Turk, E. (2005). Sustainability indicators for managing community tourism. *Tourism Management*, 26(3), 465–475. DOI: 10.1016/j.tourman.2003.12.003

Cohen, E. (1988). Authenticity and commoditization in tourism. *Annals of Tourism Research*, 15(3), 371–386. DOI: 10.1016/0160-7383(88)90028-X

D'Souza, C., Taghian, M., Lamb, P., & Peretiatko, R. (2007). Green decisions: Demographics and consumer understanding of environmental labels. *International Journal of Consumer Studies*, 31(4), 371–376. DOI: 10.1111/j.1470-6431.2006.00567.x

Dwyer, L., & Kim, C. (2003). Destination competitiveness: Determinants and indicators. *Current Issues in Tourism*, 6(5), 369–414. DOI: 10.1080/13683500308667962

Forsyth, M. (2013). Protecting traditional knowledge and cultural heritage: Who, what, why, and where? *Indigenous Law Bulletin*, 8(8), 8–12.

Forsyth, P. (2013). Climate change and tourism: Policy and international perspectives. *Journal of Sustainable Tourism*, 21(1), 12–22. DOI: 10.1080/09669582.2012.695842

Gervais, D. J. (2005). Traditional knowledge & intellectual property: A TRIPS-compatible approach. *Detroit College of Law at Michigan State University Law Review*, 2005(1), 137–166.

Giovannucci, D., Barham, E., & Pirog, R. (2010). Defining and marketing "local" foods: Geographical indications for US products. *The Journal of World Intellectual Property*, 13(2), 94–120. DOI: 10.1111/j.1747-1796.2009.00370.x

Gretzel, U., Fesenmaier, D. R., Formica, S., & O'Leary, J. T. (2006). Searching for the future: Challenges faced by destination marketing organizations. *Journal of Travel Research*, 45(2), 116–126. DOI: 10.1177/0047287506291598

Gretzel, U., & Jamal, T. (2009). Conceptualizing the creative tourist class: Technology, mobility, and tourism experiences. *Tourism Analysis*, 14(4), 471–481. DOI: 10.3727/108354209X12596287114219

Kuruk, P. (2007). Cultural heritage, traditional knowledge, and indigenous rights: An analysis of the Convention for the Safeguarding of Intangible Cultural Heritage. *Macquarie Journal of International and Comparative Environmental Law*, 4(2), 1–20.

Popp, D. (2019). Environmental policy and innovation: A decade of research. *Journal of Environmental Economics and Management*, 48(2), 411–434. DOI: 10.1016/j.jeem.2019.02.006

Rangnekar, D. (2004). The socio-economics of geographical indications: A review of empirical evidence from Europe. *UNCTAD/ICTSD*. Retrieved from https://unctad.org/system/files/official-document/ictsd2004ipd9_en.pdf

Richards, G. (1996). Production and consumption of European cultural tourism. *Annals of Tourism Research*, 23(2), 261–283. DOI: 10.1016/0160-7383(95)00063-1

Richards, G., & Hall, D. (Eds.). (2003). *Tourism and sustainable community development*. Routledge., DOI: 10.4324/9780203218602

Smith, M. K. (2003). *Issues in cultural tourism studies*. Routledge. DOI: 10.4324/9780203402825

Thakur, R. (2018). Cybersecurity and the digital transformation of the tourism industry: A review and research agenda. *Journal of Hospitality and Tourism Technology*, 9(3), 314–328. DOI: 10.1108/JHTT-10-2017-0106

Timothy, D. J., & Nyaupane, G. P. (2009). *Cultural heritage and tourism in the developing world: A regional perspective*. Routledge., DOI: 10.4324/9780203877753

Tussyadiah, I. P., & Wang, D. (2016). Tourism experience facilitation through mobile apps: A case study of MyTripApp. *Annals of Tourism Research*, 64, 139–152. DOI: 10.1016/j.annals.2016.03.008

United Nations World Tourism Organization. (2019). *Tourism and intellectual property rights: A guide for tourism stakeholders*. UNWTO., DOI: 10.18111/9789284421295

U.S. Copyright Office. (2021). *Copyright basics*. Retrieved from https://www.copyright.gov/circs/circ01.pdf

Vandecandelaere, E., Arfini, F., Belletti, G., & Marescotti, A. (2009). *Linking people, places and products: A guide for promoting quality linked to geographical origin and sustainable geographical indications*. FAO. Retrieved from https://www.fao.org/3/i0500e/i0500e.pdf

World Intellectual Property Organization. (2013). *Trademarks and sustainable development*. Retrieved from https://www.wipo.int/wipo_magazine/en/2013/04/article_0002.html

World Intellectual Property Organization. (2016). *Understanding patents*. Retrieved from https://www.wipo.int/patents/en/

World Intellectual Property Organization. (2017). *Intellectual property, traditional knowledge, and traditional cultural expressions*. Retrieved from https://www.wipo.int/tk/en/igc/

World Intellectual Property Organization. (2019). *Geographical indications: An introduction*. Retrieved from https://www.wipo.int/publications/en/details.jsp?id=4222

World Intellectual Property Organization. (2020). *E-commerce and intellectual property*. Retrieved from https://www.wipo.int/ecommerce/en/

World Intellectual Property Organization. (2020). *Intellectual property and sustainable tourism development*. Retrieved from https://www.wipo.int/ip-development/en/agenda/

Chapter 6 Leveraging Intellectual Property for Destination Branding and Marketing in the Tourism Sector

Bassam Samir Al-Romeedy
Faculty of Tourism and Hotels, University of Sadat City, Egypt

ABSTRACT

This chapter delves into the essential role of intellectual property (IP) in the branding and marketing of tourism destinations. It investigates how IP assets like trademarks, copyrights, and geographical indications (GIs) are instrumental in creating, safeguarding, and promoting distinctive tourism experiences. The chapter underscores the influence of IP on enhancing destination recognition and differentiation, particularly through trademarks and GIs that strengthen brand identity. It also explores the use of copyrighted content in marketing efforts, the challenges and opportunities arising from digital marketing, and the importance of integrating cultural heritage into tourism via IP. It examines how IP contributes to sustainable tourism by supporting authentic, locally-made products and preserving intangible cultural heritage. It further addresses the challenges destinations encounter in maximizing IP, such as enforcement and infringement issues, and discusses future trends and innovations, including blockchain and AI, that could improve IP management in the tourism sector.

DOI: 10.4018/979-8-3693-4171-1.ch006

INTRODUCTION

In the ever-evolving and competitive tourism industry, IP is crucial in shaping, safeguarding, and promoting the unique features and experiences that define a destination. As tourism destinations compete to stand out in an increasingly crowded market, the strategic application of IP has become essential for establishing a strong brand identity, preserving cultural heritage, and supporting sustainable tourism development. This introduction delves into the diverse role of IP in the tourism sector, emphasizing its importance in destination branding, marketing, and the promotion of local products and traditions (Tien et al., 2019; Hodson, 2021; Al-Romeedy & Hashem, 2024).

IP in tourism includes various assets such as trademarks, copyrights, patents, and GIs, all of which contribute to a destination's uniqueness. These IP assets are vital in creating and protecting the distinctive experiences that draw visitors, ranging from iconic landmarks and cultural events to local crafts and culinary traditions. By securing legal protection for these assets, destinations can prevent unauthorized use and maintain their brand value. IP not only protects the economic interests of tourism stakeholders but also plays a significant role in preserving the cultural and natural heritage that is central to many tourism experiences (Dar & Ojha, 2023; Punchihewa, 2021).

Trademarks and GIs are particularly powerful tools in destination branding. Trademarks, such as logos and slogans, help establish a recognizable and trustworthy brand image that can be used across marketing campaigns and tourism products. GIs, meanwhile, link products to their place of origin, emphasizing the unique qualities that come from that specific location. For example, the use of GIs like "Champagne" or "Swiss Made" not only elevates the perceived quality of the product but also strengthens the destination's brand identity. This strategic use of IP can greatly enhance destination recognition and differentiation in the global tourism market, making it easier for travelers to associate particular experiences or products with a specific place (Rasmi et al., 2022; Benson, 2019; Macmillan, 2020; Ubertazzi, 2022).

Branding through IP enables destinations to gain a competitive advantage by emphasizing their unique features and creating a cohesive brand that appeals to target audiences, leading to increased visitor numbers and economic benefits. However, the success of this approach depends on the effective management and protection of IP assets, which is challenging in the globalized and digital landscape. IP rights in tourism marketing are not limited to branding; they also involve the strategic use of copyrighted materials, such as images and logos, to develop compelling campaigns. Protecting and monetizing these IP assets is crucial for ensuring that the value generated by marketing efforts benefits the rightful owners and supports the destination's economic growth (Otay Demir et al., 2022; McCabe, 2014; Prebensen et al., 2018).

In the digital era, tourism marketing increasingly depends on online platforms and social media, where IP protection becomes even more vital. The widespread sharing of content online presents both opportunities and challenges for IP management. On the one hand, digital platforms offer broader reach and engagement, allowing destinations to connect with global audiences. On the other hand, the ease of copying and distributing digital content raises concerns about IP infringement. Destinations must navigate these challenges by adopting strong IP strategies that protect their assets while taking advantage of the opportunities provided by digital marketing (Sorokina et al., 2022; Çeltek & İhan, 2018; Kozak & Baloglu, 2010; Al-Romeedy, 2024a, b).

GIs are vital in promoting local products and traditions, making them a key component of tourism marketing. They emphasize the origin and authenticity of products, while also preserving and promoting cultural heritage. For example, promoting region-specific products like “Roquefort cheese” or “Darjeeling tea” boosts local economies and strengthens regional cultural identity, attracting tourists seeking authentic experiences. Integrating cultural heritage and local products into tourism marketing through IP can enhance a destination's appeal and contribute to its sustainability. However, it is essential to balance commercialization with the preservation of cultural and natural assets to avoid exploitation or degradation of heritage (Palfrey, 2011; Yang, 2021; Dratler Jr & McJohn, 2024; Stim, 2024; Dosso & Vezzani, 2020).

The role of IP in sustainable tourism development is multifaceted, aiding destinations in achieving economic sustainability while preserving cultural and natural resources. IP tools like trademarks and GIs help market eco-friendly and culturally significant products, appealing to tourists who value sustainability and authenticity. Additionally, IP protects intangible cultural heritage, such as traditional knowledge, from misuse. However, managing IP in tourism faces challenges, especially in enforcement and dealing with globalization and digitalization, which complicate IP protection. Emerging technologies like blockchain and AI offer promising solutions for enhancing IP management and safeguarding tourism brands. Strategic IP use in tourism can strengthen destination branding, support sustainability, and ensure long-term success in a competitive global market (George, 2021; Camilleri, 2018; Horner & Swarbrooke, 2020; Morgan et al., 2022; Dar & Ojha, 2023).

INTELLECTUAL PROPERTY (IP) IN TOURISM

Definition and Types of IP Relevant to Tourism

IP refers to the legal protections granted for creations of the mind in various fields, including industrial, scientific, literary, and artistic domains. These rights enable creators and owners to control and benefit from the use of their intellectual assets, safeguarding them from unauthorized exploitation. In the tourism sector, IP encompasses a variety of assets that are essential for building and maintaining a destination's brand, preserving cultural heritage, and promoting distinctive experiences. The primary forms of IP relevant to tourism include trademarks, copyrights, patents, and GIs.

Trademarks are among the most prominent types of IP in tourism. A trademark is a unique sign, symbol, or phrase that distinguishes the goods or services of one entity from those of others. In tourism, trademarks often manifest as logos, slogans, or brand names tied to specific destinations, hotels, tour operators, or tourism products. For example, the logo of a well-known hotel chain or the name of a popular tourist site can be trademarked to prevent unauthorized use by others, thereby protecting brand integrity and maintaining consumer trust (Birdir et al., 2018; Rathee & Rajain, 2022; Benson, 2019; Tien et al., 2019).

Copyrights protect original works of authorship, including literary, artistic, and musical creations. Within the tourism industry, copyrights are crucial for protecting creative content such as promotional materials, websites, photographs, videos, and guidebooks. For instance, images used in a destination's marketing campaign or written content in a travel guide are safeguarded by copyright, ensuring that others cannot reproduce or distribute them without permission. Copyrights ensure creators are compensated for their work while maintaining the authenticity and quality of the tourism experience (Camilleri, 2024; Kozak & Kozak, 2015).

Patents provide protection for inventions and innovations, giving the patent holder exclusive rights to use and commercialize their invention for a specified period. Although patents are less common in tourism compared to other forms of IP, they can be relevant for developing new technologies or processes that improve the tourism experience. For instance, a company that creates a unique software application for managing hotel bookings or a novel method for sustainable tourism practices could obtain a patent to prevent competitors from copying their innovation (Punchihewa, 2020; Pike & Page, 2014).

GIs are a type of IP that links a product's name to a specific geographical origin, emphasizing qualities or a reputation tied to that location. In tourism, GIs play a significant role in promoting local products such as wines, cheeses, handicrafts, and agricultural goods that are unique to a particular region. For example, the term

"Champagne" is exclusively used for sparkling wine produced in the Champagne region of France, and "Roquefort" refers only to cheese made in Roquefort-sur-Soulzon. GIs protect the authenticity of these products, prevent misrepresentation, and enhance the destination's branding and appeal by highlighting its unique cultural and natural attributes (Ruiz-Real et al., 2020; Hanna et al., 2021; Gursoy & Chi, 2018; Camilleri, 2018a).

The role of IP in Creating and Protecting Unique Tourism Assets and Experiences

IP plays a central role in both developing and safeguarding the distinctive assets and experiences that characterize a tourism destination. By securing IP rights, destinations and tourism businesses can set themselves apart from competitors, strengthen their brand identity, and protect the integrity of their cultural and natural heritage. IP enables destinations to craft unique tourism offerings that stand out in a competitive global market. For instance, trademarks help destinations create recognizable brands that embody specific values, qualities, and experiences associated with a place. A well-established trademark can evoke notions of luxury, adventure, or cultural depth, attracting tourists who seek those particular experiences. Likewise, GIs foster a sense of authenticity and exclusivity around local products, appealing to tourists interested in discovering the unique characteristics of a region. Additionally, copyrights safeguard the creative content integral to the tourism experience. Whether it's the design of promotional materials or the creation of original artistic performances and cultural exhibitions, copyrights ensure that creators are compensated for their work, helping to maintain the uniqueness and appeal of the tourism experience. This protection encourages ongoing creativity and innovation within the tourism sector, leading to the development of new attractions, events, and experiences that draw tourists to a destination (Vellas, 2016; Dratler, 2023; Hodson, 2021; Bagiastuti, 2023; Dharmawan et al., 2020).

Moreover, the protection offered by IP is essential for preserving the value and integrity of tourism assets. Without IP protection, the unique elements that make a destination special could be easily copied or misused by others, resulting in brand dilution and a loss of competitive advantage. For example, the unauthorized use of a destination's trademark by subpar service providers could damage the destination's reputation and erode tourists' trust. GIs play a crucial role in protecting traditional products and practices from imitation, which is vital for maintaining the cultural heritage of a destination. When local products are protected by GIs, they are shielded from misappropriation by those who might produce inferior copies or falsely claim the same quality and characteristics. This protection not only safeguards the economic interests of local producers but also ensures that tourists receive an authentic experience that remains true to the destination's heritage. Additionally, IP protection helps destinations and tourism businesses address challenges such as counterfeiting and the unauthorized commercial use of their assets. For example, a popular tourist attraction may face unauthorized exploitation through unlicensed merchandise or the unapproved use of its images in marketing materials. By enforcing IP rights, the destination can prevent such practices, ensuring that its assets are used in ways that align with its brand values and business goals (Macmillan, 2020; Ubertazzi, 2022; Palfrey, 2011; Pike & Page, 2014; Gursoy & Chi, 2018; Camilleri, 2018a).

IP is a foundational element of successful tourism development, allowing destinations to create unique offerings that resonate with travelers while protecting those assets from unauthorized use and exploitation. By strategically utilizing trademarks, copyrights, patents, and GIs, tourism stakeholders can build strong, distinctive brands, preserve cultural heritage, and deliver authentic, high-quality experiences that attract and satisfy tourists (Dosso & Vezzani, 2020; Camilleri, 2024).

THE ROLE OF IP IN DESTINATION BRANDING

How Trademarks and GIs can Enhance a Destination's Brand Identity

Trademarks and GIs are integral elements in the strategy of destination branding, playing a critical role in solidifying a destination's brand identity. In the highly competitive global tourism industry, where destinations vie for travelers' attention, a strong, recognizable brand identity is essential for standing out and attracting visitors. Trademarks and GIs help shape and reinforce this identity by embodying the unique attributes, values, and experiences that a destination offers.

Trademarks serve as the visual and symbolic representation of a destination's brand. They include logos, slogans, symbols, and even sounds that distinguish one destination from another. For instance, the silhouette of the Eiffel Tower is more than just a globally recognized trademark; it is a powerful symbol of Paris and France, evoking images of romance, culture, and history. Similarly, the "I NY" slogan and logo are inextricably linked with New York City, encapsulating the city's dynamic and vibrant character. These trademarks are not just marketing tools; they are foundational elements of a destination's identity, creating an immediate connection in the minds of potential tourists (Yang, 2021; Dratler Jr & McJohn, 2024; Stim, 2024).

When used effectively, trademarks highlight a destination's unique selling points, whether they are related to luxury, adventure, cultural depth, or natural beauty. They serve as a promise to travelers, signaling the type of experience they can anticipate. A well-designed trademark can also foster an emotional connection with the destination, turning it into a sought-after brand that people aspire to visit. Additionally, trademarks can be deployed across various platforms and marketing materials, ensuring consistency in branding efforts and reinforcing the destination's identity at every touchpoint (Kozak & Kozak, 2015; Punchihewa, 2020).

GIs, in contrast, are used to highlight the unique characteristics of products that are inherently linked to a specific location. In the context of destination branding, GIs can significantly enhance the perceived authenticity and exclusivity of a destination's offerings. For example, products like "Champagne" from the Champagne region of France or "Darjeeling tea" from India are more than just goods; they represent the heritage, quality, and tradition of their respective regions. These GIs create a strong association between the product and the place, contributing to the destination's overall brand identity.

By promoting GI-protected products, destinations can craft a compelling narrative around their unique cultural and natural assets, which in turn strengthens their brand identity. Tourists seeking authentic experiences are drawn to destinations that offer products and experiences that are unavailable elsewhere. For example, the Parma region in Italy has successfully leveraged the GI status of "Parma Ham" to position itself as a premier destination for gourmet food tourism. The protection and promotion of GIs ensure that these products maintain their reputation for quality and authenticity, thereby enhancing the destination's appeal and reinforcing its identity (Otay Demir et al., 2022; McCabe, 2014; Prebensen et al., 2018; Morrison, 2013).

The Impact of Branding Through IP on Destination Recognition and Differentiation

Utilizing IP for branding, especially through trademarks and GIs, significantly influences how a destination is recognized and differentiated. In a global market crowded with similar travel options, the ability to stand out is essential for attracting tourists and gaining a competitive edge. IP plays a crucial role in this by establishing unique, identifiable identities that appeal to target audiences. Trademarks and GIs are vital in enhancing a destination's visibility by offering distinct, consistent symbols and names that are easily associated with specific attributes. For example, a strong trademark ensures that potential visitors immediately connect the logo or slogan with the destination and its offerings. This immediate recognition is critical for building brand awareness and ensuring the destination remains prominent in tourists' minds during their decision-making process. The widespread application of trademarks across marketing efforts, social media, merchandise, and digital platforms helps solidify the destination's brand in the minds of prospective travelers. For instance, the "Incredible India" campaign effectively used a memorable slogan and unique visual elements to position India as a diverse and culturally rich destination. The persistent use of this trademark across various media has enhanced India's recognition and attracted millions of visitors globally (Birdir et al., 2018; Rathee & Rajain, 2022; Hanna et al., 2021; Morgan et al., 2022; Camilleri, 2018b).

Likewise, GIs boost recognition by directly linking products to their place of origin, making it easier for consumers to associate these products with specific regions. This recognition not only highlights the products but also enhances the overall visibility of the destination on the global stage. For instance, Tuscany's connection with "Chianti wine" or Scotland's with "Scotch whisky" not only elevates the recognition of these products but also enhances the regions' profiles, attracting tourists interested in the heritage and tradition behind these renowned products (Camilleri, 2018c; Horner & Swarbrooke, 2020; Vellas, 2016).

Beyond boosting recognition, IP-based branding is crucial for differentiation, which involves making a destination stand out from others with similar offerings. Trademarks and GIs are key tools in this process, helping destinations highlight their unique attributes, such as cultural heritage, natural landscapes, culinary traditions, or artisanal products. By showcasing these distinct features, destinations can set themselves apart in travelers' minds, making them more attractive amidst numerous options (Kozak & Baloglu, 2010; Ruiz-Real et al., 2020).

For example, New Zealand's "100% Pure New Zealand" trademark has effectively positioned the country as a premier destination for pristine nature and outdoor adventure. This consistent branding has established New Zealand as a top choice for eco-tourists and adventure enthusiasts, distinguishing it from other locations with similar landscapes but lacking equivalent branding and recognition (https://www.newzealand.com/nz/).

GIs also play a vital role in differentiation by protecting and promoting products that are uniquely tied to specific regions. These products act as representatives of their destinations, offering experiences that cannot be found elsewhere. GI protection ensures that such products remain exclusive to their regions, preventing imitation and preserving the destination's unique appeal. For instance, the GI status of "Tequila" not only protects the product's authenticity but also reinforces Mexico's identity as the origin of this famous spirit, differentiating it from other regions that produce similar beverages (Sorokina et al., 2022; Çeltek & İhan, 2018).

Strategically leveraging IP in destination branding is crucial for enhancing both recognition and differentiation in the competitive global tourism market. Trademarks and GIs are powerful tools for establishing a strong brand identity, ensuring that destinations capture attention and maintain their competitive edge. Effective use of these IP assets can create a lasting impact on potential visitors, driving tourism growth and sustaining the destination's appeal over time (Hall, 2014; George, 2021).

IP RIGHTS AND TOURISM MARKETING

Utilizing Copyrighted Materials in Marketing Campaigns

Copyrighted materials, such as images, videos, logos, and other creative content, are essential components of successful tourism marketing campaigns. These assets help to communicate the core qualities of a destination, forging a visual and emotional bond with prospective travelers. Copyright protection ensures that the creators or owners have exclusive rights to use, reproduce, and distribute these works. In tourism marketing, effectively utilizing copyrighted materials can significantly boost a destination's attractiveness and memorability to target audiences (Dratler, 2023; Dar & Ojha, 2023).

Images and videos are especially impactful in tourism promotion. High-quality, captivating visuals can showcase the beauty and distinctiveness of a destination, evoking emotions that drive potential tourists to visit. For example, a professionally crafted video highlighting a destination's vibrant culture and breathtaking scenery can be the deciding factor for someone considering a trip. Copyright protection of these visual elements ensures that they are not used without authorization, preserving the marketing message's integrity and preventing unauthorized use that might weaken the brand (Punchihewa, 2021; Rasmi et al., 2022; Benson, 2019).

Logos are also crucial in destination branding. A well-crafted logo can become closely associated with the destination, providing instant recognition and reinforcing the brand's identity. For instance, the "Incredible India" logo is widely recognized and symbolizes India's rich cultural heritage. Copyrighting logos prevents unauthorized copying or misuse by others, which could confuse consumers or diminish the brand's value.

Moreover, copyrighted slogans, jingles, and written content are vital in creating a compelling narrative for tourism marketing. These elements help convey important messages that resonate with potential visitors. By securing these creative works through copyright, tourism marketers ensure that their unique messaging remains exclusive, distinguishing their destination from competitors (Tien et al., 2019; Hodson, 2021; Bagiastuti, 2023).

Strategies for Protecting and Monetizing IP Assets in Tourism Marketing

Protecting and monetizing IP assets is vital for optimizing the value derived from tourism marketing efforts. Without adequate protection, the creative and branding elements that define a destination may be misappropriated or exploited, leading to diminished brand value, revenue losses, and potential harm to the destination's reputation.

A key strategy for safeguarding IP assets is to ensure legal registration and enforcement of all copyrighted materials, trademarks, and other IP elements. Registering copyrights creates a public record of ownership and enhances the legal standing of the rights holder in case of infringement. Trademark registration is crucial for securing exclusive rights to brand symbols, logos, and slogans, preventing others from using similar marks that might confuse consumers (Dharmawan et al., 2020; Macmillan, 2020).

Utilizing licensing agreements is another effective strategy to manage how IP assets are used by third parties. Licensing permits IP owners to authorize other entities, such as tour operators, travel agencies, or souvenir makers, to use their copyrighted materials or trademarks in return for fees or royalties. This approach not only generates revenue but also ensures that the IP is used in ways that align with the destination's branding and marketing objectives. For instance, a destination might license its logo to a local artisan group for use on handcrafted items, thereby generating income while promoting local culture (Dratler Jr & McJohn, 2024; Stim, 2024; Dosso & Vezzani, 2020).

Ongoing monitoring and enforcement are essential for effective IP protection. Destinations and tourism marketers must vigilantly track the use of their IP assets both online and offline to identify unauthorized usage. This can be accomplished through manual searches, automated monitoring tools, or by hiring IP enforcement agencies. If infringement is detected, prompt measures such as issuing cease-and-desist letters, initiating legal action, or negotiating settlements can prevent further misuse and maintain the brand's integrity (Gursoy & Chi, 2018; Camilleri, 2018a; Birdir et al., 2018).

Monetizing IP assets involves more than just licensing; it includes leveraging these assets for various revenue-generating opportunities. For example, destinations can sell exclusive rights to use specific images or videos in third-party marketing efforts. Additionally, IP assets can be used to create and sell branded merchandise, such as apparel, accessories, and souvenirs, providing additional revenue streams while enhancing the destination's visibility (Rathee & Rajain, 2022; Sorokina et al., 2022).

Challenges and opportunities in using IP for digital marketing and online platforms

The digital realm presents both substantial challenges and opportunities for utilizing IP in tourism marketing. As destinations increasingly turn to online platforms to connect with global audiences, it is crucial to safeguard IP assets while maximizing their impact. One major challenge is the ease with which digital content can be copied and disseminated without authorization. Images, videos, and other copyrighted materials posted on websites, social media, and various digital platforms are prone to unauthorized use, often without the original creator's or rights holder's knowledge. This can result in widespread IP infringement, where content is used in ways that diminish the brand or misrepresent the destination. For instance, a striking photo of a destination shared on social media might be duplicated and utilized by another company in its marketing efforts without permission or acknowledgment of the original photographer. Such misuse not only devalues the content but also undermines the brand's exclusivity (Otay Demir et al., 2022; McCabe, 2014; Prebensen et al., 2018; Horner & Swarbrooke, 2020; Vellas, 2016; Dratler, 2023).

To counter these challenges, tourism marketers need to implement effective digital rights management (DRM) strategies. DRM tools can protect digital content by embedding watermarks, metadata, and usage restrictions that prevent unauthorized copying or distribution. Additionally, IP monitoring services can track the online use of content, allowing for prompt action against infringement. Social media platforms and content-sharing sites also offer mechanisms for reporting and removing infringing content, which can help protect IP assets (Ubertazzi, 2022; Palfrey, 2011; Yang, 2021; Çeltek & İhan, 2018; Kozak & Baloglu, 2010).

Despite these challenges, digital platforms offer remarkable opportunities for leveraging IP assets in tourism marketing. The global reach of the internet enables destinations to share their content with a vast audience, creating brand awareness and engagement on an unprecedented scale. Social media, in particular, serves as a powerful platform for distributing copyrighted images, videos, and logos, driving interest through viral content and user-generated posts. For instance, a destination might encourage visitors to share their own photos and experiences with a branded hashtag, amplifying the reach of its marketing campaign (Ruiz-Real et al., 2020; Hanna et al., 2021; Camilleri, 2018a; Birdir et al., 2018; Rathee & Rajain, 2022).

Digital marketing also provides greater flexibility in utilizing and monetizing IP assets. For example, destinations can create subscription-based access to exclusive content, such as high-quality video tours or virtual experiences, generating new revenue streams while protecting IP. Additionally, online platforms allow destinations to experiment with various formats and channels for distributing their IP assets, from influencer partnerships to interactive content, reaching diverse audiences in innovative ways.

IP rights are crucial for successful tourism marketing, offering both protection and opportunities for creative content and branding elements. By strategically using copyrighted materials, safeguarding IP assets, and navigating the digital marketing landscape, destinations can strengthen their brand identity, distinguish themselves from competitors, and forge meaningful connections with travelers. Success lies in balancing IP protection with innovative digital strategies to engage and inspire a global audience (Palfrey, 2011; Yang, 2021; Dratler Jr & McJohn, 2024; Stim, 2024).

GIs AND CULTURAL HERITAGE

The Significance of GIs in Promoting Local Products and Traditions

GIs are essential for promoting local products and safeguarding cultural heritage by associating products with their specific geographic origins. A GI is a type of IP that identifies a product as coming from a particular area, where its quality, reputation, or other attributes are intrinsically linked to that location. This association not only emphasizes the distinctiveness of local products but also serves as a valuable tool for preserving traditional knowledge, skills, and cultural practices related to their production.

The importance of GIs lies in their ability to protect and enhance the authenticity of local products, which is increasingly valued in the global market. Consumers often seek out and are willing to pay more for products that are certified as genuine and tied to a specific geographic area, as they associate these products with superior quality, tradition, and cultural identity. For example, "Champagne" from the Champagne region in France, "Roquefort" cheese from Roquefort-sur-Soulzon, and "Darjeeling" tea from India are globally recognized for their unique qualities directly linked to their geographical origins. GI protection ensures that only products genuinely from these regions can use these names, thus preserving their reputation and market value (Dharmawan et al., 2020; Macmillan, 2020; Ubertazzi, 2022; Rasmi et al., 2022; Benson, 2019; Tien et al., 2019).

GIs also play a crucial role in supporting rural economies by benefiting local producers and communities. By protecting the exclusivity of a product, GIs prevent imitation and misuse, which could undermine traditional production methods and market value. Additionally, GIs can boost tourism by attracting visitors interested in experiencing and purchasing authentic local products. For instance, wine tourism in regions such as Bordeaux and Tuscany is closely linked to the prestige of their GIs, drawing tourists who want to visit vineyards, taste wines, and learn about the local heritage of wine production (Otay Demir et al., 2022; McCabe, 2014; Prebensen et al., 2018).

Beyond economic advantages, GIs are vital for preserving cultural heritage. They help ensure that traditional production methods, often passed down through generations, are recognized and sustained. This protection of intangible cultural heritage—such as traditional farming techniques, artisanal craftsmanship, and culinary practices—is crucial for maintaining the cultural identity of a region. By safeguarding these traditions through GIs, communities can retain their cultural uniqueness amidst globalization, while also capitalizing on the increasing demand for authentic, culturally-rich products (Hanna et al., 2021; Morgan et al., 2022; Camilleri, 2018b).

Strategies for Integrating Cultural Heritage and Local Products into Tourism Marketing using IP

Incorporating cultural heritage and local products into tourism marketing using IP, especially GIs, requires a well-thought-out strategy that showcases the distinct features of the region while safeguarding and promoting its cultural assets. Here are several effective strategies for destinations to integrate GIs and cultural heritage into their tourism marketing efforts: A key method is to focus on authentic experiences that enable visitors to engage with the local culture directly. This can involve promoting tours, workshops, and events that highlight the production processes of GI-protected products. For example, destinations might offer guided tours of vineyards, olive orchards, or cheese factories, where tourists can observe traditional production techniques, sample the products, and learn about their historical and cultural importance. Such experiences not only enhance the attractiveness of the destination but also deepen visitors' appreciation for the cultural heritage associated with these products (Dosso & Vezzani, 2020; Camilleri, 2024; Kozak & Kozak, 2015; Punchihewa, 2020).

Creating cultural heritage trails that connect GI-protected products with cultural landmarks can offer tourists a curated experience of the region's cultural and gastronomic diversity. For instance, a wine route in Burgundy or a cheese trail in Switzerland could guide visitors through various towns and villages, each offering distinct products and experiences. Marketing these trails can draw tourists interested in exploring the area's cultural richness, boosting local visitation and economic benefits. Partnering with local producers and artisans is also crucial for effectively incorporating GIs into tourism marketing. Destinations can collaborate with these stakeholders to create joint marketing campaigns that promote both the destination and the GI-protected products. This might include branded packaging that features the destination's logo alongside the GI or developing promotional materials that share the story of the product and its cultural heritage. Additionally, organizing festivals, fairs, and markets that celebrate local products can provide a platform for artisans and producers to showcase their goods to tourists (Sorokina et al., 2022; Çeltek & İhan, 2018).

Digital marketing offers a powerful avenue for communicating the stories behind GI-protected products and the cultural heritage of the region. Destinations can produce engaging content, such as videos, blogs, and social media posts, to highlight the history, production methods, and cultural significance of these products. Sharing these narratives online allows destinations to reach a global audience, attract culturally-minded tourists, and build a strong emotional connection between the product, the place, and potential visitors. Digital storytelling can also help clarify any misconceptions and educate consumers about the value of authenticity and heritage in their product choices (Camilleri, 2018c; Horner & Swarbrooke, 2020; Vellas, 2016).

Additionally, protecting cultural heritage through IP is essential to ensure that the benefits of tourism and product promotion remain with local communities. This involves registering and enforcing GIs to prevent unauthorized use and ensuring that all marketing activities respect the region's values and traditions. By doing so, destinations can protect their cultural assets while enhancing their market position. Promoting ethical production and sustainable tourism practices linked to GI-protected products can also strengthen the destination's reputation as a responsible and culturally-rich travel spot (Yang, 2021; Dratler Jr & McJohn, 2024).

GIs are a valuable tool for promoting local products and preserving cultural heritage in tourism marketing. By strategically incorporating GIs into their marketing strategies, destinations can craft a compelling narrative that attracts tourists, supports local economies, and ensures the protection of cultural traditions. This approach not only enhances the destination's brand but also contributes to the long-term sustainability and authenticity of its tourism offerings (Stim, 2024; Dosso & Vezzani, 2020; Camilleri, 2024).

IP AS A TOOL FOR SUSTAINABLE TOURISM DEVELOPMENT

How IP can support sustainable tourism by promoting authentic and locally-produced goods

IP is crucial in fostering sustainable tourism by promoting authentic, locally-produced goods that form the cultural and economic backbone of tourism destinations. Securing IP rights, such as trademarks and GIs, enables destinations to protect and market products that are deeply embedded in local environments and cultural practices. This not only preserves the distinctiveness of these products but also supports sustainable economic practices that benefit local communities. Tourists often seek genuine experiences, which are embodied by authentic and locally-made goods, such as traditional crafts, artisanal foods, and indigenous products. When these items are protected by IP, particularly through GIs, their origin, quality, and traditional production methods are safeguarded. This ensures that only products meeting specific standards can use these designations, preventing the market from being flooded with inferior imitations that could damage the reputation of the genuine products and the destination itself. Promoting IP-protected goods encourages sustainable practices that bolster local economies and reduce environmental impacts. For instance, GIs help preserve traditional agricultural methods that are often more environmentally friendly than large-scale industrial farming. In areas like Tuscany or Bordeaux, the GI protection of wine not only maintains the unique characteristics of the vineyards but also supports small-scale, sustainable farming practices passed down through generations. This link between product, place, and practice ensures that tourism supports the local economy in a manner that is both environmentally and culturally sustainable.

Moreover, marketing authentic, IP-protected goods attracts tourists who value sustainability and are willing to pay a premium for ethically sourced products that are genuinely connected to the destination's heritage. This approach boosts revenue for local producers and promotes the preservation of traditional knowledge and skills, contributing to the overall sustainability of the destination. By incorporating IP into tourism development strategies, destinations can ensure that tourism growth enhances rather than compromises local cultures and environments, supporting their long-term sustainability (Kozak & Kozak, 2015; Punchihewa, 2020; Pike & Page, 2014).

The role of IP in preserving and promoting intangible cultural heritage in tourism

IP is essential for preserving and promoting intangible cultural heritage, which encompasses the practices, representations, expressions, knowledge, and skills transmitted within communities. This form of heritage is often threatened by globalization and mass tourism, where commercialization can lead to the dilution or misrepresentation of traditional practices. IP rights, including GIs, trademarks, and copyrights, offer a means to protect these intangible assets and ensure they remain a vital part of a destination's cultural identity. GIs, for instance, safeguard not only the names of products associated with specific regions but also the traditional knowledge and production methods. This is crucial in tourism, where the authenticity of cultural experiences attracts visitors. For example, the GI designation for "Darjeeling tea" protects both the name and the traditional cultivation and processing techniques that have been used in the Darjeeling region for centuries. This protection ensures that tourists can experience the genuine culture and heritage of tea production rather than a diluted or commercialized version.

Trademarks and copyrights also play a key role in safeguarding intangible cultural heritage by ensuring that traditional designs, music, dance, and other cultural expressions are not exploited without permission from the original creators. For instance, traditional textile patterns or indigenous music can be protected by trademarks or copyrights to prevent their unauthorized use in commercial products that do not benefit the creators. This helps maintain the integrity of cultural expressions while allowing communities to gain economic rewards from their heritage (Dratler, 2023; Dar & Ojha, 2023; Punchihewa, 2021; Rasmi et al., 2022; Benson, 2019).

Highlighting intangible cultural heritage through IP-protected tourism experiences can enhance a destination's appeal by offering tourists unique and meaningful interactions with local cultures. IP-protected cultural festivals, traditional performances, and artisanal workshops provide authentic experiences while ensuring that cultural practices remain vibrant and relevant within their communities. This approach not only attracts culturally-conscious tourists but also contributes to the sustainability of heritage by making it economically viable (Gursoy & Chi, 2018; Camilleri, 2018a; Birdir et al., 2018).

Balancing commercialization with the protection of cultural and natural assets

While IP can significantly advance the promotion and protection of cultural and natural assets in tourism, it is crucial to maintain a balance between commercialization and preservation. While the commercial success of IP-protected goods and experiences can enhance tourism and provide economic benefits for local communities, there is a risk that commercialization may lead to overexploitation of resources, cultural commodification, and the degradation of the unique attributes that define a destination (Otay Demir et al., 2022; McCabe, 2014; Prebensen et al., 2018).

A major challenge is ensuring that the commercialization of cultural heritage does not result in its trivialization or misrepresentation. When cultural practices or products are marketed primarily for tourism, they may be altered to fit tourist expectations, potentially compromising their authenticity. For example, a traditional dance might be shortened or simplified to suit tourists' schedules, or traditional crafts might be mass-produced to meet demand, losing the original craftsmanship and attention to detail. To address these issues, it is vital that IP protections are supported by guidelines and standards that preserve the integrity of cultural expressions (Camilleri, 2018c; Horner & Swarbrooke, 2020; Vellas, 2016).

Furthermore, balancing commercialization with environmental stewardship is essential. Promoting IP-protected natural products, such as wines, cheeses, or agricultural goods, can boost production and attract tourists to the regions where these products are made. While this can be economically advantageous, it may also exert pressure on local ecosystems and resources. To mitigate these effects, sustainable tourism practices should be implemented, including limiting visitor numbers, encouraging off-season travel, and supporting environmentally-friendly production methods (Dratler Jr & McJohn, 2024; Stim, 2024; Dosso & Vezzani, 2020).

Additionally, it is important that the economic benefits of IP protection and commercialization are fairly distributed among all stakeholders, especially the local communities that safeguard cultural and natural assets. Ensuring that these communities receive a fair share of the economic rewards and are involved in decision-making processes is crucial for maintaining social sustainability. Community-based tourism initiatives, cooperative models, and transparent licensing agreements can help empower local people and preserve their cultural and natural heritage (Hodson, 2021; Bagiastuti, 2023; Dharmawan et al., 2020).

Overall, IP is a valuable tool for fostering sustainable tourism development by protecting and promoting authentic, locally-produced goods and intangible cultural heritage. However, to achieve true sustainability, it is essential to balance the commercial opportunities offered by IP with the need to protect cultural and natural assets. By doing so, destinations can build a tourism industry that is economically viable, culturally respectful, and environmentally responsible, ensuring that the benefits of tourism are sustained for current and future generations (Ruiz-Real et al., 2020; Hanna et al., 2021).

CHALLENGES IN LEVERAGING IP FOR DESTINATION BRANDING

Common challenges faced by destinations in protecting and utilizing IP

Utilizing IP for destination branding involves several challenges, especially concerning the protection and effective use of these assets. One major challenge is enforcing IP rights. Even if destinations successfully register trademarks, GIs, or copyrights, enforcing these rights can be complex and costly. For example, if a destination's trademark is violated by counterfeiters selling fake merchandise with the destination's logo, tracking down and taking legal action against these infringers—particularly those operating in different jurisdictions—can be difficult. Enforcement issues are exacerbated by the fact that many destinations lack the legal infrastructure and resources necessary for effective IP protection. Small or developing destinations may particularly struggle with the financial and logistical demands of IP enforcement. Without adequate enforcement, the risk of IP infringement rises, potentially harming the destination's brand reputation. For instance, if unauthorized low-quality products are sold using a destination's trademark, it could damage the destination's image and erode consumer trust in the brand (Rathee & Rajain, 2022; Sorokina et al., 2022; Macmillan, 2020; Ubertazzi, 2022; Palfrey, 2011; Yang, 2021).

Another challenge involves managing GIs. Although GIs are effective in protecting products associated with specific regions, they require strict adherence to production methods, quality standards, and geographical boundaries. Ensuring that all producers within the designated area meet these standards can be challenging, particularly with numerous small-scale producers. Variability in quality or practices among producers can weaken the GI's effectiveness and, by extension, the destination's brand. Additionally, managing and enforcing GIs entails considerable administrative effort, including continuous oversight and coordination among various stakeholders.

Destinations also often face difficulties in maximizing the potential of their IP assets. While IP rights offer legal protection, integrating these assets into branding and marketing strategies requires a thorough understanding of the destination's unique qualities and the global market. Many destinations may lack the expertise or resources to develop and implement effective branding campaigns that fully leverage their IP assets. For instance, a destination with a valuable GI may find it challenging to communicate the product's significance and uniqueness to international audiences, thus limiting the impact of the IP on the destination's overall brand (Çeltek & İhan, 2018; Kozak & Baloglu, 2010; Morgan et al., 2022; Camilleri, 2018b; Morrison, 2013; Hall, 2014; George, 2021).

The impact of globalization and digitalization on IP management in tourism

Globalization and digitalization have profoundly impacted the tourism sector, offering both benefits and hurdles for managing IP. On one hand, these developments have broadened the exposure of tourism brands, enabling destinations to reach a global audience. On the other hand, they have introduced new challenges in safeguarding and managing IP assets. Globalization has increased the cross-border flow of goods, services, and information, complicating IP enforcement. For example, a trademark registered in one country may not be acknowledged or protected elsewhere. This discrepancy can lead to international infringement issues, where unauthorized entities in different countries use the trademark without permission. Legal proceedings in multiple jurisdictions can be extremely costly and time-consuming, especially for smaller destinations. Furthermore, varying IP laws and enforcement practices across countries create legal uncertainties, making consistent global protection of IP rights difficult.

Digitalization exacerbates these challenges by making it easier for infringers to copy and disseminate IP-protected content without authorization. The expansion of the internet and social media allows destination brands to reach extensive audiences, but it also increases the risk of IP theft. Digital assets such as images, videos, and logos can be easily duplicated and shared online, often without the IP owner's consent. This can result in widespread unauthorized use of a destination's branding materials, diluting the brand and complicating image control. Moreover, digital platforms facilitate the distribution of counterfeit goods, including fake souvenirs or merchandise that misuse a destination's trademark or GI. These counterfeit items are frequently sold on e-commerce platforms or social media, making it challenging for IP owners to detect and address the infringement. The spread of such counterfeit goods can damage the destination's reputation and devalue its IP assets.

Digitalization also provides advanced tools and technologies to support IP management. For example, blockchain technology offers the potential to improve IP protection by creating a transparent, immutable ledger for recording IP ownership and transactions. This can assist destinations in tracking the use of their IP assets more effectively and proving ownership in disputes. Additionally, artificial intelligence (AI) and machine learning can be utilized to monitor online platforms for unauthorized IP use, facilitating faster detection and response to infringements.

Although globalization and digitalization have broadened the scope for destinations to capitalize on their IP assets internationally, they have also brought significant challenges in safeguarding and managing these assets. To address these challenges, destinations need to adopt comprehensive IP strategies that encompass international registration, digital monitoring, and enforcement measures. By implementing these strategies, destinations can protect their brand identity, preserve the integrity of their cultural and natural assets, and succeed in an increasingly interconnected global environment.

FUTURE TRENDS AND INNOVATIONS IN IP AND TOURISM MARKETING

Emerging trends in IP management and potential impact on tourism branding

As the tourism industry adapts to global shifts, new trends in IP management are emerging that could significantly influence destination branding and marketing. A key trend is the increasing emphasis on sustainability and ethical practices in IP management. Consumers are becoming more interested in brands that reflect their values, particularly regarding environmental responsibility and cultural preservation. Destinations that manage their IP to highlight sustainability—such as safeguarding GIs linked to organic or eco-friendly products—can set themselves apart in the market and attract a more environmentally conscious traveler.

Another trend is the integration of IP with experiential marketing strategies. Destinations are moving beyond protecting logos, trademarks, and product names to creating immersive experiences tied to their IP assets. For example, a destination might organize a branded cultural festival or culinary event featuring GI-protected products, offering visitors a unique and memorable experience. This shift from static IP assets to dynamic, experience-driven branding fosters deeper engagement and enhances brand loyalty.

Moreover, the globalization of the tourism sector is driving the need for stronger international IP protection strategies. Destinations are increasingly aware of the necessity to secure IP rights not only domestically but also in important international markets. This is particularly crucial for trademarks and GIs, which are prone to infringement in foreign markets where legal protection may be lacking. As a result, there is a growing trend towards collaboration between destinations and international bodies, such as the World Intellectual Property Organization (WIPO), to streamline registration processes and enhance enforcement across borders (Camilleri, 2018c; Horner & Swarbrooke, 2020; Vellas, 2016; Bagiastuti, 2023; Dharmawan et al., 2020; Macmillan, 2020).

The role of technology in enhancing IP protection and utilization

Technology is increasingly vital in improving IP protection and utilization in tourism marketing. Two of the most promising technologies are blockchain and artificial intelligence (AI), which address many long-standing issues in IP management. Blockchain technology offers a decentralized, immutable ledger that can record and verify IP rights and transactions. This technology enhances tourism branding by providing transparency, security, and traceability. For instance, blockchain can create a secure record of ownership for trademarks, copyrights, and GIs, simplifying the process of proving ownership and defending against infringement. It can also track the use of IP assets across different platforms and jurisdictions, ensuring compliance with licensing agreements and preventing unauthorized use. Additionally, blockchain can improve consumer trust by providing verifiable information about the origin and authenticity of products associated with GIs. For example, a bottle of Champagne could feature a blockchain-based QR code that allows consumers to verify its authenticity, ensuring they are purchasing a genuine product. This transparency strengthens the link between the destination's brand and its products, meeting the growing demand for authenticity from tourists (Gaafar & Al-Romeedy, 2024a, b).

AI is also transforming IP management in tourism. It can automate the monitoring of IP assets across digital platforms, detecting infringements more swiftly and accurately than manual methods. For instance, AI algorithms can search social media, e-commerce sites, and other online platforms for unauthorized use of a destination's trademarks or copyrighted material. When an infringement is detected, the system can automatically alert the IP owner and initiate takedown procedures, reducing the time and resources required to protect IP rights. Furthermore, AI enhances the personalization of tourism marketing by analyzing large datasets to discern consumer behavior patterns. This allows marketers to develop more targeted and effective campaigns. For example, AI can tailor marketing messages based on specific interests and preferences, such as promoting GI-protected local foods to culinary enthusiasts or highlighting eco-friendly lodging to environmentally conscious travelers. This personalized approach not only improves marketing efficiency but also strengthens the destination's brand identity (Punchihewa, 2021; Rasmi et al., 2022; Benson, 2019; Tien et al., 2019; Hodson, 2021).

Predictions for the future of IP in destination branding and marketing

Looking ahead, the significance of IP in destination branding and marketing is expected to grow as the tourism sector adapts to technological innovations, evolving consumer preferences, and global challenges. One major forecast is that IP will increasingly be regarded not merely as a protective tool but as a strategic asset that fosters innovation and market differentiation. With sustainability becoming a key focus for both consumers and policymakers, destinations that use their IP to highlight sustainable practices and products are likely to gain a competitive advantage. GIs, in particular, will be pivotal in showcasing the environmental and cultural sustainability of local products, appealing to tourists who value these principles. Destinations that can effectively use IP to demonstrate their commitment to preserving natural and cultural heritage will be well-positioned in a market that increasingly prioritizes authenticity and sustainability.

Technology will play a crucial role in the future of IP management in tourism. The adoption of blockchain and AI in IP management systems is expected to increase, offering improved protection and more efficient use of IP assets. As these technologies become more accessible, even smaller destinations will be able to better safeguard their IP rights and confidently engage in the global tourism market. Future branding efforts will likely focus more on creating immersive, experience-oriented tourism products closely connected to IP assets. Destinations will emphasize developing branded experiences, such as cultural festivals, culinary tours, and artisan workshops, that highlight their unique IP-protected products and heritage. These experiences will enhance the destination's brand and offer deeper engagement with tourists, promoting long-term brand loyalty.

Moreover, as the global tourism market becomes more interconnected, the need for international collaboration in IP protection will increase. Destinations will need to collaborate with international organizations to create unified IP frameworks that ensure protection of IP rights across borders. This cooperation will be crucial for preserving brand identity and cultural assets in a globalized market.

The future of IP in destination branding and marketing will be shaped by emerging trends in sustainability, technology, and global cooperation. By leveraging these trends and viewing IP as a strategic asset, destinations can enhance their brand identity, protect their cultural heritage, and succeed in a rapidly evolving tourism landscape (Dratler, 2023; Dar & Ojha, 2023; Rathee & Rajain, 2022; Sorokina et al., 2022; Hall, 2014; George, 2021).

CONCLUSION AND RECOMMENDATIONS

The examination of IP in destination branding and marketing highlights its crucial role in establishing, safeguarding, and promoting the unique characteristics of tourism destinations. IP elements, such as trademarks, copyrights, and GIs, are essential tools for differentiating destinations in a competitive global marketplace. Trademarks and GIs contribute to building a strong, recognizable brand identity that appeals to potential tourists, while copyrights protect creative content that narrates a destination's story and values. Effective IP management allows destinations to protect their cultural and natural assets, ensuring their use enhances the brand and attracts discerning travelers. Incorporating IP into marketing strategies not only enhances destination recognition and distinction but also supports sustainable tourism by promoting authentic, locally-produced goods and preserving intangible cultural heritage.

However, leveraging IP in destination branding involves several challenges, such as the complexities of IP enforcement, risks of infringement, and the effects of globalization and digitalization on IP management. As the tourism industry evolves, the importance of IP will grow in addressing these challenges and seizing new opportunities, particularly through advanced technologies like blockchain and artificial intelligence (AI).

To fully harness IP in branding and marketing, destination marketers should ensure comprehensive registration and protection of all relevant IP assets, including trademarks, GIs, and copyrights, in key markets. This process involves conducting detailed IP audits to identify valuable assets and securing legal protections through registration. Additionally, robust enforcement strategies are necessary, including vigilant monitoring for infringement and prompt action against unauthorized use. IP should be integral to the destination's branding approach, with trademarks and GIs highlighting the destination's unique qualities and values. Marketers should strive for a unified brand identity that integrates all IP assets, ensuring consistency across marketing channels and platforms. This includes incorporating IP-protected logos, slogans, and products into all promotional materials and marketing campaigns.

Destination marketers should also utilize IP to highlight authentic and culturally significant experiences that appeal to tourists seeking unique and meaningful travel opportunities. This can be accomplished by promoting IP-protected local products, such as GI-certified foods or crafts, in marketing efforts and by developing branded experiences like cultural festivals or culinary tours that celebrate the destination's heritage. Advanced technologies, including blockchain and AI, can further enhance IP protection and application. Marketers should consider using blockchain for secure IP management and traceability, especially for GIs, and AI for monitoring digital platforms to detect potential IP infringements. Additionally, digital marketing tools should be leveraged to narrate the stories behind IP-protected products and experiences, reaching a global audience and fostering stronger connections with prospective tourists.

Governments and tourism organizations play a crucial role in ensuring the effective use of IP in the tourism industry by providing comprehensive and enforceable IP laws, particularly for trademarks, copyrights, and GIs. They should enhance IP registration processes and enforcement, especially in tourism-dependent regions, and promote international cooperation through organizations like the World Intellectual Property Organization (WIPO) to standardize IP laws globally. Additionally, these entities should advocate for the use of IP to support sustainable tourism, encourage ethical commercialization of cultural assets, and invest in educational programs to improve IP management among tourism stakeholders, helping businesses and destinations protect and maximize their IP assets.

To fully leverage Intellectual Property (IP) in tourism, it is essential to integrate IP management into broader tourism development strategies that align with economic growth, cultural preservation, and sustainability goals. This involves identifying key IP assets, such as GIs, and incorporating them into regional tourism strategies like food, wine, or cultural heritage tourism. Collaboration between public and private sectors, including partnerships with businesses, local communities, and IP professionals, is crucial for developing effective IP strategies. Destination marketing should include plans for leveraging IP assets to build strong brand identities, while addressing challenges like IP protection in the digital age. Regular monitoring and assessment of IP's impact on tourism can help refine strategies and ensure successful outcomes. Overall, IP serves as a vital tool for destination branding, offering opportunities for differentiation, sustainability, and economic growth, which are key to securing long-term success in the global tourism market.

REFERENCES

Al-Romeedy, B. S. (2024a). Tomorrow's Travel Companion: The Role of Artificial Intelligence in Shaping the Future of Tourism. In Hashem, T., Albattat, A., Valeri, M., & Sharma, A. (Eds.), *Marketing and Big Data Analytics in Tourism and Events* (pp. 162–182). IGI Global., DOI: 10.4018/979-8-3693-3310-5.ch010

Al-Romeedy, B. S. (2024b). Unlocking the Power of Data: Exploring the Dynamic Role of MKIS in Revolutionizing Tourism Marketing. In Hashem, T., Albattat, A., Valeri, M., & Sharma, A. (Eds.), *Marketing and Big Data Analytics in Tourism and Events* (pp. 183–204). IGI Global., DOI: 10.4018/979-8-3693-3310-5.ch011

Al-Romeedy, B. S., & Hashem, T. (2024). From Insight to Advantage: Harnessing the Potential of Marketing Intelligence Systems in Tourism. In Hashem, T., Albattat, A., Valeri, M., & Sharma, A. (Eds.), *Marketing and Big Data Analytics in Tourism and Events* (pp. 80–98). IGI Global., DOI: 10.4018/979-8-3693-3310-5.ch005

Bagiastuti, N. K. (2023). Denpasar City Branding as Tourism Development Strategy: Law Branding Aspect Point of View. *International Journal of Social Science and Human Research*, 6(04), 2462–2469. DOI: 10.47191/ijsshr/v6-i4-60

Benson, T. J. (2019). Intellectual property rights in gastronomic tourism. In *The Routledge Handbook of Gastronomic Tourism* (pp. 499–505). Routledge. DOI: 10.4324/9781315147628-60

Birdir, S. S., Dalgic, A., & Birdir, K. (2018). Destination marketing and destination image. In *The Routledge handbook of destination marketing* (pp. 71–81). Routledge. DOI: 10.4324/9781315101163-7

Camilleri, M. A. (2018a). *Strategic perspectives in destination marketing*. IGI Global.

Camilleri, M. A. (2018b). *The branding of tourist destinations: Theoretical and empirical insights*. Emerald Publishing Limited. DOI: 10.1108/9781787693739

Camilleri, M. A. (2018c). *Travel marketing, tourism economics and the airline product: An introduction to theory and practice*. Springer International Publishing. DOI: 10.1007/978-3-319-49849-2

Camilleri, M. A. (2024). *Tourism planning and destination marketing*. Emerald Publishing Limited. DOI: 10.1108/9781804558881

Çeltek, E., & İhan, . (2018). Innovations in destination marketing. In *The Routledge handbook of destination marketing* (pp. 417–428). Routledge. DOI: 10.4324/9781315101163-32

Dar, M. A., & Ojha, M. (2023). Destination imaging, compatibilities with intellectual property rights-based tourism industry. *The Journal of World Intellectual Property*, 26(2), 328–335. DOI: 10.1111/jwip.12268

Dharmawan, N. K. S., Kasih, D. P. D., Dewi, A. A. I. A. A., & Kurniawan, I. (2020). Trademark protection for small-medium enterprises in Bali: Strengthening Community-based tourism in the era of fourth industrial revolution. *J. Legal Ethical & Regul. Isses*, 23, 1.

Dosso, M., & Vezzani, A. (2020). Firm market valuation and intellectual property assets. *Industry and Innovation*, 27(7), 705–729. DOI: 10.1080/13662716.2019.1685374

Dratler, J. (2023). *Licensing of intellectual property*. Law Journal Press.

Dratler, J.Jr, & McJohn, S. M. (2024). *Intellectual property law: Commercial, creative and industrial property*. Law Journal Press.

Gaafar, H. A., & Al-Romeedy, B. S. (2024a). Bridging the Digital Divide: Unleashing the Power of Big Data Analytics for Touristic Destination Promotion. In Hashem, T., Albattat, A., Valeri, M., & Sharma, A. (Eds.), *Marketing and Big Data Analytics in Tourism and Events* (pp. 17–37). IGI Global., DOI: 10.4018/979-8-3693-3310-5.ch002

Gaafar, H. A., & Al-Romeedy, B. S. (2024b). Data Fusion for Destination Success: Exploring the Integration of MKIS and BDA in Marketing Touristic Destinations. In Hashem, T., Albattat, A., Valeri, M., & Sharma, A. (Eds.), *Marketing and Big Data Analytics in Tourism and Events* (pp. 38–60). IGI Global., DOI: 10.4018/979-8-3693-3310-5.ch003

George, R. (2021). *Marketing tourism and hospitality: Concepts and cases*. Springer Nature. DOI: 10.1007/978-3-030-64111-5

Gursoy, D., & Chi, C. G. (2018). *The Routledge handbook of destination marketing*. Routledge. DOI: 10.4324/9781315101163

Hall, C. M. (2014). *Tourism and social marketing*. Routledge. DOI: 10.4324/9780203854259

Hanna, S., Rowley, J., & Keegan, B. (2021). Place and destination branding: A review and conceptual mapping of the domain. *European Management Review*, 18(2), 105–117. DOI: 10.1111/emre.12433

Hodson, J. M. (2021). *Connecting Brand Identity and Consumer-Based Brand Equity for Tourism Destinations*. Springer Fachmedien Wiesbaden. DOI: 10.1007/978-3-658-33057-6

Horner, S., & Swarbrooke, J. (2020). *Consumer behaviour in tourism*. Routledge. DOI: 10.4324/9781003046721

Kozak, M., & Baloglu, S. (2010). *Managing and marketing tourist destinations: Strategies to gain a competitive edge* (Vol. 21). Routledge. DOI: 10.4324/9780203842300

Kozak, M., & Kozak, N. (2015). *Destination marketing: An international perspective*. Routledge. DOI: 10.4324/9781315720050

Macmillan, F. (2020). *Intellectual and cultural property: between market and community*. Routledge. DOI: 10.4324/9780429425844

McCabe, S. (2014). *The Routledge handbook of tourism marketing*. Routledge. DOI: 10.4324/9781315858265

Morgan, N., Pritchard, A., & Pride, R. (2011). *Destination brands: Managing place reputation*. Routledge.

Morrison, A. M. (2013). *Marketing and managing tourism destinations*. Routledge. DOI: 10.4324/9780203081976

Morrison, A. M. (2013). *Marketing and managing tourism destinations*. Routledge. DOI: 10.4324/9780203081976

Otay Demir, F., Yavuz Görkem, Ş., & Rafferty, G. (2022). An inquiry on the potential of computational literary techniques towards successful destination branding and literary tourism. *Current Issues in Tourism*, 25(5), 764–778. DOI: 10.1080/13683500.2021.1887100

Palfrey, J. (2011). *Intellectual property strategy*. Mit Press. DOI: 10.7551/mitpress/9066.001.0001

Pike, S., & Page, S. J. (2014). Destination Marketing Organizations and destination marketing: A narrative analysis of the literature. *Tourism Management*, 41, 202–227. DOI: 10.1016/j.tourman.2013.09.009

Prebensen, N. K., Chen, J. S., & Uysal, M. S. (2018). *Creating experience value in tourism*. Cab International. DOI: 10.1079/9781786395030.0000

Punchihewa, N. S. (2020). Exploring the use of intellectual property tools to promote tourism industry in Sri Lanka: A legal perspective. [JMTR]. *Journal of Management and Tourism Research*, 3, 27–30.

Punchihewa, N. S. (2021). Branding of tourism-related products and services for a competitive advantage in Sri Lanka: An intellectual property perspective. *South Asian Journal of Tourism and Hospitality*, 1(1), 138–157. DOI: 10.4038/sajth.v1i1.31

Rasmi, A. A., Phuoc, J. C., Othman, Z., & Azman, N. (2022). Geographical indication for gastronomy tourism: Maximising intellectual property value and branding. *Academy of Strategic Management Journal*, 21(2), 1–13.

Rathee, R., & Rajain, P. (2022). *Destination marketing: creating memorable tourism experiences*. Apple Academic Press. DOI: 10.1201/9781003282501

Ruiz-Real, J. L., Uribe-Toril, J., & Gázquez-Abad, J. C. (2020). Destination branding: Opportunities and new challenges. *Journal of Destination Marketing & Management*, 17, 100453. DOI: 10.1016/j.jdmm.2020.100453

Sorokina, E., Wang, Y., Fyall, A., Lugosi, P., Torres, E., & Jung, T. (2022). Constructing a smart destination framework: A destination marketing organization perspective. *Journal of Destination Marketing & Management*, 23, 100688. DOI: 10.1016/j.jdmm.2021.100688

Stim, R. (2024). *Patent, copyright & trademark: an intellectual property desk reference*. Nolo.

Tien, N. H., Dung, H. T., & Tien, N. V. (2019). Branding building for Vietnam tourism industry reality and solutions. *International journal of research in marketing management and sales, 1*(2), 63-68.

Ubertazzi, B. (2022). *Intangible cultural heritage, sustainable development and intellectual property: international and European perspectives* (Vol. 18). Springer Nature. DOI: 10.1007/978-3-031-08104-0

Vellas, F. (2016). *The international marketing of travel and tourism: A strategic approach*. Bloomsbury Publishing.

Yang, D. (2021). *Understanding and profiting from intellectual property in international business: Strategies across borders*. Springer Nature. DOI: 10.1007/978-3-030-54034-0

Chapter 7
Synergising Brands:
Licensing and Collaboration Strategies in Tourism

Rajeev Semwal
https://orcid.org/0000-0003-4572-5411
Amity University, Noida, India

Nandita Tripathi
Amity University, Noida, India

Priyanka Tyagi
https://orcid.org/0000-0002-7898-2708
Chandigarh University, India

Amrik Singh
https://orcid.org/0000-0003-3598-8787
Lovely Professional University, Punjab, India

ABSTRACT

Tourism marketing relies more on licensing and collaboration for brand expansion and market penetration. In this chapter, licensing and collaboration in the tourism industry are shown to boost growth and innovation. Tourism brands can expand their reach by licensing their intellectual property to third parties, increasing revenue and brand visibility. Collaboration between businesses, governments, and local communities promotes resource sharing and innovation, improving marketing campaigns and visitor experiences. It discusses the pros and cons of these strategies, including the need for clear agreements, risk management, and partner goal alignment. It also discusses digital licensing, sustainability, and how technology will shape future strategies. Tourism brands can use licensing and collaboration to complement their strengths, create unique offerings, and gain a competitive edge.

DOI: 10.4018/979-8-3693-4171-1.ch007

The chapter explains how these strategies can be used to navigate the changing tourism landscape through case studies and practical insights.

1. INTRODUCTION

Licenses and collaboration are critical components of the tourism industry's marketing landscape, offering unique opportunities for brand expansion and market penetration. Licensing involves the granting of rights to use intellectual property, such as trademarks, logos, or other brand assets, to another entity in exchange for a fee or royalty(Kaushik, 2013). This strategy allows tourism brands to extend their influence, enter new markets, and increase revenue without directly managing all aspects of their operations. On the other hand, collaboration in tourism involves strategic partnerships between various entities, including tourism businesses, local governments, or even cross-industry partners such as technology or entertainment companies(Luongo et al., 2023). These collaborations can lead to joint marketing campaigns, the development of new tourism products, and enhanced visitor experiences, pooling resources and expertise to create synergies that drive innovation and competitiveness.

Intellectual property plays a vital role in tourism marketing by protecting the distinctive elements that define a brand(Dosso & Vezzani, 2020). In a competitive industry where branding and experiences are key differentiators, safeguarding intellectual property is essential for maintaining a brand's uniqueness and reputation. Through licensing, tourism brands can control how their intellectual property is used while benefiting from the expertise and market reach of their licensees. This not only helps in expanding brand visibility but also in reinforcing brand identity and building customer trust. Collaborative efforts often involve shared use of intellectual property, such as in co-branding initiatives or joint promotions, where multiple brands come together to create a stronger market presence. The strategic use of intellectual property in these partnerships ensures that all involved parties benefit from the collective brand equity, leading to more effective and impactful tourism marketing strategies(Huynh et al., 2021).

In today's globalised and increasingly digital world, the importance of licensing and collaboration in tourism cannot be overstated. Licensing offers tourism brands a powerful tool for diversifying their offerings and entering new markets with reduced risk(Azmi et al., 2023). By partnering with local entities through licensing agreements, brands can leverage local market knowledge and operational expertise while maintaining control over their brand image and standards. This approach allows for rapid scaling and market entry, making licensing an essential strategy in the modern tourism landscape. Collaboration, meanwhile, is crucial for innovation and adaptation in a market where consumer preferences are constantly evolving. By working together, tourism businesses can combine their strengths, whether through shared marketing efforts, the co-development of new products, or improving service delivery, ultimately leading to enhanced customer satisfaction and loyalty.

However, while licensing and collaboration offer significant benefits, they also present challenges that tourism brands must navigate carefully. Licensing agreements must be meticulously crafted to avoid issues such as brand dilution, mismanagement, or legal disputes. Ensuring that partners adhere to agreed-upon brand standards is crucial for maintaining the brand's integrity and reputation. Similarly, successful collaborations require clear communication, aligned objectives, and mutual trust between partners. Differences in business cultures, operational practices, or legal environments can create obstacles that need to be addressed through careful planning, well-defined agreements, and ongoing management. Despite these challenges, when executed effectively, licensing and collaboration can provide tourism brands with a competitive edge, increased market presence, and the ability to deliver enhanced experiences to their customers.

This chapter will explore the strategic value of licensing and collaboration in tourism marketing, offering insights into the benefits, challenges, and best practices for leveraging these approaches. By understanding the complexities and opportunities associated with licensing and collaboration, tourism professionals can better navigate the intellectual property landscape and harness these strategies to drive growth and success in the industry.

2. UNDERSTANDING LICENSING IN TOURISM

Licensing in tourism is a strategic approach where a brand grants permission to another entity to use its intellectual property under defined terms(Hernández-Chea et al., 2020). This process is crucial for expanding a brand's presence and revenue streams without direct investment in new markets or products. There are several types of licensing commonly employed in the tourism industry:

Brand Licensing involves allowing another company to use a brand's name, logo, or other identity elements(Erjansola et al., 2021). This type of licensing is often used for marketing purposes or to endorse related tourism products and services. For example, a well-known theme park may license its brand to hotels and merchandise retailers to create themed products and services that attract visitors and enhance brand visibility.

Product Licensing allows a company to produce and sell goods under another brand's name(Farronato et al., 2024). In tourism, this could involve a travel agency licensing a destination's brand to offer exclusive tour packages or a souvenir manufacturer licensing a destination's logo to produce branded merchandise. This type of licensing helps brands reach new markets and generate additional revenue without the complexities of managing production and distribution.

Franchising is another form of licensing where a brand permits an operator to use its business model, including its name, systems, and trademarks(Alon et al., 2021). This model is common among hotel chains and restaurant brands in the tourism sector, allowing them to maintain brand consistency while expanding rapidly through franchisees who adhere to established standards and operational guidelines.

Figure 1. Types of Licensing in Tourism industry

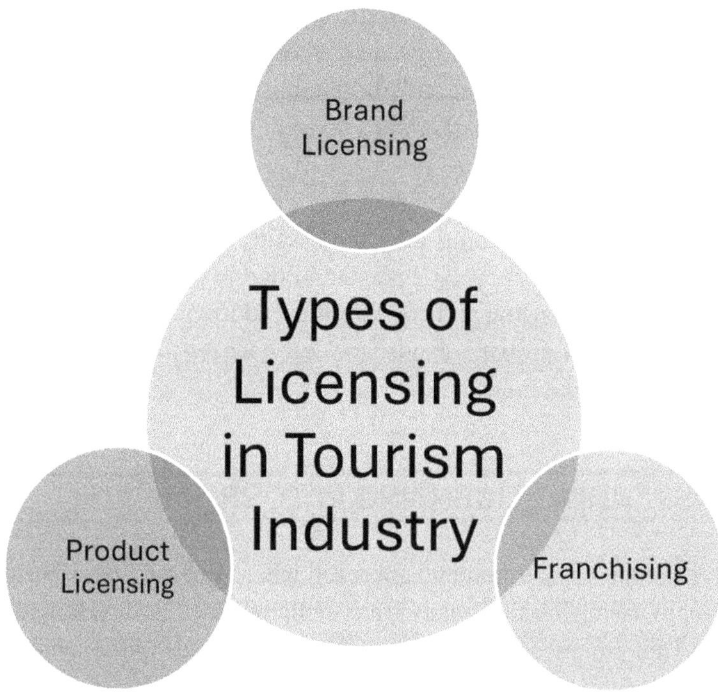

Source: Authors Own Compilation

Each type of licensing offers distinct benefits and opportunities, enabling tourism brands to leverage their intellectual property effectively while achieving broader market reach and enhancing their overall brand presence.

2.1 Benefits of Licensing for Tourism Brands

Licensing offers significant benefits for tourism brands, contributing to their growth and market presence in several key ways.

Expanding Brand Reach and Visibility: Licensing allows tourism brands to extend their influence into new markets and demographics without the need for direct investment(Kyrylov et al., 2020). By granting other entities the rights to use their intellectual property, brands can leverage local expertise and infrastructure to penetrate markets that may otherwise be challenging to access. For example, a global hotel chain can license its brand to local operators in various regions, thus increasing its footprint and visibility. This expansion helps brands tap into new customer bases and enhance their presence in diverse geographical locations.

Generating Additional Revenue Streams: Licensing provides an additional source of income through fees and royalties paid by licensees(Aksoy & Beaudry, 2021). These financial returns can be substantial, especially for well-established brands with strong market appeal. For instance, a tourism destination that licenses its logo for use on merchandise or promotional products can earn royalties while minimising the costs and complexities associated with product development and distribution. This additional revenue stream can support the brand's marketing efforts, fund new initiatives, and contribute to overall profitability.

Enhancing Brand Reputation and Credibility: Licensing can bolster a brand's reputation by associating it with reputable partners and high-quality products or services(Gregorič et al., 2021). When a trusted brand licenses its intellectual property to other businesses, it can enhance its credibility and reinforce its position as an industry leader. For example, a prestigious travel brand that licenses its name to a luxury hotel operator can boost the perceived value and trustworthiness of the hotel. This positive association not only strengthens the brand's image but also builds customer loyalty and confidence.

Overall, licensing enables tourism brands to broaden their reach, generate revenue, and enhance their reputation, making it a valuable strategy for achieving sustained growth and success.

2.2 Challenges and Risk of Licensing

While licensing offers numerous benefits for tourism brands, it also comes with inherent challenges and risks that need careful management.

Brand dilution is a significant risk associated with licensing(Grimm & Wagner, 2022). If a licensee does not adhere to the brand's quality standards or misuses its intellectual property, the brand's reputation can suffer. For example, if a licensed merchandise line does not meet consumer expectations or reflects poorly on the brand, it can diminish the perceived value and integrity of the brand. This dilution can negatively impact customer trust and loyalty, ultimately affecting the brand's market position.

Legal disputes are another potential risk in licensing agreements(Laplane & Mazzucato, 2020). Disagreements over contract terms, intellectual property rights, or the scope of the license can lead to costly and time-consuming legal battles(Gandhi, 2022). Disputes may arise over issues such as unauthorised use of intellectual property, non-compliance with contractual obligations, or breaches of licensing agreements. These legal challenges can strain resources and divert focus from strategic business goals.

To mitigate these risks, several strategies can be employed:

1. **Thorough due diligence:** Before entering into a licensing agreement, brands should carefully vet potential licensees to ensure they have a solid reputation and a track record of compliance(Hinchliffe et al., 2024). This includes assessing their financial stability, operational capabilities, and commitment to upholding brand standards.
2. **Detailed Contracts:** Clear and comprehensive licensing agreements are crucial(Dabbous et al., 2020). These contracts should outline specific terms regarding brand usage, quality control, financial arrangements, and dispute resolution mechanisms. Well-defined terms help prevent misunderstandings and provide a basis for resolving any issues that arise.
3. **Regular Monitoring:** Ongoing oversight and regular evaluations of the licensee's performance can help maintain brand integrity(Meschnig et al., 2023). Implementing quality control measures and conducting periodic audits ensure that the licensee adheres to the brand's standards and contractual obligations.

By addressing these challenges proactively, tourism brands can effectively manage the risks associated with licensing and leverage the strategy for long-term success.

2.3 Successful Licensing in Tourism

One prominent example of successful licensing in tourism is the partnership between Disney and various hospitality brands(Hua et al., 2021). Disney's licensing agreements extend the company's iconic characters and themes to a range of products and services, including hotels, merchandise, and entertainment experiences. A notable case is the licensing of Disney characters and themes to hotels and resorts worldwide, such as the Disney-themed hotels in Orlando and Paris. These partnerships have significantly enhanced the guest experience, driving brand loyalty and increasing visitation to Disney parks. The success of this licensing strategy lies in

Disney's ability to maintain strict quality control and ensure that all licensed products and services align with its brand standards, creating a consistent and immersive experience for customers.

Another successful case is the collaboration between the city of Las Vegas and various entertainment and retail brands(Vargas-Sánchez et al., 2022). Las Vegas has leveraged its brand through licensing agreements with companies to create themed attractions, merchandise, and promotional campaigns. For example, licensing agreements have led to the development of Las Vegas-themed slot machines, casino games, and branded merchandise that capitalise on the city's vibrant image. These agreements not only extend the reach of the Las Vegas brand but also generate additional revenue streams and enhance the city's appeal to visitors.

Lessons Learnt

- **Brand Consistency:** Ensuring that all licensed products and services maintain the brand's quality and image is crucial. Both Disney and Las Vegas demonstrate the importance of strict quality control to preserve brand integrity and customer trust.
- **Strategic Partnerships:** Selecting licensees and partners who align with the brand's values and standards can enhance the effectiveness of licensing agreements. Successful case studies highlight the benefits of partnering with reputable and experienced entities.
- **Innovative Integration:** Leveraging licensing agreements to create unique and immersive experiences can significantly boost brand visibility and customer engagement. Innovation in licensing applications helps to differentiate brands and attract new audiences.

These case studies illustrate the potential of licensing to drive growth and success in tourism by expanding brand reach, enhancing customer experiences, and generating new revenue opportunities.

3. COLLABORATION STRATEGIES IN TOURISM

Collaboration is essential for fostering innovation and promoting growth in the tourism business(Perkins et al., 2021). Collaboration facilitates the exchange of ideas, resources, and expertise among various stakeholders, such as businesses, governments, and community organisations(Eweje et al., 2021). This exchange can result in the creation of new tourism products, improved customer experiences, and more efficient marketing strategies. Strategic alliances play a crucial role in tourist marketing, as they enhance marketing endeavours and expand the reach into untapped areas by collaborating with compatible companies or organisations(Meyer et al., 2022). For instance, a tourism board may form partnerships with airlines, hotels, and tour operators to develop cohesive marketing campaigns that not only draw in tourists but also enhance the promotion of the location in a more efficient manner than any one organisation could accomplish independently. These collaborations not only increase the prominence of the participating companies but also contribute to the development of a unified and captivating storyline that deeply connects with the intended consumers.

Various forms of cooperation exist within the tourist sector, each presenting distinct benefits and difficulties. Public-private partnerships (PPPs) are a prevalent practice in which government entities and private sector enterprises collaborate to construct and advance tourist infrastructure, such as airports, resorts, or cultural attractions(Biygautane et al., 2020). These partnerships may be extremely advantageous since they merge the resources and regulatory assistance of the public sector with the creativity and effectiveness of the commercial sector. Another common type of cooperation is cross-industry collaborations, in which tourist brands join up with enterprises from different industries, such as entertainment, technology, or retail(Klimas et al., 2023). As an illustration, a tourism area may collaborate with a prominent film studio to establish themed attractions or events that attract enthusiasts of the series. These agreements have the potential to broaden the range of tourist options and appeal to a more diverse group of people. Furthermore, partnerships between local and international entities are crucial in the tourist sector, especially in terms of marketing a location to worldwide markets. Local partnerships may entail cooperation between tourist operators and local companies or cultural organisations, while international partnerships may involve coordinated marketing initiatives between distinct nations or regions to allure long-haul travellers.

The advantages of cooperative marketing in the tourist industry are substantial and diverse. One key benefit is the ability to share resources and knowledge, resulting in more streamlined and impactful marketing initiatives. Through the consolidation of their resources, partners that collaborate can attain a larger size and exert a more significant influence than if they were to operate alone. In a highly competitive business such as tourism, it is crucial to make a significant investment and introduce innovative strategies in order to differentiate oneself from the competition in a saturated market(Klimas et al., 2023). Collaborative endeavours also facilitate expanded market penetration and enhanced consumer involvement. Tourism businesses may expand their consumer base and enhance their market position by collaborating with brands or organisations that have similar target demographics. Moreover, forming strategic partnerships may boost brand equity by linking a tourism brand with reputable and long-standing partners. This can result in heightened customer confidence and allegiance, as well as a more robust overall brand perception. When implemented proficiently, collaborative marketing may result in a mutually beneficial outcome for all stakeholders, fostering expansion and triumph in the tourist sector.

Nevertheless, collaborative tourist marketing is not without its obstacles. One of the primary challenges is effectively managing the expectations and objectives of all partners involved (MacDonald et al., 2022). Each participating organisation in a cooperation may own distinct aims, deadlines, and success indicators, which can result in disputes if not effectively handled. Establishing clear communication lines and agreeing on common goals and performance metrics from the beginning is of utmost importance for all parties. Managing cultural and operational disparities is an additional obstacle, especially when engaging in multinational partnerships(Gray et al., 2022). Variations in corporate practices, legal frameworks, and cultural norms might lead to misinterpretations and conflicts, impeding the partnership's success(Zhao & Stiles, 2024). In cross-border partnerships, there might be legal and regulatory problems that need to be addressed, particularly when there are differences in laws and regulations that need to be resolved. These problems need meticulous strategising, resolute guidance, and a readiness to make concessions and adjust in order to guarantee the triumph of cooperation.

Analysing case studies of successful cooperation in the tourist sector may offer significant insights and lessons for professionals in the business. An exemplary instance is the collaboration between Airbnb and the city of Paris, when Airbnb cooperated with local officials to boost the city's appeal as a tourist hotspot while simultaneously tackling regulatory issues pertaining to temporary rentals(Serrano et al., 2020). This partnership not only enhanced the tourist industry in Paris but also established a standard for how internet platforms might collaborate with local governments to create mutually advantageous results. An additional instance is the collaboration between the New Zealand tourist board and the "Lord of the Rings" film series. This relationship entailed the development of specialised tours, attractions, and marketing strategies that took advantage of the movie's immense worldwide appeal. This partnership greatly enhanced New Zealand's reputation as a sought-after tourist destination and yielded major economic advantages for the nation. The key lessons learnt from these case studies include the significance of harmonising the objectives and principles of all collaborators, upholding honest and clear communication, and demonstrating flexibility and adaptability when confronted with obstacles. To achieve enduring success in the tourist business, firms may optimise the potential of collaborative marketing by adhering to these recommended strategies.

4. INTEGRATING LICENSING AND COLLABORATION STRATEGIES

Licensing and collaboration can significantly complement each other, creating synergies that amplify brand impact and market reach(Cozzolino et al., 2021). Licensing allows a brand to extend its intellectual property to third parties, while collaboration involves working directly with partners to achieve shared objectives(Ghamat et al., 2021). Integrating these strategies can enhance their effectiveness. For instance, a tourism brand might collaborate with a travel agency to co-create a new tour package and then license the branded tour to other operators in different regions. This approach leverages the strengths of both strategies: the collaborative effort ensures a well-designed product or service, while licensing extends its reach and generates additional revenue.

To integrate licensing into collaborative marketing efforts effectively, brands should focus on several strategies. Firstly, ensure that collaborative partners understand and agree on how licensing will be applied within the partnership. This includes defining the scope of intellectual property usage and aligning on brand standards. Secondly, establish clear roles and responsibilities in the collaboration to avoid conflicts and ensure that all parties are working towards common goals. Lastly, use licensing agreements to support the collaborative effort by providing access to additional markets or resources, thereby enhancing the overall impact of the joint initiative.

4.1 Developing a Licensing and Collaboration Strategy

Creating an effective licensing and collaboration strategy involves several key steps. Begin by assessing the brand's objectives and identifying areas where licensing and collaboration can add value. This includes determining which intellectual property assets are suitable for licensing and where strategic partnerships could enhance brand goals. Next, identify potential partners and licensees who align with the brand's values and have the capability to contribute effectively to the collaboration.

Negotiating and structuring agreements is crucial for success. Draft detailed contracts that specify terms related to intellectual property usage, quality control, financial arrangements, and the roles and responsibilities of each party. Ensure that the agreements align with the brand's strategic objectives and provide a clear framework for managing the partnership. Effective negotiation involves balancing the interests of all parties while maintaining the integrity of the brand.

4.2 Measuring the Success of Licensing and Collaboration

Evaluating the success of licensing and collaboration efforts requires tracking specific key performance indicators (KPIs)(Housawi et al., 2020). For licensing, important KPIs include revenue generated from licensing fees and royalties, the number of new markets entered, and the impact on brand recognition. For collaborative efforts, measure the effectiveness of joint marketing campaigns, the return on investment (ROI) from shared resources, and customer engagement levels. Additionally, evaluate qualitative factors such as the partnership's strength and alignment with strategic objectives.

Financial performance metrics, such as revenue growth and profitability attributed to licensing and collaboration(Lee, 2021). Customer feedback and market research can also provide insights into the effectiveness of these strategies. To review and adjust the strategies based on performance data to optimise outcomes and ensure that both licensing and collaboration efforts are meeting their intended goals.

4.3 Overcoming Common Pitfalls

Combining licensing and collaboration can present several challenges. Common pitfalls include misalignment between partners on goals and expectations, difficulties in maintaining consistent brand standards, and legal complexities(Parida & Jovanovic, 2022). To overcome these challenges, establish clear communication channels and align expectations from the outset. Ensure that all parties have a mutual understanding of the goals and responsibilities associated with the collaboration and licensing agreements.

Maintaining brand consistency requires rigorous quality control and regular monitoring of licensed products or services(Sardella et al., 2021). Implement robust mechanisms for oversight and compliance to prevent brand dilution. To address legal complexities, invest in comprehensive contracts and legal support to handle intellectual property issues and resolve disputes efficiently. Flexibility and adaptability are also crucial; be prepared to adjust strategies and agreements as needed to address evolving market conditions and partnership dynamics. By proactively managing these challenges, brands can successfully integrate licensing and collaboration strategies, achieving greater impact and sustained growth.

5. FUTURE TRENDS IN LICENSING AND COLLABORATION IN TOURISM

5.1 Emerging Trends in Tourism Licensing

Technology is revolutionising tourism licensing through digital advancements that streamline processes and open new possibilities. Digital licensing allows brands to manage their intellectual property online, making it easier to track, enforce, and monetise licenses. Digital platforms facilitate real-time updates, broad distribution, and more efficient contract management, reducing administrative burdens and expanding market reach. For instance, virtual goods and digital experiences are becoming significant, with brands licensing virtual assets and experiences for use in online environments and gaming platforms.

Sustainability is also becoming a crucial factor in licensing agreements. As consumers increasingly prioritise environmental and social responsibility, brands are incorporating sustainability criteria into their licensing practices. Future licensing agreements are likely to emphasise eco-friendly production processes, ethical sourcing, and support for local communities. This trend reflects a broader industry shift towards sustainability, ensuring that licensed products and services align with the growing demand for responsible tourism practices.

5.2 Evolving Collaboration Models

The tourism industry is seeing a shift towards new forms of collaboration that leverage diverse partnership models. Co-branding involves two or more brands working together to create a unified product or experience that combines their strengths. For example, a destination might partner with a popular lifestyle brand to develop exclusive travel packages or themed experiences that appeal to their shared audiences. Joint ventures are also gaining traction, where companies collaborate to launch new projects or ventures, pooling resources and sharing risks to achieve mutual benefits.

Global trends are influencing tourism collaborations, with an increasing emphasis on cross-border partnerships. These collaborations bring together entities from different countries or regions to create unique offerings and foster cultural exchange. Such international partnerships can enhance a destination's appeal, attract diverse visitors, and stimulate economic growth by tapping into global markets.

5.3 The Role of Innovation in Licensing and Collaboration

Innovation is driving new opportunities in tourism marketing, transforming how brands engage with consumers and create value. Advances in virtual reality (VR) and augmented reality (AR) are enabling brands to offer immersive and interactive experiences that captivate audiences and enhance their travel experiences. For example, VR can provide virtual tours of destinations, while AR can enhance real-world interactions with digital content, creating unique and engaging marketing opportunities.

The future of intellectual property in tourism will increasingly involve integrating these technological innovations. Brands will explore new ways to protect and monetise their digital assets, such as virtual goods and experiences. Innovation in data analytics and artificial intelligence (AI) is also playing a role, offering personalised and targeted marketing strategies that enhance customer engagement and optimise business performance(Bhatt et al., 2024).

Overall, embracing emerging trends and technological advancements will be crucial for tourism brands to stay competitive and capitalise on new opportunities in licensing and collaboration. By leveraging these innovations, brands can enhance their market presence, create compelling experiences, and achieve sustainable growth in an evolving industry landscape.

6. CONCLUSION

The integration of licensing and collaboration strategies in tourism represents a powerful approach for brands aiming to expand their reach, enhance their market presence, and drive innovation. As the tourism industry evolves, these strategies are becoming increasingly critical for achieving sustained growth and success. Licensing offers significant advantages, including the ability to extend a brand's influence into new markets and generate additional revenue streams. By granting third parties the rights to use their intellectual property, brands can leverage local expertise and infrastructure, creating a broader and more diversified market presence. This approach not only boosts brand visibility but also opens up new avenues for income through licensing fees and royalties.

Collaboration, on the other hand, fosters strategic partnerships that enable brands to pool resources, share expertise, and co-create unique offerings. Collaborative efforts can lead to innovative marketing campaigns, enhanced customer experiences, and a stronger competitive edge. Whether through public-private partnerships, cross-industry collaborations, or local and international alliances, working together with other entities allows tourism brands to amplify their impact and reach diverse audiences. The synergy between licensing and collaboration can be particularly powerful, as licensing agreements can support and enhance collaborative marketing efforts, and vice versa.

However, the successful implementation of these strategies requires careful management of potential risks and challenges. Brand dilution, legal disputes, and misalignment of goals can undermine the effectiveness of licensing and collaboration efforts. To mitigate these risks, brands must engage in thorough due diligence, establish clear and comprehensive agreements, and maintain rigorous quality control. Regular monitoring and flexible adaptation are also essential for addressing any issues that arise and ensuring that both licensing and collaboration strategies align with the brand's objectives.

Emerging trends and technological advancements will shape the landscape of licensing and collaboration in tourism in the future. Digital licensing is revolutionising how intellectual property is managed and distributed, while sustainability is becoming a crucial factor in licensing agreements. New forms of collaboration, such as co-branding and joint ventures, are creating innovative opportunities for brands to connect with consumers and enhance their offerings. Technological innovations, including virtual reality (VR) and augmented reality (AR), are driving new marketing possibilities and reshaping the way brands engage with their audiences.

Innovation will continue to play a key role in the evolution of licensing and collaboration strategies. As brands explore new technologies and data-driven approaches, they will have the opportunity to create more immersive and personalized experiences for travelers. The future of intellectual property in tourism will likely involve the integration of these innovations, offering new ways to protect and monetise digital assets while enhancing customer engagement and brand value.

In conclusion, the effective integration of licensing and collaboration strategies offers tourism brands a path to growth, innovation, and competitive advantage. By leveraging these approaches, brands can extend their market reach, enhance their reputation, and create compelling experiences that resonate with today's travelers. Embracing emerging trends and technological advancements will be crucial for navigating the evolving tourism landscape and achieving long-term success. As the industry continues to adapt to changing market conditions and consumer expectations, the strategic use of licensing and collaboration will remain essential for driving progress and maintaining a strong market presence.

REFERENCES

Aksoy, A. Y., & Beaudry, C. (2021). How are companies paying for university research licenses? Empirical evidence from university-firm technology transfer. *The Journal of Technology Transfer*, 46(6), 2051–2121. DOI: 10.1007/s10961-020-09838-x

Alon, I., Apriliyanti, I. D., & Henríquez Parodi, M. C. (2021). A systematic review of international franchising. *Multinational Business Review*, 29(1), 43–69. DOI: 10.1108/MBR-01-2020-0019

Azmi, E., Che Rose, R. A., Awang, A., & Abas, A. (2023). Innovative and Competitive: A Systematic Literature Review on New Tourism Destinations and Products for Tourism Supply. *Sustainability 2023, Vol. 15, Page 1187, 15*(2), 1187. DOI: 10.3390/su15021187

Bhatt, V., Singh, P., Mishra, S., Bhartiya, S., & Tyagi, P. (2024). A Retrospective Analysis of Information Technology in Tourism Research. *African Journal of Hospitality, Tourism and Leisure*, 13(2), 410–420. DOI: 10.46222/ajhtl.19770720.523

Biygautane, M., Clegg, S., & Al-Yahya, K. (2020). Institutional work and infrastructure public–private partnerships (PPPs): The roles of religious symbolic work and power in implementing PPP projects. *Accounting, Auditing & Accountability Journal*, 33(5), 1077–1112. DOI: 10.1108/AAAJ-04-2019-3982

Cozzolino, A., Corbo, L., & Aversa, P. (2021). Digital platform-based ecosystems: The evolution of collaboration and competition between incumbent producers and entrant platforms. *Journal of Business Research*, 126, 385–400. DOI: 10.1016/j.jbusres.2020.12.058

Dabbous, M., Chachoua, L., Caban, A., & Toumi, M. (2020). Managed Entry Agreements: Policy Analysis From the European Perspective. *Value in Health*, 23(4), 425–433. DOI: 10.1016/j.jval.2019.12.008 PMID: 32327159

Dosso, M., & Vezzani, A. (2020). Firm market valuation and intellectual property assets. *Industry and Innovation*, 27(7), 705–729. DOI: 10.1080/13662716.2019.1685374

Erjansola, A. M., Lipponen, J., Vehkalahti, K., Aula, H. M., & Pirttilä-Backman, A. M. (2021). From the brand logo to brand associations and the corporate identity: Visual and identity-based logo associations in a university merger. *Journal of Brand Management*, 28(3), 241–253. DOI: 10.1057/s41262-020-00223-5

Eweje, G., Sajjad, A., Nath, S. D., & Kobayashi, K. (2021). Multi-stakeholder partnerships: A catalyst to achieve sustainable development goals. *Marketing Intelligence & Planning*, 39(2), 186–212. DOI: 10.1108/MIP-04-2020-0135

Farronato, C., Fradkin, A., Larsen, B. J., & Brynjolfsson, E. (2024). Consumer Protection in an Online World: An Analysis of Occupational Licensing. *American Economic Journal. Applied Economics*, 16(3), 549–579. DOI: 10.1257/app.20210716

Gandhi, V. H. (2022). Intellectual Property Disputes and Resolutions. [JIPR]. *Journal of Intellectual Property Rights*, 26(1), 14–19. DOI: 10.56042/jipr.v26i1.39447

Ghamat, S., Pun, H., Critchley, G., & Hou, P. (2021). Using intellectual property agreements in the presence of supplier and third-party copycatting. *European Journal of Operational Research*, 291(2), 680–692. DOI: 10.1016/j.ejor.2020.09.041

Gray, B., Purdy, J., & Ansari, S. (2022). Confronting Power Asymmetries in Partnerships to Address Grand Challenges. *Organization Theory*, 3(2). Advance online publication. DOI: 10.1177/26317877221098765

Gregorič, A., Rabbiosi, L., & Santangelo, G. D. (2021). Diaspora ownership and international technology licensing by emerging market firms. *Journal of International Business Studies*, 52(4), 671–691. DOI: 10.1057/s41267-020-00324-y

Grimm, M. S., & Wagner, R. (2022). Challenging the linearity assumption of intrabrand image confusion. *Journal of Marketing Analytics 2022 12:2, 12*(2), 355–374. DOI: 10.1057/s41270-022-00202-6

Hernández-Chea, R., Vimalnath, P., Bocken, N., Tietze, F., & Eppinger, E. (2020). Integrating Intellectual Property and Sustainable Business Models: The SBM-IP Canvas. *Sustainability 2020, Vol. 12, Page 8871, 12*(21), 8871. DOI: 10.3390/su12218871

Hinchliffe, S., Bard, A., Chan, K. W., Adam, K., Bruce, A., Reyher, K., & Buller, H. (2024). Regulating antimicrobial resistance: Market intermediaries, poultry and the audit lock-in. *Agriculture and Human Values*, 41(2), 801–814. DOI: 10.1007/s10460-023-10525-4

Housawi, A., Amoudi, A. Al, Alsaywid, B., Lytras, M., Moreba, Y. H. B., Abuznadah, W., & Alhaidar, S. A. (2020). Evaluation of Key Performance Indicators (KPIs) for Sustainable Postgraduate Medical Training: An Opportunity for Implementing an Innovative Approach to Advance the Quality of Training Programs at the Saudi Commission for Health Specialties (SCFHS). *Sustainability 2020, Vol. 12, Page 8030, 12*(19), 8030. DOI: 10.3390/su12198030

Hua, Z., Song, H., & Zou, K. (2021). Research on Disney's Possible Expansion Strategy in Asian Market. *Proceedings of the 2021 3rd International Conference on Economic Management and Cultural Industry (ICEMCI 2021), 203*, 2618–2625. DOI: 10.2991/assehr.k.211209.426

Huynh, H. T. N., Trieu, H. D. X., Van Nguyen, P., Tran, T. G., & Lam, L. N. H. (2021). Explicating Brand Equity in the Information Technology Sector in Vietnam. *Administrative Sciences 2021, Vol. 11, Page 128, 11*(4), 128. DOI: 10.3390/admsci11040128

Kaushik, N. (2013). Intellectual Property: Licensing and Franchising. SSRN *Electronic Journal*. https://doi.org/DOI: 10.2139/SSRN.2315960

Klimas, P., Czernek-Marszałek, K., Wójcik, D., & Juszczyk, P. (2023). The Two-Sided Effect of the Sharing Economy and Its Impacts on Inter-organizational Cooperation in the Tourism Sector. *Contributions to Management Science*, 351–383. DOI: 10.1007/978-3-031-18134-4_17

Kyrylov, Y., Hranovska, V., Boiko, V., Kwilinski, A., & Boiko, L. (2020). International Tourism Development in the Context of Increasing Globalization Risks: On the Example of Ukraine's Integration into the Global Tourism Industry. *Journal of Risk and Financial Management 2020, Vol. 13, Page 303, 13*(12), 303. DOI: 10.3390/jrfm13120303

Laplane, A., & Mazzucato, M. (2020). Socializing the risks and rewards of public investments: Economic, policy, and legal issues. *Research Policy*, 49, 100008. DOI: 10.1016/j.repolx.2020.100008

Lee, R. (2021). The Effect of Supply Chain Management Strategy on Operational and Financial Performance. *Sustainability 2021, Vol. 13, Page 5138, 13*(9), 5138. DOI: 10.3390/su13095138

Luongo, S., Sepe, F., & Del Gaudio, G. (2023). Regional innovation systems in tourism: The role of collaboration and competition. *Journal of Open Innovation*, 9(4), 100148. DOI: 10.1016/j.joitmc.2023.100148

MacDonald, A., Clarke, A., & Huang, L. (2022). Multi-stakeholder Partnerships for Sustainability: Designing Decision-Making Processes for Partnership Capacity. *Business and the Ethical Implications of Technology*, 103–120. DOI: 10.1007/978-3-031-18794-0_7

Meschnig, A., Decker-Lange, C., & Dubiel, A. (2023). Burning the candle at both ends: How to balance potential profitability and brand protection when licensing brands. *European Journal of Marketing*, 57(9), 2407–2431. DOI: 10.1108/EJM-01-2021-0016

Meyer, C., Gerlitz, L., & Klein, M. (2022). Creativity as a Key Constituent for Smart Specialization Strategies (S3), What Is in It for Peripheral Regions? Co-creating Sustainable and Resilient Tourism with Cultural and Creative Industries. *Sustainability 2022, Vol. 14, Page 3469, 14*(6), 3469. DOI: 10.3390/su14063469

Parida, V., & Jovanovic, M. (2022). Servitization in global markets: Role alignment in global service networks for advanced service provision. *R & D Management*, 52(3), 577–592. DOI: 10.1111/radm.12505

Perkins, R., Khoo-Lattimore, C., & Arcodia, C. (2021). Collaboration in marketing regional tourism destinations: Constructing a business cluster formation framework through participatory action research. *Journal of Hospitality and Tourism Management*, 46, 347–359. DOI: 10.1016/j.jhtm.2021.01.004

Sardella, M., Belcher, G., Lungu, C., Ignoni, T., Camisa, M., Stenver, D. I., Porcelli, P., D'Antuono, M., Castiglione, N. G., Adams, A., Furlan, G., Grisoni, I., Hall, S., Boga, L., Mancini, V., Ciuca, M., Chonzi, D., Edwards, B., Mangoni, A. A., & Le Louet, H. (2021). Monitoring the manufacturing and quality of medicines: A fundamental task of pharmacovigilance. *Therapeutic Advances in Drug Safety*, 12. Advance online publication. DOI: 10.1177/20420986211038436 PMID: 34394910

Serrano, L., Sianes, A., & Ariza-Montes, A. (2020). Understanding the Implementation of Airbnb in Urban Contexts: Towards a Categorization of European Cities. *Land 2020, Vol. 9, Page 522, 9*(12), 522. DOI: 10.3390/land9120522

Vargas-Sánchez, A., Fotiadis, A., Manuel Alcaraz, J., Castellanos-Verdugo, M., Manuel Hernández-Mogollón, J., Pierre Levy-Mangin, J., Manuel Berbel-Pineda, J., José Martínez-López, F., Riquel-Ligero, F., Miguel Rodríguez-Antón, J., Francesc Valls-Giménez, J., Abbate, T., Aguas, P., Jere Jakulin, T., Morvillo, A., Nigro, C., Allee, J., Chung-chi Wu, S., Jafari, J., & Sheldon, P. (2022). MACAO'S NON-GAMING ENTERTAINMENT, CULTURE AND CITY BRANDING. *ENLIGHTENING TOURISM. A PATHMAKING JOURNAL, 12*(1), 304–336. DOI: 10.33776/et.v12i1.5432

Zhao, X., & Stiles, D. R. (2024). Stuck in Limbo: How sensemaking discrepancy over strategy-related performance leads to disjointed collaboration in an international joint venture. *Asia Pacific Journal of Management*, 41(2), 903–945. DOI: 10.1007/s10490-023-09877-6

Chapter 8
Collaborative Marketing Strategies for Tea Tourism:
Leveraging Local and Global Networks

Shuvasree Banerjee
https://orcid.org/0000-0001-5255-2489
Chandigarh University, India

Pankaj Kumar Tyagi
https://orcid.org/0000-0001-9504-541X
Chandigarh University, India

ABSTRACT

This chapter's purpose is to perform an analysis of the importance of these approaches in order to study the relevance of collaborative marketing strategies in the process of increasing tea tourism through the usage of both local and extended networks. This will be accomplished by conducting an investigation into the significance of these techniques. Because of this, it will be feasible to analyze the relevance of the several solutions that are offered. Integrated marketing programs that connect local tea farmers, tourism boards, and foreign partners are growing increasingly in demand as the need for initiatives of this sort continues to rise. foreign partners are also becoming increasingly important. The level of competition among these programs is gradually growing. In particular, this necessity is becoming an increasingly significant phenomena, particularly in light of the fact that tea tourism is continuing to acquire extra appeal from time to time.

DOI: 10.4018/979-8-3693-4171-1.ch008

1. INTRODUCTION

In an increasingly interconnected world, the dynamics of marketing within tea tourism are being reshaped by both local and global influences. As digital economies expand to even the most remote regions, the potential for tea tourism destinations to tap into new markets and audiences has grown exponentially. Graham (2019) highlights how changing connectivity at global margins is altering economic landscapes, providing opportunities for regions traditionally on the periphery to engage with broader audiences. In this context, tea tourism destinations are well-positioned to leverage these shifts by employing collaborative marketing strategies that bridge local traditions with global networks.

However, these opportunities come with unique challenges, especially for smallholders and SMEs in developing economies. Ho, Quang, and Miles (2022) discuss the concept of "liability of poorness," where limited resources and market access constrain the ability of these entities to compete on a larger scale. By adopting entrepreneurial marketing processes, these small players can overcome such limitations, creating value through strategic collaborations that amplify their reach.

Hudson (2017) emphasizes the importance of a global and digital approach to marketing in the tourism industry, noting that effective strategies must balance global appeal with local authenticity. This balance is crucial in tea tourism, where the cultural and historical significance of tea is central to the visitor experience. Hoppen, Brown, and Fyall (2014) also underscore the role of cultural narratives in destination branding, arguing that successful marketing in niche tourism sectors, like tea tourism, requires a deep understanding of local heritage alongside innovative promotional techniques.

As collaborative marketing strategies evolve, the role of intellectual property (IP) in protecting and enhancing the unique assets of tea tourism destinations becomes increasingly important. Intellectual property, which includes trademarks, copyrights, and geographical indications (GIs), plays a vital role in safeguarding the cultural and commercial value of tea regions (Graham, 2019). For instance, geographical indications like "Darjeeling" or "Ceylon" tea not only protect the reputation of these regions but also ensure that only products genuinely originating from these areas can be marketed under these prestigious names. This protection enhances the brand value of the tea and by extension, the tourism experiences associated with these regions (Chasomeris et al., 2015; Dona & Nelshani, 2023).

Moreover, by effectively managing IP, stakeholders in tea tourism can ensure that the economic benefits are shared fairly among all participants, including small-scale farmers and local communities. This is particularly important in developing economies, where IP can be leveraged to protect traditional knowledge and promote local products in the global market (Ho, Quang, & Miles, 2022).

In the context of collaborative marketing, integrating IP considerations helps to strengthen market positioning and promote sustainable tourism. By protecting the unique attributes of tea tourism destinations—whether it's the name, logo, or even traditional tea-making techniques—stakeholders can create a distinct identity that is not only attractive to tourists but also resilient in the face of competition and market changes (Hudson, 2009; Mtapuri, Giampiccoli, & Jugmohan, 2017). This approach ensures that the cultural and natural heritage of tea regions is preserved and that the benefits of tourism are long-lasting and inclusive.

By weaving together these perspectives, this chapter explores how tea tourism destinations can craft collaborative marketing strategies that leverage both local and global networks. These strategies not only enhance the visibility of tea tourism offerings but also ensure that they resonate with diverse audiences, ultimately driving sustainable growth in this unique sector.

2. SIGNIFICANCE OF THE STUDY

This study on sustainable development through collaborative marketing in tea tourism is significant for several reasons, particularly in its integration of intellectual property (IP) as a crucial component of these efforts. The tea tourism industry is deeply intertwined with cultural heritage, regional identity, and environmental sustainability. As tea-producing regions seek to capitalize on their unique attributes to attract global tourists, the protection and management of these assets through IP become essential.

a. **Protection of Cultural Heritage and Authenticity:** Tea tourism often revolves around the unique cultural practices, traditional knowledge, and regional identities associated with tea production. By integrating intellectual property tools such as geographical indications (GIs), trademarks, and copyrights into marketing strategies, stakeholders can safeguard these cultural elements from misappropriation and exploitation. This not only preserves the authenticity of the tea tourism experience but also enhances the market value of products and services linked to specific regions (Chasomeris et al., 2015). Protecting such assets ensures that the economic benefits derived from these cultural practices are reinvested into the communities that have maintained them for generations.
b. **Economic Empowerment through Brand Equity:** The strategic use of intellectual property in collaborative marketing can significantly enhance the brand equity of tea tourism destinations. For instance, geographical indications like "Darjeeling" or "Assam" tea add considerable value to the product, distinguishing it from generic alternatives and attracting premium prices in the global market

(Dona & Nelshani, 2023). This, in turn, empowers local producers and tourism operators by providing them with a competitive edge that can be leveraged in both domestic and international markets. The study highlights how IP, when managed effectively, can drive economic development and provide sustainable livelihoods for communities involved in tea tourism.

c. **Sustainability and Fair Distribution of Benefits:** The study emphasizes the role of collaborative marketing in promoting sustainability within the tea tourism sector. Intellectual property plays a pivotal role in ensuring that the benefits of tourism are fairly distributed among all stakeholders, including small-scale farmers, local artisans, and community members. By protecting locally produced goods and services, IP helps prevent the commodification of cultural assets and ensures that tourism revenues are channeled back into local development, supporting long-term sustainability (Ho, Quang, & Miles, 2022). This is particularly important in developing economies where the tourism industry can be a significant driver of poverty alleviation and social inclusion.
d. **Innovation and Market Differentiation:** Intellectual property fosters innovation by encouraging tea tourism stakeholders to develop unique products and experiences that are protected from imitation. This innovation is critical for market differentiation, allowing tea tourism destinations to stand out in a competitive global market. By integrating IP into collaborative marketing strategies, destinations can offer exclusive experiences, such as guided tours of protected tea estates or access to trademarked tea ceremonies, that are not available elsewhere. This differentiation attracts tourists seeking authentic and unique experiences, further boosting the destination's appeal and sustainability (Hudson, 2017).
e. **Global Competitiveness and Long-Term Resilience:** Finally, the study highlights the role of intellectual property in enhancing the global competitiveness and resilience of tea tourism destinations. In an increasingly interconnected and digital world, protecting IP is crucial for maintaining control over how a destination's brand is perceived and ensuring that it remains competitive on a global scale (Graham, 2019). By linking IP management with collaborative marketing, the study demonstrates how tea tourism destinations can build strong, resilient brands that are capable of withstanding market fluctuations and adapting to changing consumer preferences.

In summary, the study underscores the importance of integrating intellectual property into collaborative marketing strategies for tea tourism. By doing so, stakeholders can protect cultural heritage, enhance brand equity, promote sustainability, foster innovation, and ensure the fair distribution of economic benefits, ultimately contributing to the long-term success and resilience of tea tourism destinations.

3. OBJECTIVES OF THE STUDY

The study on sustainable development through collaborative marketing in tea tourism, with a focus on intellectual property (IP), aims to achieve the following key objectives:

1. Examine the Role of Collaborative Marketing in Tea Tourism:
    - To analyze how collaborative marketing strategies can enhance the global appeal of tea tourism destinations by leveraging partnerships among tea producers, tourism operators, local communities, and government bodies.
    - To understand the ways in which these strategies can contribute to sustainable tourism practices, benefiting both the local economy and environment.
2. Investigate the Integration of Intellectual Property in Marketing Efforts:
    - To explore how intellectual property tools, such as trademarks, geographical indications (GIs), and copyrights, can be effectively integrated into collaborative marketing strategies to protect and promote the unique cultural and regional assets of tea tourism destinations.
    - To assess the impact of IP protection on the authenticity, brand equity, and competitiveness of tea tourism products and services.
3. Evaluate the Economic and Social Benefits of IP-Driven Collaborative Marketing:
    - To evaluate the extent to which intellectual property-based collaborative marketing strategies contribute to the economic empowerment of local communities involved in tea tourism, particularly small-scale farmers and artisans.
    - To investigate how these strategies can ensure a fair distribution of tourism revenues, fostering social inclusion and community development.
4. Identify Best Practices for Sustainable Tourism Development:
    - To identify and document best practices in the use of collaborative marketing and intellectual property for sustainable tourism development in tea-producing regions.
    - To provide recommendations for stakeholders on how to effectively manage IP and implement collaborative marketing initiatives that support long-term sustainability.
5. Analyze the Challenges and Opportunities of IP in Tea Tourism:
    - To examine the challenges associated with protecting intellectual property in the tea tourism industry, including issues related to enforcement, awareness, and international recognition.

- To explore opportunities for innovation and differentiation through IP protection, and how these can be leveraged to enhance the competitiveness of tea tourism destinations.

6. Propose a Framework for Sustainable Development:
    - To propose a comprehensive framework that integrates collaborative marketing and intellectual property as core components of sustainable development in tea tourism.
    - To outline strategies for stakeholders to collaborate effectively in promoting and protecting tea tourism destinations, ensuring that the industry remains viable, resilient, and equitable in the long term.

These objectives aim to provide a holistic understanding of how collaborative marketing and intellectual property can be harnessed to promote sustainable development in the tea tourism sector, ensuring that it benefits both local communities and global consumers.

4. THEORETICAL FRAMEWORK AND LITERATURE REVIEW

The growing intersection of tea tourism and intellectual property (IP) has emerged as a vital area of focus in the broader field of tourism marketing. As tea-producing regions increasingly turn to tourism as a means of economic diversification and cultural preservation, the role of IP in safeguarding these assets and enhancing market competitiveness becomes more prominent. This literature review examines key themes related to collaborative marketing, sustainable tourism, and the strategic use of intellectual property within the tea tourism industry.

- **Collaborative Marketing in Tea Tourism**

Collaborative marketing, which involves the partnership of multiple stakeholders, is increasingly recognized as a powerful tool for promoting tourism destinations, particularly in niche markets like tea tourism. Hoppen, Brown, and Fyall (2014) highlight the importance of collaborative efforts in developing marketing strategies that promote the cultural and natural assets of a destination. In the context of tea tourism, these collaborations often include tea producers, local communities, tourism operators, and governmental bodies working together to create a unified brand that attracts tourists. Hudson (2017) further underscores the significance of such partnerships in enhancing a destination's visibility and competitiveness on a global scale.

However, while collaborative marketing strategies can effectively promote tea tourism, the integration of intellectual property protection within these efforts is essential for safeguarding the unique attributes of the destination. For example, the use of geographical indications (GIs) in marketing tea from specific regions like Darjeeling or Ceylon adds authenticity and value to the product, distinguishing it from competitors and enhancing the overall brand equity of the destination (Chasomeris et al., 2015).

- **Intellectual Property and Geographical Indications**

Intellectual property, particularly in the form of geographical indications, plays a critical role in the tea tourism sector. Geographical indications protect the reputation and quality of products associated with specific regions, thereby preserving the cultural heritage and authenticity of those areas. Graham (2019) discusses how digital economies at the global margins can benefit from IP protections that enhance connectivity and market access for small producers. In the tea tourism context, GIs not only protect the integrity of the product but also serve as a marketing tool that draws tourists seeking authentic experiences.

For instance, the GI status of "Darjeeling Tea" ensures that only tea produced in the Darjeeling region can be marketed under this prestigious name, thereby safeguarding the region's cultural heritage and providing economic benefits to local producers. Similarly, Dona and Nelshani (2023) highlight how IP protection, particularly through GIs, has been instrumental in promoting the Sri Lankan tea industry in international markets. These protections allow tea producers to command premium prices, thereby supporting the economic sustainability of tea tourism destinations.

- **Economic and Social Impact of IP in Tea Tourism**

The integration of intellectual property into collaborative marketing strategies has significant economic and social implications. Ho, Quang, and Miles (2022) emphasize the role of entrepreneurial marketing processes in supporting smallholders and SMEs in developing economies. In the tea tourism sector, IP protection can empower local communities by providing them with the legal means to protect and monetize their cultural and natural assets. This is particularly important in regions where tea tourism serves as a critical source of income and employment.

Mtapuri, Giampiccoli, and Jugmohan (2017) further explore how marketing community-based tourism ventures can create pathways for local empowerment and economic development. By ensuring that the benefits of tourism are equitably distributed and reinvested into local communities, IP-driven collaborative marketing strategies can foster social inclusion and sustainability. This is especially relevant in the tea tourism sector, where local farmers and artisans play a central role in creating the tourism experience.

- **Challenges in Protecting Intellectual Property in Tea Tourism**

Despite the clear benefits of intellectual property protection in tea tourism, several challenges remain. Jantapoon and Saenchaiyathon (2023) discuss the difficulties faced by tea entrepreneurs in Thailand in protecting their products from imitation and maintaining the authenticity of their offerings. These challenges are often exacerbated by the global nature of the tourism industry, where enforcing IP rights across borders can be complex and resource-intensive.

Furthermore, the lack of awareness and understanding of IP among local stakeholders can hinder the effective implementation of IP protections. As highlighted by Khaokhrueamuang and Chueamchaitrakun (2019), many small-scale tea producers are unaware of the potential benefits of GIs and other forms of IP protection. Addressing these challenges requires targeted education and capacity-building efforts, as well as stronger legal frameworks that support the enforcement of IP rights in the tourism sector.

- **Innovation and Differentiation through IP**

Intellectual property also fosters innovation and differentiation in tea tourism. By protecting unique products, practices, and experiences, IP enables tea tourism destinations to offer exclusive experiences that cannot be replicated elsewhere. For example, Lee et al. (2024) discuss how tea farms in Vietnam have leveraged IP protection to differentiate their agritourism offerings and attract tourists seeking authentic, high-quality experiences. This innovation not only enhances the destination's appeal but also contributes to its long-term sustainability.

O'Grady (2014) further explores how rural tourism businesses can use IP to develop and adopt marketing strategies that differentiate their offerings from competitors. In the tea tourism sector, this differentiation is crucial for standing out in an increasingly competitive global market. By integrating IP into their collaborative marketing efforts, tea tourism destinations can create strong, resilient brands that attract tourists while protecting their cultural and natural assets.

- **Sustainable Development through IP and Collaborative Marketing**

Ultimately, the integration of intellectual property into collaborative marketing strategies supports the sustainable development of tea tourism destinations. Prevolšek, Kukurin, and Golja (2024) propose a model of cooperation between local stakeholders and tourism businesses that emphasizes the importance of IP in creating elevated destination experiences. This approach not only enhances the economic viability of tea tourism but also promotes environmental sustainability and cultural preservation.

By protecting the unique attributes of tea tourism destinations, IP ensures that the benefits of tourism are long-lasting and equitable. Syahban and Marsasi (2024) emphasize that IP-driven marketing programs can also align with broader sustainable development goals, contributing to the resilience and competitiveness of the tea tourism industry in the face of global challenges.

This integrates the concept of intellectual property into the broader discussion of collaborative marketing and sustainable development in the tea tourism industry. By examining the role of IP in protecting cultural assets, enhancing economic opportunities, and promoting innovation, the review highlights the critical importance of IP in ensuring the long-term success and sustainability of tea tourism destinations.

5. CHALLENGES IN THE TEA TOURISM INDUSTRY IN CONNECTION WITH INTELLECTUAL PROPERTY

The tea tourism industry faces several challenges that can hinder its growth and sustainability, particularly when it comes to the integration and protection of intellectual property (IP). These challenges span across issues related to authenticity, market competition, legal frameworks, and stakeholder awareness. Addressing these challenges is crucial for ensuring that tea tourism destinations can effectively leverage their cultural and natural assets, protect their unique offerings, and maintain their competitiveness in the global market.

Protecting Authenticity and Cultural Heritage

One of the significant challenges in tea tourism is the protection of authenticity and cultural heritage. Tea-producing regions often rely on their unique cultural practices and traditional knowledge to attract tourists. However, without proper IP protection, these cultural assets are vulnerable to misappropriation and commodification by third parties. For example, traditional tea-making techniques or ceremonial practices may be copied and commercialized without proper recognition or compensation to the original communities (Chasomeris et al., 2015).

Intellectual property tools such as geographical indications (GIs) can play a crucial role in protecting these cultural assets. However, many tea tourism destinations face challenges in obtaining and enforcing GIs due to limited legal infrastructure and a lack of awareness among local stakeholders. This can lead to the erosion of cultural authenticity, as mass-produced imitations flood the market, diluting the value of the original product.

Market Competition and Brand Dilution

Tea tourism destinations often face intense market competition, both from within the industry and from other forms of tourism. This competition can lead to brand dilution, where the unique identity of a tea region is overshadowed by cheaper, lower-quality imitations. For instance, teas falsely labeled as originating from prestigious regions like Darjeeling or Uji can undermine the reputation of these regions and reduce their appeal to tourists (Dona & Nelshani, 2023).

Intellectual property protection, particularly through trademarks and GIs, can help mitigate this challenge by ensuring that only authentic products from specific regions are marketed under those names. However, enforcing these protections across international borders is often challenging, especially in countries with weak IP laws. This makes it difficult for tea tourism destinations to maintain their brand integrity and protect their market share.

Legal and Regulatory Challenges

The legal and regulatory landscape surrounding intellectual property in the tea tourism industry is complex and varies significantly across different regions. Many tea-producing countries lack robust IP laws or the resources needed to enforce them effectively. This creates a significant challenge for tea tourism stakeholders who seek to protect their products and practices through IP (Ho, Quang, & Miles, 2022).

Moreover, the process of obtaining IP protection, such as GIs or trademarks, can be time-consuming and costly, especially for small-scale tea producers and community-based tourism ventures. These legal hurdles often discourage stakeholders from pursuing IP protection, leaving their cultural and natural assets vulnerable to exploitation.

Limited Awareness and Capacity Among Local Stakeholders

A critical challenge in integrating intellectual property into tea tourism is the limited awareness and capacity among local stakeholders. Many tea producers, especially in developing economies, are not fully aware of the potential benefits of IP protection or the processes involved in obtaining it (Khaokhrueamuang & Chueamchaitrakun, 2019). This lack of knowledge can result in missed opportunities for enhancing the value of their products and protecting their cultural heritage.

Capacity-building efforts are needed to educate local stakeholders about IP and its role in tourism development. Without this knowledge, tea producers and tourism operators may continue to rely on traditional marketing methods that do not fully leverage the potential of IP, thereby limiting their ability to compete in the global market.

Balancing Commercialization with Sustainability

Another challenge in tea tourism is balancing the commercialization of tea-related products and experiences with the need for sustainability. While intellectual property can help protect and promote tea tourism products, there is a risk that over-commercialization could lead to the exploitation of cultural assets and environmental degradation (Mtapuri, Giampiccoli, & Jugmohan, 2017).

For instance, the mass production of goods bearing a geographical indication can strain local resources and disrupt traditional practices, undermining the sustainability of the destination. Therefore, it is crucial to implement IP strategies that not only protect the commercial interests of tea tourism stakeholders but also promote sustainable tourism practices that preserve the cultural and natural heritage of the region.

Adapting to Digital Economies

In today's digital world, tea tourism faces the challenge of adapting to online marketplaces and digital platforms. The rise of e-commerce and digital marketing has created new opportunities for tea tourism destinations to reach global audiences, but it has also increased the risk of IP infringement. Online platforms are often used to sell counterfeit products or unauthorized replicas of traditional tea-related experiences (Graham, 2019).

Addressing these challenges requires a comprehensive approach to IP management that includes digital monitoring and enforcement strategies. Tea tourism stakeholders must be equipped with the tools and knowledge to protect their IP in the digital space, ensuring that their brands and products are not exploited by online counterfeiters.

The challenges faced by the tea tourism industry in protecting and integrating intellectual property are multifaceted and require a coordinated effort among stakeholders. By addressing issues related to authenticity, market competition, legal frameworks, awareness, sustainability, and digital adaptation, tea tourism destinations can better protect their cultural and natural assets, enhance their global competitiveness, and ensure long-term sustainability. Intellectual property, when effectively managed and enforced, can be a powerful tool in overcoming these challenges and promoting the growth and resilience of the tea tourism industry.

6. SUSTAINABLE DEVELOPMENT THROUGH COLLABORATIVE MARKETING

Sustainable development in the tea tourism industry is essential for preserving cultural heritage, supporting local economies, and ensuring environmental stewardship. One of the most effective ways to achieve sustainability is through collaborative marketing, where various stakeholders—such as tea producers, tourism operators, government bodies, and local communities—work together to promote a unified brand and sustainable practices. The integration of intellectual property (IP) into these collaborative efforts further strengthens sustainability by protecting and enhancing the unique attributes of tea tourism destinations.

i. Collaborative Marketing as a Catalyst for Sustainable Development

Collaborative marketing involves creating partnerships among diverse stakeholders to jointly promote a destination or product, combining resources and expertise to achieve shared goals. In the context of tea tourism, this approach can lead to more sustainable outcomes by:

Pooling Resources for Better Marketing Efforts: Collaborative marketing allows smaller tea producers and community-based tourism ventures to pool their resources and compete more effectively in the global market. By working together, stakeholders can create stronger marketing campaigns that highlight the unique cultural and environmental aspects of their destinations (Hoppen, Brown, & Fyall, 2014).

Promoting Sustainable Practices: Collaboration encourages stakeholders to adopt sustainable tourism practices that protect the environment and preserve cultural heritage. For example, eco-friendly tea cultivation methods, responsible waste management, and the promotion of local traditions can be emphasized in marketing campaigns. These efforts contribute to the long-term sustainability of the destination and help attract tourists who prioritize ethical and sustainable travel.

Ensuring Fair Distribution of Benefits: Collaborative marketing can help ensure that the economic benefits of tea tourism are equitably distributed among all stakeholders, including small-scale farmers, artisans, and local communities. By promoting products and experiences that are tied to specific regions, stakeholders can secure higher returns, which supports local development and reduces inequalities (Mtapuri, Giampiccoli, & Jugmohan, 2017).

ii. The Role of Intellectual Property in Enhancing Collaborative Marketing

Intellectual property plays a critical role in enhancing the effectiveness of collaborative marketing in tea tourism. IP protection, particularly through geographical indications (GIs), trademarks, and copyrights, helps safeguard the unique cultural and natural assets that form the foundation of tea tourism destinations. Here's how IP connects with collaborative marketing and sustainable development:

Protecting Authenticity through Geographical Indications (GIs): GIs are a form of IP that protect the names and characteristics of products tied to specific geographic regions. In the tea tourism industry, GIs ensure that only tea produced in certain regions, following specific methods, can use the region's name. This protection not only enhances the brand value of the destination but also preserves the cultural heritage and authenticity of the product. For example, the GI status of "Darjeeling Tea" guarantees that only tea produced in the Darjeeling region can be marketed under this prestigious name, protecting it from counterfeiting and ensuring that the benefits of its reputation are retained within the local community (Chasomeris et al., 2015).

Enhancing Brand Equity and Market Differentiation: Trademarks and GIs allow tea tourism destinations to differentiate themselves in a crowded market. By using IP to protect unique symbols, logos, and regional names, destinations can build strong brands that resonate with consumers seeking authentic and exclusive experiences. This differentiation supports sustainable tourism by attracting high-value visitors who are willing to pay premium prices for genuine products, thereby supporting local economies (Dona & Nelshani, 2023).

Encouraging Innovation and Quality Improvement: IP protection incentivizes stakeholders to invest in quality improvements and innovation. When tea producers know that their unique products are protected, they are more likely to innovate and maintain high standards, knowing that their efforts will not be undermined by imitations. This focus on quality and innovation contributes to the sustainability of tea tourism by ensuring that the destination remains competitive and continues to attract discerning tourists (Lee et al., 2024).

Fostering Long-Term Partnerships: IP protection fosters trust among stakeholders, as it ensures that their contributions are recognized and protected. This trust is essential for building long-term partnerships that are necessary for effective collaborative marketing. For example, when local artisans know that their traditional designs are protected by copyright, they are more likely to collaborate with tourism operators to develop new products and experiences that appeal to tourists while preserving their cultural heritage (Ho, Quang, & Miles, 2022).

While collaborative marketing and IP protection offer significant benefits for sustainable development in tea tourism, several challenges remain. Legal and regulatory hurdles, limited awareness among stakeholders, and the cost of obtaining IP protection can hinder the effectiveness of these strategies (Jantapoon & Saenchaiyathon, 2023). To overcome these challenges, capacity-building initiatives, stronger legal frameworks, and more accessible IP registration processes are needed.

Looking ahead, tea tourism destinations can further enhance sustainability by integrating digital tools into their collaborative marketing efforts. Digital platforms can help protect IP, promote transparency, and engage global audiences in more meaningful ways. By continuing to innovate and collaborate, the tea tourism industry can ensure that it remains a viable and sustainable sector for years to come.

Sustainable development in tea tourism can be significantly enhanced through collaborative marketing and the strategic use of intellectual property. By protecting cultural and natural assets, fostering innovation, and promoting fair economic practices, IP-driven collaborative marketing ensures that tea tourism destinations can thrive in the global market while preserving their unique identities and contributing to the well-being of local communities. As the industry continues to evolve, the integration of IP and collaborative marketing will remain key to achieving long-term sustainability.

7. CASE EXAMPLES OF SUSTAINABLE DEVELOPMENT THROUGH IP-DRIVEN COLLABORATIVE MARKETING

Several tea tourism destinations have successfully integrated IP into their collaborative marketing efforts to promote sustainable development:

To illustrate the impact and potential of sustainable development through collaborative marketing in tea tourism, this section presents several case studies from different regions. These case studies highlight how collaborative efforts among stakeholders can lead to successful outcomes in sustainability, economic growth, and cultural preservation.

I. The Darjeeling Tea Tourism Initiative, India

Background: The Darjeeling tea industry has effectively used its GI status to protect the authenticity of its tea and promote the region as a premier tea tourism destination. Collaborative marketing campaigns that emphasize the unique characteristics of Darjeeling tea, along with responsible tourism practices, have helped preserve the region's cultural and environmental heritage while supporting local economies. Darjeeling, known globally for its premium tea, has leveraged its rich cultural heritage and natural beauty to develop a thriving tea tourism industry. The Darjeeling Tea Tourism Initiative is a collaborative effort involving tea estates, local communities, government agencies, and tourism operators.

Collaborative Marketing Efforts: The initiative focuses on promoting sustainable tourism practices by integrating tea production with cultural and eco-tourism. Marketing campaigns highlight the unique appeal of staying at heritage tea bungalows, participating in tea plucking and processing activities, and exploring the surrounding Himalayan landscape. These efforts are supported by partnerships with international travel agencies and online platforms that target eco-conscious travelers.

Outcomes: The initiative has successfully attracted a global audience, leading to increased tourist footfall and economic benefits for local communities. Moreover, it has contributed to the preservation of Darjeeling's cultural and natural heritage. The collaborative marketing strategy has not only enhanced the region's brand but also promoted sustainable development by encouraging organic farming and conservation efforts across tea estates.

Challenges: Despite its success, the initiative faces challenges related to infrastructure development and ensuring equitable benefits for all stakeholders, particularly small-scale farmers and marginalized communities. Ongoing efforts are needed to address these issues through inclusive and sustainable practices.

II. The Mae Salong Tea Tourism Project, Thailand

Background: Mae Salong, a mountainous region in Northern Thailand, is famous for its Oolong tea. The region has developed a unique tea tourism model that integrates the area's ethnic diversity and natural beauty with sustainable agricultural practices.

Collaborative Marketing Efforts: The Mae Salong Tea Tourism Project is a collaboration between local tea farmers, ethnic minority communities, tourism operators, and government agencies. Marketing strategies emphasize the cultural richness of the region, with tourists invited to experience traditional tea ceremonies, learn about the ethnic Akha and Yunnanese cultures, and explore the picturesque tea terraces. The project also promotes sustainable farming practices, such as organic cultivation, which are highlighted in the marketing materials.

Outcomes: The project has successfully positioned Mae Salong as a key destination for cultural and eco-tourism in Thailand. Collaborative marketing has led to increased international visibility, attracting tourists interested in authentic cultural experiences and sustainable tourism. The economic benefits have been significant, with tea sales and tourism-related income providing livelihoods for local communities.

Challenges: The project faces challenges related to maintaining cultural authenticity while accommodating the growing number of tourists. There is also a need to enhance infrastructure and provide training for local communities to ensure that the benefits of tourism are widely distributed.

III. The Nuwara Eliya Tea Tourism Collaboration, Sri Lanka

Background: Sri Lanka has leveraged the GI of Ceylon Tea to enhance its global brand image and promote tea tourism. Collaborative efforts between the Sri Lankan Tea Board, local producers, and tourism operators have focused on promoting sustainable tea farming practices, which attract eco-conscious tourists and ensure the long-term viability of the industry (Dona & Nelshani, 2023).Nuwara Eliya, often referred to as "Little England" for its colonial-era architecture and cool climate, is a major hub for tea production in Sri Lanka. The region's tea estates have long been a tourist attraction, and recent collaborative efforts have focused on enhancing the sustainability of this tourism sector.

Collaborative Marketing Efforts: The Nuwara Eliya Tea Tourism Collaboration involves partnerships between tea estates, the Sri Lanka Tourism Development Authority, local communities, and international travel agencies. Marketing campaigns emphasize the environmental and social responsibility of the tea industry, with a focus on fair-trade practices, organic tea production, and eco-friendly tourism accommodations. The collaboration also promotes tea-themed tours that include visits to tea factories, heritage sites, and nature reserves.

Outcomes: The collaborative marketing efforts have successfully increased tourist numbers while promoting sustainable development. The initiative has helped preserve the region's natural and cultural heritage, improved the livelihoods of tea workers through fair-trade agreements, and enhanced the global reputation of Sri Lankan tea tourism. The economic impact has been positive, with increased revenue from both tea sales and tourism-related activities.

Challenges: Key challenges include managing the environmental impact of increased tourism and ensuring that all stakeholders, particularly local communities and tea workers, benefit equitably from the industry. The collaboration continues to seek solutions to these challenges, such as implementing more stringent environmental regulations and promoting community-based tourism initiatives.

IV. The Uji Tea Tourism Experience, Japan

Background: Uji, known for its high-quality matcha tea, has used geographical indications and trademarks to protect its tea products and promote tea tourism. The region's collaborative marketing efforts highlight the traditional tea culture, attracting tourists who are interested in authentic Japanese tea ceremonies and practices, thereby supporting cultural preservation and sustainable tourism.Uji, located near Kyoto, is one of Japan's oldest and most famous tea-producing regions, known for its high-quality matcha (powdered green tea). The Uji Tea Tourism Experience is a collaborative effort to promote sustainable tourism while preserving the region's tea heritage.
Collaborative Marketing Efforts: The collaboration involves tea producers, local government, tourism operators, and cultural institutions. Marketing campaigns focus on the historical and cultural significance of Uji tea, offering tourists immersive experiences such as tea ceremonies, visits to traditional tea houses, and tours of tea plantations. The collaboration also promotes the environmental sustainability of Uji tea production, highlighting practices such as organic farming and the use of traditional, low-impact cultivation methods.
Outcomes: The Uji Tea Tourism Experience has successfully attracted both domestic and international tourists, enhancing the region's economy and promoting the cultural heritage of Uji tea. The collaborative marketing efforts have helped Uji maintain its status as a premium tea destination while supporting sustainable agricultural practices. The initiative has also contributed to the preservation of traditional tea-making techniques and the promotion of cultural tourism in the region.
Challenges: The primary challenge faced by the Uji Tea Tourism Experience is balancing the commercialization of tea tourism with the preservation of cultural and environmental integrity. As tourism grows, there is a need to manage the impact on local communities and the environment, ensuring that tourism development remains sustainable and respectful of Uji's heritage.

These case studies demonstrate the effectiveness of collaborative marketing in promoting sustainable development within the tea tourism industry. By working together, stakeholders in different regions have been able to create unique, sustainable tourism experiences that benefit local communities, preserve cultural and natural heritage, and enhance the global reputation of their tea products. However, these case studies also highlight the ongoing challenges that must be addressed to ensure the long-term sustainability of tea tourism.

8. FUTURE IMPLICATIONS OF COLLABORATIVE MARKETING AND INTELLECTUAL PROPERTY IN TEA TOURISM

The future of tea tourism, particularly in the context of collaborative marketing and intellectual property (IP), holds significant potential for both growth and sustainability. As global tourism trends evolve and consumers become increasingly conscious of authenticity, sustainability, and cultural heritage, tea tourism destinations can leverage these shifts to enhance their appeal. However, several future implications must be considered to ensure that the industry can adapt to changing demands while maintaining its unique identity.

i. Increased Importance of Digital Platforms and E-Commerce

As digitalization continues to transform the global economy, tea tourism destinations will need to integrate digital platforms and e-commerce into their marketing strategies. The rise of online marketplaces, social media, and virtual experiences offers new opportunities for tea producers and tourism operators to reach global audiences. However, this also increases the risk of IP infringement, such as the sale of counterfeit products and unauthorized use of trademarks.

To address these challenges, tea tourism stakeholders will need to invest in digital IP protection strategies. This includes monitoring online platforms for potential infringements, engaging in digital marketing campaigns that emphasize the authenticity and uniqueness of their offerings, and utilizing digital tools to enhance the visitor experience. By doing so, tea tourism destinations can capitalize on the growing demand for online experiences while safeguarding their intellectual property.

ii. Growing Demand for Sustainable and Ethical Tourism

The global shift towards sustainable and ethical tourism is expected to continue, with travelers increasingly seeking destinations that prioritize environmental protection, cultural preservation, and social responsibility. Tea tourism destinations that embrace sustainable practices and highlight their commitment to these values will likely attract a growing segment of eco-conscious tourists.

Collaborative marketing efforts that emphasize sustainability, such as promoting organic tea farming, eco-friendly accommodations, and community-based tourism initiatives, will be crucial in meeting this demand. Additionally, IP tools like geographical indications (GIs) can reinforce the authenticity and sustainability of tea products, further enhancing their appeal to ethically-minded consumers.

iii. Strengthening Legal and Regulatory Frameworks

As the importance of intellectual property in tea tourism grows, so too will the need for stronger legal and regulatory frameworks. Governments and industry bodies must work together to create policies that support IP protection, streamline the registration process for geographical indications and trademarks, and enforce IP rights across borders.

In the future, international cooperation on IP issues will become increasingly important, particularly in protecting tea tourism destinations from counterfeiting and brand dilution. Efforts to harmonize IP laws and strengthen enforcement mechanisms will be essential in ensuring that tea tourism destinations can fully benefit from their intellectual property.

iv. Enhancing Stakeholder Awareness and Capacity

For tea tourism to thrive, local stakeholders—including tea producers, artisans, and tourism operators—must be equipped with the knowledge and tools to protect their intellectual property and engage in collaborative marketing. Future efforts should focus on capacity-building initiatives that educate stakeholders about the benefits of IP, the process of obtaining protection, and the role of collaborative marketing in promoting sustainable tourism.

By empowering local communities to take ownership of their intellectual property and participate in marketing efforts, tea tourism destinations can create a more inclusive and resilient industry. This approach will help ensure that the economic benefits of tea tourism are shared equitably and that cultural heritage is preserved for future generations.

v. Innovation and Adaptation in Response to Global Trends

As global tourism trends continue to evolve, tea tourism destinations will need to innovate and adapt to stay competitive. This includes exploring new tourism models, such as experiential tourism, where visitors engage directly with tea cultivation and production processes, or wellness tourism, which integrates tea-related experiences with health and relaxation.

Innovation in product development, marketing strategies, and visitor experiences will be essential in attracting new audiences and meeting the changing expectations of travellers. Intellectual property will play a key role in protecting and promoting these innovations, ensuring that tea tourism destinations can maintain their unique identities while adapting to global trends.

vi. Opportunities for Global Collaboration

The future of tea tourism will also be shaped by opportunities for global collaboration. Cross-border partnerships between tea-producing regions, international tourism organizations, and global brands can create synergies that enhance the visibility and appeal of tea tourism destinations. These collaborations can help promote best practices in sustainable tourism, share knowledge on IP protection, and create joint marketing campaigns that reach broader audiences.

In addition, global collaborations can support the development of new IP frameworks that address the unique needs of tea tourism. For example, international agreements on the protection of geographical indications or new models for collective IP ownership could provide tea tourism destinations with more robust tools for protecting their cultural and natural assets.

The future implications of collaborative marketing and intellectual property in tea tourism are far-reaching, offering both opportunities and challenges. As the industry continues to evolve, tea tourism destinations must embrace digital transformation, sustainability, legal reforms, and innovation to remain competitive and sustainable. By leveraging IP as a tool for protection and promotion, and by fostering collaboration among stakeholders, the tea tourism industry can ensure a vibrant and resilient future that benefits both local communities and global travelers.

9. CONCLUSION

The integration of collaborative marketing and intellectual property (IP) in tea tourism represents a powerful strategy for driving sustainable development and preserving cultural heritage. As tea tourism destinations navigate the complexities of a globalized market, the protection and promotion of their unique assets through IP tools such as geographical indications (GIs) and trademarks become increasingly vital. Collaborative marketing efforts that involve stakeholders across the value chain—from tea producers and tourism operators to local communities and government bodies—can amplify the impact of these IP protections, ensuring that the benefits of tea tourism are distributed equitably and that destinations maintain their authenticity.

The challenges facing the tea tourism industry, such as counterfeiting, brand dilution, and the need for stronger legal frameworks, highlight the importance of ongoing efforts to educate stakeholders, enhance capacity, and innovate in response to global trends. As sustainability and ethical tourism become more prominent, tea tourism destinations must continue to emphasize eco-friendly practices and cultural preservation in their marketing strategies.

Looking ahead, the future of tea tourism will be shaped by digital transformation, international collaboration, and a growing demand for unique, authentic experiences. By leveraging IP and collaborative marketing, tea tourism destinations can secure their place in the global tourism landscape, attract discerning visitors, and contribute to the long-term well-being of their communities. In doing so, they will not only protect their rich heritage but also ensure that tea tourism remains a thriving and sustainable industry for generations to come.

- **Key Takeaways:**

  i. **Enhanced Market Positioning:** Collaborative marketing enables tea tourism destinations to leverage their unique cultural and environmental attributes, enhancing their global competitiveness. By pooling resources and expertise, destinations can create compelling value propositions that attract and retain discerning tourists seeking authentic and sustainable experiences.

  ii. **Commitment to Sustainability:** The focus on sustainability is paramount for the future of tea tourism. Collaborative marketing strategies that emphasize sustainable practices—such as organic farming, water conservation, and fair-trade certification—align with the growing consumer demand for eco-friendly and socially responsible tourism. These efforts not only contribute to the preservation of natural resources but also strengthen the overall sustainability of the tea tourism industry.

  iii. **Economic and Community Benefits:** Collaborative marketing fosters economic growth and community empowerment by ensuring that tourism revenues are equitably distributed and reinvested into local development. By engaging local communities in the tourism development process, stakeholders can build stronger, more resilient economies and enhance social inclusion.

  iv. **Technological Integration:** The integration of technology and innovation is crucial for the future of tea tourism. Collaborative marketing strategies that leverage digital tools and data analytics can improve marketing effectiveness, enhance customer engagement, and streamline operations, providing a competitive edge in an increasingly digital world.

v. **Cultural Preservation:** Maintaining authenticity and cultural heritage is essential for differentiating tea tourism destinations. Collaborative marketing efforts that highlight traditional tea practices and cultural experiences contribute to the preservation of local heritage and provide tourists with genuine, immersive experiences.

vi. **Adaptability to Global Challenges:** The ability to adapt to global challenges—such as climate change, economic shifts, and evolving consumer preferences—is vital for the long-term success of tea tourism. Collaborative marketing fosters resilience by enabling stakeholders to develop adaptive strategies and communicate their efforts effectively to a global audience.

The chapter illustrates that collaborative marketing is not just a tool for promoting tea tourism but a fundamental approach for achieving sustainable development. The future of tea tourism will be shaped by these collaborative efforts, driving progress toward a more sustainable and inclusive industry that celebrates the rich heritage of tea while addressing the pressing challenges of our time.

REFERENCES

Chasomeris, M., Munapo, E., Khumalo, T., & Adeyeye, O. (2015). The South African tea industry: challenges and business strategies. *Environmental economics*, (6, Iss. 4 (contin.), 133-142.

Dona, S. A., & Nelshani, S. (2023). Implementation of Export Business Strategy for Internationalization Entrepreneurial Startups to achieve Competitive Advantage in an Emerging Economy.: Evidence from Sri Lankan SMEs Textile and Tea Industry.

Graham, M. (2019). Changing connectivity and digital economies at global margins. *Digital economies at global margins*, 1-18.

Ho, K. L. P., Quang, H. T., & Miles, M. P. (2022). Leveraging entrepreneurial marketing processes to ameliorate the liability of poorness: The case of smallholders and SMEs in developing economies. *Journal of Innovation & Knowledge*, 7(4), 100232. DOI: 10.1016/j.jik.2022.100232

Hoppen, A., Brown, L., & Fyall, A. (2014). Literary tourism: Opportunities and challenges for the marketing and branding of destinations? *Journal of Destination Marketing & Management*, 3(1), 37–47. DOI: 10.1016/j.jdmm.2013.12.009

Hudson, S. (2009). Tourism and hospitality marketing: A global perspective. *Sage (Atlanta, Ga.)*.

Hudson, S. (2017). Marketing for tourism, hospitality & events: a global & digital approach.

Jantapoon, K., & Saenchaiyathon, K. (2023). Supply chain strategy under VUCA world for Sustainable of the Tea Entrepreneur in Thailand. In *E3S Web of Conferences* (Vol. 440, p. 06006). EDP Sciences. DOI: 10.1051/e3sconf/202344006006

Khaokhrueamuang, A. (2020). International exchange in tea tourism: reconceptualizing Japanese green tourism for sustainable farming communities. In *Tourism Development in Japan* (pp. 140–159). Routledge. DOI: 10.4324/9780429273513-8

Khaokhrueamuang, A., & Chueamchaitrakun, P. (2019). Tea cultural commodification in sustainable tourism: perspectives from Thai and Japanese farmer exchange. *Special Issue of Rajabhat Chiang Mai Research Journal*, 104-117.

Lee, K., Nguyen, A. T., Nguyen, N. P., Nguyen, T. H., Tran, N., Nguyen, T. L., ... & Vu, T. T. (2024). Determinants of agritourism development in green tea farms of the northern mountains of Vietnam: A hybrid approach based on the combination of diffusion of Innovation (DOI) theory and PLS-SEM. *Multidisciplinary Science Journal, 6*(4).

Mingjing, Q. (2023). Barriers and opportunities for women in tea tourism: A qualitative examination of policy context in Yaoqu township, China. *Jurnalul Practicilor Comunitare Pozitive*, 23(3), 67–82.

Mtapuri, O., Giampiccoli, A., & Jugmohan, S. (2017). Marketing community-based tourism ventures: Pathways in a marketing route model. *Journal for New Generation Sciences*, 15(1), 385–401.

Ngo, T., Hales, R., & Lohmann, G. (2019). Collaborative marketing for the sustainable development of community-based tourism enterprises: A reconciliation of diverse perspectives. *Current Issues in Tourism*, 22(18), 2266–2283. DOI: 10.1080/13683500.2018.1446919

O'Grady, D. (2014). Marketing rural tourism-an analysis of the development and adoption of marketing strategies by small, family owned, peripheral, rural-tourism businesses.

Prevolšek, D., Kukurin, Ž., & Golja, T. (2024). Collaborative Synergies for Elevated Destination Experiences: A Model of Cooperation between Hotel Companies, DMOs, and Local Stakeholders. *Organizacija*, 57(1), 20–38. DOI: 10.2478/orga-2024-0002

Sheth, J. N., Sinha, M., & Shah, R. (2016). *Breakout strategies for emerging markets: Business and marketing tactics for achieving growth.* FT Press.

Simkhada, S., Kattel, R. R., Dhakal, S. C., & Koirala, A. (2020). Determinants of Organic Tea Cultivation and Selection of Efficient Marketing Channels by the Orthodox Tea Growers in Nepal. *Journal of the Institute of Agriculture and Animal Science*, •••, 31–40. DOI: 10.3126/jiaas.v36i1.48380

Syahban, K. R., & Marsasi, E. G. (2024). Implementation of Integrated Marketing Communication Based on Purchase Intention in The Artisan Tea Marketing Program. *Jurnal Manajemen Bisnis, 11*(1), 01-13.

Tan, C. C., & Sitikarn, B. (2018). *Coffee-and-Tea based and Social Entrepreneurship-Oriented Community-based Tourism (CBT) in Northern Thailand: Contributing towards a Theory*. International Multidisciplinary Research Foundation.

Chapter 9
The Role of Trademarks in Tourism:
A Study With Special Reference to Non-Traditional Marks

Karun Sanjaya
VIT School of Law, Vellore Institute of Technology, Chennai, India & Symbiosis Law School, Nagpur, India

P. R. L. Rajavenkatesan
VIT School of Law, Vellore Institute of Technology, Chennai, India

ABSTRACT

Trademarks are vital elements of tourism that empower the industry by enabling destination differentiation, branding, and identification. This chapter evaluates trademarks' influence on tourism while focusing on the current non-traditional trademarks trend. In the tourism context, non-traditional trademarks comprise sensory features that create emotions, memories, and sensory experiences. This chapter examines how trademarks shape tourists' perceptions and decisions and improve their experiences. This research also studies how traditional trademarks, such as logos and slogans, have diversified to incorporate non-traditional features as sensory experiences and marketing gain popularity. This chapter will further investigate the legal and organizational implications of non-traditional trademarks. This chapter concludes by discussing the possibilities and risks associated with non-traditional trademarks in promoting or maintaining sustainable destination development and cultural signifiers.

DOI: 10.4018/979-8-3693-4171-1.ch009

1. INTRODUCTION

In the context of tourism, trademarks are essential elements for distinguishing and identifying destinations, products, and services in the industry (Usakli & Baloglu, 2011). According to the United States Patent and Trademark Office (USPTO) (2021), a trademark is defined as any word, name, symbol, or device used to identify and distinguish goods or services. It includes sounds, scents, colours, and unique shapes used to identify goods or services (USPTO, 2021). In tourism, the dynamics of operations have identified unique roles for trademarks beyond traditional identification. They include creating brand awareness, enforcing marketing strategies, and ensuring a competitive market for different destinations. They are crucial in destination branding since they encapsulate the destination's central values and unique selling features. Trademark registration is essential in destination branding since it helps potential tourists identify with a particular destination. They are essential in establishing the destination's quality, history, and overall commitment. They are powerful marketing assets promoting a shared commitment towards a brighter future.

Trademarks are central in destination branding since they suggest the essence, experience, and values linked with the place (Morgan et al, 2003). Munar and Jacobsen (2014) indicated that the establishment of an official trademark influences how the destination will appear in people's choices. Good trademarks are helping travellers make faster travel decisions. Morgan, Pritchard, and Piggott (2003) added that a trademark is an effective marketing tool when strategically based on memory or learning. A destination trademark should evoke a desire to go on a fantastic adventure before people even know where that place is. Along with other symbols, it builds a visual language that reflects the complexity and dynamism of the location. According to Munar and Jacobsen (2014), a trademark is the key accelerator for tourist decisions. Moreover, a well-thought trademark facilitates expert guides who enhance tourist marketing. A trademark becomes the basis for banners, advertisements, and stationery.

Non-traditional trademarks are a rapidly growing and developing domain of trademark law and practice, integrating several unconventional components, such as sounds, scents, colors, shapes, and even motions (World Intellectual Property Organization, 2017) . While traditional trademarks mostly manifest in words and logos, non-traditional ones rely on sensory experiences to position a product or service in a unique way (Klink, 2000). In tourism, non-traditional trademarks are a unique opportunity for a destination to create an unforgettable and engaging experience that will leave visitors with strong emotional links to the place (Adeyinka-Ojo et al., 2014). Therefore, for destination marketers, policymakers, and industry professionals, it is crucial to have a deep understanding of the role of non-traditional trademarks in tourism.

2. TRADEMARKS IN TOURISM

In tourism, trademarks constitute unique signs, symbols, or expressions used by businesses and destinations to differentiate their products and services from competitors (Hosany et al., 2006). The USPTO (2021) defined trademarks as symbols, devices, names, combinations of words, and any other identifiers which act as source indicators. In addition to enabling consumer recognition, trademarks are also used to strengthen brand loyalty and protect intellectual property rights (Morgan et al., 2003). Generally, by effectively outside trademarks, tourism businesses and destinations develop recognizable market images and establish reputations based on consumer-perceived trust and unique identifiability.

Within the tourism industry, trademarks have been altered as the change of consumers havior, technological capabilities, and legal regulations occurred. Traditionally, tourism trademarks in visual form of logos, emblems, insignias, were mostly employed by hotels, airlines, and travel agencies such as insignias on airplanes and hotel names (Munar & Jacobsen, 2014). Today, the traditional visual representations are expanding their nature into non-traditional and sensory-intensive indicators, such as, for example, smells and sounds. These indicators are capable of getting consumers to experience emotions and, as a result, increase the level of emotional connection to consumers (Klink, 2000). Additionally, with the rapid development of digital technologies, trademarks get easy access to the public, making it an online trend.

Trademarks also have a profound impact on the perception and decision-making of tourists. By being a visual trigger, they are also a source of information as they tell about attributes, quality, and authenticity of a destination (Morgan et al., 2003). According to recent studies, tourists use such trademarks as indicators of one's reputation and trustworthiness when choosing a destination or using tourism services (Munar & Jacobsen, 2014). Furthermore, trademarks also affect the image of destinations and brand associations and therefore the expectation and experience of tourists at a certain destination (Adeyinka-Ojo et al., 2014). Destination marketers can use knowledge about the influence of trademarks on tourist behavior to design effective branding strategies that would be appealing to target audiences and competitive enough.

3. MEANING AND CONCEPT OF NON-TRADITIONAL TRADEMARKS

Non-traditional trademarks are a group of different elements of intellectual property that extend from the standard understanding of just words or logos. Instead, non-traditional trademarks include some sensory elements such as sounds, scents, colours, shapes, and even motions, which help in distinguishing one's goods or services from the ones of competitors (World Intellectual Property Organization, 2017). This type of trademark employs multiple senses instead of vision, which is used in the case of standard trademarks, and is becoming increasingly popular (Adeyinka-Ojo et al., 2014).

Non-traditional trademark types of sounds, scents, colours, shapes, etc. Non-traditional trademarks come in many forms and can be anything that produces a unique sensory experience. For instance: 1. Sounds – intellectual property in a form of ringing emanating from a mobile device, for example, the Nokia ringtone. Scents, including the aromas or fragrances that create a unique feel associated with a product or service provision, like the smell of fresh bread in a bakery. Colours, specific colour combinations or schemes that brands utilize as brand signifiers, like red and white as Coca-Cola colours. Shapes, product designs or packaging configurations that are easily replicable and instantly recognizable, like the Coca-Cola bottle. Motions, dynamic or animated movements that are associated with a brand or product, such as MGM lion. Each type of non-traditional trademark has its own advantages and can be very beneficial for branding and differentiation of a brand or destination owing to enhancing the sensory experience.

Non-traditional trademarks must be distinctive and recognizable or easily identified to be eligible for trademark registration and protection. Distinctiveness signifies the ability of a mark to distinguish its origin or source from others or create a uniqueness element for it. Recognizability means that it is easily deducible for the end consumers to whom it belongs. For non-traditional trademarks, distinctiveness and recognizability are also necessary rooms to allow a mark to be registered and protectable (Calboli, 2018). Non-traditional marks that are well recognized and distinctive demonstrate the optimal capability of conveying the intended brand symbol and message to customers. Nevertheless, it is particularly difficult for some sensory non-traditional marks to establish distinctiveness on their own, mainly due in part to the likelihood of scent and sounds not being notably unique on their own authority. Thus, marks linked to these sensory elements often face greater requirements to demonstrate acquired distinctiveness (Gangjee, 2010).

4. NON-TRADITIONAL TRADEMARKS' IMPORTANCE IN TOURISM

Besides, non-traditional trademarks support differentiate many destinations that are otherwise indistinguishable from each other and define a distinct destination claim in the over-saturated tourism marketplace (Indulia, 2022). They evoke experiences and emotions through the effective use of the senses – sound, scent, color, or shape

– that could enhance a sense of visitor remembrance (Thakkar, 2023). Such things could be a special sound of a regional music implement, a unique aroma from a specific dish, etc. Consequently, non-traditional trademarks are an essential basis for discouraging competition, cultivating the brand image of destinations and their value, tradition, and history, sensations of meaningfulness, and tourist satisfaction (Kurup & Pradeep, 2020).

The Contribution of Sensory Branding to Visitor Experience Sensory branding that is enabled by the non-traditional trademark contributes to the visitor experiences of multiple sensations and establishes an immersive atmosphere to provoke and evoke feelings and remembrances (Shahid et al., 2022). It uses different aspects like sound, scent, or colour to develop responses that produce moods, activate recall, and stimulate a sense of place. For example, sounds of ocean waves or the scent of tropical blossoms fosters of relaxation and serenity state. Therefore, the foundations of sensory branding in tourism are such devices innovating holy feelings and visitor challenges, which also may raise loyalty (Sarıbaş & DEMİR, 2022).

Today, destinations are operating in fiercely competitive and overcrowded tourism markets. Against this backdrop, non-traditional trademarks serve as a unique opportunity to differentiate themselves and capture the market's attention (Lukose, 2015). By fostering sensory experiences and branding, a destination can create a unique experience for a targeted market segment (Hudson & Ritchie, 2009). For example, a destination known for distinct use of graffiti and murals on the streets can use murals not only as a facade but also as a non-traditional trademark that would appeal to visually oriented and artistically inclined travellers. In contrast to traditional forms of trademarks, non-traditional ones provide a mechanism of portraying a destination as innovative and on trend, allowing a destination to remain relevant within its targeted markets. Indeed, non-traditional trademarks offer a "critical core of differentiation in the global market" for a destination (Ruiz-Real et al., 2020).

5. CASE STUDIES: APPLICABILITY OF THE CONCEPT OF NON-TRADITIONAL TRADEMARKS TO TOURISM

5.1 *Sonic branding: Destination Soundscapes*

A classic example of sonic branding is that of the NYC Subway Chimes. New York is widely associated with a fast-paced lifestyle and its subway system. The sounds of the closing door chimes at the subway entrances have become an integral part of the NYC experience, and the cities energy and buzz were captured through this chime (Haigney et al., 2021). People are instantly taken to the streets of New York and a feeling of anticipation and excitement when hearing it. Thus, NYC, as seen through its subway chime, has developed a powerful audible trademark that attracts and retains tourists in promoting its dynamic and lively character.

5.2 *Olfactory Branding: Utilizing Scents to Evoke Memories and Emotions*

Olfactory branding involves applying unique scents to the cabin atmosphere and making the scent a remarkable experience. Singapore Airline's signature cabin fragrance stands out as an apt example of olfactory branding. Singapore Airlines is well known for its excellent service and attention to detail. By collaborating with well-known designers, Singapore Airlines created its scent and puffed it gently around its planes. The smells are both delicate and expensive, and they give the planes a feeling of relaxation and opulence. This concept contributes to smooth integration, comfort and an overall better experience for passengers. This olfactory branding plays a significant role in the differentiation of services offered by competing airlines (Heracleous & Wirtz, 2010).

Another example of olfactory branding is the practice of Westin Hotels & Resorts' use of a signature scent, White Tea, throughout its hotel lobbies globally. Specifically, the fragrance mixes fresh and calming ingredients to foster a serene and warm ambiance for guests on arrival. As such, the odor produced by White Tea can help travelers, weary from a long voyage or a hectic day of travel, to relax. Since the aroma is sprayed in all of Westin's properties, the hotel chain can ensure that guests, whether first time or loyal, receive the same optimal experience in all of them (Nast, 2019).

5.3 *Visual Trademarks: Iconic Landmarks and Colour Associations*

The Eiffel Tower stands as an enduring symbol of romance, elegance, and French culture. Its distinctive silhouette and wrought-iron lattice design have made it one of the most recognizable landmarks in the world. Beyond its architectural significance, the Eiffel Tower is also associated with a specific colour palette, characterized by shades of brown and beige. This visual trademark reinforces Paris's identity as a timeless and sophisticated destination, attracting millions of tourists each year who seek to experience the city's charm and allure (Holter, 2024). The Eiffel Tower's iconic status and visual appeal have cemented its place as a hallmark of Parisian culture and a symbol of French pride.

5.4 *Experiential Trademarks: Interactive Installations and Performances*

Iceland's stunning scenery and incredible natural phenomena, such as the enchanting Northern Lights, draw visitors from across the world, seeking unique and unforgettable experiences. In an effort to amplify the experience of observing the Northern Lights, Icelandic tour operators are integrating the viewing of the spectacle with interactive installations and performances. For example, people can enjoy colorful light shows, music presentations, and storytelling sessions while observing the lights dance across the night sky (Thaler, 2022). Such experiential hallmarks serve both to entertain and enlighten guests as well as to create memories that they will remember for a lifetime. Through such unique experiences, Iceland has solidified its reputation as one of the top destinations for both the Northern Lights and adventure seekers.

6. LEGAL AND REGULATORY CONSIDERATIONS

6.1 Trademark Registration Requirements for Non-traditional Marks

Registration requirements for non-traditional trademarks are quite challenging because they differ significantly from traditional marks. While traditional marks, such as words and logos, are relatively easy to register due to their nature, non-traditional marks, such as sounds, scents, or colours, may be more complicated due to the need for additional evidence of uniqueness and labelling (Mishra, 2008). Trademarks must identify and delineate one enterprise's products and services from others while avoiding being too generic or simple. Moreover, applicants may be required to present testimony that a non-traditional mark has become distinct because they have been extensively used and advertised within commercial marketplaces. These processes can be extremely challenging and may require the use of specialist expertise to achieve full protection (Mishra, 2008).

Protecting and enforcing non-traditional trademarks are challenging due to their intangible and sensory nature. While traditional marks are easily recognizable, non-traditional marks can easily be mimicked, and often, it is hard to determine the same (Mishra, 2008). For example, it is not easy to determine when an unauthorized body uses a sound or a smell to imitate a trademark. In addition, sensory experiences are more ubiquitous now, mediated by technology in digital and virtual environments, which makes it difficult to distinguish. International borders also pose a challenge due to different countries having different legal and enforcement standards. Therefore, one possible solution is for the trademark owners to be proactive in their enforcement efforts. This includes monitoring their marks and identifying when they are infringed upon. This then could result in the awarding of compensation for damages and legal enforcement. Additionally, educating consumers and other actors is an alternative solution that can be undertaken to ensure that the marks are protected.

6.2 *International Perspectives on Trademark Protection in Tourism*

Trademark protection emanates from national laws and international treaties such as the Paris Convention for the Protection of Industrial Property, 1883 and the Agreement on Trade-Related Aspects of Intellectual Property Rights, 1994. While the international legal system provides a foundation for the protection of the mark, there has always been a disparity in national enforcement and cultural beliefs for intellectual property rights. The international legal system may provide a robust legal framework for the protection of non-traditional marks, but the same may not be applicable to all nations (Jain, 1996). The same is because the international agreements and conventions pertaining to Intellectual Property often give what we commonly call as "flexibilities" to the member states. The member state may be at liberty to either follow a particular obligation or not to follow it, or they may have the liberty as to the method of implementation of an obligation or so. Though these flexibilities adversely affect the harmonization of intellectual property regulations at the global level, they are much needed keeping in mind the diversified socio-economic and cultural surroundings of every state.

7. NON-TRADITIONAL TRADEMARKS FOR DESTINATION DEVELOPMENT

7.1 *Collaborative Branding Strategies*

One of the best ways to use non-traditional trademarks for destination development is to promote collaborative branding among the stakeholders. Branding initiatives between destination management organizations, businesses, and local communities help develop integrated campaigns to promote intellectual capital and create unique sensory experiences (Acheampong, 2020). For example, tourism boards and local artisans can partner up to develop a product that emphasizes cultural identity and provides an enhanced visitor experience. Collaborative branding initiatives keep stakeholders engaged and excited about promoting their regions and make them more competitive in the global tourism marketplace (Acheampong, 2020).

Non-traditional trademarks also promote sustainable tourism and preserve cultural heritage (World Intellectual Property Organization & World Tourism Organization, 2021). Tourism stakeholders can promote authentic experiences and visitor responsibility by appealing to their senses. For example, responsible tour operators can use smells and sounds associated with the natural world to arouse responsible tourism attitudes . Additionally, the IP can serve as a symbol of pride and conscious cultural identification that helps preserve practice and knowledge for future generations (World Intellectual Property Organization & World Tourism Organization, 2021). By enhancing sustainable tourism initiatives, tourism stakeholders attract a new type of visitor who is committed to supporting socially conscious operations.

7.2 *Technological Innovations and Digital Experiences in Trademark Promotion*

Advancements in technology, such as AR, VR, and interactive multimedia, present new opportunities for promoting non-traditional trademarks and enhancing visitor experiences. Digital platforms and immersive technologies allow destination marketers to provide interactive and engaging brand experiences that defy the limitations of time and space (Aras, 2023). For example, through AR applications, destination marketers can add virtual scents and sounds to physical environments, allowing visitors to experience multisensory explorations of destination attractions . Similarly, with VR simulations and 360-degree videos on social media, viewers can be virtually transported to destinations across the world and experience a sensory view of their attractions. Technological innovation has allowed destinations to use digital storytelling to capture the imagination of audiences, attract more people, and develop deeper emotional connections with people in an increasingly digital world (Robin, 2016).

8. RECENT DEVELOPMENTS

8.1 *Emerging Trends in Non-traditional Trademark Development and Utilization*

The future of non-traditional trademarks in tourism will be influenced by emerging trends such as experiential branding, sensory personalization, and interactive technologies. The rising and falling consumer preferences will drive destinations and other tourism players to create experiences that reflect the senses and the individual preference for them (Balaji, 2024). Further, the rising data analytics and AI capabilities will support targeted sensory branding initiatives that promote tailored experiences and experiences among different kinds of tourists. Similarly, the upcoming integration of non-traditional trademarks into coming digital platforms and virtual environments will create many chances for tourists to engage in platforms and explore new opportunities. Knowing and embracing any of these developments will provide the necessary insight and capability to establish and use temporary trademarks, thereby assisting stakeholders in the sector to succeed (Haleem et al., 2022).

Technology and globalization are likely to impact trademark strategies dramatically in tourism. They are likely to change how destinations brand themselves and interact with visitors . For example, the proliferation of digital platforms, social media, and online marketplaces has made information more accessible and enabled consumers to participate more actively in the definition of the destination brand (Yılmaz & Tekeli, 2021). Accordingly, destinations would have to develop versatile and responsive trademark strategies that will use tech to amplify messages and auto-reform in line with the values of the target clients (Chakraborty & Jain, 2022). Similarly, globalization has allowed the collaboration of cultures and people, leading to diversity in trademark creation. As businesses operate in a global market, tourism stakeholders need to ensure that they remain authentic while leveraging innovations from around the world.

8.2 *Recommendations for maximizing the effectiveness of trademarks in tourism*

Stakeholders can maximize the effectiveness of trademarks in tourism by adopting an integrated approach that merges branding, marketing, and the experience design. Recommended steps include:

1. Intensive market research on the target market to understand preference, persuasion, and behaviour.
2. Creation of an unforgettable and stylish non-traditional trademarks that draw the audience and uphold the values and identity.
3. Deploy an integrated brand strategy by designing a strikingly recognizable logo for forging a unique and consistent identity at every contact possibles.
4. Launch experiential branding through designing complete visitor experience to stimulate sense to narrate the brand.
5. Engaging with tourism stakeholders, local communities, and government agencies to ensure collaborative and consistent branding approaches. 6. Using digital and technological tools to amplify brand messages, engage new audiences, and monitor the outcomes of branding efforts. Adhering to the recommendations

and suggestions outlined in the chapter will enable tourism stakeholders to improve their brand positioning, create more inviting experiences for visitors, and successfully compete in the global tourism marketplace.

9. CONCLUSION AND RECOMMENDATIONS

This subsection concludes the chapter by putting forth its findings and results. The areas explored in this chapter include the definition and application of trademarks with a focus on non-traditional examples and their importance for destination branding and experience production. The study also covered the types of non-traditional marks within the realm of tourism, discussed prominent case examples, reviewed relevant legal considerations, and provided perspectives on the future evolution of trademarks. The chapter is intended to aid practitioners understand the role of trademarks and develop informed branding strategies that can improve destination experiences and competitiveness. Policymakers will appreciate legislative perspectives, and considerations about trademarks that underline the necessity of having proper legal frameworks. The trends section will guide policymakers in using their legal power to enforce branding through trademarks.

As the field of trademarks and tourism continues to develop and change, a number of opportunities exist for future study. Future works may address new trademark strategies for young tourism markets, the effects of nontraditional trademarks on tourist attitudes and conduct, and the influence of trademarks on user-friendly tourism and culture conservation. Such exciting fields as trademarks in connection to such fields of tourism as destination appearance, marketing communication, and destination management may provide substantial additional value in the broad understanding of tourism branding and competitiveness. Generally, the tourism cases of trademarks are an excellent field for interdisciplinary investigation and practice, and this research offers a variety of applications.

REFERENCES

Acheampong, H. (2020). *Destination Branding: Focusing on Events Contribution on an Urban Level.* https://www.diva-portal.org/smash/get/diva2:1520475/FULLTEXT02

Adeyinka-Ojo, S. F., Nair, V., & Khoo-Lattimore, C. (2014). Case Studies Approach in Tourism Destination Branding Research. *SHS Web of Conferences, 12*. DOI: 10.1051/shsconf/20141201061

Aras, S. (2023). AR and VR technology: Transforming our lives through immersive experiences. *The Times of India*. https://timesofindia.indiatimes.com/readersblog/reflective-ruminations/ar-and-vr-technology-transforming-our-lives-through-immersive-experiences-52485/

Balaji, G. (2024, March 27). *Unconventional Trademarks in India: Protection Challenges & Prospects*. Depenning & Depenning. https://depenning.com/blog/unconventional-trademarks-evolution/

Calboli, I. (2018). Introduction. In Calboli, I., & Senftleben, M. (Eds.), *Oxford University Press eBooks* (pp. 1–10). Oxford University Press., DOI: 10.1093/oso/9780198826576.003.0001

Chakraborty, A., & Jain, V. (2022). Leveraging Digital Marketing and Integrated Marketing Communications for Brand Building in Emerging Markets. In Adeola, O., Hinson, R. E., & Sakkthivel, A. M. (Eds.), *Marketing Communications and Brand Development in Emerging Economies* (Vol. I). Palgrave Studies of Marketing in Emerging Economies. Palgrave Macmillan., DOI: 10.1007/978-3-030-88678-3_13

Gangjee, D. (2010). Non Conventional Trade Marks in India. *National Law School of India Review, 22*(1), 67–95. https://www.jstor.org/stable/44283714

Haigney, S., Lu, D., Gianordoli, G., & Syam, U. (2021, August 13). The Hidden Melodies of Subways Around the World. *The New York Times*. https://www.nytimes.com/interactive/2021/08/13/arts/subway-train-sounds.html

Haleem, A., Javaid, M., Qadri, M. A., Singh, R. P., & Suman, R. (2022). Artificial Intelligence (AI) Applications for marketing: a literature-based Study. *International Journal of Intelligent Networks, 3*(3), 119–132. sciencedirect. DOI: 10.1016/j.ijin.2022.08.005

Heracleous, L., & Wirtz, J. (2010). *The Globe: Singapore Airlines' Balancing Act.* Harvard Business Review. https://hbr.org/2010/07/the-globe-singapore-airlines-balancing-act

Holter, M. G. (2024, January 30). Branding the City of Light's Signature Landmark. *Washington Post.* https://www.washingtonpost.com/archive/politics/2005/05/15/branding-the-city-of-lights-signature-landmark/139104a8-a81c-4e32-9dcd-c43899c928c9/

Hosany, S., Ekinci, Y., & Uysal, M. (2006). Destination image and destination personality: An application of branding theories to tourism places. *Journal of Business Research*, 59(5), 638–642. DOI: 10.1016/j.jbusres.2006.01.001

Hudson, S., & Ritchie, J. R. B. (2009). Branding a memorable destination experience. The case of "Brand Canada.". *International Journal of Tourism Research*, 11(2), 217–228. DOI: 10.1002/jtr.720

Indulia, B. (2022, September 16). *A Perspective on Non-Conventional Trademarks and the Difficulties in Extending IP Protection to Them.* SCC Times. https://www.scconline.com/blog/post/2022/09/16/a-perspective-on-non-conventional-trademarks-and-the-difficulties-in-extending-ip-protection-to-them/

Jain, S. C. (1996). Problems in International Protection of Intellectual Property Rights. *Journal of International Marketing*, 4(1), 9–32. https://www.jstor.org/stable/25048632. DOI: 10.1177/1069031X9600400103

Klink, R. R. (2000). Creating Brand Names With Meaning: The Use of Sound Symbolism. *Marketing Letters*, 11(1), 5–20. DOI: 10.1023/A:1008184423824

Kurup, R., & Pradeep, N. A. (2020). NON-CONVENTIONAL TRADEMARKS IN INDIA: THE WHAT, THE WHY AND THE HOW. *Journal of Academic Innovation and Research in Intellectual Property Assets (E-JAIRIPA, 1*(01), 131–148. https://cnlu.ac.in/wp-content/uploads/2022/08/9-Rachna-R-Kurup-and-Nimita-Aksa-Pradeep.pdf

Lukose, L. P. (2015). NON-TRADITIONAL TRADEMARKS: A CRITIQUE. *Journal of the Indian Law Institute*, 57(2), 197–215. https://www.jstor.org/stable/44782501

Mishra, N. (2008). Registration of Non-Traditional Trademarks. *Journal of Intellectual Property Rights*, 13(1), 43–50. https://nopr.niscpr.res.in/bitstream/123456789/407/1/JIPR%2013(1)%20(2008)%2043-50.pdf

Morgan, N. J., Pritchard, A., & Piggott, R. (2003). Destination branding and the role of the stakeholders: The case of New Zealand. *Journal of Vacation Marketing*, 9(3), 285–299. DOI: 10.1177/135676670300900307

Munar, A. M., & Jacobsen, J. Kr. S. (2014). Motivations for sharing tourism experiences through social media. *Tourism Management, 43*(0261-5177), 46–54. DOI: 10.1016/j.tourman.2014.01.012

Nast, C. (2019, August 2). *How a Hotel Gets Its Signature Scent*. Condé Nast Traveler. https://www.cntraveler.com/story/how-a-hotel-gets-its-signature-scent

Robin, B. (2016). *The Power of Digital Storytelling to Support Teaching and Learning*. https://files.eric.ed.gov/fulltext/EJ1125504.pdf

Ruiz-Real, J. L., Uribe-Toril, J., & Gázquez-Abad, J. C. (2020). Destination Branding: Opportunities and New Challenges. *Journal of Destination Marketing & Management*, 17(1), 100453. DOI: 10.1016/j.jdmm.2020.100453

Sarıbaş, Ö., & Demír, C. (2022). The Impact of Sensory Branding on Tourist Experience. *Journal of Tourism and Gastronomy Studies*, 10(4), 4. Advance online publication. DOI: 10.21325/jotags.2022.1118

Shahid, S., Paul, J., Gilal, F. G., & Ansari, S. (2022). The role of sensory marketing and brand experience in building emotional attachment and brand loyalty in luxury retail stores. *Psychology and Marketing*, 39(7), 1398–1412. DOI: 10.1002/mar.21661

Thakkar, A. (2023, November 3). *What & Why Sensory Marketing is used to attract customers?* Infidigit. https://www.infidigit.com/blog/sensory-marketing/

Thaler, S. (2022, March 16). *The Northern Lights at NYC's Hudson Yards*. BizBash. https://www.bizbash.com/production-strategy/event-production-fabrication/article/22118556/the-northern-lights-at-nycs-hudson-yards

Usakli, A., & Baloglu, S. (2011). Brand personality of tourist destinations: An application of self-congruity theory. *Tourism Management*, 32(1), 114–127. DOI: 10.1016/j.tourman.2010.06.006

USPTO. (2021). *What is a trademark?*Www.uspto.gov. https://www.uspto.gov/trademarks/basics/what-trademark#:~:text=A%20trademark%20can%20be%20any

World Intellectual Property Organization. (2017). *Making a Mark: An Introduction to Trademarks for Small and Medium-Sized Enterprises*. Wipo.

World Intellectual Property Organization, & World Tourism Organization. (2021). *Boosting tourism development through intellectual property*. World Intellectual Property Organization ; Madrid.

Yılmaz, G., & Tekeli, N. (2021). The Importance and Role of Digital Marketing in the Preference of Touristic Products in Turkey. *University of South Florida M3 Center Publishing, 18*(9781732127586). DOI: 10.5038/9781732127586

Chapter 10
Savoring Safeguards: Intellectual Property Protection in Gastronomy Tourism

Norhidayah bt Azman
Management and Science University, Malaysia

Iylia Dayana Mohamed Izwan
https://orcid.org/0000-0003-2018-3257
Management and Science University, Malaysia

Nur Amalina Binti Abdul Ghani
https://orcid.org/0000-0001-9751-0055
Multimedia University, Malaysia

Shalieza Binti Razali
Management and Science University, Malaysia

ABSTRACT

The tourist industry of the twenty-first century has been shaped by significant trends that are affected by advancements in technology and innovative marketing strategies. Gastronomy tourism is one among them. The objective of this research is to discover the factors that impact the expansion of astronomy tourism, with the goal of predicting the factors that determine the availability of resources for global marketing efforts. An effective approach to categorizing food items can be achieved by considering the geographic sources of a particular gourmet cuisine. Consequently, the increasing reliance and utilization of "geographical indicators" (GIs) may encompass unique characteristics associated with a particular location or differentiating attributes derived from the history, culture, and folklore of a given geographic region. This study examines the economic significance and impact of

DOI: 10.4018/979-8-3693-4171-1.ch010

geographical indication (GI) indicators on gourmet tourism, as well as the utilization of GI as a novel branding technique.

INTRODUCTION

The majority of items used and endorsed in gourmet tourism, as well as the overall tourist industry, are safeguarded by Intellectual Property Rights (IPRs) in the present global context. Intellectual property, in its whole, confers substantial benefits and advantages to all participants in the field of gourmet tourism (Seyitoğlu & Ivanov, 2020). The recognition is given to inventors and innovators who have successfully transformed concepts into actual products that have greatly transformed and improved the tourist industry in the Asia-Pacific region. This includes advancements in mobile phones and more fuel-efficient automobiles (Liu & Jiang, 2020; Vandecandelaere et al., 2020). Intellectual property is widely recognized as a key catalyst for innovation (Dutta et. al., 2020). Undoubtedly, intellectual property plays a crucial role in the culinary tourism business by ensuring the continuous generation of new, high-quality ideas in society. This, in turn, benefits lives, stimulates economies, and safeguards the environment (Dewalska-Opitek & Hofman-Kohlmeyer, 2021). Individuals ranging from scientists conducting experiments in laboratories to inventors brainstorming in their garages utilize intellectual property (IP) to advance their work. Gastronomy, within the realm of tourism, is not an exception (Yongxun & Lulu, 2021; Rejeb et. al., 2021; Sottile, Massaglia & Peano, 2020).

Ever since the World Tourism Organization (WTO) acknowledged tourism as a crucial driver of trade and progress (Nurani, Nurjanah & Prihantoro, 2021), the tourism industry has had consistent growth within the service sector. Tourism is asserted to have emerged as a significant component of the world economy and a large revenue generator for nations of varying economic statuses (Yongxun & Lulu, 2021; Rejeb et. al., 2021; Sottile, Massaglia & Peano, 2020). The components of the IP system have diverse uses in the tourism business, specifically in culinary tourism. Establishing and leveraging brands is essential for the service sector, including the tourist industry as a whole (Nurani, Nurjanah & Prihantoro, 2021). In order to establish and profit from a brand in the field of gourmet tourism, it is crucial to utilize various intellectual property rights (IPRs) such as trademarks, geographical indications, certified marks, collective markings, and industrial designs. Additionally, patents, copyrights, and trade secrets play a significant role in this process (Ghouri et. al., 2021). Gastronomy tourism notably benefits from the legal protection of intellectual property rights, which grant exclusive usage rights and the capacity to prevent unauthorized third parties from profiting from such rights (Yongxun & Lulu, 2021; Rejeb et. al., 2021; Sottile, Massaglia & Peano, 2020).

GEOGRAPHICAL INDICATIONS(GIs)

Geographical indicators are a recent concept in the field of marketing and are considered a form of intellectual property. Geographical indications (GIs) are defined as indications that identify a product as originating from a specific member's territory, region, or locality. These indications are used when a particular quality, reputation, or characteristic of the product is primarily linked to its geographic origin. This definition is based on the WTO Agreement on Trade-Related Aspects of Intellectual Property Rights (TRIP) (Fernández-Zarza et. al., 2021; Ranjan, 2021 and Defossez, 2017). The globalization of trade necessitated the urgent need to harmonize the various methods and standards employed by countries for the registration of Geographical Indications (GIs) (Supriatna et. al., 2021). The Paris Convention on trademarks, established in 1883 and still in force with 176 members, was the initial endeavor in this area. It was then followed by a more comprehensive provision in the 1958 Lisbon Agreement on the Protection of Appellations of Origin and their Registration, as referenced by Friedmann (2020) and de Almeida & Carls (2021). Algeria, Bosnia and Herzegovina, Bulgaria, Burkina Faso, Congo, Costa Rica, Cuba, Czech Republic, North Korea, France, Gabon, Georgia, Haiti, Hungary, Iran, Israel, Italy, Macedonia, Mexico, Moldova, Montenegro, Nicaragua, Peru, Portugal, Serbia, Slovakia, Togo, and Tunisia are among the 28 countries that have ratified the Lisbon Treaty (Delimatsis, 2021). The Lisbon Agreement has recorded more than 9000 geographical indicators (Silva & Paul, 2021). Upon the conclusion of the WTO TRIPS negotiations in 1994, all 164 member nations of the WTO (as of August 2016) unanimously agreed to establish essential regulations for safeguarding Geographical Indications (GIs) in all member countries. Under the TRIPS agreement, member countries of the World Trade Organization (WTO) have two important obligations regarding Geographical Indications (GIs).

According to Article 22 of the TRIPS Agreement, it is mandatory for all governments to incorporate provisions in their national laws that allow the owner of a Geographical Indication (GI) registered in that country to take legal action against the use of trademarks that deceive the public regarding the true geographical origin of the product. This encompasses the prevention of using a geographical name that, although factually accurate, misleadingly implies that the product originates from a different location. According to Article 22 of TRIPS, governments have the authority to reject the registration of a trademark or cancel an existing trademark (if their laws allow or upon the request of another government) if it deceives the public regarding the actual source of a product. (Richards, 2020). As per Article 23 of the TRIPS Agreement, it is mandatory for all governments to grant geographical indicator (GI) owners the legal authority to prohibit the use of a geographical indicator for wines that do not originate from the designated location indicated by the GI. This applies in cases when there is no deception of the public, no unfair competition, and the true origin of the product is disclosed or accompanied by language such as "kind," "type," "style," "imitation," or similar expressions. Geographical markers pertaining to spirits should have equal protection, as stated by Motari et al. (2021) and Richards (2020). Article 23 states that governments have the authority to reject or revoke the registration of a trademark if it directly competes with a geographical indication (GI) for wine or spirits. This applies regardless of whether the trademark is misleading or not. This information is supported by Motari et al. (2021) and Richards (2020).

Moreover, TRIPS Article 24 grants certain exemptions to the safeguarding of geographical indications, particularly pertaining to wines and spirits geographical indications (Motari, et. al., 2021 and Richards, 2020). Members are exempt from protecting a geographical indicator if it has become a generic term for describing the product in question. Efforts to enforce these regulations should not endanger existing trademark rights. Additionally, in certain situations, such as when there is a well-established history of using a specific geographical indicator for wines or spirits, the ongoing use of that indicator may be allowed to continue without significant changes in scope or nature. (Motari, et. al., 2021 and Richards, 2020). Member nations of the World Trade Organization (WTO) are currently discussing the establishment of a "multilateral registry" for geographical indications. This is being done as part of the Doha Development Round, which commenced in December 2001 (Motari, et. al., 2021 and Richards, 2020). Certain countries, like the European Union (EU), are promoting the implementation of a register that has legal force, but others, like the United States (US), are advocating for a system that is not legally binding. In this system, the World Trade Organization (WTO) would only be informed about the geographical indications of its member countries, without any need to enforce them. (Motari, et. al., 2021 and Richards, 2020).

Certain states participating in the negotiations, particularly the European Communities, are interested in expanding the discussion to include Geographical Indications (GIs) on products other than wines and spirits, as outlined in TRIPS Article 23 (Motari, et. al., 2021 and Richards, 2020). These governments argue that the expansion of Article 23 will enhance the global safeguarding of these trademarks. Other countries, including the United States, oppose this proposal, raising doubts about the need to expand the heightened safeguard of Article 23 to include other products. Concerns arise regarding the inadequacy of Article 23 protection in providing consumers with the desired benefits outlined in GIs legislation. Malaysia expressed concerns regarding gourmet tourism, as highlighted by Motari et al. (2021) and Richards (2020).

GI PRACTICES IN UNITED STATES, SOUTH EAST ASIAN AND EUROPEAN UNION

In the United States, Geographical Indications (GIs) are commonly recognized as brands and trademarks. The protection of GIs is overseen by the United States Patent and Trademark Office (USPTO). Additionally, regulations regarding the labeling of wine, malt drinks, beer, and distilled spirits are enforced by the Alcohol and Tobacco Tax and Trade Bureau (Aronzon, 2020; Rosas, 2020 and Gan, 2020). ASEAN has adopted the TRIPS Agreement in a manner that is comparable to the United States. However, certain countries within ASEAN, such as the Philippines, Brunei, and Myanmar, have extended the protection of geographical indications (GI) to include gastronomy tourism through trade mark or certification laws (Rahmah, 2018). Although TRIPS does not mandate nations to establish a distinct system for protecting Geographical Indications (GIs), the majority of WTO members have either already done so or are in the process of doing so (Motari, et. al., 2021 and Richards, 2020). Designing a distinct system only for geographical indications (GIs) was unnecessary because the United States had already been protecting them for many years before to the implementation of TRIPS (Schipper, Tchoukarine & Bechmann Pedersen, 2018). Moreover, the trademark system was widely recognized by professionals, interested parties, and legal authorities. Consequently, the United States made the decision to maintain the protection of GIs as trademarks through registration with the United States Patent and Trademark Office (USPTO) and under US common law. This decision is further elaborated by Aronzon (2020), Rosas (2020), and Gan (2020).

Geographical indications (GIs) that serve as certification and collective marks to indicate regional origin are safeguarded by Section 4 of the modified Trademark Act of 1946 (Aronzon, 2020; Rosas, 2020; Gan, 2020; Situmeang & Murniarti, 2021; and Rahmah, 2018). Geographical indications (GIs) can be safeguarded as trademarks if they can demonstrate their distinctive nature via usage. While most GIs are protected under Section 4 of several sources (Aronzon, 2020; Rosas, 2020; Gan, 2020; Situmeang & Murniarti, 2021; and Rahmah, 2018), others may require further evidence of acquired distinctiveness. Collective trademarks are mainly employed to guarantee specific characteristics of a product, such as its geographical origin. These trademarks are owned by either a public or private organization, such as a trade association, which grants its members the right to use them for commercial purposes (Aronzon, 2020; Rosas, 2020; Gan, 2020; Situmeang & Murniarti, 2021; Rahmah, 2018). Certification markings are utilized to indicate that a product has been manufactured in adherence to specific criteria, such as the geographical origin of production. These marks are owned by a corporation that does not sell the product, but rather certifies its compliance with the established standards. In the United States and ASEAN, GIs are mainly seen as brands and trademarks. However, the European Union safeguards GIs through different quality standards, as mentioned by Aronzon (2020), Rosas (2020), Gan (2020), Situmeang and Murniarti (2021), and Rahmah (2018). Within the European Union, Geographical Indications (GIs) are employed to safeguard the names of products and highlight their unique characteristics, which are closely linked to their geographical origin and traditional expertise in culinary tourism (Zappalaglio, 2021). EU quality schemes provide protection for things whose product qualities or traits are inherently linked to their geographical origin. Access as a hyperlink to an external source. There are several:

1. PDOs (protected designations of origin) for agricultural and culinary items, as well as wines.
2. PGIs (protected geographical indications) for agricultural and culinary goods, as well as wines.
3. Geographical indications (GI) for alcoholic beverages and scented wines

The recognition of Geographical Indications (GIs) enables buyers to have confidence in and distinguish these products, while also helping manufacturers to efficiently promote their products in the market. The geographical indicators system in the European Union safeguards the designations of products originating from certain locations, possessing unique characteristics, or being associated with the manufacturing region's reputation. This practice is widely employed in the European Union for the purpose of gourmet tourism (Aronzon, 2020; Rosas, 2020; Gan, 2020; Situmeang & Murniarti, 2021; Rahmah, 2018; and Zappalaglio, 2021).

DIFFERENCES IN IMPLEMENTATION OF GI AMONG UNITED STATES, SOUTH EAST ASIAN AND EUROPEAN UNION

An disparity in perspective regarding the criteria for determining a "authentic" product is a contributing factor to the conflicts between the United States, ASEAN, and the European Union (Zappalaglio, 2021). In Europe, the prevailing concept is that of terroir, which refers to the idea that a specific geographic location possesses a unique characteristic that requires the precise application of geographical designations. Therefore, individuals possessing the appropriate sheep breeds have the ability to produce Roquefort cheese, but only if they reside in the specific region of France. However, individuals outside of that particular area are not permitted to produce a blue sheep's milk cheese and label it as Roquefort, even if they precisely replicate the method described in the Roquefort definition. In contrast, both in the United States and Southeast Asia, the concept of name is frequently considered a matter of intellectual property. The cited sources include Aronzon (2020), Rosas (2020), Gan (2020), Situmeang and Murniarti (2021), and Rahmah (2018). Meadowcreek Farms possesses the legal ownership of the name Grayson and has the authority to utilize it as a registered trademark (Süess, 2012). It is prohibited for anybody, including those in Grayson County, Virginia, to use the name "Grayson" for their cheese. However, if Meadowcreek Farms were to acquire another farm in a different location inside the United States, they would be allowed to use the name "Grayson" for their cheese, even if the property is not in Grayson County (Süess, 2012). Preserving a company's reputation is seen to be a guarantee of quality. The primary source of friction between the United States and Europe about geographical names arises from this discrepancy (Aronzon, 2020; Rosas, 2020; Gan, 2020; Situmeang & Murniarti, 2021; and Rahmah, 2018). Nevertheless, there is significant convergence, particularly with American products from a European standpoint (Aronzon, 2020; Rosas, 2020; Gan, 2020; Situmeang & Murniarti, 2021; and Rahmah, 2018). The crops that are most widely recognized include Vidalia onions, Florida oranges, and Idaho potatoes (Lucier & Parr, 2020). For each of these scenarios, the state governments of Georgia, Florida, and Idaho have applied for trademarks. These trademarks grant permission to their growers, or in the case of the Vidalia onion, only those located in a particular and clearly defined geographic area within the state, to use the name. However, these trademarks also prohibit others from using the name (Lucier & Parr, 2020). Vintners in various American Viticultural Areas are striving to establish unique and well-defined identities as New World wine gains popularity in the industry. Additionally, American viticulture is gradually embracing the European concept. This information is supported by Aronzon (2020), Rosas (2020), Gan (2020), Situmeang & Murniarti (2021), and Rahmah (2018). The United States has a well-established tradition of imposing highly stringent regulations on its domestic varieties of whiskey. Of particular importance are the criteria for labeling a product as whiskey, which necessitates that the whiskey is produced in the United States in accordance with specific standards. Additionally, federal law and various international agreements, such as NAFTA, enforce the requirement that any product labeled as Tennessee whiskey must be a straight Bourbon (Pacult, 2021).

Figure 1. Selected Examples of GIs around the world

EUROPEAN UNION	ASEAN COUNTRIES	OTHER COUNTRIES AROUND THE WORLD
Wachauer (Marille apricot – Austria)	**Kampong Speu Palm Sugar** / ស្ករត្នោតកំពង់ស្ពឺ (Sugar – Cambodia)	**Vale dos Vinhedos** (Wine – Brazil)
Brussels grondwitloof (Chicory heads – Belgium)	**Kampot pepper** / ម្រេចកំពត (Pepper – Cambodia)	**Café de Colombia** (Coffee – Colombia)
Šoltansko maslinovo ulje (Olive oil – Croatia)	**Kopi Arabika Gayo** (Coffee – Indonesia)	**Habanos** (Tobacco – Cuba)
Chamomilla bohemica (Spices – Czech Republic)	**Madu Sumbawa** (Honey – Indonesia)	**Café de Valdesia** (Coffee – Dom. Republic)
Champagne (Wine – France)	**Sabah Tea** (Tea – Malaysia)	**Ron de Guatemala** (Spirits – Guatemala)
Bremer Bier (Beer – Germany)	**Surat Thani Oyster PGI** / หอยนางรมสุราษฎร์ธานี (Oysters – Thailand)	**Penja pepper** (Cameroon)
Parmigiano Reggiano (Cheese – Italy)	**Lamphun Brocade Thai Silk PGI** / ผ้าไหมยกดอกลำพูน (Silk – Thailand)	**Tequila** (Spirits – Mexico)
Daujėnų naminė duona (Bread – Lithuania)	**Huế Palm-Leaf Conical** Hat (Hat – Vietnam)	**Argan Oil** (Plant oil – Morocco)
Karp zatorski (Fish – Poland)	**Buôn Ma Thuột coffee** (Coffee – Vietnam)	**Pisco** (Spirits – Peru)
Porto / Port / vinho do Porto / Port Wine / vin de Porto / Oporto / Portvin / Portwein / Portwijn (Wine – Portugal)	**Lạng Sơn Star Aniseed** (Star anise – Vietnam)	**Rheintaler Ribelmais** (Corn – Switzerland)
Ternera Gallega PGI (Veal – Spain)	**Hoà Lộc mango** (Mango – Vietnam)	**Longjing cha** 龙井茶 (Tea – China)
Irish Whiskey / Uisce Beatha Eireannach / Irish Whisky GI (Spirits – Ireland)	**Bình Thuận dragon fruit** (Dragon fruit – Vietnam)	**Napa Valley** (Wines – USA) (Protected under a Legislative Act in the USA)

Sources; European Commission(2020).

GASTRONOMY TOURISM

Indulging in local cuisine and beverages, discovering unfamiliar food and drinks, savoring extraordinary culinary creations, witnessing the preparation of diverse dishes, enjoying a meal prepared by a renowned chef, visiting notable restaurants and wine cellars, or at the very least simulating these experiences during the trip (Çetin, 2021; Visković & Komac, 2021 and Celebi, Pirnar & Eris, 2020). Tourism developments are currently giving priority to cultural and historical features. Consequently, tourists now favor areas that possess notable cultural attributes. The tourism program has prioritized the preservation of indigenous tourist values (Yalin, 2021). Due to the adverse impacts of mass tourism on the natural environment, there has been a rise in the popularity of tourism practices that prioritize the preservation of nature and cultural values. Gastronomy tourism, agrotourism, and rural tourism have become increasingly popular in recent years (Çetin, 2021; Visković & Komac, 2021; Celebi, Pirnar & Eris, 2020). Food and beverage outlets located at the tourist destination are considered a significant aspect of the tourist experience, making up 33% of the money spent by visitors. In order to address the increasing popularity of indigenous values within the country and globally, a tourist legislation has been developed to reduce misunderstandings. This law has been mentioned in the works of Çetin (2021), Visković and Komac (2021), and Celebi, Pirnar, and Eris (2020).

PROTECTION OF GEOGRAPHICAL INDICATIONS IN GASTRONOMY TOURISM

In the knowledge-based economy, competition is intense, and individuals who see the potential of intangible assets to differentiate and enhance the value of physical objects are rewarded (Başaran, 2021 ; Jaelani, Handayani & Karjoko, 2020). The intellectual property system serves as a framework and employs procedures to safeguard, preserve, monetize, and enforce intangible assets (Török et. al., 2020). Millennial tourists are increasingly opting to visit destinations renowned for their authentic regional cuisines (Pavlidis & Markantonatou, 2020). Gourmet tourism has emerged as a result of tourists' inclination towards regional cuisine. Conversely, local cuisine is insufficient to sustain the growth of this particular form of tourism. The presence of local products, along with the culinary traditions of the region, entice tourists, aid in establishing the destination's identity, and contribute to its economic well-being (Ianioglo & Rissanen, 2020). The indigenous people's way of life, the destination's history, and its customs and traditions contribute significantly to the development of gourmet tourism (Richards, G. (2021).

Gastronomy tourism plays a significant role in shaping the geographical landscape. This process involves the incorporation of worldwide aspects into specific local environments, taking into account both their advantages and disadvantages, and redefining the concept of place through cultural advancements. Consequently, the conventional scenery undergoes a metamorphosis into a gastronomic scenery that mirrors the complexities of contemporary lifestyles, as well as the geographical and cultural variety fostered by diverse cultural traditions (Başaran, 2021 ; Jaelani, Handayani & Karjoko, 2020). Gourmet tourism enables places to capitalize on their cultural uniqueness and variety as a competitive edge in an ever more interconnected globe. The expansion of gastronomy tourism is a direct consequence of the processes of globalization and increased mobility (Derek, 2021). Consequently, gastronomy has emerged as a significant determinant in choosing holiday destinations, and it also plays a pivotal role in experience tourism, such as wine tourism (Pavlidis & Markantonatou, 2020). In order to achieve success, destinations need to effectively promote and market the unique products and resources that contribute to their image, such as different cultural and natural commodities (Török et. al., 2020). Food distribution, both in physical and ethereal forms, significantly influences and molds geographical locations, mostly through alterations in social and economic systems, as well as land utilization. Explaining the ways in which legacy functions as a resource for territorial development is challenging due to the intricate nature of legacy (Pavlidis & Markantonatou, 2020).

This holds particularly true as the territory is a complex entity in which numerous stakeholders (residents, visitors, and investors) engage with each other based on their individual views, motives, knowledge, experiences, and expectations (Török et. al., 2020). Multiple research on gastronomy tourism indicate that the economic benefits of food might create divisions among host cities (Török et al., 2020 and Ketter, 2020). Birch and Memery (2020) view local food as a means to enhance cultural tourism and promote local identity through the sale of local food products. However, Visković and Komac (2021) caution that gastronomy tourism may not always lead to the anticipated levels of cultural, social, economic, or territorial development. This holds particularly true in the present era of heightened global competition (Török et. al., 2020; Ketter, 2020; Visković & Komac, 2021). Considering the significant number of urban dwellers who have a background in rural environments, it is crucial to examine the complexities of urban-rural interactions, including a focus on local landscapes and terroir (Visković, N. R., & Komac, 2021). Gastronomy tourism reduces the spatial and technological gaps caused by industrialization and globalization of agricultural food supply chains by engaging local food system participants such as farmers, producers, processors, chefs, caterers, festival organizers, managers, policymakers, authorities, and the community (Payandeh et al., 2020). By engaging in product creation, processing, and transformation, individuals acquire indigenous skills, historical and cultural practices, as well as traditional knowledge (Duxbury et al., 2021). As a result, regional disparities arise due to the significance of food as a crucial component. Urban regions typically exhibit this phenomenon more prominently, but its impact on spatial development and regional identity in rural areas may be less apparent. One example of this influence is the establishment of a tourist gourmet region and a tourism scape (Lee, et. al., 2020).

GEOGRAPHICAL INDICATION AS NEW MARKETING STRATEGY IN TOURISM INDUSTRY

Čehić, Mesić, and Oplanić (2020) found that consumers who purchase regional products highly appreciate labels that include regional certification. Their research revealed that geographical indication (GI) labels significantly increase consumers' willingness to pay a higher price for products that are protected by regional regulations. According to a study conducted by Jarma Arroyo, Hogan, Ahrent Wisdom, Moldenhauer, and Seo (2020), the inclusion of provenance information greatly enhances the acceptance of virgin olive oil. Katt and Meixner (2020) examine the inclinations of German consumers towards regional cuisine and their readiness to pay an additional cost for such products, often known as willingness to pay (WTP). The previous literature review illustrates the perspective of the Western school of thought regarding GI products and their perception. The role of GI protection in marketing is evident from its significant contributions. To ascertain the attributes of GI in a commercial context, the subsequent elements are emphasized:

1. Geographical Brand

Branding and establishing a brand throughout the business cycle require a significant amount of time. Geographic markers have a long history and a dedicated customer base. However, research indicates that these brands have been established in the Western world for a significant period of time. This suggests that buyers are more familiar with these markers and hold a positive attitude towards regional brands (Duxbury et al., 2021; Čehić, Mesić & Oplanić, 2020; Török et al., 2020; Ketter, 2020; Visković & Komac, 2021). According to Teuber, individual devotion to geographical markers is subject to change. Belonging to a group results in a prevailing optimistic outlook in the market.

2. Product differentiation.

Refers to the process of distinguishing a product from its competitors by highlighting unique features, characteristics, or benefits. Differentiation plays a key role in the marketing of a product. The system of attributes employed to distinguish the product is likewise encompassed in the context of geographical indications. The prominence and support for GI marketing is increasing due to the differentiation of products and legal protection. Exclusive rights provide producers a unique opportunity to develop a distinct marketing approach. Geographical indicators are increasingly acknowledged as valuable instruments for distinguishing products, and they can contribute to improving economic efficiency by incentivizing producers to meet market demand adequately (Duxbury et al., 2021; Čehić, Mesić & Oplanić, 2020; Török et al., 2020; Ketter, 2020; Visković & Komac, 2021).

3. Enhancing the Worth of Marketing.

Effective marketing and promotional strategies that shape customer perceptions of the product's quality and worth are essential for successfully commercializing a Geographical Indication (GI). However, it is challenging to build a positive reputation for a GI product. In order to establish a significant geographical indication (GI), several key factors must be considered, including a substantial investment of time, patience, financial resources, meticulous quality control measures, and a carefully devised marketing strategy. For instance, it is asserted that the process of establishing the esteemed reputation of "Champagne" took approximately 150 years to accomplish (Duxbury et al., 2021; Čehić, Mesić & Oplanić, 2020; Török et al., 2020; Ketter, 2020; Visković & Komac, 2021).

4. Expertise in the field of marketing.

GIs support and promote cultural contributions and recognize the creativity of cultural and traditional knowledge by establishing exclusive markets for well-known products of indigenous peoples and preventing others from exploiting their reputation (Duxbury et al., 2021; Čehić, Mesić & Oplanić, 2020; Török et al., 2020; Ketter, 2020; Visković & Komac, 2021).

GI FOR INDIGENOUS GASTRONOMY TOURISM

Most of the foods protected by geographical indications (GIs) are derived from land, indicating strong historical and symbolic connections between the specific area and the product (Başaran, 2021 and Jaelani, Handayani & Karjoko, 2020). Given that GIs own a form of exclusive market control, it is possible to implement niche marketing and differentiate food products by using the understanding of the specific cultural and geographical origins of these food items. This provides a dual advantage by allowing food product manufacturers in the country to differentiate their products in the market and also serving as a barrier to entry for other companies in the same market sector. The standards outlined in the GI registration specify the precise methods, locations, and ingredients used in the manufacturing of the food product. Geographical indications (GIs) provide a means to exploit the inherent value associated with the designation given to a certain group of producers and their products, which meet certain criteria for protection (Başaran, 2021 and Jaelani, Handayani & Karjoko, 2020).

However, protecting Geographical Indications (GIs) might have unexpected repercussions as it may inadvertently disclose the specific locations and territories associated with their names. The region of Burgundy is famed for its wine, which is considered one of the world's best-known wines and is named after the region itself (Majerčáková & Greguš, 2021). Dutfield and Suthersanen (2019) highlight the inherent conflicts between modern intellectual property rights systems and customary law and traditional cultural property rights. However, they also recognize the beneficial aspects of Geographical Indications (GIs) in safeguarding indigenous peoples' knowledge related to the producers and origins of traditional cuisine. While indigenous communities may have similar concepts to 'property rights,' conflicts arise between contemporary intellectual property rights (IPRs) norms, practices, and economics, and the cultural rights and customary practices of indigenous communities due to their 'informal innovation system' and cultural exchange systems (Kuruk, 2020). Geographical indications (GIs) has distinct attributes that make them particularly well-suited for safeguarding the traditional practices of indigenous groups, when compared to other forms of intellectual property rights (IPRs);

1. Data is stored in the public domain:

The knowledge or information contained within the protected indication or product remains in the public domain as no organization, whether a firm or an individual, possesses exclusive monopolistic control over it. Therefore, worries regarding the commercialization of conventional knowledge due to geographical indications (GIs) are exaggerated. The process of converting established practices into regulations that are well known to the public (Başaran, 2021 and Jaelani, Handayani & Karjoko, 2020; Majerčáková & Greguš, 2021 and Dutfield and Suthersanen, 2019) serves as a form of safeguarding. Nevertheless, because to the lack of protection for the information included in the item, there are apprehensions regarding the unauthorized use of traditional knowledge. However, the codified standards do not encompass all of the indigenous knowledge associated with the product and its manufacturing process.

2. Rights may be of endless duration.

The particular indication remains safeguarded as long as the relationship between the good and the place of origin is maintained and the indication is not diluted to become generic. Indigenous cultures often regard their knowledge as a valuable cultural asset that must be conserved to ensure the survival of their culture. It is important to note that the regulations associated with a GI may differ and change over time, which should be taken into account when considering compatibility. This undoubtedly brings up fundamental issues regarding the fundamental qualities of a "traditional" practice/food product, as well as the extent to which alteration is deemed acceptable (Başaran, 2021 and Jaelani, Handayani & Karjoko, 2020; Majerčáková & Greguš, 2021 and Dutfield and Suthersanen, 2019).

3.The extent of protection is in line with cultural and traditional rights.

Geographical indications (GIs) are a shared entitlement held by all producers in the supply chain who adhere to specified regulations and produce within a specific geographic area (Başaran, 2021; Jaelani, Handayani & Karjoko, 2020; Majerčáková & Greguš, 2021; Dutfield and Suthersanen, 2019). The individuals who possess a Geographical Indication (GI) do not possess the authority to transfer the indication.

This authority is exclusively granted to holders of trademarks and patents, as stated in Article 21, 22, 23, and 24 of the TRIPs Agreement. Consequently, the relationship between product quality and place, which forms the basis of Geographical Indication (GI) protection, effectively prohibits the indication from being used by manufacturers outside the specified territory. The indication is not applicable to 'similar' things that originate from outside the specified geographical area or are produced differently when they originate from inside the territory. By protecting an indicator, it restricts the group of people who are able to use it, in terms of their class and/or location (Başaran, 2021 and Jaelani, Handayani & Karjoko, 2020; Majerčáková & Greguš, 2021 and Dutfield and Suthersanen, 2019).

GI AS COMPETITIVE EDGE FOR BRANDING

Regrettably, relying on GI-based tactics for establishing and sustaining competitive market advantages entails drawbacks (Punchihewa, 2020). Geographical identifiers are possessed by a group of firms that operate within a specific geographic region, rather than being owned by a single manufacturer. Therefore, it is necessary for every manufacturer to furnish both their corporate/brand name and a location. In other words, General Influencers (GIs) are more inclined to stimulate the overall demand for a specific product category rather than the specific demand for a single brand inside that category (Styvén, Mariani & Strandberg, 2020). Businesses are motivated to precisely define their geographical scope in order to enhance their capacity to distinguish their items. Local cuisine and products, it might be argued, have a significant impact on visitor engagement. To ensure the transmission of these goods to future generations, it is necessary to document geographic indicators on them. Geographical designations have a crucial role in safeguarding the culture, traditions, customs, tourism attractions, and cultural history of a region. They also contribute to the region's sustainability in the long run (Panda et. al., 2020).

This scenario exemplifies how regional designations contribute to the advancement of tourism. When a geographical indication is associated with culinary tourism, it generates significant revenue for the region by attracting tourists to locations where commodities are produced. Additionally, it serves as a magnet by highlighting the tourism assets of the region, and it has the potential to contribute to its expansion (Marescotti et. al., 2020). Considering all of these factors, it is reasonable to deduce that there is a strong correlation between locally made products and culinary tourism. Geographical indicators significantly influence the formation of the region's culinary identity. In addition, they safeguard the conventional manufacturing methods and the fundamental character of the locality, which is transmitted through successive generations (Özdemir, 2018). The developers of a GI identity are unable to retain all of the advantages linked to the GI identity (which they contributed to establishing). Once a GI "brand" achieves success, additional participants will enter the geographical area with the intention of capitalizing on the brand equity of the GI (Fusté-Forné, 2020). For instance, the Idaho potato brand can be utilized by any potato producer in Idaho, without restriction to a specific producer or a collective of farmers who initially created and promoted it (Lu et al., 2021). This could result in an increase in output within the GI sector, reducing product scarcity and hence lowering rates.

Consequently, geographical indications (GIs) may not always provide protection against competition, as other enterprises are allowed to enter the market as long as they adhere to the restrictions set by the GI collective. Punchihewa (2020), Styvén, Mariani, and Strandberg (2020), Panda et al. (2020), Marescotti et al. (2020), Fusté-Forné (2020), Başaran (2021), Jaelani, Handayani, and Karjoko (2020), Majerčáková and Greguš (2021), and Dutfield and Suthersanen (2019). There may be a propensity to broaden the geographical scope of where the identification is issued. From a technical standpoint, it can be challenging to draw a boundary and assert a geographical advantage in producing a specific high-quality product on one side of the boundary but not on the other. The only choice manufacturers have to decrease the excessive number of producers and the risk of weakening the brand property of the GI is to restrict the geographical area linked to the GI. Implementing and upholding Geographical Indication (GI) classification in the European Union, for instance, could require non-EU companies to eliminate all mentions of these GI descriptors from their promotional materials. This could weaken a crucial aspect of brand value for these enterprises. The following references were cited: Aronzon (2020), Rosas (2020), Gan (2020), Situmeang and Murniarti (2021), Rahmah (2018), and Zappalaglio (2021). In certain instances, global food companies may have officially recorded such names in their respective nations. It is important to mention that organizations may utilize geographic associations in their brand positioning that are not officially registered as trademarks. Implementing Geographical Indication (GI) strategies may pose challenges for existing businesses that have used GIs without discrimination to promote their products, such as Chinese cuisine or Italian dressing. It may also affect multinational food companies that have relied on these designations to classify their products. (Punchihewa, 2020; Styvén, Mariani & Strandberg, 2020; Panda et. al., 2020; Marescotti et. al., 2020; Fusté-Forné, 2020; Başaran, 2021 and Jaelani, Handayani & Karjoko, 2020; Majerčáková & Greguš, 2021 and Dutfield and Suthersanen, 2019).

CONCLUSION

Gastronomy tourism in any destination's culture is incomplete without sampling the regional specialties. It is crucial to ensure that items from a specific region or area are offered with the same level of unique quality and taste as those that are locally available. In a knowledge-driven economy, a comprehensive grasp of Geographical Indications is essential for the continued expansion and development of local and rural culinary tourism, in order to effectively serve a wide range of tourists and clients. Geographical Indications are regarded as a novel form of intellectual property that can be utilized to obtain a competitive advantage in the marketing and branding of culinary tourism. Every region has a legitimate right to be acknowledged in the field of culinary tourism, and this right should be safeguarded through Geographical Indications (GIs). Geographic indications are more significant in both economic and political contexts. Culinary tourism is becoming increasingly popular in both developed and developing nations, offering the opportunity to enhance national and rural tourism revenues. They have recognized the GIs' capacity to generate cash through gourmet tourism. Geographical indicators are associated with culinary tourism as they draw in foreign visitors and contribute to the sustainability and expansion of local tourist communities. Enhancing the utilization and conservation of GIS is crucial for ensuring the proper development of domestic culinary tourism and gaining a competitive advantage in branding and marketing.

REFERENCES.

Aronzon, S. M. (2020). Blockchain and geographical indications: a natural fit?. Journal of Intellectual Property Law & Practice.

Başaran, B. (2020). Perceptions, Attitudes and Behaviours of Consumers Towards Traditional Foods and Gastronomy Tourism: The Case of Rize. *Journal of Tourism and Gastronomy Studies*, 8(3), 1752–1769. DOI: 10.21325/jotags.2020.632

Bhati, D. (2020). Agribusiness module of value added underutilized food products towards livelihood support of hills population (Doctoral dissertation).

Birch, D., & Memery, J. (2020). Tourists, local food and the intention-behaviour gap. *Journal of Hospitality and Tourism Management*, 43, 53–61. DOI: 10.1016/j.jhtm.2020.02.006

Čehić, A., Mesić, Ž., & Oplanić, M. (2020). Requirements for development of olive tourism: The case of Croatia. *Tourism and Hospitality Management*, 26(1), 1–14. DOI: 10.20867/thm.26.1.1

Celebi, D., Pirnar, I., & Eris, E. D. (2020). Bibliometric analysis of social entrepreneurship in gastronomy tourism. Tourism. *Tourism (Zagreb)*, 68(1), 58–67. DOI: 10.37741/t.68.1.5

Çetin, B. (2021). Gastronomy Tourism. TOURISM STUDIES AND SOCIAL SCIENCES, 16.

de Almeida, A. R., & Carls, S. (2021). The Criteria to Qualify a Geographical Term as Generic: Are We Moving from a European to a US Perspective? *IIC; International Review of Industrial Property and Copyright Law*, 52(4), 444–467. DOI: 10.1007/s40319-021-01045-x

Defossez, D. A. L. (2017). Global regulation of international intellectual property through Agreement on Trade-Related Aspects of Intellectual Property Rights (TRIPS): The European Union and Brazil. Revista de Direito Setorial e Regulatório= Journal of Law and Regulation, 3(2), 131-160.

Delimatsis, P. (2021). A Partnership of Equals?'Deeper'Economic Integration Between the EU and Northern Africa. *European Foreign Affairs Review*, 26(4).

Derek, M. (2021). Nature on a Plate: Linking Food and Tourism within the Ecosystem Services Framework. *Sustainability (Basel)*, 13(4), 1687. DOI: 10.3390/su13041687

Dewalska-Opitek, A., & Hofman-Kohlmeyer, M. (2021). Players As Prosumers-How Customer Engagement In Game Modding May Benefit Computer Game Market. Central European Business Review, 10(1).

Dutfield, G., & Suthersanen, U. (2019). Traditional knowledge and genetic resources: Observing legal protection through the lens of historical geography and human rights. *Washburn Law Journal*, 58, 399.

Dutta, P., Choi, T. M., Somani, S., & Butala, R. (2020). Blockchain technology in supply chain operations: Applications, challenges and research opportunities. Transportation research part e: Logistics and transportation review, 142, 102067.

Duxbury, N., Bakas, F. E., Vinagre de Castro, T., & Silva, S. (2021). Creative Tourism Development Models towards Sustainable and Regenerative Tourism. *Sustainability (Basel)*, 13(1), 2. DOI: 10.3390/su13010002

Fernández-Zarza, M., Amaya-Corchuelo, S., Belletti, G., & Aguilar-Criado, E. (2021). Trust and Food Quality in the Valorisation of Geographical Indication Initiatives. *Sustainability (Basel)*, 2021(13), 3168. DOI: 10.3390/su13063168

Friedmann, D. (2020). Grafting the Old and New World: Towards a Universal Trademark Register that Cancels Generic IGO Terms. In Wine Law and Policy (pp. 311-345). Brill Nijhoff.

Fusté-Forné, F. (2020). Savouring place: Cheese as a food tourism destination landmark. Journal of Place Management and Development.

Gan, R. (2020). "Pure Michigan" and "Napa Valley 100%": Is Protection of American Origin Wines as Geographic Indications on Fertile Ground? In Wine Law and Policy (pp. 392-414). Brill Nijhoff.

Ghouri, A. M., Mani, V., Jiao, Z., Venkatesh, V. G., Shi, Y., & Kamble, S. S. (2021). An empirical study of real-time information-receiving using industry 4.0 technologies in downstream operations. *Technological Forecasting and Social Change*, 165, 120551. DOI: 10.1016/j.techfore.2020.120551

Ianioglo, A., & Rissanen, M. (2020). Global trends and tourism development in peripheral areas. *Scandinavian Journal of Hospitality and Tourism*, 20(5), 520–539. DOI: 10.1080/15022250.2020.1848620

Jaelani, A. K., Handayani, I. G. A. K. R., & Karjoko, L. (2020). Development of tourism based on geographic indication towards to welfare state. *International Journal of Advanced Science and Technology*, 29(3s), 1227–1234.

Jarma Arroyo, S. E., Hogan, V., Ahrent Wisdom, D., Moldenhauer, K. A., & Seo, H. S. (2020). Effect of geographical indication information on consumer acceptability of cooked aromatic rice. *Foods*, 9(12), 1843. DOI: 10.3390/foods9121843 PMID: 33322325

Katt, F., & Meixner, O. (2020). A systematic review of drivers influencing consumer willingness to pay for organic food. *Trends in Food Science & Technology*, 100, 374–388. DOI: 10.1016/j.tifs.2020.04.029

Ketter, E. (2020). Millennial travel: tourism micro-trends of European Generation Y. Journal of Tourism Futures.

Kuruk, P. (2020). *Traditional Knowledge, Genetic Resources, Customary Law and Intellectual Property: A Global Primer*. Edward Elgar Publishing. DOI: 10.4337/9781785368486

Lee, C. K., Ahmad, M. S., Petrick, J. F., Park, Y. N., Park, E., & Kang, C. W. (2020). The roles of cultural worldview and authenticity in tourists' decision-making process in a heritage tourism destination using a model of goal-directed behavior. *Journal of Destination Marketing & Management*, 18, 100500. DOI: 10.1016/j.jdmm.2020.100500

Liu, C. H., & Jiang, J. F. (2020). Assessing the moderating roles of brand equity, intellectual capital and social capital in Chinese luxury hotels. *Journal of Hospitality and Tourism Management*, 43, 139–148. DOI: 10.1016/j.jhtm.2020.03.003

Lu, L., Nguyen, R., Rahman, M. M., & Winfree, J. (2021). Demand Shocks and Supply Chain Resilience: An Agent Based Modelling Approach and Application to the Potato Supply Chain (No. w29166). National Bureau of Economic Research.

Lucier, G., & Parr, B. (2020). *Vegetable and pulses outlook*. United States Department of Agriculture. April.

Majerčáková, D., & Greguš, M. (2021). The Analysis of the Investment Opportunities into the Wine. In *Eurasian Business and Economics Perspectives* (pp. 189–201). Springer. DOI: 10.1007/978-3-030-65147-3_13

Marescotti, A., Quiñones-Ruiz, X. F., Edelmann, H., Belletti, G., Broscha, K., Altenbuchner, C., Penker, M., & Scaramuzzi, S. (2020). Are protected geographical indications evolving due to environmentally related justifications? An analysis of amendments in the fruit and vegetable sector in the European Union. *Sustainability (Basel)*, 12(9), 3571. DOI: 10.3390/su12093571

Motari, M., Nikiema, J. B., Kasilo, O. M., Kniazkov, S., Loua, A., Sougou, A., & Tumusiime, P. (2021). The role of intellectual property rights on access to medicines in the WHO African region: 25 years after the TRIPS agreement. *BMC Public Health*, 21(1), 1–19. DOI: 10.1186/s12889-021-10374-y PMID: 33706726

Nurani, N., Nurjanah, R., & Prihantoro, I. (2021). Competence of Human Resources of Small and Medium Enterprises (MSMEs) of West Java through Intellectual Property Rights (IPR) Protection in the COVID-19 Pandemic Era. *Psychology and Education Journal*, 58(3), 251–264.

Özdemir, B. P. (2018). Branding a Millennia-old Turkish City: Case of Gaziantep. *Ankara Üniversitesi İlef Dergisi*, 5(2), 121–140.

Pacult, F. P. (2021). Buffalo, Barrels, & Bourbon: The Story of How Buffalo Trace Distillery Became The World's Most Awarded Distillery. John Wiley & Sons.

Panda, T. K., Kumar, A., Jakhar, S., Luthra, S., Garza-Reyes, J. A., Kazancoglu, I., & Nayak, S. S. (2020). Social and environmental sustainability model on consumers' altruism, green purchase intention, green brand loyalty and evangelism. *Journal of Cleaner Production*, 243, 118575. DOI: 10.1016/j.jclepro.2019.118575

Pavlidis, G., & Markantonatou, S. (2020). Gastronomic tourism in Greece and beyond: A thorough review. *International Journal of Gastronomy and Food Science*, 21, 100229. DOI: 10.1016/j.ijgfs.2020.100229 PMID: 32834883

Payandeh, E., Allahyari, M. S., Fontefrancesco, M. F., & Surujlale, J. (2020). Good vs. Fair and Clean: An Analysis of Slow Food Principles Toward Gastronomy Tourism in Northern Iran. *Journal of Culinary Science & Technology*, •••, 1–20.

Punchihewa, N. S. (2020). Branding of Tourism-Related Products and Services for a Competitive Advantage in Sri Lanka: An Intellectual Property Perspective.

Rahmah, M. (2018). The Protection of Geographical Indication for Agricultural Development: Challenges for ASEAN.

Ranjan, P. (2021). Trade-Related Aspects of Intellectual Property Rights Waiver at the World Trade Organization: A BIT of a Challenge. Available at *SSRN*. DOI: 10.2139/ssrn.3888980

Rejeb, A., Rejeb, K., Simske, S., & Treiblmaier, H. (2021). Blockchain Technologies in Logistics and Supply Chain Management: A Bibliometric Review. *Logistics (Basel)*, 5(4), 72. DOI: 10.3390/logistics5040072

Richards, D. G. (2020). *Intellectual property rights and global capitalism: The political economy of the TRIPS agreement*. Routledge. DOI: 10.4324/9781003063650

Richards, G. (2021). Evolving research perspectives on food and gastronomic experiences in tourism. *International Journal of Contemporary Hospitality Management*, 33(3), 1037–1058. DOI: 10.1108/IJCHM-10-2020-1217

Rosas, R. (2020). A Comparative Study of Trademarks: USMCA (US-Mexico-Canada Agreement) and NAFTA (North American Free Trade Agreement). *BU Int'l LJ*, 38, 38.

Schipper, F., Tchoukarine, I., & Bechmann Pedersen, S. (2018). *The history of the European travel comission*. European Travel Commission.

Seyitoğlu, F., & Ivanov, S. (2020). A conceptual framework of the service delivery system design for hospitality firms in the (post-) viral world: The role of service robots. International Journal of Hospitality Sottile, F., Massaglia, S., & Peano, C. (2020). Ecological and economic indicators for the evaluation of almond (Prunus dulcis L.) orchard renewal in sicily. *Agriculture*, 10(7), 301.

Silva, V., & Paul, N. (2021). Potential impact of earthquakes during the 2020 COVID-19 pandemic. *Earthquake Spectra*, 37(1), 73–94. DOI: 10.1177/8755293020950328

Situmeang, T., & Murniarti, E. (2021). Asean Attitudes Toward Patent Protection of The Covid-19 Vaccine Versus Humanitarian Interests. Jurnal Hukum dan Peradilan, 10(2), 255-276.

Styvén, M. E., Mariani, M. M., & Strandberg, C. (2020). This is my hometown! The role of place attachment, congruity, and self-expressiveness on residents' intention to share a place brand message online. *Journal of Advertising*, 49(5), 540–556. DOI: 10.1080/00913367.2020.1810594

Süess, A. (2012). Feta and chablis-what's in a name?: systems of GI protection under the aspect of genericness (Master's thesis, University of Cape Town).

Supriatna, A. D., Tresnawati, D., Kurniadi, D., & Cahyana, R. (2021, March). Web-based geographic information system for mapping religious tourism object. [). IOP Publishing.]. *IOP Conference Series. Materials Science and Engineering*, 1098(3), 032071. DOI: 10.1088/1757-899X/1098/3/032071

Török, Á., Jantyik, L., Maró, Z. M., & Moir, H. V. (2020). Understanding the real-world impact of geographical indications: A critical review of the empirical economic literature. *Sustainability (Basel)*, 12(22), 9434. DOI: 10.3390/su12229434

Vandecandelaere, E., Teyssier, C., Barjolle, D., Fournier, S., Beucherie, O., & Jeanneaux, P. (2020). Strengthening sustainable food systems through geographical indications: Evidence from 9 worldwide case studies. Journal of Sustainability Research, 4(3). *Management*, 91, 102661.

Visković, N. R., & Komac, B. (2021). Gastronomy tourism: A brief introduction. *Acta Geographica Slovenica*, 61(1), 95–105.

Yalin, G. (2021). An Overview of Gastronomy Tourism. TOURISM STUDIES AND SOCIAL SCIENCES, 134.

Yongxun, Z., & Lulu, H. (2021). Protecting Important Agricultural Heritage Systems (IAHS) by Industrial Integration Development (IID): Practices from China. *Journal of Resources and Ecology*, 12(4), 555–566. DOI: 10.5814/j.issn.1674-764x.2021.04.013

Zappalaglio, A. (2021). Sui generis, bureaucratic and based on origin: a snapshot of the nature of EU Geographical Indications. In *Intellectual Property as a Complex Adaptive System*. Edward Elgar Publishing. DOI: 10.4337/9781800378384.00018

Chapter 11
Leveraging Geographical Indications for Tourism Development and Destination Branding

Pramendra Singh
https://orcid.org/0000-0002-9142-265X
Lovely Professional University, India

Vaibhav Bhatt
https://orcid.org/0000-0003-2859-7913
Central University of Tamil Nadu, India

ABSTRACT

This chapter explores the pivotal role of Geographical Indications (GIs) in advancing tourism development and enhancing destination branding. This review aims to investigate how GIs can be strategically utilized to boost tourism and create distinctive brand identities for destinations. It also examines how GIs contribute to destination branding by defining branding concepts, exploring branding strategies that incorporate GIs, and reviewing successful campaigns. Challenges and considerations related to authenticity, commercialization, and maintaining the integrity of GIs are also discussed. Additionally, the chapter evaluates the economic, social, and cultural impacts of GIs on local communities. Leveraging GIs offers a powerful approach to enriching tourism experiences and strengthening regional identities, with significant implications for both local economies and cultural heritage.

DOI: 10.4018/979-8-3693-4171-1.ch011

INTRODUCTION: GEOGRAPHICAL INDICATION AND ITS SIGNIFICANCE

Geographical indications (GIs) have become a significant aspect of intellectual property, garnering increasing global attention over the past decade. A GI tag is granted to products that originate from specific geographical regions, where the qualities or reputation of these products are intrinsically linked to their place of production (Jaelani et al., 2020). This designation not only ensures product differentiation based on quality but also plays a crucial role in preserving local cultural heritage and traditions. The impact of GIs extends beyond product value; they offer vital opportunities for rural development. By fostering economic activities, supporting local businesses, and improving living standards, GIs contribute to the revitalization of rural areas (Arion, 2024). The presence of GIs helps sustain traditional and environmentally sustainable agricultural practices, which are essential components of a region's cultural heritage. As such, GIs play a key role in maintaining and enhancing the distinctiveness of local agro-production landscapes.

When GIs are integrated with gastronomy tourism, their benefits are magnified. As noted by Pamukçu et al. (2021), GIs significantly boost regional tourism revenue by attracting visitors interested in authentic, locally produced goods. This integration not only highlights the region's culinary assets but also serves as a major draw for tourists, thereby supporting local development and enhancing tourism appeal. Tourism initiatives such as food and wine routes or local agritourism experiences are often directly linked to the presence of GIs, demonstrating how these indications can stimulate a diverse range of tourism-related activities (Hadelan et al., 2021).

Moreover, GIs increase the perceived value of local products through assured quality and official certification, which in turn protects consumers and enhances marketing opportunities (Suh & MacPherson, 2007). Countries with a significant tourism sector often have a higher prevalence of GIs, as these indications contribute to a richer and more varied tourism experience. Yıkmış & Ünal (2016) emphasize that the protection of GIs is crucial for safeguarding both consumers and producers, while also ensuring product quality and maximizing economic contributions. They highlight that engaging with local flavors is a key aspect of experiencing a destination's gastronomic culture, and maintaining product quality can help countries attract international visitors and boost their global tourism revenue.

The creation of traditional products marked with protected GIs is closely linked to traditional and sustainable agricultural methods, contributing to the preservation of cultural heritage and the enhancement of regional identity. This connection supports the growth of gastronomic tourism and fosters economic prosperity in rural communities. By certifying product quality and establishing a unique link to the production area, GIs not only promote tourism but also aid in building a distinctive and appealing brand for the destination (Arion, 2024).

Geographical indications serve as a powerful tool for valorizing local products and cultural heritage. They play a crucial role in tourism development by enhancing the attractiveness of destinations and supporting economic growth. By leveraging GIs, regions can effectively promote their unique attributes, attract tourists, and contribute to broader economic and cultural benefits (Nizam & Tatari, 2022).

The primary aim of this review is to investigate how Geographical Indications (GIs) can be effectively harnessed to support tourism development and bolster destination branding. It focuses on understanding the role GIs play in enhancing the attractiveness of tourist destinations by showcasing unique local products, which in turn can drive visitor interest and boost regional economic activity. The review will delve into how GIs contribute to the creation and reinforcement of a destination's brand identity, making it stand out in the global tourism arena. It will also explore how GIs intersect with local cultural and traditional practices, supporting tourism initiatives by preserving and promoting regional heritage. By examining successful implementations and identifying key strategies, the review aims to offer practical insights into leveraging GIs for tourism growth. Additionally, it will address the challenges and opportunities associated with integrating GIs into tourism and branding strategies, providing a well-rounded perspective on their impact and potential benefits.

GEOGRAPHICAL INDICATIONS AND TOURISM DEVELOPMENT

The integration of GIs into tourism has proven highly beneficial, generating substantial income and creating employment opportunities across various sectors. Recognized GIs drive increased tourism activity, which in turn benefits local producers and related industries such as accommodation services, gift shops, and restaurants (Dogan & Gokovali, 2012). By leveraging the geographical name of a product, GIs effectively draw attention to local identity, enhancing the appeal of the destination. One significant advantage of GIs in tourism is their role in the creation of enogastronomic tourist routes. These routes integrate national history, culture, and local culinary traditions into a cohesive tourism product. This approach not only enhances tourist numbers and profitability but also boosts employment, attracts investment in domestic producers, stimulates the national economy, and elevates global recognition (Matviichuk et al., 2023). The establishment of such routes underscores the potential of GIs to enrich the tourism experience and drive regional development.

Local communities are instrumental in the registration and protection of GIs for new regional innovations. They help manage and safeguard these indications while assisting the government in their implementation. Tourism intellectual property-based GIs can effectively brand unique destinations, attracting both local and international tourists. They also play a crucial role in shaping tourism policy by showcasing a diverse range of products (Saputro et al., 2023). Furthermore, authentic GI-based souvenirs from tourist destinations enhance tourists' perceived value and purchase intention. These souvenirs reflect local heritage, history, and craftsmanship, contributing to local economic growth by increasing resident income, creating jobs, and supporting local entrepreneurship (Das & Dileep, 2023). The positive impact of GIs extends to the handicraft industry, supporting the growth and development of both tourism and local crafts, particularly in rural areas (Török et al., 2020).

The recognition of GIs fosters trust in product differentiation, aiding producers in market positioning and enhancing regional marketing efforts. It promotes prosperity, income, and regional appeal by highlighting the unique products and services of a territory, supporting tourism through distinctive advertising, and enriching tourist experiences with local souvenirs (Covalkchuck & Medeiros, 2023). By connecting food, place, and culture, GIs encourage visits to regions and interactions with local producers, thereby extending economic benefits beyond agriculture to include tourism and artisanal activities (Van Caenegem et al., 2014).

As the tourism industry evolves, offering valuable opportunities for business, employment, and state revenue, both the creative and tourism sectors become essential national assets. Protecting these assets through intellectual property registration, especially for GIs, is crucial for maximizing their long-term benefits (Ferdian, 2021). Promoting GIs can serve as a strategic investment, fostering the creation of value-enhancing local businesses and providing a unified approach to regional promotion (Cei, 2018).

Geographical Indications (GIs) offer substantial benefits for tourism by generating income and creating jobs across various sectors such as accommodation, gift shops, and restaurants. They enhance local identity and appeal through product names linked to specific regions, facilitate the development of gastronomic tourism by integrating history and culinary traditions, and boost regional tourism and economic growth. GIs assist in branding unique destinations, attracting both local and international tourists, and influencing tourism policy. They also increase the perceived value of authentic souvenirs, support the handicraft industry, and enrich regional marketing and tourism experiences.

GEOGRAPHICAL INDICATIONS AND DESTINATION BRANDING

Destination branding can be defined as the set of marketing activities that support the creation of a distinctive identity for a destination, while also conveying expectations of a memorable travel experience uniquely associated with that place. As conceptualized by Blain, Levy & Ritchie (2005), these activities serve multiple purposes: they help create and reinforce an emotional connection between visitors and the destination, reduce consumer search costs and perceived risks, and ultimately influence destination choice. This definition builds on earlier work by scholars such as Aaker (1991), who emphasized the importance of identification and differentiation in branding, and Ritchie & Ritchie (1998), who highlighted the role of conveying expectations about the travel experience. It also incorporates insights from Berry (2000) on emotional connections in branding, and Woodside (1982) on reducing consumer search costs. The authors arrived at this comprehensive definition by synthesizing concepts from branding literature and incorporating input from destination marketing organization (DMO) practitioners, reflecting both theoretical underpinnings and practical applications in the field of destination marketing.

Destination branding is essential for attracting tourists by establishing a unique identity and image for a place, distinguishing it from competitors, and influencing visitor choice. As Blain et al. (2005) highlight, effective destination branding serves multiple purposes: it aids in identification and differentiation by creating a distinctive identity in a saturated market (Blain et al., 2005); it sets expectations by conveying the promise of a memorable experience, which affects visitor decision-making (Ritchie & Ritchie, 1998); it fosters an emotional connection between visitors and the destination, which can motivate and encourage repeat visits (Berry, 2000); it reduces perceived risk by offering a consistent image and quality promise, crucial for a product that cannot be tested before purchase (Blain et al., 2005); it enhances the destination's overall image, influencing potential visitors' perceptions (Lee et al., 2002, as cited in Blain et al., 2005); it facilitates marketing efforts by providing a unifying element for promotional activities (Blain et al., 2005); and ultimately, it aims to influence consumer choice by creating a strong, positive, and distinctive image that boosts a destination's appeal (Blain et al., 2005).

Geographical Indications (GIs) are signs or labels used on products that have a specific geographical origin and possess qualities, characteristics, or reputation essentially attributable to that origin. According to the World Intellectual Property Organization (WIPO), as cited in the document, "A geographical indication (GI) is a sign used on products that have a specific geographical origin and possess qualities or a reputation that are due to that origin." GIs serve as a form of intellectual property right, differing from other such rights like trademarks or patents in their collective nature (Delphine, 2008). They identify goods where a given quality, reputation, or other characteristic is essentially linked to its geographical origin, often resulting from environmental factors, traditional processing methods, or manufacturing skills unique to that area (Blakeney, 2001). GIs can apply to a wide range of products, including agricultural goods, foodstuffs, handicrafts, and industrial products, providing a crucial link between product quality and place of origin.

In the context of destination branding and tourism, GIs can significantly enhance a location's appeal by highlighting its unique local offerings and cultural heritage (Akın, 2006; Şentürk, 2011). GIs allow destinations to differentiate themselves in competitive markets by highlighting products with specific qualities tied to their geographical origin (Blakeney, 2001). This not only adds value to local products but also preserves cultural heritage and traditional know-how (Barjolle et al., 2009; Cerdan et al., 2009). The GI system protects local producers and often leads to premium pricing, thereby supporting local economies (Addor and Grazioli, 2002). Furthermore, GI products are frequently associated with higher quality and sustainable practices, enhancing the overall perceived quality of the destination (Mascarello et al., 2015). GIs directly influence the development of local and nation-wide economies, marketing of tourism activities and branding of destination. By linking quality, reputation, and authenticity to geographical origin, GIs create a strong, differentiated brand identity that can attract tourists and enhance the destination's overall appeal in the tourism market (Delphine, 2008; Oraman, 2015).

STRATEGIES TO LEVERAGE GIS FOR DESTINATION BRANDING

Geographical Indications (GIs) offer powerful branding opportunities for products with strong ties to specific locations. Effective strategies for leveraging GIs in branding include creating branded experiences through cultural tourism, experiential marketing, and immersive storytelling. Partnerships with local producers can lead to collaborative branding, joint marketing campaigns, and product bundling. The GI certification itself can be used as a quality assurance mark in branding materials and educational marketing efforts. Sustainability and ethical branding can emphasize traditional production practices and community support. Digital and e-commerce strategies, such as specialized online platforms and influencer collaborations, can enhance the reach of GI products. GIs can also play a crucial role in destination branding, incorporating regional branding and GI-focused tourism routes. Innovative retail and packaging approaches, including premium packaging design and exclusive retail partnerships, can further elevate the perceived value of GI products. By implementing these strategies, brands can harness the unique value of GIs to develop strong, distinctive, and culturally resonant identities that appeal to consumers seeking authentic, place-based experiences and products.

Geographical Indications (GIs) have been effectively utilized in India not only to promote products but also to enhance the branding of tourism destinations. Here are some examples of successful tourism destination branding campaigns in India that have leveraged GIs are Darjeeling (Darjeeling Tea), Kutch (Kutch Embroidery and Rogan Art), Kashmir (Pashmina Shawls and Kashmiri Saffron), Mysore (Mysore Silk and Mysore Betel Leaf), Varanasi (Banarasi Sarees) etc.

IMPACT OF GIS ON LOCAL ECONOMIES AND COMMUNITIES

Geographical Indications (GIs) significantly impact local economies and communities through various channels. Economically, GIs enhance the market value of products, such as French Champagne or Italian Parmesan cheese, leading to higher incomes for producers. They also improve market access and protect against counterfeiting, benefiting small-scale producers and local businesses. Additionally, GIs promote rural development by driving tourism and investment in rural areas, creating jobs, and diversifying local economies. Socially and culturally, GIs help preserve traditional production methods and cultural practices, strengthen community identity, and improve quality of life by supporting local economies and infrastructure. Environmentally, GIs often involve sustainable production practices that protect ecosystems and preserve landscapes integral to the product's identity.

CONCLUSION

Geographical Indications (GIs) have emerged as a vital tool for enhancing both tourism development and destination branding. By tying products to their geographical origins, GIs provide a unique identity that differentiates destinations in the competitive tourism market. As outlined in this chapter, GIs contribute significantly to local economies by supporting traditional practices, boosting regional tourism, and fostering rural development. They create added value for local products, enhance the appeal of tourist destinations through authentic experiences, and support the preservation of cultural heritage. The integration of GIs into tourism strategies, such as the development of local souvenirs, underscores their potential to drive economic growth and enrich the tourism experience. Furthermore, GIs play a crucial role in shaping destination branding by establishing a strong, distinctive identity that attracts visitors and supports local branding efforts. As demonstrated by successful examples in India, GIs not only enhance product quality and market positioning but also contribute to regional development and global recognition. Therefore, leveraging GIs effectively can lead to a more vibrant, sustainable tourism sector and a richer, more culturally connected travel experience.

REFERENCES

Aaker, D. A. (1991). *Managing Brand Equity*. Free Press.

Addor, F., & Grazioli, A. (2002). Geographical indications beyond wines and spirits: A roadmap for a better protection for geographical indications in the WTO TRIPS Agreement. *The Journal of World Intellectual Property*, 5(6), 865–897. DOI: 10.1111/j.1747-1796.2002.tb00185.x

Akın, E. B. (2006). Coğrafi işaret olarak tescil edilmiş Malatya kayısısının teknolojik özelliklerinin saptanması ve gıda güvenliği açısından araştırılması [Doctoral dissertation]. Hacettepe University.

Arion, O. V. (2024). Geographical indications and traditional products as the basis of enogastronomic tourism: Significance for the development of rural communities (on the example of Italy). *Journal of Geology Geography and Geoecology*, 33(1), 3–13. DOI: 10.15421/112401

Barjolle, D., Paus, M., & Perret, A. (2009). Impacts of geographical indications - review of methods and empirical evidences. International Association of Agricultural Economists Conference, Beijing, China.

Berry, L. L. (2000). Cultivating Service Brand Equity. *Journal of the Academy of Marketing Science*, 28(1), 128–137. DOI: 10.1177/0092070300281012

Blain, C., Levy, S. E., & Ritchie, J. R. B. (2005). Destination Branding: Insights and Practices from Destination Management Organizations. *Journal of Travel Research*, 43(4), 328–338. DOI: 10.1177/0047287505274646

Blakeney, M. (2001). Proposals for the international regulation of geographical indications. *The Journal of World Intellectual Property*, 4(5), 629–652. DOI: 10.1111/j.1747-1796.2001.tb00131.x

Cei, L., Defrancesco, E., & Stefani, G. (2018). From Geographical Indications to Rural Development: A Review of the economic effects of European Union policy. *Sustainability (Basel)*, 10(10), 3745. DOI: 10.3390/su10103745

Cerdan, C., Vitrolles, D., Delfosse, C., Velloso, C. Q., Nabinger, C., & Silva, A. L. (2009). Penser la conservation des ressources bioculturelles sous l'angle de la valorisation de l'origine: La mise en place d'indications géographiques dans le Sud Brésil. *Autrepart (La Tour d'Aigues)*, 50, 153–166. DOI: 10.3917/autr.050.0153

Covalkchuck, G. C. & Medeiros, M. D. L. (2023). Geographical indication of Sao Matheus as a boost to gastronomic tourism. Tourism & heritage journal, 5, 37-55. DOI: .DOI: 10.1344/THJ.2023.5.3

Das, D., & Dileep, M. R. (2023). Geographical Indication and Tourism: A Study on the Awareness, Factors Influence, and the Scope of GI Tagging in Kerala as a Rural Tourism Development Tool. *International Journal of Hospitality and Tourism Systems*, 16(4), 25–34.

Delphine, M. V. (2008). From plant variety definition to geographical indication protection: A search for the link between Basmati rice and India/Pakistan. *The Journal of World Intellectual Property*, 11(4), 321–344. DOI: 10.1111/j.1747-1796.2008.00341.x

Dogan, B., & Gokovali, U. (2012). Geographical indications: The aspects of rural development and marketing through the traditional products. *Procedia: Social and Behavioral Sciences*, 62, 761–765. DOI: 10.1016/j.sbspro.2012.09.128

Ferdian, M. (2021). Legal Protection of Geographical Indications for Local Handicrafts in Tourism Activities in Indonesia. *Advances in Social Science, Education and Humanities Research*, 605, 333–336.

Hadelan, L.. (2021). Food geographical indication in enhancing agricultural and tourism performance. *Scientific Papers. Series Management, Economic, Engineering in Agriculture and Rural Development*, 21(1), 361–368.

Jaelani, A. K., Handayani, I. G. A. K. R. & Karjoko, L. (2020). Development of tourism based on geographic indication towards to welfare state. International journal of advanced science and technology, 29(3), 1227-1234.

Mascarello, G., Pinto, A., Parise, N., Crovato, S., & Ravarotto, L. (2015). The perception of food quality. Profiling Italian consumers. *Appetite*, 89, 175–182. DOI: 10.1016/j.appet.2015.02.014 PMID: 25681654

Matviichuk, L. Y., Lepkyi, M. I., Dashchuk, Y. Y., Sydoruk, S. V., & Mezentseva, I. V. (2023). Approach to formation of enogastronomic tourism based on the geographical indication system. *Journal of Geology Geography and Geoecology*, 31(4), 689–701. DOI: 10.15421/112265

Nizam, D., & Tatari, M. F. (2022). Rural revitalization through territorial distinctiveness: The use of geographical indications in Turkey. *Journal of Rural Studies*, 93, 144–154. DOI: 10.1016/j.jrurstud.2020.07.002

Oraman, Y. (2015). Türkiye'de coğrafi işaretli ürünler. *Balkan and Near Eastern Journal of Social Sciences*, 1(1), 76–85.

Pamukçu, H., Saraç, Ö., Aytuğar, S., & Sandıkçı, M. (2021). The Effects of Local Food and Local Products with Geographical Indication on the Development of Tourism Gastronomy. *Sustainability (Basel)*, 13(12), 6692. DOI: 10.3390/su13126692

Ritchie, J. R. B., & Ritchie, R. J. B. (1998). The Branding of Tourism Destinations: Past Achievements and Future Challenges. *Proceedings of the 1998 Annual Congress of the International Association of Scientific Experts in Tourism, Destination Marketing: Scopes and Limitations*, Marrakech, Morocco, 89-116.

Saputro, T. A., Pujiyono, P., & Latifah, E. (2023). The Role of the Local Community in Geographic Indications based on Tourism Intellectual Property. *ICLSSE*, 2022. Advance online publication. DOI: 10.4108/eai.28-10-2022.2326401

Şentürk, B. (2011). Coğrafi işaretlerin ekonomik etkileri: Mikro ve makro açıdan bir değerlendirme [Master's thesis]. Muğla University.

Suh, J., & MacPherson, A. (2007). The impact of geographical indication on the revitalisation of a regional economy: A case study of 'Boseong' green tea. *Area*, 39(4), 518–527. DOI: 10.1111/j.1475-4762.2007.00765.x

Török, Á., Jantyik, L., Maró, Z. M., & Moir, H. V. J. (2020). Understanding the Real-World Impact of Geographical Indications: A Critical review of the Empirical Economic literature. *Sustainability (Basel)*, 12(22), 9434. DOI: 10.3390/su12229434

Turkish Patent Institute. (n.d.). Coğrafi işaretler. Retrieved from http://www.turkpatent .gov.tr

Van Caenegem, W., Cleary, J. A., & Drahos, P. (2014). Pride and profit: Geographical indications as regional development tools in Australia. *Journal of Economic and Social Policy*, 16(1), 1–25.

Woodside, A. (1982). Positioning a Province Using Travel Research. *Journal of Travel Research*, 20(3), 2–6. DOI: 10.1177/004728758202000301

Yıkmı, S. & Ünal, A. (2016). The importance of geographical indication in gastronomy tourism: Turkey. International Journal of Agricultural and Life Sciences- IJALS (2016), Volume 2(4) pp.73-79.

Chapter 12
The Power of Place:
Geographical Indicators as a Marketing Tool in Indian Tourism

Rajeev Semwal
https://orcid.org/0000-0003-4572-5411
Amity University, Noida, India

Priyanka Tyagi
https://orcid.org/0000-0002-7898-2708
Chandigarh University, India

Tirthajani Panda
Government Autonomous College, Rourkela, India

ABSTRACT

Geographical indicators (GIs) promote tourism by highlighting regional characteristics and local product cultural significance. This chapter looks at Indian tourism marketing with GIs. Indian GIs like Darjeeling Tea, Kanjeevaram Silk, and Basmati Rice are defined, important, and statused. The chapter discusses how GIs promote regional identity and attract tourists seeking authentic, place-based experiences. It examines how GIs can boost destination branding, product differentiation, and sustainable tourism. This chapter discusses successful tourism GI applications and marketing campaigns using case studies. It addresses GI marketing issues like misuse, brand dilution, and quality control and offers solutions. The chapter discusses innovative trends like digital marketing, virtual tours, and regional collaboration. These opportunities help destinations increase appeal, attract niche markets, and promote sustainable tourism. The chapter illustrates how GIs boost tourism and regional development.

DOI: 10.4018/979-8-3693-4171-1.ch012

1. INTRODUCTION

Geographical indicators (GIs) are intellectual property rights safeguarding goods from certain geographical areas where their original qualities are inextricably connected to their source (Dagne, 2010). These markers of regional authenticity, quality, and tradition help to differentiate goods and experiences whose unique characteristics come from their local setting (Basile & Cavallo, 2020). Within the framework of tourism, GIs may be rather important for advancing regional identity, safeguarding cultural legacy, and improving the attractiveness of locations.

Fundamentally, GIs are meant to safeguard the prestige of locally distinctive items like the renowned Darjeeling Tea or the opulent Kanjeevaram Silk of India. These markers guarantee that only goods really from these areas may be sold under these designations, therefore preserving the integrity of regional farming methods and artisanal work. Linking the quality and reputation of a product to its geographical source helps GIs not only ensure authenticity but also support regional businesses and cultural traditions (Bartoli et al., 2022a).

In travel, GIs are a useful instrument for producing unique and real trip experiences. They help places to take advantage of their special regional qualities and attract visitors eager to discover local history and handicap work. For example, a trip to Darjeeling's tea farms or a tour stressing the ancient methods underlying Kanjeevaram Silk may give visitors unique experiences transcending ordinary tourism. Those who search for real and culturally rich connections find these events more interesting, which helps niche tourism sectors grow.

The preservation of cultural legacy depends especially on the help of GIs (Santos et al., 2021). GIs assist in preserving the continuation of cultural traditions that could otherwise be in danger of fading by supporting regional specialities and traditional ways of life. Apart from giving local communities financial incentives, this preservation enhances the cultural fabric of the travel sector by giving guests a better knowledge of the places they go to. This chapter seeks to investigate how the Indian tourist industry may make best use of GIs as a marketing tool. We will investigate the strategic advantages of including GIs in tourist marketing efforts, offer case studies of effective implementations, and look at the possible advantages and difficulties. We want to show how GIs could improve destination branding, increase tourist involvement, and support sustainable tourism growth by examining how they are included in tourism plans.

Although GIS have several advantages for tourism, their use presents certain difficulties. Maintaining the quality and validity of the indicators, negotiating legal and regulatory complexity, and resolving problems like possible misrepresentation or abuse help to guarantee that GIs are used properly. As we investigate these facets, the chapter will offer ideas on how tourism players could overcome obstacles to maximise the benefits of GIs.

Emphasising their function in improving regional authenticity, maintaining cultural legacy, and generating distinctive travel experiences, the chapter will provide a thorough review of the value of geographical indicators in Indian tourism overall. Understanding and intelligently using GIs can help tourism businesses and destinations to stand out in a crowded market and create closer relationships with guests.

2. UNDERSTANDING GEOGRAPHICAL INDICATORS

Geographical indicators (GIs) are a type of intellectual property whereby a specific geographical area is identified from which a certain quality, reputation, or other attribute of the product is naturally connected (Menggala et al., 2021). GIs help to safeguard goods whose special qualities come from their geographical surroundings: the soil, temperature, and traditional manufacturing techniques specific to the area.

Legally, GIs resemble trademarks but concentrate on the geographical source rather than the brand name (Mao, 2022). They give special rights to use certain names or symbols connected to a geographical area, therefore guaranteeing that only goods really from that place will have the GI designation. For instance, "Darjeeling Tea" is GI; hence, only tea produced in the Darjeeling area of India may be sold under this label. This legal protection guarantees that consumers get items that are authentic to their regional beginnings and helps stop abuse.

Economically, GIs greatly increase the marketability and attractiveness of items, therefore adding great value. They enable manufacturers to charge premium pricing and get a competitive edge depending on the special qualities connected with their geographic origin, therefore helping to differentiate products in competitive marketplaces (Sood & Sharma, 2024). The economic importance also reaches to regional development, as GIs may boost local businesses by means of tourism, support of traditional sectors, and endorsement of sustainable practices. GIs, for example, may boost tourism by drawing guests eager for real, place-based activities such as guided tours of vineyards or courses on traditional handicaps.

All things considered, GIs are rather important for maintaining the quality and reputation of goods connected to their geographical sources and for helping areas economically as well as for producers.

2.1 Geographical indicators in India

Geographical indicators (GIs) are a major feature of India's intellectual property scene and help to preserve and promote the nation's many regional goods (Marie-Vivien, 2020). The Geographical Indications of Goods (Registration and Protection) Act, 1999, controls the GI system in India by providing legal protection to goods with traits or reputations linked to their geographical source.

One of the most well-known GIs in India, Darjeeling Tea, shows the results of this approach (Das, 2006). Only tea grown in West Bengal's Darjeeling area may be sold under this brand, which is protected as a GI. By guaranteeing that buyers get the real product and thereby supporting local tea farms and farmers, this protection helps preserve the high quality and distinctive taste character of the tea. By drawing visitors and tea drinkers to the area, the GI rating also improves the marketability of the product, both locally and globally.

Kanjeevaram Silk is another renowned GI that reflects Tamil Nadu's rich textile legacy (Nithyaprakash et al., 2021). Only Kanjeevaram spins this opulent silk fabric, renowned for its vivid colours and complex patterns. Since only real Kanjeevaram Silk may wear the GI mark, the GI protection supports the local weaving community and helps to maintain traditional weaving practices. This, in turn, promotes both regional development and cultural tourism.

Celebrated for its unique scent and large grain, basmati rice is a GI-protected food from particular areas of India, including sections of Punjab, Haryana, and Uttarakhand. The GI classification guarantees that only rice farmed in specified regions may be sold as basmati, therefore limiting abuse and improving the value of this basic food. This safeguard not only benefits nearby rice growers but also enhances India's position in the global rice market.

The GI system in India generally plays a crucial role in preserving the originality of regional products, boosting local businesses, and aiding economic growth through both domestic and international markets.

2.2 Role in Tourism

Geographical indicators (GIs) improve regional identity and attract visitors looking for real, place-based experiences, thus transforming the travel industry(Alaux et al., 2023; Owen et al., 2020). GIs give strong arguments for visitors to come and experience particular places by stressing the special qualities of goods and customs connected to different locales.

GIs improve tourism mostly by encouraging regional identity, which helps to strengthen travel (Pazhuhan & Shiri, 2020a). GI's products frequently reflect the natural resources, cultural legacy, and traditional methods of their areas (Angelstam et al., 2021). This connection between a product and its location enhances the travel experience by providing guests with a deeper understanding of the local customs and culture. For instance, the GI classification of Darjeeling Tea has become a major attraction for visitors. In addition to the tea itself, Darjeeling's breathtaking scenery and the opportunity to explore tea plantations and discover age-old tea-making techniques draw visitors. This immersive experience helps visitors appreciate the local culture more and connects them with the area's legacy.

Similarly, Kanjeevaram Silk supports tourism by highlighting Tamil Nadu's rich textile legacy. Visitors to the area may participate in events that include seeing silk weaving factories, browsing historic marketplaces, and seeing the complex process of silk manufacturing. Because visitors are certain of the quality and traditional workmanship behind the items, Kanjeevaram Silk's GI certification gives legitimacy to these encounters. This benefits nearby artists as well as entices visitors to buy genuine native items.

The GI status of Basmati rice also influences tourism, especially in areas like Punjab and Haryana where rice farming is a pillar of local life. Tourism projects that emphasize agricultural tours offer unique and instructive opportunities, allowing guests to witness the farming process and participate in harvest celebrations. These visits allow visitors to interact with the nearby agricultural people and learn about the significance of basmati rice in the area's cultural and commercial life.

GIs generally improve tourism by providing unique and real experiences that honor regional legacy (Angelstam et al., 2021). Using the special features linked with GIs, locations may draw visitors interested in cultural immersion and help to preserve regional customs and businesses. By using well-chosen tourism experiences connected to GIs, areas can efficiently highlight their special qualities and establish unforgettable interactions with tourists.

3. LEVERAGING GIS FOR TOURISM MARKETING

Incorporating Geographical Indicators (GIs) into tourism marketing strategies offers several strategic advantages, enhancing destination branding, differentiating tourism products, and supporting sustainable tourism development(Bartoli et al., 2022b). GIs can effectively amplify a region's unique attributes, providing a compelling narrative that attracts tourists and creates a distinct competitive edge.

Enhancing Destination Branding: GIs help build strong, authentic destination brands by emphasising the unique qualities associated with a specific place (Dadashpour Moghaddam et al., 2022). For example, Darjeeling Tea's GI status not only promotes the tea itself, but also reinforces Darjeeling's branding as a premier tea tourism destination. This association between the product and the destination helps create a cohesive brand identity that resonates with tourists seeking authentic experiences. By aligning a destination's brand with its GI-protected products, marketers can craft compelling stories that highlight regional uniqueness and cultural heritage.

Differentiating Tourism Products: In a competitive market, GIs provide a valuable tool for differentiating tourism products(Chen et al., 2022). By leveraging the exclusivity and authenticity associated with GIs, tourism operators can create unique offerings that stand out. For instance, tourism operators in Tamil Nadu have developed specialised textile tours using Kanjeevaram Silk. These tours provide visitors with exclusive access to traditional weaving workshops and marketplaces, showcasing the region's craftsmanship. The GI status of Kanjeevaram Silk not only guarantees the products authenticity, but also enhances the appeal of these tours by linking them to a revered cultural heritage.

Supporting Sustainable Tourism Development: GIs contribute to sustainable tourism by promoting local industries and preserving cultural practices(Pazhuhan & Shiri, 2020b). By focussing on GI-protected products, tourism marketing can drive demand for locally produced goods and support traditional industries. This approach helps maintain regional craftsmanship and supports the economic development of local communities. For example, in Punjab, the promotion of Basmati rice through agricultural tourism not only educates visitors about the rice cultivation process, but also promotes sustainable farming practices. This form of tourism generates income for local farmers and encourages environmentally friendly practices, aligning with the principles of sustainable tourism.

Case Studies:

- **Darjeeling Tea**:The successful marketing of Darjeeling Tea as a premium product has driven tourism to the region, where visitors can engage in tea-tasting experiences and explore tea estates. This approach leverages the GI status to enhance the destination's brand and attract niche markets interested in tea tourism.
- **Kanjeevaram Silk**: Specialised textile tours in Tamil Nadu capitalise on the GI status of Kanjeevaram Silk, offering tourists immersive experiences in traditional weaving and textile arts. This strategy differentiates the region's tourism products and supports the preservation of local craftsmanship.

In conclusion, integrating GIs into tourism marketing strategies provides significant benefits by enhancing destination branding, differentiating tourism products, and supporting sustainable development. By leveraging the unique attributes associated with GIs, destinations can create compelling, authentic experiences that attract and engage tourists while promoting regional heritage and local economies.

3.2 Case Studies in India

3.2.1 Darjeeling Tea

Darjeeling Tea, recognized as one of India's most prestigious GIs, is a prime example of leveraging geographical indicators in tourism marketing. The Darjeeling region of West Bengal cultivates the tea, known for its distinct flavour and aromatic qualities. The GI status of Darjeeling Tea has been effectively used to enhance tourism by creating immersive experiences centred around tea production (Dubey, 2020).

Tourism operators in Darjeeling have capitalised on the GI status to develop tea tourism packages that attract visitors from around the world. These packages frequently include guided tours of tea estates, where tourists can witness the traditional tea-making process, from plucking to processing. Visitors also have the opportunity to participate in tea tastings, exploring the unique flavours of different Darjeeling tea varieties. Additionally, some tours offer stays at heritage tea bungalows, providing an authentic experience of life on a tea estate.

The promotion of Darjeeling Tea as a premium product with a unique GI status has not only boosted the region's tourism, but also reinforced its global brand. This strategy has successfully differentiated Darjeeling from other tea-growing regions, creating a niche market for tea enthusiasts and travellers interested in experiencing the region's cultural and agricultural heritage.

3.2.2 Kanjeevaram Silk

Kanjeevaram Silk, a traditional silk fabric from Tamil Nadu, is another exemplary case of using GIs in tourism marketing (De Mattos Fagundes et al., 2012). The Kanjeevaram Silk GI status protects the authenticity of this luxurious textile, which is renowned for its vibrant colours and intricate patterns. Tourism initiatives in Tamil Nadu have leveraged this GI to attract visitors interested in traditional crafts and textiles.

Heritage tours focused on Kanjeevaram Silk provide tourists with a deep dive into the history and craftsmanship of silk weaving. These tours often include visits to weaving workshops, where tourists can observe skilled artisans at work and learn about the traditional techniques passed down through generations. Some tours also include interactive workshops where visitors can try their hand at weaving or dyeing fabrics, providing a hands-on experience of the craft.

Various cultural festivals and exhibitions have featured Kanjeevaram Silk, further promoting the textile and its GI status. These events showcase the fabric's significance in local culture and attract tourists interested in fashion and traditional arts.

3.2.3 Basmati Rice

Another example of effectively using geographical indicators in tourism marketing is Basmati Rice, given its GI status (Arif et al., 2021). In regions such as Punjab and Haryana, tourism initiatives focus on agricultural experiences related to rice cultivation. These tours offer visitors the opportunity to explore rice fields, participate in harvest festivals, and learn about traditional farming practices.

These agricultural tourism experiences promote Basmati Rice, which not only highlights the GI-protected product but also educates tourists about sustainable farming practices and the cultural significance of rice cultivation in the region. This approach supports local farmers and contributes to the preservation of traditional agricultural methods while enhancing the overall tourism experience.

These case studies demonstrate how effectively leveraging GIs can create unique and compelling tourism experiences, attract niche markets, and support local economies and cultural heritage.

3.3 Integrating GIs into Tourism Campaigns

Integrating Geographical Indicators (GIs) into tourism marketing campaigns requires strategic planning and execution to effectively leverage their unique qualities (Bartoli et al., 2022c). Practical strategies for integrating GIs involve branding, promotional activities, and partnerships that create compelling narratives and attract niche markets.

Branding Strategies: Integrating GIs into destination branding involves highlighting the unique attributes associated with a region's GI-protected products(Török et al., 2020). Tourism campaigns should emphasise how these products embody the cultural and historical essence of the area. For example, a branding strategy for **Darjeeling Tea** might include visual elements like the lush tea gardens and the heritage of tea cultivation, combined with storytelling that conveys the tea's unique flavour profile and the region's tradition. Using GIs as a central theme in branding helps create a distinctive identity for the destination, making it stand out in a crowded market.

Effective promotional activities use the GI status to create engaging and memorable tourism experiences (Panas et al., 2022). This can include designing specialised tours that showcase the production processes of GI-protected products, such as guided tours of **Kanjeevaram silk** weaving workshops or tea estates. Marketing materials should feature high-quality imagery and videos that capture the essence of these experiences. Digital marketing campaigns can leverage social media platforms to share stories and testimonials from tourists who have experienced the region's

GI-related attractions. Additionally, organising events like food festivals or textile exhibitions that focus on GI products can generate buzz and attract media attention.

Partnerships with Local Businesses and Tourism Boards: Collaborating with local businesses and tourism boards is crucial for successfully integrating GIs into tourism campaigns (Kalvet et al., 2020). Partnerships with local producers and artisans can enhance the authenticity of tourism offerings, such as including GI-protected products in souvenir shops or local markets. Working with tourism boards helps align marketing efforts with regional development goals and ensures a cohesive promotional strategy. For instance, tourism boards can collaborate with tea estates in Darjeeling to develop joint marketing campaigns that promote both the tea and the destination.

Crafting compelling narratives around GIs involves narrating the connection between these products and their geographical origins. Highlighting the craftsmanship, traditions, and local communities behind GI products adds depth to the tourism experience. A campaign focusing on Basmati rice, for example, might include stories of the farmers and the traditional methods used in rice cultivation, offering tourists a glimpse into the cultural significance of the product.

Attracting niche markets: GIs can effectively target niche markets interested in cultural and culinary experiences (Nizam & Tatari, 2022). By showcasing the unique attributes and heritage of GI-protected products, tourism campaigns can appeal to travellers seeking authentic and specialised experiences. Tailoring marketing efforts to these niche audiences ensures that campaigns resonate with their specific interests and preferences.

Integrating GIs into tourism campaigns involves leveraging branding strategies, engaging promotional activities, and forming strategic partnerships. By creating compelling narratives and targeting niche markets, tourism marketers can effectively use GIs to enhance destination appeal and offer unique, authentic experiences.

4. CHALLENGES AND RISK

Using Geographical Indicators (GIs) in tourism marketing presents several challenges and risks that need careful management. These potential pitfalls can impact the effectiveness of GI-based marketing strategies and the overall value of the GI-protected products and destinations.

Misuse and Misrepresentation: One of the primary challenges in GI marketing is the potential misuse or misrepresentation of GIs. If we fail to properly enforce the GI status, we risk marketing products not genuinely originating from the designated geographical area under the GI label. This misrepresentation can undermine the credibility of the GI and dilute its value. For example, if non-Darjeeling teas are sold as "Darjeeling Tea," consumers may become sceptical about the authenticity of the product, leading to a loss of trust in the GI and its associated tourism offerings.

Brand Dilution: Another significant risk is brand dilution. As tourism marketing efforts expand, especially through mass-market channels, there is a danger that the unique qualities of GI-protected products may become overexposed or generalized. If we use the GI too broadly or neglect to emphasize its authentic attributes, this can happen. For instance, if the marketing of Kanjeevaram Silk becomes too commercialised or if its availability spreads beyond traditional sources, the exclusivity and premium perception associated with the silk may diminish. This dilution can affect not only the product's market value but also the effectiveness of related tourism campaigns.

Maintaining Quality Standards: Ensuring consistent quality standards for GI-protected products is crucial yet challenging. For GIs to remain credible and valuable, products must adhere to strict quality standards and traditional methods that define their uniqueness. In tourism marketing, promoting a GI product requires demonstrating that it consistently meets these standards. However, maintaining quality across various production sites and ensuring compliance with GI regulations can be difficult, especially as demand grows. For example, if the quality of basmati rice produced in different regions does not consistently meet the high standards associated with the GI, it can affect consumer perceptions and the overall success of related tourism initiatives.

Navigating the legal and regulatory landscape associated with GIs can also present challenges. Ensuring that all stakeholders, including local producers and tourism operators, adhere to GI regulations requires effective enforcement mechanisms and collaboration with regulatory bodies. Inconsistent application or enforcement of GI protections can lead to disputes and legal complications, impacting the stability of marketing efforts.

Cultural Sensitivity: Lastly, there is the challenge of ensuring cultural sensitivity and authenticity in GI marketing. Misrepresenting or oversimplifying the cultural significance of GI-protected products can lead to negative perceptions and alienate local communities. Tourism campaigns must carefully balance promotional activities with respect for local traditions and practices.

GIs offer valuable marketing opportunities, addressing the challenges of misuse, brand dilution, maintaining quality standards, regulatory complexities, and cultural sensitivity is essential for successful and sustainable GI-based tourism marketing. Effective management and strategic planning can help mitigate these risks and maximise the benefits of using GIs in tourism.

4.1 Legal and regulatory Issues

The protection and enforcement of geographical indicators (GIs) in tourism face several legal and regulatory challenges that are crucial for maintaining the integrity and value of GI-protected products. Addressing these challenges requires a robust legal framework and effective enforcement mechanisms to safeguard against infringement and misuse.

Intellectual Property Issues: To uphold their value and authenticity, GIs, as a form of intellectual property, require strong legal protections. The primary legal issue is preventing unauthorized use or infringement of products that do not genuinely originate from the designated geographical area under the GI label. These practices mislead consumers and dilute the value of the Geographical Indication (GI). For instance, selling non-Darjeeling tea as "Darjeeling Tea" undermines the credibility of the GI, harming both the product's reputation and the tourism marketing efforts associated with it.

To effectively protect GIs, countries must have robust legal frameworks in place. In India, the Geographical Indications of Goods (Registration and Protection) Act, 1999, provides a legal basis for registering and protecting GIs. However, the implementation of this framework requires rigorous enforcement to address issues of infringement and counterfeiting. Different jurisdictions may have varying levels of protection and enforcement capabilities, making it particularly challenging to extend and enforce GI protections across international borders.

Enforcement Challenges: Effective enforcement of GI protections involves monitoring and regulating the use of GI labels, conducting investigations into potential infringements, and taking legal action against violators. This can be resource-intensive and complex, especially when dealing with cross-border infringements. Coordination between local authorities, legal professionals, and international organisations is essential to address these challenges and ensure consistent protection of GIs.

International cooperation is necessary for protecting GIs, given the global nature of trade and tourism. Bilateral and multilateral agreements, such as those under the World Trade Organisation (WTO) agreements, can facilitate the enforcement of GI protections across borders. Collaborative efforts among countries can help harmonise standards and practices for GI protection, making it easier to address issues of infringement and misuse on a global scale.

Addressing legal and regulatory challenges related to GIs in tourism requires a comprehensive and well-enforced legal framework, effective enforcement mechanisms, and international cooperation. By strengthening these aspects, stakeholders can better protect GI integrity and support the successful marketing of GI-protected products in the tourism sector.

4.2 Strategies for Mitigation

Overcoming the challenges associated with Geographical Indicators (GIs) in tourism requires a multi-faceted approach that includes strengthening legal protections, ensuring consistent quality, and educating stakeholders. Implementing these strategies can help maintain the integrity of GIs and maximise their effectiveness in tourism marketing.

Developing Strong Legal Protections: To address issues of misuse and infringement, it is crucial to establish and maintain robust legal frameworks for GI protection. This involves updating and enforcing legislation to cover all aspects of GI protection, including clear definitions of geographic origin and quality standards. Regular audits and monitoring mechanisms can help detect and address unauthorised use or counterfeiting of GI-protected products. Additionally, strengthening international cooperation through bilateral and multilateral agreements can enhance cross-border enforcement and protect GIs globally. Engaging with intellectual property experts and legal professionals to navigate and enforce GI protections can also contribute to more effective legal safeguards.

Ensuring Consistent Quality: For GI-protected products, maintaining high and consistent quality standards is critical for preserving their value and reputation. Implementing rigorous quality control measures and certification processes can achieve this. Establishing clear guidelines and standards for GI products ensures that all producers adhere to the defined criteria. Regular inspections and quality assessments can help maintain these standards and prevent deviations that could impact the GI's credibility. Collaborating with local producers and industry associations to provide training and resources on quality maintenance can further support these efforts.

Educating stakeholders: Education plays a key role in maintaining the integrity of GIs. Stakeholders, including producers, tourism operators, and consumers, need to understand the significance of GIs and their impact on regional branding and tourism. Conducting awareness campaigns and training programs can help stakeholders recognise the value of GIs and the importance of compliance with GI regulations. Providing producers and tourism operators with resources and support on best practices for marketing and protecting GI products can also reinforce the commitment to maintaining GI integrity.

Addressing the challenges of GI marketing involves developing strong legal protections, ensuring consistent quality, and educating stakeholders. By implementing these strategies, stakeholders can better manage the risks associated with GIs and leverage their potential to enhance tourism and regional branding.

5. FUTURE TRENDS AND OPPORTUNITIES

5.1 Emerging Trends in GI Utilisation

The use of Geographical Indicators (GIs) in tourism is evolving in response to emerging trends driven by technological advancements and shifting consumer preferences. These trends offer new opportunities for leveraging GIs to enhance destination marketing and create unique travel experiences.

The rise of digital marketing and social media has significantly impacted the promotion and utilisation of GIs in tourism. Digital platforms provide a powerful means to reach global audiences and create engaging content that highlights the unique attributes of GI-protected products. For instance, social media campaigns featuring visually appealing images and videos of **Darjeeling tea** plantations or **Kanjeevaram silk** weaving processes can capture the interest of potential tourists. Influencer partnerships and user-generated content can further amplify the reach of GI-related marketing efforts, fostering a broader awareness and appreciation of these products.

Virtual Tours and Augmented Reality: Technological innovations such as virtual tours and augmented reality (AR) offer immersive ways to experience GI-protected products and destinations(Bhatt et al., 2024). Virtual tours allow potential visitors to explore tea estates, silk weaving workshops, or rice paddies from anywhere in the world, providing a taste of the authentic experiences they can expect. AR applications can enhance on-site experiences by overlaying digital information about the history, production processes, and significance of GI products, enriching the tourist's understanding and engagement. For example, an AR app at a **Basmati rice** field could provide interactive information about traditional cultivation methods and the cultural importance of rice in the region.

Integration into Experiential Travel: As consumer preferences shift towards experiential travel, curated travel experiences that emphasise authenticity and cultural immersion are increasingly incorporating **GIs.** Travel packages that feature GI-related activities—such as participating in tea harvesting, attending traditional silk weaving workshops, or engaging in culinary tours centred around GI products—are becoming popular. These experiences cater to travellers seeking deeper connections with local cultures and traditions. By integrating GIs into experiential travel, destinations can offer unique, hands-on activities that differentiate their tourism products and attract niche markets.

Growing consumer awareness of sustainability and ethical tourism is influencing the promotion of GIs. Tourists are increasingly interested in products and experiences that support local communities and environmental conservation. These values are aligned with GI marketing strategies that emphasize sustainable production practices and the positive impact of tourism on local economies. For example, promoting the sustainable practices of **Darjeeling Tea** estates or highlighting eco-friendly initiatives in **Kanjeevaram Silk** production can appeal to environmentally conscious travellers.

Data-Driven Insights: Advances in data analytics and customer insights are also shaping GI strategies. By analysing data on consumer preferences, behaviour, and feedback, tourism marketers can tailor their GI promotions to better meet the needs of their target audiences. Personalised marketing campaigns and targeted outreach can enhance the effectiveness of GI-related tourism efforts and drive greater engagement.

Emerging trends like digital marketing, virtual tours, experiential travel, sustainability, and data-driven insights are revolutionizing the use of GIs in tourism. By leveraging these trends, destinations can enhance their marketing strategies, offer compelling experiences, and effectively connect with modern travellers.

5.2 Opportunities for Innovation

The evolving landscape of tourism presents several opportunities for innovatively utilising Geographical Indicators (GIs) to create unique experiences and foster regional collaboration. Embracing these opportunities can enhance the appeal of GI-protected products and contribute to sustainable tourism development.

a. **New Types of Tourism Experiences**: One significant opportunity is to develop novel tourism experiences centered around GIs. Beyond traditional tours, destinations can create immersive and interactive experiences that showcase the unique aspects of GI-protected products. For example, **Darjeeling Tea** estates could offer bespoke experiences such as tea blending workshops, where visitors create their own custom blends under the guidance of expert tea makers. Similarly, fashion tours featuring Kanjeevaram Silk could offer opportunities to design or tailor garments using traditional techniques. These personalised experiences cater to travellers seeking deeper engagement and create memorable interactions with GI products.
b. **Collaborative Marketing Efforts**: There is considerable potential for innovation through collaborative marketing efforts between regions with complementary GI-protected products. For instance, regions known for different GI products—such as **Basmati Rice** in Punjab and **Kanjeevaram Silk** in Tamil Nadu—can partner to create joint marketing campaigns. These collaborations can include cross-promotional activities, combined travel packages, and shared events that highlight the cultural and economic ties between the regions. Such initiatives not only enhance the visibility of GI products but also attract tourists interested in exploring diverse aspects of Indian heritage.

c. **Sustainable Tourism Initiatives**: Leveraging GIs in sustainable tourism initiatives offers another innovative opportunity. As sustainability becomes a key concern for travellers, incorporating GI products into eco-friendly tourism practices can attract environmentally conscious visitors. For example, tourism operators can develop eco-tours that focus on sustainable production methods of GI products, such as organic tea cultivation or eco-friendly silk production. Highlighting the environmental benefits of GI-protected products and their role in supporting sustainable practices can resonate with travellers seeking to make responsible choices.
d. **Digital and Interactive Experiences:** Using digital technologies to improve the GI tourism experience can drive innovation. Creating virtual reality (VR) experiences that allow users to explore GI product production processes from their homes or developing mobile apps that provide augmented reality (AR) tours can make GI-related tourism more accessible and engaging. These digital innovations can provide educational content, interactive features, and virtual interactions with local artisans, enriching the tourist experience and broadening the reach of GI marketing efforts.
e. **Culinary and Cultural Fusion**: Another innovative opportunity is the fusion of GI products into culinary and cultural experiences. Creating culinary tours that include cooking classes with GI ingredients, such as dishes made with Basmati rice or Darjeeling tea, can provide travelers with unique gastronomic experiences. Additionally, cultural festivals or themed events that celebrate GI products and their origins can create vibrant platforms for showcasing regional traditions and attracting tourists.

Opportunities for innovation in the use of GIs in tourism include creating new types of interactive experiences, fostering regional collaborations, integrating sustainability, and leveraging digital technologies. By exploring these avenues, destinations can enhance the appeal of GI-protected products, attract diverse audiences, and contribute to sustainable tourism development.

6. CONCLUSION

Using Geographic Indicators (GIs) in tourism offers a wonderful chance to broaden and enhance the travel experience while supporting regional authenticity and local economy development. GIs—markers of distinctive regional traits—offer great value by highlighting the cultural and historical relevance of local goods such as Darjeeling Tea, Kanjeevaram Silk, and Basmati Rice. Including GIs in travel marketing plans helps to improve destination branding, provide unique and engaging travel experiences, and strengthen the closer relationship between visitors and the locations they go to.

Using GIs in tourism presents difficulties, even if the overall advantages are quite clear. Possible abuse, trademark dilution, and upholding quality standards are examples of problems that require strong legal systems and attentive administration. Dealing with these issues means creating robust legal safeguards, guaranteeing constant quality, and teaching interested parties the need to maintain GI integrity. These techniques help stakeholders reduce risks and maximize the potential of GIs as a marketing tool.

Looking ahead, new trends and creative ideas present intriguing chances for GI-based travel. The emergence of digital marketing, virtual tours, and augmented reality offers fresh approaches to interact with worldwide consumers and build immersive experiences anchored on GI-protected products. If areas cooperate, integrate GIs into sustainable tourism projects, and develop participatory and culturally rich events, GI-related tourism could become even more appealing. Accepting these ideas would not only draw niche audiences but also promote ethical and environmentally friendly travel methods.

All things considered, the efficient use of GIs in tourism has enormous potential to promote regional development, protect cultural legacy, and provide significant and unforgettable travel opportunities. Destinations can leverage GIs to achieve success in a competitive and dynamic tourism environment by navigating related challenges and seizing opportunities for creativity.

REFERENCES

Alaux, C., Dioko, D., Morgan, N., Florek, M., Carmouze, L., Dessendier, C., Dinnie, K., Fan, H., Freire, J., Hereźniak, M., Lucarelli, A., Mauri, C., Zavattaro, S., & Zenker, S. (2023). *Unpacking the dynamic nature of Geographical Indications (GIs): a longitudinal study on Prosecco as a territorial brand.* 81–82. https://iris.unive.it/handle/10278/5020941

Angelstam, P., Manton, M., Yamelynets, T., Fedoriak, M., Albulescu, A. C., Bravo, F., Cruz, F., Jaroszewicz, B., Kavtarishvili, M., Muñoz-Rojas, J., Sijtsma, F., Washbourne, C. L., Agnoletti, M., Dobrynin, D., Izakovicova, Z., Jansson, N., Kanka, R., Kopperoinen, L., Lazdinis, M., & Zagidullina, A. (2021). Maintaining natural and traditional cultural green infrastructures across Europe: Learning from historic and current landscape transformations. *Landscape Ecology*, 36(2), 637–663. DOI: 10.1007/s10980-020-01161-y

Arif, M., Chilvers, G., Day, S., Naveed, S. A., Woolfe, M., Rodionova, O. Y., Pomerantsev, A. L., Kracht, O., Brodie, C., Mihailova, A., Abrahim, A., Cannavan, A., & Kelly, S. D. (2021). Differentiating Pakistani long-grain rice grown inside and outside the accepted Basmati Himalayan geographical region using a 'one-class' multi-element chemometric model. *Food Control*, 123, 107827. DOI: 10.1016/j.foodcont.2020.107827

Bartoli, C., Bonetti, E., & Mattiacci, A. (2022a). Marketing geographical indication products in the digital age: A holistic perspective. *British Food Journal*, 124(9), 2857–2876. DOI: 10.1108/BFJ-03-2021-0241

Bartoli, C., Bonetti, E., & Mattiacci, A. (2022b). Marketing geographical indication products in the digital age: A holistic perspective. *British Food Journal*, 124(9), 2857–2876. DOI: 10.1108/BFJ-03-2021-0241

Bartoli, C., Bonetti, E., & Mattiacci, A. (2022c). Marketing geographical indication products in the digital age: A holistic perspective. *British Food Journal*, 124(9), 2857–2876. DOI: 10.1108/BFJ-03-2021-0241

Basile, G., & Cavallo, A. (2020). Rural Identity, Authenticity, and Sustainability in Italian Inner Areas. *Sustainability 2020, Vol. 12, Page 1272, 12*(3), 1272. DOI: 10.3390/su12031272

Bhatt, V., Singh, P., Mishra, S., Bhartiya, S., & Tyagi, P. (2024). A Retrospective Analysis of Information Technology in Tourism Research. *African Journal of Hospitality, Tourism and Leisure*, 13(2), 410–420. DOI: 10.46222/ajhtl.19770720.523

Chen, J., Jiang, L., Luo, J., Tian, L., Tian, Y., & Chen, G. (2022). Characteristics and Influencing Factors of Spatial Differentiation of Market Service Industries in Rural Areas around Metropolises—A Case Study of Wuhan City's New Urban Districts. *ISPRS International Journal of Geo-Information 2022, Vol. 11, Page 170, 11*(3), 170. DOI: 10.3390/ijgi11030170

Dadashpour Moghaddam, M., Ahmadzadeh, H., & Valizadeh, R. (2022). A GIS-Based Assessment of Urban Tourism Potential with a Branding Approach Utilizing Hybrid Modeling. *Spatial Information Research*, 30(3), 399–416. DOI: 10.1007/s41324-022-00439-4

Dagne, T. W. (2010). Harnessing the development potential of geographical indications for traditional knowledge-based agricultural products. *Journal of Intellectual Property Law & Practice*, 5(6), 441–458. DOI: 10.1093/jiplp/jpq002

Das, K. (2006). International Protection of India's Geographical Indications with Special Reference to "Darjeeling" Tea. *The Journal of World Intellectual Property*, 9(5), 459–495. DOI: 10.1111/j.1422-2213.2006.00300.x

De Mattos Fagundes, P., Padilha, A. C. M. H., Sluszz, T., & Padula, A. D. (2012). Geographical indication as a market orientation strategy: An analysis of producers of high-quality wines in Southern Brazil. *Journal of Database Marketing and Customer Strategy Management*, 19(3), 163–178. DOI: 10.1057/dbm.2012.18

Dubey, A. (2020). An Analysis of the Challenges Faced by India in the Protection and Enforcement of Geographical Indication through the Case Study of Darjeeling Tea. *International Journal of Law Management & Humanities*, 3(6). https://heinonline.org/HOL/Page?handle=hein.journals/ijlmhs8&id=833&div=&collection=

Kalvet, T., Olesk, M., Tiits, M., & Raun, J. (2020). Innovative Tools for Tourism and Cultural Tourism Impact Assessment. *Sustainability 2020, Vol. 12, Page 7470, 12*(18), 7470. DOI: 10.3390/su12187470

Mao, D. (2022). Geographical Collective Marks in the EU: Should They Be Redefined in the EU Trade Mark Law? Or Should They Be Incorporated into the GIs Regime? SSRN *Electronic Journal*. https://doi.org/DOI: 10.2139/SSRN.4289585

Marie-Vivien, D. (2020). Protection of Geographical Indications in ASEAN countries: Convergences and challenges to awakening sleeping Geographical Indications. *The Journal of World Intellectual Property*, 23(3–4), 328–349. DOI: 10.1111/jwip.12155

Menggala, S. R., Vanhove, W., Muhammad, D. R. A., Rahman, A., Speelman, S., & Van Damme, P. (2021). The Effect of Geographical Indications (GIs) on the Koerintji Cinnamon Sales Price and Information of Origin. *Agronomy 2021, Vol. 11, Page 1410, 11*(7), 1410. DOI: 10.3390/agronomy11071410

Nithyaprakash, V., Niveathitha, S., & Shanmugapriya, V. (2021). *Indian Handloom Design Innovations and Interventions Through Sustenance Lens*. 221–249. DOI: 10.1007/978-981-16-5967-6_10

Nizam, D., & Tatari, M. F. (2022). Rural revitalization through territorial distinctiveness: The use of geographical indications in Turkey. *Journal of Rural Studies*, 93, 144–154. DOI: 10.1016/j.jrurstud.2020.07.002

Owen, L., Udall, D., Franklin, A., & Kneafsey, M. (2020). Place-Based Pathways to Sustainability: Exploring Alignment between Geographical Indications and the Concept of Agroecology Territories in Wales. *Sustainability 2020, Vol. 12, Page 4890, 12*(12), 4890. DOI: 10.3390/su12124890

Panas, G., Thrasidi, N., Halkiopoulos, C., & Gkintoni, E. (2022). Consumer Behavior and Cognitive Factors in Relation to Gastronomic Tourism and Destination Marketing in Greece. *Springer Proceedings in Business and Economics*, 655–677. DOI: 10.1007/978-3-030-92491-1_40

Pazhuhan, M., & Shiri, N. (2020a). Regional tourism axes identification using GIS and TOPSIS model (Case study: Hormozgan Province, Iran). *Journal of Tourism Analysis*, 27(2), 119–141. DOI: 10.1108/JTA-06-2019-0024

Pazhuhan, M., & Shiri, N. (2020b). Regional tourism axes identification using GIS and TOPSIS model (Case study: Hormozgan Province, Iran). *Journal of Tourism Analysis*, 27(2), 119–141. DOI: 10.1108/JTA-06-2019-0024

Santos, B., Gonçalves, J., Martins, A. M., Pérez-Cano, M. T., Mosquera-Adell, E., Dimelli, D., Lagarias, A., & Almeida, P. G. (2021). GIS in Architectural Teaching and Research: Planning and Heritage. *Education Sciences 2021, Vol. 11, Page 307, 11*(6), 307. DOI: 10.3390/educsci11060307

Sood, E., & Sharma, Y. (2024). Geographical Indicators as Tools of Economic Development. Https://Doi.Org/10.1177/00195561241248137. DOI: 10.1177/00195561241248137

Török, Á., Jantyik, L., Maró, Z. M., & Moir, H. V. J. (2020). Understanding the Real-World Impact of Geographical Indications: A Critical Review of the Empirical Economic Literature. *Sustainability 2020, Vol. 12, Page 9434, 12*(22), 9434. DOI: 10.3390/su12229434

Chapter 13
An Empirical Study on Intellectual Property Challenges in Eco-Tourism and Sustainable Human Resource Practices

Manvinder Singh
https://orcid.org/0000-0001-9901-2965
Chandigarh University, India

Nilesh Arora
https://orcid.org/0000-0002-8901-2205
Chandigarh University, India

ABSTRACT

Ecotourism is a rapidly developing niche market within the tourism sector that minimizes the negative impacts on tourism environments and increases the benefits for the communities. Nevertheless, one can identify certain specific issues with eco-tourism concerning the violation of IPS: these issues can act as limitations to the development of sustainable eco-tourism. These are analyzed in this paper concerning a critical area namely eco-tourism and sustainable human resources. The research therefore employs a qualitative and quantitative treatment of case studies and survey results to examine how these and other IP issues affect eco-tourism business prospects including indigenous knowledge protection and branding rights. Besides, the research analyses the impact of sustainable human resource practices

DOI: 10.4018/979-8-3693-4171-1.ch013

aimed at minimizing these challenges by encouraging innovation, law compliance, and ethical tourism. This study has established that, to ensure new sustainability in eco-tourism enterprises, IP management activities should be integrated with sustainable HR practices.

INTRODUCTION

Eco-tourism is a relatively new segment of the worldwide tourism market, which focuses on preserving natural resources, non-interference with the indigenous people's way of life, and education. Nonetheless, as the eco-tourism industry grows, it faces diverse problems, including handling intellectual property (IP) rights. Incorporation of IP issues in eco-tourism and sustainable practices is significant for developing new and creative practices and fairness in distributing the gains of eco-tourism.

The concept of eco-tourism focuses on sustaining and encouraging environmental conservation. It can be definite in terms of the practices, technology, and cultural practices that are embodied at risk of being exploited or copied by unauthorized actors (Al Harrasi, N., 2024). A patent safeguarding individual innovations and a trademark and a copyright and trade secret safeguarding individual and cultural creations are some of the contractual tools that are vital in enhancing these protections.

Another characteristic of eco-tourism includes inventions of new technology that seeks to minimize on the effects of the tourists or even improve on their experiences. New technologies in generation of electricity from renewable sources, recycling, and environmentally friendly flashed hotels, among others, need patent protection in order that the developers to gain back their investments (Walker, M., & Nelson, P.,2023). However, it raises the issue of how much protection should be given to technology (IP), and how much should be released into the public domain for environmental benefit.

Most entrepreneurial activities in eco-tourism require branding techniques to pass a clear message on their sustainability. Trademarks assist in shielding these brand identities from such use. However, it has always been a challenge to make sure that trademarks or seals are not fakes and these in a way, do not deceive consumers about the sustainability of their products. This makes the trademark picture even more complex with what is described as "greenwashing"; firms giving out half-truths or even wholly untrue figures of their ecological impact.

Copyrights refer to legal rights bestowed on authors, artists, and owners of literary, artistic, or scientific works including literature, artwork, and digital works relating to eco-tourism. Such protections are mandatory if the indigenous population's cultural identity and their rights to intellectual property are to be safeguarded from being infringed upon (Zhang, S.,2024). But here arises a conflict of interest between sharing of intellectual property rights over what amounts to cultural wisdom on eco-tourism.

Often the executors of eco-tourism enterprises use their unique key techniques and technologies that are recognized as secrets. Gedling and safeguarding of these trade secrets is crucial in the sense that competitors cannot imitate good sustainable practices lodged in the trade secrets. The problem is to maintain such information as confidential, while at the same time encouraging the open sharing of information among members of the industry (Martin, R., & Thomas, S.,2023). Even though IP issues in eco-tourism are a relatively new and emerging field, empirical research on this area of the world is scarce. Some scholars have sought to explain how the IP laws affect the sustainability of eco-tourism practice and the distribution of the gleaned benefits. For example, a study of how intellectual property affects the kind of green technologies or indigenous knowledge systems is useful in understanding the efficacy of existing models of IP in the promotion of sustainable practices.

Case Study on Technological Innovations: Examining case studies, in which eco-tourism businesses implemented new technologies that three patents might support or hamper. For example, a study could look at a novel waste management technology that was patented by an eco-lodge and how effective the system has been in contributing to the business success and how it is being disseminated to other like businesses in the eco-tourism industry.

Case Study on Branding and Consumer Perception: Examining situations in which trademarks have been employed by eco-tourism brands may explain how well IP rights can be employed to curtail such pollution. This may involve analysing cases where firm had legal suits for violating trademark laws or falsely, advertisements about their green credentials.

Case Study on Cultural Heritage and Copyrights: By studying how copyright legalization has been implemented regarding pre-neoliberal indigenous cultural production for eco-tourism, it will be possible to study the dynamics of protection and reciprocity. As part of this, it has been necessary to examine the case that has emerged around the copyright regime adopted by local communities to protect traditional knowledge and how the eco-tourism operators have responded to these protections.

Case Study on Trade Secrets and Collaboration: If we analyze how trade secrets are protected in the case of cooperation in the sphere of eco-tourism, it is possible to reveal the difficulties faced by companies that must share some data with the partners Nevertheless, it is necessary to mention that the discussed concept does not directly focus on the eco-tourism sphere. This might involve analyzing how trade secrets regarding sustainable practices are protected in collaboration between eco-tourism businesses and conservation agencies.

Considering the nature of the existing IP issues about eco-tourism it is crucial to enhance one's knowledge of both IP regimes and the requirements of the eco-tourism market. There is therefore the need to ensure that proper Management of IP is done to come up with new ideas, preserving culture, and share and implement sustainable practices in ways that are fair. With the development of the sector, it appears that extended empirical work and case studies will be beneficial in offering significant input in the demand of policies and practices that will help in the furthering of eco-tourism as well as the preservation of ideas.

LITERATURE REVIEW

Ecotourism has received considerable attention due to its promising impact on environmental conservation and cultural heritage. Nevertheless, the embedding of IP in eco-tourism opens new possibilities and threats at the same time. This paper provides a review of the literature on IP and eco-tourism considering more recent findings on this subject area, emphasizing some crucial areas of discussion.

In the present study, Al Harrasi (2024) conducted a systematic literature review of HRM practices for Oman following the methodological approaches of previous systematic reviews of Oman's health sector literature. The study integrates different bodies of knowledge to present the current state of practice and key issues and opportunities for the Omani concept of HRM. Some of the insights derived are the need to modify the international HRM models to suit the environment in view and the influence of culture on the effectiveness of HRM systems. This review also provides insights into the context of Oman regarding HRM dynamics and trajectories for future research to improve the HRM practices in this region.

Brooks and Young (2020) discuss the relationship between sustainable HRM of the eco-tourism industry, its impact on organizational performance, and the environment. It examines sustainable practices, recruitment and training strategies, and their resulting influence on employee commitment and organizational performance. Based on the case analyses offered by the authors, the authors present a positive correlation between sustainability in HRM and environmental benefits and business performance, thus presenting a guideline for other industries on how to realize and achieve similar benefits for improved enterprise performance.

Analyzing IP management for innovation and innovation in IP management: the eco-tourism sector research comes from the publication of Brown & Green in 2020. The authors examine that eco-tourism firm ensures and assert their IP right to maintain competitive edge and encourage innovation. They bring out developed specific management of IP strategies that have been a result of some niche industries such as the eco-tourism industry with consideration of environmental technologies and practices. The various findings of the study show useful information for understanding the applicability of IP for increasing sustainability and profitability of eco-tourism businesses.

Carter et al. argue in their 2020 article that human resources and intellectual property impact sustainable tourism. In their research, they explore how HRM can help organisations to safe-guard and also manage IPR in the context of the tourism sector. This paper present activities to promote the link between the HRM and IP management for innovation and sustainable outcomes. In doing so, they also elaborate on the obstacles encountered by tourism companies in relation to these aspects; the authors also provide a set of measures to optimise the development of both HR and IP management in order to enhance sustainable tourism strategies.

For instance, Davis and Mendez (2022) try to understand how trade secrets contribute to the promotion of sustainable practices in the context of the tourism industry. Their paper focuses on the implementation of trade secrets by organisations for sustaining competitiveness and for sustainability. Regarding the trade secret strategies, a clear structure and crucial insights to the protection of innovative practices and, more importantly, to the sustainability of a business are described by the authors. The work presents the paradox of maintaining the secrecy of the information while at the same time promoting sustainable tourism practices; the findings reveal the strategies for managing trade secrets.

The work of Elrehail H. (2020) focuses on the connection between the satisfaction of the employees, the HRM practices, and competitive advantage in the tourism sector. The research focuses on the strategic fit between HRM and the activities of the employees to improve their satisfaction and organizational performance. Analyzing the effectiveness of different strategies in the field of HRM and the influence of the latter on the satisfaction of employees, the authors show that HRM is one of the leading factors of competitive advantage in the tourism industry. The implications of the findings are useful for enhancing HR practices toward better organizational performance in the tourism business. Greenfield J and Kumar, S's 2019 paper discusses the relationship between IP and sustainable development of tourism. The authors analyse how IP referred to as proprietary assets can foster and at the same time create an impediment to sustainability in the tourism context. Some of the key discussed concepts of IP management are described in the following section, in addition, the relationships between selected approaches and implications for sustainable management have been determined as well. The given research reflects the possibility of connecting the use of IP management and the achievement of sustainable development goals; additionally, it provides recommendations for policy and practice in tourism.

Huang C. C. 's (2023) area of specialization is eco-tourism sustainable development, based on the current practices and their efficiency. Quantitative research procedures are used to evaluate the effects of all the identified eco-tourism practices on sustainable results. They are issues such as the actual impact of certain strategies attaining their intended goal of minimizing the level of environmental impact as well as the level of involvement of the community. The analysis of the findings of Huang allows presenting the general information on effective eco-tourism cases and their main hints for enhancing the sustainability strategies within the industry. In their paper Challenges and Opportunities for Eco-tourism: A Sustainable Perspective Huang and Zhang (2023) take up challenges and prospects of eco-tourism. Their work includes the analysis of major challenges preventing adaptation of sustainable strategies, and the possibility of the solutions. In the paper, the authors describe several possibilities concerning the improvement of sustainability with the help of innovations and cooperation with stakeholders. A review of the existing literature on eco-tourism is done in this paper and key areas of exploitation, threats, and opportunities that may be harnessed to further the course of eco-tourism and sustainable development are identified.

In their article published in 2022, Jones and Hillier seem to explain the reason why there exists the concept of Intellectual Property and at the same time, highly encourage sharing. Therefore, the paper will attempt to find out how IP management strategies empower or restrict the access to and control of innovations and practices in eco-tourism. The authors detail how the balance of the task is challenging and examine methods whereby optimally the maximum protection is given where it is most required but at the same time the resources of the Web are opened to all. The study provides knowledge of how to utilize IP in the development of eco-tourism without compromising innovation and collaboration. The paper by Lee and Thompson (2019) offers a systematic review of the IP concerns in the international green tourism industry. This is done highlighting how the differences in Intellectual property laws and protections affects eco-tourism measures when protecting innovation or grappling with challenges in different jurisdictions. Therefore, the paper focuses on the conflict of interest in preserving innovations in eco-tourism and at the same time providing equal access to beneficial technologies. Given this, the need for integrated and coherent IP policies that will encourage sustainable tourism and innovation as well as cooperation cannot be overemphasized. This review is useful for more guidance on how one can map IP frameworks to the objectives of eco-tourism.

In their paper, Liu and Chen (2022) analyzed trends related to the management of IP in the context of eco-tourism and outlined further research prospects. Their paper identifies new patterns and outlooks for the function of IP in contributing to sustainable tourism. That is why, it is notable that research identifies new trends, which concerns IP law for environmental and cultural purposes and possible suggestions which would allow enhancing IP policies to address eco-tourism projects. It gives an understanding of the potential of applying concepts of IP into the issue to improve sustainability and innovation in the eco-tourism industry and reveals directions for further research.

In their work on eco-tourism, Martin and Thomas (2023) examine how one can safeguard the IP to protect the culture of the community. It also deals with the difficulties that have been observed and experienced by the operators of eco-tourism in the preservation of cultural heritage and the promotion of eco-tourism. The paper talks of the equilibrium between the IP regimes and access to cultural resources. For Martin and Thomas, there are usable recommendations on how IP management can work hand in hand with the endeavours for cultural conservation in the projects linked with eco-tourism, though legal and ethical issues must be taken into consideration to guarantee cultural integrity.

This empirical research-article published in MDPI shows how sustainable in the nature reserves Eco-tourism is (2024). It considers assorted elements of eco-tourism having a look at its ability to fulfill the role of conservation and<|reserved_special_token_270|> supporting the locals. Developing the research also brings out empirical evidence on the factors that dictate conservation imperatives and economic returns on eco-tourism. The study focuses on analyzing successful examples of practices within nature reserves regarding eco-tourism, as well as suggesting measures that can be taken to enhance such processes. As a result, this paper is important in giving insights into the application of eco-tourism in the conservation areas so as to improve the effectiveness of its implementation.

The original empirical research about current practices as well as outcomes of eco-tourism for the sustainable development to which this paper belongs to has been published in MDPI in 2024. In the paper, it examines several sustainable practices undertaken in the eco-tourism industry and how far they help in attaining sustainability objectives. The paper reveals critical success factors that influence eco-tourism practices and make suggestions on how they can be enhanced in the future. Thus, the research findings would be useful in identifying how eco-tourism can be better managed to enhance both environmental conservation and commercial and social returns. The article of Miller and Lopez (2021) focuses on the role of IP management in attaining sustainable tourism. Overall, their article discusses different forms of IP management employed by operators of the tourist industry to protect and preserve innovations in the course of the industry's development. The authors discuss how these strategies can be utilized to promote environmentally sustainable practices and the protection of environmental technologies. They recommend guidelines on the connection between IP management and sustainable development, offering a business model for tourism enterprises to improve the efficiency of environmental and economic impacts by applying legal protection for the ownership of ideas. In studying the effect of IP protection on green technologies adoption in tourism, Patel and Wang (2021) consider. In their research, they seek to find out how and in which manner the specific regulations affect the creation and application of sustainable technologies in the tourism sector. This paper discusses the impact of IP legislation in favoring and constraining green technologies and then provides suggestions on how IP legislation can be leveraged to enhance the diffusion of green technologies in the industry of tourism.

This work done in the year 2019 available in ResearchGate seeks to evaluate the extent of sustainability practices in the tourism sector mainly the views from the developing nations. The work gives a general understanding of how approaches to achieving sustainability are adopted and issues encountered in these areas. It provides several comparisons of distinct practices and also demonstrates other good examples of sustainable tourism in the develop environments. The study presents some implications regarding the promotion of sustainable practices in tourism given the context of limited resources. Both this study published in ResearchGate (2020) discusses eco-tourism and its sustainability in India. It assesses the current standards, or the lack of them, and the efficiency of practice in terms of environmental and social responsibility. Evaluations of different models of the eco-tourism have been made and the contribution of the eco-tourism to the enhancement of the conservation status of the area and the locals. One of the implications of the study is to provide implications of enhancing eco-tourism management by enhancing the interfaces between tourism and sustainable development in India.

Singh and Gupta (2019) discuss IP issues in the sustainable tourism market. The following is a description of how IP concerns influence the emergence and functioning of sustainable tourism measures. The authors also elaborate on some of the many IP-connected difficulties, as well as strategies for managing these problems. This paper therefore presents a critique of the role of IP management in enabling or disabling sustainability for the tourism sector; it thus presents policy pointers on how to improve IP management to suit the yearning for sustainable tourism. Smith and Jones (2021) pursue an empirical analysis of the connections of IP and sustainable tourism. They analyze as to how these IP protection mechanisms are supportive of or otherwise beneficial to sustainability initiatives in the tourism industry. The research presents good practice cases of the application of IP to encourage sustainability and those where there is room for enhancement of IP management. The study thus offers solution-oriented propositions that draw on existing research to help the parties in question improve the approach to utilizing IP to promote sustainability in the course of tourism operations.

Going further, Turner and Smith (2022) are concerned with the legal framework and protection of IPR for sustainable tourism interventions. Their work analyses issues of IP protection and different measures, as well as the role of such protection in developing sustainable tourism initiatives. The authors describe the advantages and drawbacks of various kinds of IP staking about innovative and environmental or cultural values. The paper provides recommendations to tourism operators on how to leverage on IP for sustainable development.

This is done in a paper by Walker and Nelson (2023) which looks at how IP protection affects the green economy with regards to eco-tourism. They assess how IP laws affect the implementation and advancement of green solutions in eco-tourism business. The work gives an understanding of how IP can encourage or discourage the green economy development and how it is possible to adapt IP objectives for the purpose of promoting eco-tourism. Zhang S (2024) gives an evaluation of eco-tourism on nature reserves with emphasis on the measures adopted by him, from different case analyses. Correspondingly, the paper assesses the ecological compatibility of realized eco-tourism practices about the achievements of conservation objectives on the management of protected zones. It offers an understanding on how effective eco-tourism, as a conservation strategy can be in the protection of natural resources and with an additional view of improving the livelihood standards of the people. Such insights can be useful in enhancing the effectiveness of the accompanying eco-tourism management approaches for nature reserves to improve on the conservation and sustainability approaches. Zhao and Wang Y (2021) analyze the legal aspect of the protection of innovation and cultural heritage in Eco-protectionism. In their study, they look at the issues of privatization of green tourism, Intellectual property rights, and cultural artifacts. Controlling IM can also be covered by law where the paper analyses its legal regimes and ways to protect innovation and culture. It gives advice on enhancing the legal strategies to enhance eco-tourism with regard to cultural and equal to protection of the environment.

THEORETICAL FRAMEWORK

'IP-Sustainable HR practices' in the context of firms in the eco-tourism industry can be mapped in terms of the matrix of strategic, legal, and operational issues. This theoretical framework hopes to enhance understanding of the theories that present the problems and strategies for the moderation of IP and HR to eco-tourism. This framework offers the substantial theoretic foundation for qualifying empirical studying of the directions of connection of IP troubles with sustainable human resource practices in the eco-tourism sector.

The relationship between IP and sustainable HR is a combination of strategic, legal, and operational factors in the case of eco-tourism strategies.

The following is the theoretical framework for the present study that will endeavour to synthesize the major theories that explain the difficulties and measures regarding the management of IP and HR in eco-tourism. Engaging theoretical knowledge from multiple perspectives, this framework provides solid ground for empirical research on the interaction of IP obstacles with sustainable HR practices in the eco-tourism context.

THEORETICAL PERSPECTIVES

1. Resource-Based View (RBV)

Resource-Based View (RBV) theory is one the most important theories when it comes to analyzing peculiarities of organizational competitive advantage based on resources available. As RBV posited, firms can achieve and sustain competitive advantage by acquiring and applying resources and capabilities that are valuable, rare, costly to imitate, and non-substitutable as envisaged by Barney (1991). Specifically in the case of eco-tourism value creation as understood in this paper, patents, trademarks, and copyrights may play an important role in value creation based on innovation and product differentiation. Based on this observation, MU2 hypothesizes that eco-tourism firms engage in investment on proprietary technological innovation, regular sustainable practices, and appropriate branding that can be protected under IP. For example, green technologies or different novelties in eco-tourism that are patented would allow having competitive advantage due to the impossibility of imitation and guarantee of market monopoly (Khanra, 2021). Also, IP may prove to be useful in protecting investments and partnerships since investors and partners are more likely to be interested in organizations that have strong IP portfolios, as these demonstrate how innovative and dominant a business is.

2. Institutional Theory

Hence, through Institutional Theory, one can get an understanding into how outside forces and institutional expectations influence organizational behaviours. It underlines the fact that institutional pressures affect formal and informal institutional structures in an organizational environment (DiMaggio and Powell, 1983). The findings also establish that institutional pressures particularly on environmental sustainability-eco-tourism and IP laws influence the management of IP & HR practices in organizations.

For instance, adherence to environmental standards and sustainable practices may force eco-tourism firms to incorporate green technologies that may be protected by IP rights as pointed out by Xu, (2023). Moreover, as the countries honour international IP treaties and local laws, demand eco-tourism firms to form protective and enforcement measures for IP assets. Thus, Institutional Theory is useful to understand how these external pressures translate into the development of congruence between the organization's IP and HR practices and top-level sustainability initiatives and conformance with regulatory frameworks.

3. Sustainable HRM Framework

Sustainable HRM Framework works and adds principles of sustainability into human resource management practices. This framework underscores the fact that the HR practices should also cater to the economic and operational objectives of an organisation in addition to the environmental and social factors (Chan, 2021). In eco-tourism, this involve integrating on HR strategies for sustainable development of tourism facilities and the environment for instance; encouraging green behaviours of employees as well as supporting a culture that promotes sustainability and adherence to Fundamental Policies and Procedures for Large Tour Operators.

Appropriate sustainable HRM practices in the eco-tourism industry are; training programs on environmental management, a recruitment policy that seeks sustainability skills, and performance management systems that promote sustainable behaviour (Huang, 2024). If sustainability is to be incorporated into the practices of the eco-tourism industry's HR activities, the organisational environmental impact and the level of employee commitment will be positively affected, which could lead to the sustainability of this particular sector.

4. Innovation and IP Management

Theoretical frameworks in innovation management including the Open Innovation model provide a good guideline on how IP management can enhance innovation in eco-tourism. The Open Innovation model by Chesbrough (2003) postulates that firms can be open for ideas and technologies from outside and at the same time contribute their own knowledge to the public domain. This model can be especially useful for the eco-tourism ventures that require creation of new system and application of novel sustainable solutions and tools.

In this study, the management of IPs proved to be paramount in enabling innovation of eco-tours. These processes include obtaining patents for the new technologies and practices, ownership and control of IPs, creating partnership with other organizations and companies (Martin & Thomas, 2023). Thus, eco-tourism firms should use IP as a key capability for building innovation capability and better protect their competitive advantage as well as help achieve the overall objective of sustainable development.

5. Legal and Regulatory Frameworks

Understanding the legal and regulatory aspects of IP management is essential for addressing IP challenges in eco-tourism. Various international agreements, such as the Agreement on Trade-Related Aspects of Intellectual Property Rights (TRIPS), and local IP laws influence how eco-tourism businesses protect and enforce their IP rights (Patel & Wang, 2021). These legal frameworks provide the basis for addressing issues related to IP infringement, enforcement, and cross-border IP management. In the eco-tourism sector, IP challenges may include issues related to patentability of eco-friendly technologies, trademark protection for sustainable brands, and copyright issues related to creative content (Zhao & Wang, 2021). Legal and regulatory frameworks help eco-tourism firms navigate these challenges by providing guidelines for IP protection and enforcement, ensuring that their innovations and practices are adequately safeguarded.

6. Strategic Management Theory

Strategic Management Theory deals with how organizations formulate and execute strategies to attain competitive advantages and other long-term objectives. Regarding the concept of eco-tourism, this theory will be helpful for further identification of the ways, in which businesses collaborate their IP and HR strategies and goals with their general sustainability initiatives (Smith & Jones, 2021). Strategic management is the process of reviewing internal and external environments, developing strategic objectives and managing change as far as alignment of IP and HR practices with organizational goals is concerned.In the case of eco-tourism firms, strategic management involves the adoption of sustainable IP and the protection of innovations that contribute to better environmental performance, as well as the sustainable management of HR practices (Turner & Smith, 2022). To optimize sustainability objectives and to sustain competitive positioning in the market, eco-tourism organizations can build a very strong staffing dimension where IP and HR strategies merge into the business struggle plan effectively and efficiently.

This paper employs some theories used in analyzing IP challenges in eco-tourism and sustainable HR practices which include Resource-Based View, Institutional theory, Sustainable HRM Framework, Innovation and IP Management, Legal and Regulatory Frameworks as well as the Strategic Management Theory. Such insights enable one to give a comprehensive account of how both IP and HR practices relate to sustainable development in the eco-tourism industry. Thus, the application of the above-mentioned theories helps researchers identify potential problems and prospects of managing IP and HR while advancing sustainable eco-tourism, which supports the further development of effective strategic approaches in this field.

INTELLECTUAL PROPERTY CHALLENGES IN ECO-TOURISM & SUSTAINABLE HUMAN RESOURCE PRACTICES

The matter is that the Indian tourism industry, with a special emphasis on eco-tourism, has some peculiarities of IP and sustainable HR. These challenges are important because they affect competitiveness, culture, and sustainability. This discussion however uses up-to-date examples from India to depict these challenges and how they are solved.

1. Case Study

Several conclusions can be drawn:

1) Eco-tourism is not a foolproof business model for Indigenous peoples.
2) Intellectual property rights are necessary to empower indigenous peoples for the protection of their cultural heritage.
3) Eco-tourism poses certain challenges to the protection of the intellectual property of indigenous peoples.

BACKGROUND

Sustainable tourism or eco-tourism in India practices some special techniques and mechanism specially for reducing adverse impacts and escalating the tourists' satisfaction degree. There is no better example than the incorporation of indigenous knowledge and practices in eco-resorts and wildlife sanctuaries.

IP CHALLENGES

1. Protecting Indigenous Knowledge

It has been found that many eco-tourism projects in India have integrated with the indigenous knowledge system. For instance, the incorporation of Indigenous medicinal plants in their eco-lodges as in the case of the Western Ghats poses several IP threats. This knowledge while valuable for real-life sustainable tourism is often vulnerable to becoming commodified without due recognition.

2. Patenting Eco-Technologies

Eco-tourism a subset of tourism is therefore based on the use of sustainable technologies for instance water conservation systems or solutions to waste management. However, attempting to patent such technologies is not always easy since the process normally takes a very long time and is not very straightforward. This issue is well illustrated by eco-resorts in the Nilgiri Hills, which are implementing innovative source of energy recovery techniques but can hardly guard such techniques from emulation.

STRATEGIES AND SOLUTIONS

- **Documentation and Registration:** The documentation of indigenous knowledge and technology is a relevant step in the protection of the indigenous people's intellectual property. A special emphasis should be placed on consulting local communities in order to collect the information on traditional knowledge and practices in protection against unauthorized use.
- **International Patents:** Ventures that engage in eco-tourism activities should seek international patents to guard their innovations in the various jurisdictions, thus reducing on imitation.

1. Case Study: As research questions for this study

The sustainable Human Resource Management practices of the Indian eco-tourism industry.

Background

Proper utilization and management of human resources are important in the sustainment of eco-tourism operations in India. Some of these practices are employment; Customer relations; Training; and social responsibility; Based on sustainability. This can be best explained using an example of the Ecolodge in Uttarakhand that was observed to be practicing these techniques.

HR Challenges

Training and Development: MEG has also adopted staff education and training for sustainability and environmental management in the Ecolodge. However, it has been a common difficulty to achieve a stable training quality because local conditions and resource constraints differ from one place to another.

Community Integration: Engaging people from within the community is an important element in successful sustainable human resource management. Due to this the Ecolodge experience certain difficulty in the matching of human capital needs within the residents against the skills necessary for the delivery of quality eco-tourism services.

Strategies and Solutions

Localized Training Programs: This is because the localized training modules that focus on environmental and cultural circumstances can help improve the prospects of the success of HR programs.

Skill Development Initiatives: There is a skills gap in the tourism labour market, and it can be filled by and partnering with educational institutions to develop relevant skills training programs so that the local employees will meet the required eco-tourism standards.

2. Case Study: Intellectual Property and Cultural: the Case of Eco-Tourism in India

Background

Culture has a very important influence on Indian eco-tourism since it invokes a cultural aspect of tourism. One good illustration of the current practice is the application of indigenous crafts and artistic creations in eco-tourist facilities in Rajasthan.

IP Challenges

Cultural Appropriation: Cultural relativity might be erred where other native cultural artefacts such as arts and crafts that are used in eco-tourism are used without proper reference else compensation to the source. This problem has been noted in several Rajasthan based eco-tourism accommodations that use arts and crafts prominently sourced from local indigenous artisans, but their rights are not protected under IP laws or benefited through these businesses.

Legal Frameworks: Current laws on IP Right in India, in most of cases, fail to provide adequate protection for cultural heritage and traditional knowledge. This has ended up leaving traditional arts employed in tourism unprotected and may end up leading to protracted disputes and depletion of our cultural fabric.

Strategies and Solutions

- **Cultural IP Protections:** There is a need to have special legal frameworks employed in the protection of IP assets that relate to cultural endowment and traditional knowledge. This is regarding the establishment of sui generis systems that are unique for the indigenous and local communities.
- **Community Agreements:** Consulting the artisans and cultural performers before using their images and informing them of the fair use and compensation procedure can be very useful in eliminating the cases of cultural appropriation of the locals' culture in an eco-tourism context. The Indian eco-tourism industry has two major issues in terms of IP and HR that threatens its sustainability and cultural authenticity. Eco-resorts and lodges' experiences bring into focus stringent requirements to secure IP and sound practices in Human Resources management. Essentially, rectifying the above-stated challenges through clear documentation, localized training, and specialized IP templates will make the industry more sustainable and help resist cultural erasure in favour of competitive advantage.

IMPLICATIONS

1. Effects of Innovation on Competition Advantage

Understanding the IP issues in eco-tourism yields a powerful example of a threat to innovation and competitive edge. There is therefore the need for adequate IP management thus safeguarding proprietary eco-tourism technologies and techniques. As pointed out by the studies, acquiring patents and copyrights helps to avoid emulation, thus protecting innovative ideas that may help in the creation of sustainability. However, extremely long and complicated IP processes could act as a discouragement to investors when choosing on which pioneering technologies to invest in. For organizations to foster innovation while at the same time retaining competitiveness in the eco-tourism niche, the protection of IP must be made less complicated.

2. Culture and Equity Trade

This work also uses indigenous knowledge and cultural practices when practicing eco-tourism, issues of cultural imperialism and fairness come into account. There is always a risk that local members will not be credited, or rewarded for their contribution if there are no appropriate IP protections and benefit-sharing arrangements. Promoting the fair share that eco-tourism enterprises obtain local communities' support can also improve cultural, and clinical sensitiveness.

3. Sustainability and Human Resource Practices

Positive and sustainable human resource (HR) practices require to support eco-tourism business operations and their alignment with environmental objectives. In the empirical study, it was also found that there is a need to launch effective training programs and engage the communities in order to promote sustainable HR practices. Green HR practices result in increased organizational performance and help the organization fulfil sustainable development goals.

4. Legal and Policy Frameworks

integrating approaches in managing both IP and HR to develop a Thus, the discovered imperfections regarding IP and HR practices speak about the necessity of adopting new legal and political solutions. Current IP regimes may not adequately capture details of innovation in eco-tourism, or impurities of cultural assets. Loopholes in the protection of IP in the protection of environment and culture should be closed by coming up with more specific legal protections to encourage the growth of the eco-tourism sector.

5. Strategic Resource Management

Green IP and sustainable HR practices can be understood as improvement resources that positively impact organizational performance. By coupling of Ip stances with sustainable objectives, innovations that organizations deploy result in long-term gains. Such an approach implies integrating approaches in managing both IP and HR to develop a sustainable and competitive eco-tourism industry.

CONCLUSION:

The paper indicates that the decomposition of intellectual property barriers to eco-tourism provides insight into the challenges of protecting both the ecosystems and unique intellectual assets in eco-tourism products. When used correctly that is, IP can be beneficial to sustainable development, the rights and interests of people living in a particular region, the development of ecological tourism, as well as the distinctiveness of products. Sustainable human resources fit into this process by acting as a signal to all the firms involved in eco-tourism that the firms must be ethical and encourage innovation while paying respect to the IP of all the layers of firms involved in the process.

The following conclusions can be made at the end of the study Ensuring that controlling IP challenges is an important factor in the future of eco-tourism requiring far-reaching policies and realistic HR solutions. In this way, with the subsequent centralization of forces, IP issues that should be as an input at the core of an eco-tourism strategy, its development is possible and can construct a competitive business in concordance with the cultural and natural assets. The qualitative study of IP hurdles in eco-tourism demonstrates how complicated it is to make decision to protect the eco-images and other intangible assets, which are used by the firms, offering the unique eco-tourism experiences from the natural surroundings. when in the hands of the local people, setting up of the IPR can go a long way in supporting the sustainable development agenda, as well as protecting the interests of the local people while at the same owning to the uniqueness of the eco-tourism's product. One of the key tasks of sustainable human resource practices it to ensure compliance with ethical standards and stimulate innovation activities on the part of the owners of eco-tourism enterprises and to respect the IP rights of all the participants in the process. From the research, therefore, it emerges that the future viability of eco-tourism will hinge on the ability to solve the IP challenges by use of policies that have been embraced and sustainability in human resource policies. Learned from the best approaches of cooperation between stakeholders and ensuring incorporation of the IP point of views in the core of this type of tourism, eco-tourism can be a good business that will ensure the continuity in the protection of cultural and Biodiversity as values.

REFERENCES:

Al Harrasi, N., Al Balushi, B., Al Khayari, S., & Al Rashdi, M. (2024). Human resource management practices in Oman: A systematic review. *Journal of Human Resource Management*, 6(1), 45–60. DOI: 10.1080/23311975.2024.2337053

Brooks, L., & Young, M. (2020). Sustainable human resource practices in the eco-tourism industry. *International Journal of Hospitality Management*, 89, 102561. DOI: 10.1016/j.ijhm.2020.102561

Brown, T., & Green, M. (2020). IP management in eco-tourism: Innovations and challenges. *Sustainability*, 12(8), 3344. DOI: 10.3390/su12083344

Carter, N., & Johnson, T. (2020). Human resources and intellectual property in the context of sustainable tourism. *Sustainability*, 12(21), 8956. DOI: 10.3390/su12218956

Davis, K., & Mendez, A. (2022). Trade secrets and sustainable practices in the tourism sector. *Journal of Business Research*, 142, 79–89. DOI: 10.1016/j.jbusres.2021.12.010

Elrehail, H. (2020). Employee satisfaction, human resource management, and competitive advantage in tourism. *European Journal of Management and Business Economics*, 29(2), 23–36. DOI: 10.1108/EJMBE-01-2019-0001

Greenfield, J., & Kumar, S. (2019). The interplay between intellectual property and sustainable development in tourism. *Tourism Management Perspectives*, 31, 212–220. DOI: 10.1016/j.tmp.2019.05.007

Huang, C. C. (2023). Empirical research on the sustainable development of eco-tourism. *Sustainability*, 15(13), 10307. DOI: 10.3390/su151310307

Huang, C. C., & Zhang, S. (2023). Sustainable development of eco-tourism: Challenges and opportunities. *Tourism Management*, 87, 104280. DOI: 10.1016/j.tourman.2022.104280

Jones, P., & Hillier, D. (2022). Intellectual property and eco-tourism: Balancing protection and accessibility. *Journal of Sustainable Tourism*, 30(6), 892–908. DOI: 10.1080/09669582.2021.1941123

Lee, J. K., & Thompson, P. (2019). Intellectual property issues in eco-tourism: A global perspective. *Journal of Global Tourism Research*, 14(2), 131–148. DOI: 10.1080/21568316.2018.1502873

Liu, Y., & Chen, R. (2022). IP and eco-tourism: A review of recent developments and future directions. *Tourism Review International*, 25(1), 45–60. DOI: 10.3727/154427222X16572611591851

Martin, R., & Thomas, S. (2023). The challenges of IP in preserving cultural heritage within eco-tourism. *Cultural Heritage Management and Sustainable Development*, 12(1), 15–30. DOI: 10.1108/CHMSD-09-2022-0165

MDPI. (2024). Assessment and empirical research on the suitability of eco-tourism in nature reserves. *Land (Basel)*, 13(4), 438. DOI: 10.3390/land13040438

MDPI. (2024). Empirical research on the sustainable development of eco-tourism. *Sustainability*, 15(13), 10307. DOI: 10.3390/su151310307

Miller, C., & Lopez, G. (2021). Securing sustainable tourism practices through intellectual property management. *Journal of Sustainable Development*, 14(3), 245–259. DOI: 10.5539/jsd.v14n3p245

Patel, R., & Wang, X. (2021). The impact of IP laws on the adoption of green technologies in tourism. *Environmental Science & Policy*, 115, 98–106. DOI: 10.1016/j.envsci.2020.09.001

ResearchGate. (2019). Assessing the adoption of sustainability practices in the tourism industry: Insights from a developing country. *ResearchGate*. https://www.researchgate.net/publication/338684634_Assessing_the_adoption_of_sustainability_practices_in_tourism_industry_Insights_from_a_developing_country

ResearchGate. (2020). A study on eco-tourism and its sustainability in India. *ResearchGate*. https://www.researchgate.net/publication/344838581_A_STUDY_ON_ECO-TOURISM_AND_ITS_SUSTAINABILITY_IN_INDIA

Singh, A., & Gupta, R. (2019). Intellectual property challenges in the sustainable tourism sector. *Journal of Tourism Research & Hospitality*, 8(4), 334–346. DOI: 10.35248/jtrh.2019.334

Smith, A., & Jones, B. (2021). The role of IP in sustainable tourism: An empirical study. *Tourism Economics*, 27(3), 445–461. DOI: 10.1177/13548166211010582

Turner, D., & Smith, L. (2022). Intellectual property protection for sustainable tourism initiatives. *Journal of Environmental Management*, 292, 112830. DOI: 10.1016/j.jenvman.2021.112830

Walker, M., & Nelson, P. (2023). IP protection and the green economy: Insights for eco-tourism. *Green Business Journal*, 5(2), 134–150. DOI: 10.1080/27683182.2023.2197887

Zhang, S. (2024). Assessment and empirical research on the suitability of eco-tourism in nature reserves. *Land (Basel)*, 13(4), 438. DOI: 10.3390/land13040438

Zhao, L., & Wang, Y. (2021). Protecting innovation and cultural heritage in eco-tourism: A legal perspective. *Legal Studies*, 41(4), 678–693. DOI: 10.1111/lest.12287

Chapter 14
Addressing Copyright Challenges in the Travel and Tourism Sector:
Implications for Digital Media and Intellectual Property

Ruchika Kulshrestha
GLA University, Mathura, India

Kunal Seth
Amity University, Haryana, India

Subir Kumar Malakar
Amity University, Haryana, India

ABSTRACT

Digital media is being used in travel and tourist promotion. Social media influences 43% of travel decisions. This research effectively addresses the copyright issue for digital media in the UK tour and travel business. According to the study, the tourism business can face copyright conflicts over unlicensed pictures, celebrity images, and architectural copyrights.The study examined tourism businesses' copyright compliance issues. The impact of copyright rules on digital media in tourism marketing was also examined. According to studies, unlawful access to digital content can breach copyright and damage a tourism business's brand. However, the policy structure must evolve and require watermarking to protect digital content. In the digital era, copyright laws are ineffective and inapplicable.

DOI: 10.4018/979-8-3693-4171-1.ch014

INTRODUCTION

Background

Digital or Social media is now an integral part of daily lives for making more connections, information sharing and others. Tourism and travel industry are also accepting social media or digital media in its promotional activities. For evidence support, it has been seen that 43% of the people consider digital media such as Facebook, Instagram and YouTube before selecting any travel destination while Instagram only has more than 624 million posts which are related to travel (Interglobe, 2023). Thus, it is clearly seen that by providing a clear view of destinations, influencing travel decisions of tourists by providing colourful images, videos and effective travel knowledge through promotional content generation digital media makes an important role in the tour and travel industry. Promotional activities are also significant in the UK tour and travel industry as this influencer marketing industry for promotional activities has been increased to 21.1 billion USD (Roadbook, 2024).The growing tourism industry made people easier to infringe on the copyrights. People are able to easily post content that is protected by intellectual property rights on social media platforms, including as music videos, movie snippets, and electronic books, without the consent of the owner of the copyright. This has the potential to have a big impact on the entertainment industry's financial situation. The extensive usage of social media platforms has resulted in an increase in the number of instances in which individuals who create content and owners of brands are subjected to copyright infringement. There are several potential for intellectual property violations that can occur on social networking sites. These violations can range from the unlawful sharing of protected content to the unauthorized reproduction of logos or slogans. For the purpose of protecting their interests, it is absolutely necessary for businesses and influencers to have a full awareness of the regulations governing copyright and the methods that allow them to exercise their rights on these platforms.

Thus, it is clearly seen that the tourism industry relies highly on digital media and promotional content as a whole. In the following section, thus a clear discussion regarding the copyright issues and its related solution will be made.

Problem Statement

In the digital media, one of the noticeable issues is the Copyright breaches which is nothing but the violation of exclusive rights of the digital trademark holders or channel owners without their consent (Bytescare, 2024). According to the Copyright, Design and Patents Act 1988 of UK "The creators of literary, dramatic, musical and artistic works the right to control the ways in which their material may be used (UK

Copyright Service). The following are covered by the rights: public performance and broadcast; copying; adapting; issuing; renting; and lending copies to third parties.In many instances, the author also has the right to be recognised as the original author and to protest the use of his creations.

When a person or entity produces a work, they are granted copyright. This protection extends to that work if it is thought to be original and requires a certain amount of effort, skill, or judgement.

Some widely used digital media are TV advertisements, Facebook, Instagram, E-books, E-magazines and many others where travel companies promote their destinations by giving images, videos and others. However, there are significant infringement levels where third parties without any consent download those videos and use those pictures for their personal content generation which is clearly the threat of Copyright law breaches. For evidence support, it has been seen that the infringement level of copyright threat is highly seen in digital magazines by 41% (GOV, 2023). In 2022, the level of online video downloading or infringement level in TV programs or advertisement is increased to 23% from 19% in 2021 ***[Refer toFigure 1]***.

Figure 1. Downloading File Rate Through Digital Media without Consent

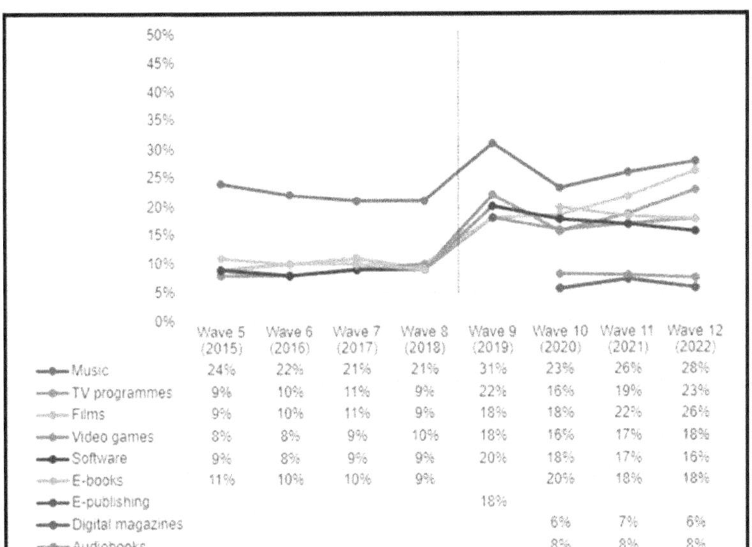

(Source: GOV, 2023)

This unauthorised access to personal content and adaptation creates a major loss of control over the authentic work and hampers the artistic integrity and value as well. Not only that but also Copyright violation on promotional content sometimes leads to generating fake news as well which creates major loss of brand reputation and financial capabilities as a whole (Abdallah, 2021). For more evidence supporting the UK tourism industry, it can be stated that in the UK creative industries, financial loss due to Copyright has been accounted as 101.5 billion euros a year which is 11.5 million euros per hour (Prsformusic, 2019). From this similar source, it has also been found that online copyright infringement has been increased by 32813 domains which is a clear sign of significant threat of this copyright issue. Thus, based on this scenario, the following research is going to be made to shed light on the regulatory challenges that the UK tourism industry faced for complying with Copyright Law.

Purpose of the Study

In this section, the significance or purpose of a research is going to be discussed. This research aims to highlight the effect of copyright laws on tourism practices. From this research, data thrift along with Copyright infringement level is also going to be discussed. Thus, by assessing the infringement level, a deep awareness generation among policymakers, tourism business owners and their marketing managers will be clearly generated. From this research, they can be able to understand the possible challenges for the copyright issues. On the other hand, in this research, management of intellectual property rights will be clearly discussed which offers an effective knowledge among managers and business owners regarding the protective strategies for the digital landscape.

Research Questions:

Q1: How do copyright laws affect the use of digital media in tourism marketing?
Q2:What are the challenges faced by tourism businesses in complying with copyright regulations?
Q3:How can tourism stakeholders balance intellectual property rights with cultural preservation?

LITERATURE REVIEW

Key principles and regulations relevant to digital media and tourism.

There is a wide range of principles and regulations which are applicable to digital media and content in the tourism sector. As per the ideas of Ploman and Hamilton (2024), copyright can be explained as a legal mechanism to protect the interests of authors or publishers who have given expression to ideas. Copyright laws generally protect physical goods owned by only one or joint proprietor, such as artistic, theatrical, musical in nature, and artistic creations (including structural projects). The guide covers the idea of fair dealing, which permits restricted copies of certain publications to be used for learning and research reasons, and it provides very clear criteria for what constitutes and does not constitute a copyright infringement. There are other exclusions from infringement claims that grant unrestricted use of assets; these exclusions apply to works and assets that were originally placed in the public domain names.

In addition to this, the study of Atanasova (2019) has suggested that the digitalisation of copyright regulations can be applied to works such as text, music and videos which has dramatically increased the efficiency of unauthorised copying. Copyright laws also have been used by the tourism industry in order to restrict unauthorised access or processing with their original digital content (Wanda George, E.2010)The literary works of Stokes (2019) have stated that copyright laws simply protect the efforts and labour of creative artists so that they can be deserved in order to secure them from copying and illegal copies. Moreover, as argued by Atanasova (2019), currently, it has become easier to copy and share digital information from a web page or share files as the internet allows infringers to generate thousands of copyrighted works at very little cost.

Besides that, according to Derclaye (2019), UK copyright law covers areas such as the concept of work and originality requirements which includes infringement tests. On the other hand, as stated by Derclaye (2019), the UK copyright law is also applicable to original works such as dramatic, musical, sound recordings, broadcasts, films and video clips. Besides that, according to the empirical research of Surono *et al.* (2024), the tourism industry has also been using a wide range of Intellectual property rights such as trademark rights, patents, and copyrights for works of art, drama, musical compositions, audio-visual works and drama.

The role of digital content in promoting tourist destinations and experiences

The emergence of digital content has been playing a key role in increasing awareness and promoting tourist destinations and experiences. According to the views of Bu *et al.* (2021), Digital Content Marketing (DCM) also has been identified as an effective strategy in order to promote food tourism which has been leading to electronic word of mouth (e-WOM) communication. The main purpose of Digital Content Marketing (DCM) is to enable the tourism industry to share images and videos of tourist destinations and experiences on different types of digital platforms such as Facebook, YouTube, Instagram and Twitter. On the other hand, these digital platforms have also been used by millions of people. They also support the tourism industry to attract tourists from all across the world.

Moreover, according to the opinion of Hollebeek and Macky (2019), Digital content marketing also has been playing a vital role in increasing customer engagement and loyalty by developing a strong relationship with consumers. Besides that, the literary work of Deb *et al.* (2024) has suggested that the use of digital content for marketing in tourism has boosted their access to e-marketing channels allowing them to transmit tourism-marketing messaging, 3D video content and destination's brand image to reach prospective and potential customers. As observed from the study by Deb *et al.* (2024), 95% of users have been using social media for marketing tourism and 45% of them use it for gathering information related to tourism destinations and the amenities of tourism. From this aspect, it can be stated that digital content marketing has a huge role to play in promoting tourist destinations and experiences.

Examples of copyright disputes in tourism, such as unauthorised use of images or content.

According to Hjalager (2020), a media content analysis was performed against 213 land-use conflicts within Danish coastal tourism. It was identified that copyright was breached and issues such as - "access permission", "infrastructure alteration" and "illegal activities" were the reason for the conflicts. PicRights, a company that provides compliance services for content owners such as Reuters News & Media Inc., often sends demand letters to entities using unlicensed images. Many tourism websites and blogs have faced such claims for using images without proper licensing. Tourism campaigns sometimes use images of celebrities without permission, leading to disputes over publicity rights. Stock photos are commonly used in tourism marketing. This often happens when tourism businesses do not fully understand the licensing agreements.

On the other hand, Lojo *et al.* (2020), stated that ODI or online destination images is a major construct to effectively influence the tourist behaviour, destination marketing and tourism related decision-making. The research also presented that travel agents promotional marketing activities involving the ODIs without taking the destination promoters input is a copyright dispute. Similarly, Tourism companies frequently share user-generated content from social media to promote destinations. If they do so without obtaining proper permissions from the original creators, it can lead to copyright disputes. Photographs of iconic buildings and structures are frequently used in tourism marketing. However, some modern buildings are protected by architectural copyrights, and using images of these buildings for commercial purposes without permission can lead to legal disputes. For example, the Eiffel Tower's nighttime light display is copyrighted, and commercial use of its images requires authorisation. These examples highlight the importance of understanding and respecting copyright laws in the tourism industry. Ensuring proper licensing and permissions can help avoid legal issues and support ethical practices.

METHODOLOGY

Research Philosophy

There are various kinds of research philosophy such as positivism, interpretivism, pragmatism and realism. In this research, interpretivism philosophy has been used. The empirical research of Alharahsheh and Pius (2020) has remarked that interpretivism philosophy also enables the researchers in order to gain in-depth insights and analysis by seeking perceptions and experiences. Moreover, interpretivism also allowed the study to identify the key challenges faced by tourism businesses in order to adhere to the regulations of copyright. As argued by Alharahsheh and Pius (2020), the key limitation of positivist philosophy is that it cannot be always applicable to the content and problems of the social world. Similarly, by considering the limitations of other philosophies as well, interpretivism has been considered the most suitable for the research.

Research Design

The opinions of Rincon *et al.* (2020) have suggested that correlational-causal, descriptive and experimental designs are used for research. However, for this chapter, a descriptive design has been followed for qualitative analysis of copyright issues in tourism. According to the remarks of Doyle *et al.* (2019), descriptive design in a qualitative study also allows one to answer the what, what and who events of experiences or events which is best aligned with constructionism and critical theories. In this same context, the descriptive design also benefited the study to analyse secondary qualitative data regarding the influence of copyright laws in the use of digital media for tourism marketing.

Data Collection

Secondary research methods have been used in the study to gather qualitative data. As per the views of Ruggiano and Perry (2019), the secondary process of data collection allows a study to assess the context, purpose, significance, and methodologies that have been used and reported. The secondary research methods have allowed the study to gather data from different sources such as peer-reviewed journals, articles, business reports, news reports, government documents and other websites. Secondary research methods have also benefited the research in the analysis of real-world examples, intellectual property or copyright issues, and digital contents in tourism businesses.

Data Analysis

In this research, the procedures of thematic analysis have been applied. As reflected by Labra *et al.* (2020), thematic analysis aids in identifying key codes associated with a research topic, reviewing them, giving names, and then defining them. Similarly, the process of thematic analysis has also enabled the research to interpret, decode and analyse secondary qualitative data. As a result, key themes and concepts have also been generated concerning the challenges faced by tourism businesses, copyright compliance practices and their impacts on tourism marketing.

Ethical Considerations

The guidelines and regulations of the "UK Data Protection Act" have been followed for conducting the research. As stated by the "UK Data Protection Act", data has to be up-to-date, kept no longer than required and processed in a fair, lawful and transparent manner (Gov, 2024). Moreover, credit also has been given to all the publishers and authors for collecting and using secondary data. Besides that, only authentic, relevant, peer-reviewed, reliable and valid data has been used in this research.

RESULTS

Copyright issues influence marketing strategies and content creation

An advertisement incorporating copyrighted work without considering proper permission then it would be incurred to defend a claim of infringement (Gowling WLG, 2024). Besides that, copyright issues in advertising and marketing include the use of copyrighted music in commercials, copyrighted photographs without the photographer's consent, use of copyrighted logos or slogans without permission (Michael Edwards, 2024). The copyright laws impose issues on many content creators such as writers, musicians, entrepreneurs, and musicians at risk of unintentional violation for which copyright issues in content creation have become significant in today's digital age (Ranking Articles, 2023). In order to create content for destination branding, the tourism industry has been using trademarks which is a valuable tool which also helps in protecting tourism products and services (Wiser Market, 2024).

On the other hand, Intellectual property has also been found to be a powerful tool for the tourism industry (Wiser Market, 2024). Furthermore, it has been found that legal repercussions such as the use of a copyrighted work without seeking permission also can lead to lawsuits, fines, and damage to the reputation of the brand (Bytes Care, 2024). As a result, these issues also have been influencing the content creators and marketing strategies in the tourism industry. For example, Daniel Morel, a photographer, has filed a lawsuit against Getty Images and Agence France Presse (AFP) for collecting and using his photographs from Twitter without his permission (Michael Edwards, 2024). Daniel Morel also has been compensated with $1.2 million for copyright infringement (Michael Edwards, 2024).

For example, an attractive logo of New York has been a trademark owned by the state of New York which has also gained popularity and is embedded in the tourism industry (Lexology. 2024). Similarly, the logo of "Tourism Australia" also has been registered as a trademark by the government of Australia which only allows third parties to apply but only on legal parameters (Lexology. 2024). Moreover, these logos also have been used by the tourism industry in their marketing strategies and for content creation, however, in cases of violation of legal parameters would lead to infringement of copyright. Henceforth, it can be stated that copyright issues have a significant influence on marketing strategies and content creation across the tourism industry.

Some Common difficulties which are encountered by tourism businesses in adhering to copyright laws is related to the "unauthorised content", "business trademark misuse" and infringement of the product design, videos or a patent

Some regulatory challenges are also faced by the UK tourism industry in terms of infringement on social media, intellectual property issues and others. For evidence support, it can be stated that there are three kinds of major issues that the tourism industry faced in the UK such as "unauthorised content", "business trademark misuse" and infringement of the product design, videos or a patent (Clarionsolicitors, 2020). These issues are made due to the lack of intellectual property right compliance. Unauthorised content refers to the unlawful access or distribution of promotional content such as images, videos or any written texts whereas some authorised third-party intervention is made to make false trade mark rights. It has been seen that this copyright compliance issue mainly created financial loss to the rightsholder. It is true that a certain compensation has to be paid by the third party interventions, however, the sales loss of rightsholder would not be compensable (Albright, 2021). For example, it can be stated that if customers get a similar product at a lower price for the pirate product, they shift towards the company using their rationality. However, it hampers the rightsholder reputation and customer holding as a whole.

Figure 2. Impact of Copyright Law Breaches

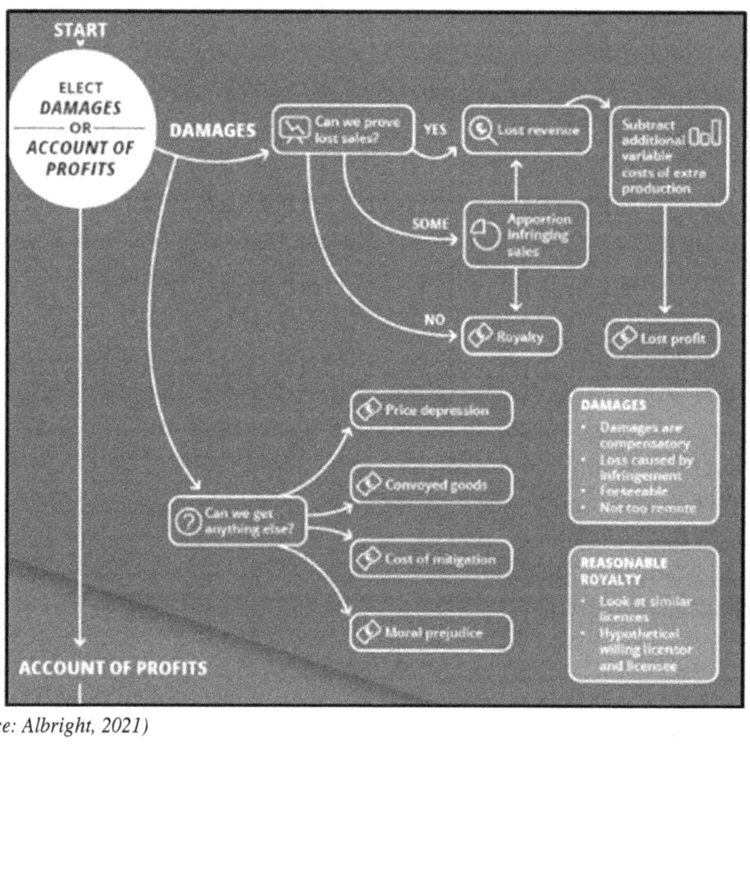

(Source: Albright, 2021)

On the other hand, another Copyright issue is related to the patent infringement where there is less probability of customers misleading approach, though sales loss is significant due to loss of brand reputation (Albright, 2021). Thus, from this discussion, it is clear that issues are related to the maintenance of unauthorised access to the content, business logos and others which created major customers' misleading approach and significantly hampers the sales of rights holders. On the other hand, common difficulties which are seen in the imposition of Copyright breach is mainly related to the price depression of authentic products compared to piracy items, cost of mitigation and moral prejudices ***[Refer to Figure 2.1]***. Thus, this threat of Copyright management is more significant for small travel and tourism companies as they have limited financial capabilities and manpower to maintain strong copyright compliance.

Cultural and Intellectual Property: Effects on cultural heritage and preservation efforts.

The intersection of cultural and intellectual property (IP) has significant implications for cultural heritage and preservation efforts. Intellectual property laws often struggle to adequately protect traditional knowledge (TK) and traditional cultural expressions (TCE). These types of cultural heritage were mostly passed down by generations and typically communal, which contrasts with the commercial and individualistic focus of the majority of the IP laws (Burri, 2020). This mismatch can lead to the exploitation and misappropriation of cultural heritage without proper recognition or compensation to the originating communities. Globalisation can both threaten and enrich cultural heritage. On one hand, it can lead to the homogenisation of cultures and the loss of unique traditions. On the other hand, it can facilitate the sharing and appreciation of diverse cultural expressions. Balancing these dynamics is essential for preserving cultural diversity. Similarly, the digitization of cultural artefacts and traditions offers both opportunities and challenges. Cultural tourism can be a double-edged sword. While it can generate economic benefits and promote cultural exchange, it can also lead to the commercialization and dilution of cultural practices. Effective management and regulation are needed to ensure that tourism supports rather than undermines cultural heritage. On one hand, it allows for broader access and preservation of cultural heritage, making it available to a global audience. On the other hand, this actively raises the challenges connected to the control and copyright of digital reproductions (Wagner and de Clippele, 2023). Ensuring that digitised cultural heritage is accessible while respecting the rights of the originating communities is a delicate balance. The commercialisation of cultural heritage can lead to its commodification, where cultural expressions are treated as marketable goods. This can undermine the cultural significance and authenticity of these expressions. The IP laws are able to facilitate this commodification through allowing the cultural heritage commercial exploitation without appropriate security for the cultural meaning and context (Steiner, 2024). Addressing these challenges requires global cooperation and culturally sensitive policies. International frameworks and agreements can help harmonise the protection of cultural heritage across borders. Researchers and institutions documenting cultural heritage must navigate ethical considerations, ensuring that their work does not exploit or misrepresent the communities involved. This includes obtaining informed consent, respecting cultural sensitivities, and providing benefits back to the communities.

DISCUSSION

Analysis of how copyright laws shape marketing practices and content usage

It was identified from the literature findings that copyright breach can happen for illegal activities, infrastructure alteration and unauthorised access permissions related practices within the tourism industry. It was also found from the literature that the online destination images used within the promotional marketing activities in tourism requires destination promoters input, unless it is considered as a copyright dispute. Most of the tourism industry organisations use copyrighted or licensed images from internet sources that can harm the company by fines and legal cases against them.On the other hand, the secondary thematic analysis of this research presented that tourism advertisements required to take proper permissions before using any copyrighted content unless it have to defend a claim of infringement. For instance, creating content over the destination marketing of tourism, major companies involve trademarks that are important equipment to support safeguarding their tourism services and products.

Recommendations for managing intellectual property in tourism, including licensing agreements and content creation strategies

The secondary thematic findings of this research effectively showcases that the IP or intellectual property laws mostly struggles to appropriately safeguard the TCE or traditional cultural expressions and the TK or traditional knowledge. The findings also presented that IP laws are capable of effectively facilitating commodification, where cultural expressions were treated as marketable goods. This can be executed by allowing the cultural heritage commercial exploitation without proper protections against the cultural context and meaning. Similarly, the findings presented that the unauthorised content refers to the unlawful access or distribution of promotional content such as images, videos or any written texts whereas some authorised third party intervention is made to make false trade mark rights. The findings also presented that issues are related to the maintenance of unauthorised access to the content, business logos and others which created major customers' misleading approach and significantly hampers the sales of rights holders.

Suggestions for policy improvements to support tourism businesses while protecting copyright holder

In the digital age, copyrights laws have created a number of challenges to the copyright holders in tourism businesses. In addition to this, it is crucial to modernise the copyright laws for the digital age as current law is not sufficient to address all the new copyright cases (innovating, 2024). Modernisation of copyright law and fair use doctrine also would be a key for the global digital age. Moreover, digital copyright laws also can be included within the Copyright Act for tourism business. The digital copyright laws also need to focus on protecting intermediaries from third party copyright infringements, address challenges in virtual reality, provide clarity on ownership rights and strike a balance between pubic rights and fair use provision (Law School Policy Review, 2024). Furthermore, the policy framework also need to be adaptive to changes of the market along with a multi-stakeholder system in order to make sure that the interests are not compromised and resources has been efficiently used to protect digital creation and distribution of copyright contents (Law School Policy Review, 2024). On the other hand, in order to protect digital contents such photographs, videos and texts, different types of tools have been used which creates a copyright watermark (Medium, 2024). Henceforth, for policy improvement, the copyright policies need to make it mandatory for the digital content creators to use tools for watermarking their contents.

CONCLUSION

Thus, it can be concluded that copyrights regulations are important for protecting the organic works and digital contents especially in the context of tourism businesses. Therefore, it is important to address the challenges which tourism industry is facing related to the copyrights. The question arises “Does the tourism practitioners and the tourism community really own its distinctive copyrights?” The challenges are vast and huge, particularly when we talk about the tourism industry to be addressed. Some of the social scientists says that the Tourism can no exist without culture (Jafari,1996). The significance of intellectual property rights such as copyrights and trademarks also has increased in tourism in order to restrict unauthorised access of digital contents.

Moreover, digital platforms such as Facebook, Instagram and YouTube are used in tourism to promote destinations and experiences. The copyright laws and principles impose a wide range of challenges on the tourism industry that also has been influencing marketing strategies and the creation of content. As a result, digital content supports in promoting tourist destinations and experiences and attracts tourists from all across the world. In addition to this, copyright is the most important Intellectual property which is also used by the advertisers and markets of the tourism industry in order to design their strategies and protect their content. Furthermore, misuse of business trademarks and infringement of the product design, videos or a patent are key challenges which have been faced by the tourism businesses in order to comply with copyright laws.

Managerial Implications

Social media plays a crucial role in the entertainment industry by facilitating artist-fan interaction and promoting their work. The users who distribute content on social media platforms without properly acknowledging its source or acquiring authorization have fostered an environment conducive to copyright infringements. Content producers and rights holders must continue to be diligent in monitoring their work and issuing takedown notifications when appropriate. However, it is necessary for social media firms and platforms to enhance regulations and enforcement in order to restrict this conduct. Individuals and brands can enhance the safeguarding of their intellectual property in the digital realm by formally registering copyrights, applying watermarks to media, and utilizing existing methods to report instances of infringement. To address the rampant infringement of copyright on social networking sites, a comprehensive approach involving education, deterrence, and continued pressure on these platforms is necessary. Creators and legal experts must continuously stay abreast of legal advancements to protect their rights and interests, given the ongoing evolution of the industry.

REFERENCES

Abdallah, A. (2021). Fake news, false advertising, social media and the tourism industry. *International Journal of Developmental Research*, 11(7), 48999–49003.

Albright 2021. Financial Compensation for Intellectual Property Infringement. Available at: https://www.albright-ip.co.uk/2021/04/financial-compensation-for-intellectual-property-infringement/ (Accessed: 22 August 2024)

Alharahsheh, H. H., & Pius, A. (2020). A review of key paradigms: Positivism VS interpretivism. *Global Academic Journal of Humanities and Social Sciences*, 2(3), 39–43.

Atanasova, I. (2019). Copyright infringement in digital environment. *Economics & Law*, 1(1), 13–22.

Bu, Y., Parkinson, J., & Thaichon, P. (2021). Digital content marketing as a catalyst for e-WOM in food tourism. *Australasian Marketing Journal*, 29(2), 142–154. DOI: 10.1016/j.ausmj.2020.01.001

Burri, M. 2020. Cultural Heritage and Intellectual Property. Oxford University Press eBooks, pp.459–482. DOI: 10.1093/law/9780198859871.003.0020

Bytes Care. 2024. Copyrights In Online Marketing // Bytescare. Available at: https://bytescare.com/copyrights-in-online-marketing(Accessed: 08 August 2024)

Bytescare 2024. What is Digital Copyright. Available at: https://bytescare.com/what-is-digital-copyright#:~:text=Digital%20copyright%20infringement%2C%20often%20termed,be%20infringed%20upon%20have%20grown. (Accessed: 19 August 2024)

Clarion solicitors 2020. Intellectual Property Infringement on Social Media – A Growing Problem. Available at: https://www.clarionsolicitors.com/articles/intellectual-property-infringement-on-social-media-a-growing-problem(Accessed: 19 August 2024)

Deb, S. K., Nafi, S. M., & Valeri, M. (2024). Promoting tourism business through digital marketing in the new normal era: A sustainable approach. *European Journal of Innovation Management*, 27(3), 775–799. DOI: 10.1108/EJIM-04-2022-0218

Derclaye, E., 2019. Assessing the Impact and Reception of the Court of Justice of the European Union case law on UK copyright law: What does the future hold?. Revue Internationale du Droit d'auteur, 2014(240).

GOV. 2023. Executive summary Online copyright infringement tracker survey (12th Wave). Available at: https://www.gov.uk/government/publications/online-copyright-infringement-tracker-survey-12th-wave/executive-summary-online-copyright-infringement-tracker-survey-12th-wave (Accessed: 21 August 2024)

Gov, 2024. The Data Protection Act. Available at: https://www.gov.uk/data-protection(Accessed: 05 August 2024)

Gowling, W. L. G. 2024. Copyright issues in advertising: what to consider? Available at: https://gowlingwlg.com/en/insights-resources/articles/2023/copyright-issues-in-advertising-what-to-consider(Accessed: 07 August 2024).

Hjalager, A. M. (2020). Land-use conflicts in coastal tourism and the quest for governance innovations. *Land Use Policy*, 94, 104566. DOI: 10.1016/j.landusepol.2020.104566

Hollebeek, L. D., & Macky, K. (2019). Digital content marketing's role in fostering consumer engagement, trust, and value: Framework, fundamental propositions, and implications. *Journal of Interactive Marketing*, 45(1), 27–41. DOI: 10.1016/j.intmar.2018.07.003

Interglobe 2023. Social Media and its impact on Travel. Available at: https://www.interglobe.com/social-media-and-its-impact-on-travel (Accessed: 22 August 2024)

Jafari, J. (1996). Tourism and culture: an inquiry into paradoxes. In *Culture, Tourism Development: Crucial Issues for the XXIst Century*. UNESCO.

Labra, O., Castro, C., Wright, R. and Chamblas, I., 2020. Thematic analysis in social work: A case study. Global social work-cutting edge issues and critical reflections, 10(6), pp.1-20.

Law School Policy Review. 2024. Need for a Digital Copyrights Act: Adjusting to the New Normal. Available at: https://lawschoolpolicyreview.com/2024/02/12/need-for-a-digital-copyrights-act-adjusting-to-the-new-normal/#(Accessed: 07 August 2024)

Lojo, A., Li, M., & Xu, H. (2020). Online tourism destination image: Components, information sources, and incongruence. *Journal of Travel & Tourism Marketing*, 37(4), 495–509. DOI: 10.1080/10548408.2020.1785370

Medium, 2024. 7 Essential Tools You Should Use to Protect Your Digital Content. Available at: https://medium.com/follower-booster-hub/7-essential-tools-you-should-use-to-protect-your-digital-content-10ca9a311363(Accessed: 06 August 2024)

Michael Edwards. 2024. Copyright Compliance in Marketing and Advertising Campaigns. Available at: https://michaeledwards.uk/copyright-compliance-in-marketing-and-advertising-campaigns/#:(Accessed: 09 August 2024)

Ploman, E. W., & Hamilton, L. C. (2024). *Copyright: Intellectual property in the information age*. Taylor & Francis. DOI: 10.4324/9781003519973

Prsformusic 2019. Piracy costs the UK economy £9bn annually. Available at: https://www.prsformusic.com/m-magazine/news/piracy-costs-uk-economy-9bn-annually (Accessed: 20 August 2024)

Ranking Articles. 2023. Navigating Copyright Issues in Content Creation. Available at: https://ranking-articles.com/navigating-copyright-issues/(Accessed: 06 August 2024)

Rincon, G. A., Cézar, R. F., & Hernandez, C. F. 2020, March. Beliefs about mathematics and academic performance: A descriptive-correlational analysis. In Journal of Physics: Conference Series (Vol. 1514, No. 1, p. 012021). IOP Publishing. DOI: 10.1088/1742-6596/1514/1/012021

Roadbook 2024. How is influencer marketing transforming the tourism industry? Available at: https://roadbook.com/travel/influencer-marketing-social-media-tourism-industry-trend/ (Accessed: 21 August 2024)

Ruggiano, N., & Perry, T. E. (2019). Conducting secondary analysis of qualitative data: Should we, can we, and how? *Qualitative Social Work: Research and Practice*, 18(1), 81–97. DOI: 10.1177/1473325017700701 PMID: 30906228

Siedlecki, S. L. (2020). Understanding descriptive research designs and methods. *Clinical Nurse Specialist CNS*, 34(1), 8–12. DOI: 10.1097/NUR.0000000000000493 PMID: 31789957

Steiner, C. 2024. INTELLECTUAL PROPERTY AND THE RIGHT TO CULTURE. Available at: https://www.wipo.int/edocs/mdocs/tk/en/wipo_unhchr_ip_pnl_98/wipo_unhchr_ip_pnl_98_2.pdf

Stokes, S. (2019). *Digital copyright: law and practice*. Bloomsbury publishing. DOI: 10.5040/9781509917327

Surono, S., Bastoni, B., Triutama, O. P., & Nisa, A. N. K. (2024). Intellectual Property Rights in Tourism Management in Cirebon. *Jurnal Toursci*, 1(4), 171–175. DOI: 10.62885/toursci.v1i4.203

Wagner, A. and de Clippele, M.-S., 2023. Safeguarding Cultural Heritage in the Digital Era – A Critical Challenge. International Journal for the Semiotics of Law - Revue internationale de Sémiotique juridique, 36(5), pp.1915–1923. DOI: 10.1007/s11196-023-10040-z

Wanda George, E. (2010). Intangible cultural heritage, ownership, copyrights, and tourism. *International Journal of Culture, Tourism and Hospitality Research*, 4(4), 376–388. DOI: 10.1108/17506181011081541

Compilation of References

Aaker, D. A. (1991). *Managing Brand Equity*. Free Press.

Abdallah, A. (2021). Fake news, false advertising, social media and the tourism industry. *International Journal of Developmental Research*, 11(7), 48999–49003.

Acheampong, H. (2020). *Destination Branding: Focusing on Events Contribution on an Urban Level*. https://www.diva-portal.org/smash/get/diva2:1520475/FULLTEXT02

Addor, F., & Grazioli, A. (2002). Geographical indications beyond wines and spirits: A roadmap for a better protection for geographical indications in the WTO TRIPS Agreement. *The Journal of World Intellectual Property*, 5(6), 865–897. DOI: 10.1111/j.1747-1796.2002.tb00185.x

Adediran, F. E., Okunade, B. A., Daraojimba, R. E., Adewusi, O. E., Bukola, A., & Igbokwe, J. C. (2024). Blockchain for social good: A review of applications in humanitarian aid and social initiatives. *International Journal of Science and Research Archive*, 11(1), 1203–1216.

Adetola, B. O., Akinola, O., & Aina, A. D. (2024). Tourism Policies and Performance of Nigerian Heritage Sites. *Advances in Research*, 25(3), 227–240. DOI: 10.9734/air/2024/v25i31067

Adeyinka-Ojo, S. F., Nair, V., & Khoo-Lattimore, C. (2014). Case Studies Approach in Tourism Destination Branding Research. *SHS Web of Conferences, 12*. DOI: 10.1051/shsconf/20141201061

Ahmed, A. (2022). Marketing 4.0: The Unseen Potential of AI in Consumer Relations. *International Journal of New Media Studies: International Peer Reviewed Scholarly Indexed Journal*, 9(1), 5–12.

Ahmed, N. (2024). Tourism Impact on the Cultural Heritage of Countries in the Middle East. *Journal of Applied Geographical Studies*, 3(1), 41–53. DOI: 10.47941/jags.1623

Akhtar, O. M. A. R. (2018). Understanding use cases for augmented, mixed and virtual reality. *Altimeter. Online verfügbar unter*https://marketing. prophet. com/acton/ct/33865/p-00b2/Bct/l-00a9/l-00a9*: 17b/ct16_0/1*.

Akın, E. B. (2006). Coğrafi işaret olarak tescil edilmiş Malatya kayısısının teknolojik özelliklerinin saptanması ve gıda güvenliği açısından araştırılması [Doctoral dissertation]. Hacettepe University.

Aksoy, A. Y., & Beaudry, C. (2021). How are companies paying for university research licenses? Empirical evidence from university-firm technology transfer. *The Journal of Technology Transfer*, 46(6), 2051–2121. DOI: 10.1007/s10961-020-09838-x

Al Harrasi, N., Al Balushi, B., Al Khayari, S., & Al Rashdi, M. (2024). Human resource management practices in Oman: A systematic review. *Journal of Human Resource Management*, 6(1), 45–60. DOI: 10.1080/23311975.2024.2337053

Alaux, C., Dioko, D., Morgan, N., Florek, M., Carmouze, L., Dessendier, C., Dinnie, K., Fan, H., Freire, J., Hereźniak, M., Lucarelli, A., Mauri, C., Zavattaro, S., & Zenker, S. (2023). *Unpacking the dynamic nature of Geographical Indications (GIs): a longitudinal study on Prosecco as a territorial brand*. 81–82. https://iris.unive.it/handle/10278/5020941

Albright 2021. Financial Compensation for Intellectual Property Infringement. Available at: https://www.albright-ip.co.uk/2021/04/financial-compensation-for-intellectual-property-infringement/ (Accessed: 22 August 2024)

Alford, P., & Jones, R. (2020). The lone digital tourism entrepreneur: Knowledge acquisition and collaborative transfer. *Tourism Management*, 81, 104139. DOI: 10.1016/j.tourman.2020.104139

Alharahsheh, H. H., & Pius, A. (2020). A review of key paradigms: Positivism VS interpretivism. *Global Academic Journal of Humanities and Social Sciences*, 2(3), 39–43.

Alon, I., Apriliyanti, I. D., & Henríquez Parodi, M. C. (2021). A systematic review of international franchising. *Multinational Business Review*, 29(1), 43–69. DOI: 10.1108/MBR-01-2020-0019

Al-Romeedy, B. (2024a). Sustainable Bytes: The Digital Literacy and Skills Revolution in Tourism. In *Dimensions of Regenerative Practices in Tourism and Hospitality* (pp. 206-221). IGI Global.

Al-Romeedy, B. (2024c). Breaking Chains, Building Futures: Blockchain's Impact on Sustainable Tourism. In *Promoting Responsible Tourism With Digital Platforms* (pp. 90-107). IGI Global.

Al-Romeedy, B. (2024d). Tomorrow's Travel Companion: The Role of Artificial Intelligence in Shaping the Future of Tourism. In *Marketing and Big Data Analytics in Tourism and Events* (pp. 162-182). IGI Global.

Al-Romeedy, B. (2024e). Unlocking the Power of Data: Exploring the Dynamic Role of MKIS in Revolutionizing Tourism Marketing. In *Marketing and Big Data Analytics in Tourism and Events* (pp. 183-204). IGI Global.

Al-Romeedy, B., & Hashem, T. (2024). From Insight to Advantage: Harnessing the Potential of Marketing Intelligence Systems in Tourism. In *Marketing and Big Data Analytics in Tourism and Events* (pp. 80-98). IGI Global.

Al-Romeedy, B. (2024b). Web of Wonders: Sustainable Digital Marketing Strategies for Unforgettable African Tourism Destinations. In *Promoting Responsible Tourism With Digital Platforms* (pp. 168–188). IGI Global. DOI: 10.4018/979-8-3693-3286-3.ch010

Al-Romeedy, B. S. (2024a). Tomorrow's Travel Companion: The Role of Artificial Intelligence in Shaping the Future of Tourism. In Hashem, T., Albattat, A., Valeri, M., & Sharma, A. (Eds.), *Marketing and Big Data Analytics in Tourism and Events* (pp. 162–182). IGI Global., DOI: 10.4018/979-8-3693-3310-5.ch010

Alyasiri, O. M., Selvaraj, K., Younis, H. A., Sahib, T. M., Almasoodi, M. F., & Hayder, I. M. (2024). A Survey on the Potential of Artificial Intelligence Tools in Tourism Information Services. *Babylonian Journal of Artificial Intelligence*, 2024, 1–8. DOI: 10.58496/BJAI/2024/001

Amam, M. (2024). Influence of Cultural Heritage Preservation on Tourism Development in Egypt. *American Journal of Arts. Social and Humanity Studies*, 4(1), 22–32. DOI: 10.47672/ajashs.2063

Ananya, S. A. (2021). Sustainable Tourism Principles and Practices in Bangladesh. In Hassan, A. (Ed.), *Tourism Products and Services in Bangladesh* (pp. 101–113). Springer Singapore., DOI: 10.1007/978-981-33-4279-8_5

Ancillai, C., Terho, H., Cardinali, S., & Pascucci, F. (2019). Advancing social media driven sales research: Establishing conceptual foundations for B-to-B social selling. *Industrial Marketing Management*, 82, 293–308. DOI: 10.1016/j.indmarman.2019.01.002

Anderson, C. K. (2012). The impact of social media on lodging performance. *Cornell Hospitality Quarterly*, 53(3), 232–244. DOI: 10.1177/1938965512459194

Angelstam, P., Manton, M., Yamelynets, T., Fedoriak, M., Albulescu, A. C., Bravo, F., Cruz, F., Jaroszewicz, B., Kavtarishvili, M., Muñoz-Rojas, J., Sijtsma, F., Washbourne, C. L., Agnoletti, M., Dobrynin, D., Izakovicova, Z., Jansson, N., Kanka, R., Kopperoinen, L., Lazdinis, M., & Zagidullina, A. (2021). Maintaining natural and traditional cultural green infrastructures across Europe: Learning from historic and current landscape transformations. *Landscape Ecology*, 36(2), 637–663. DOI: 10.1007/s10980-020-01161-y

Antons, C. (2013). Asian Borderlands and the Legal Protection of Traditional Knowledge and Traditional Cultural Expressions. *Modern Asian Studies*, 47(4), 1403–1433. https://www.jstor.org/stable/24494202. DOI: 10.1017/S0026749X12000443

Aplin, T., Aplin, T., & Davis, J. (2013). *Intellectual property law: text, cases, and materials*. Oxford University Press. DOI: 10.1093/he/9780199643301.001.0001

Aras, S. (2023). AR and VR technology: Transforming our lives through immersive experiences. *The Times of India*. https://timesofindia.indiatimes.com/readersblog/reflective-ruminations/ar-and-vr-technology-transforming-our-lives-through-immersive-experiences-52485/

Arif, M., Chilvers, G., Day, S., Naveed, S. A., Woolfe, M., Rodionova, O. Y., Pomerantsev, A. L., Kracht, O., Brodie, C., Mihailova, A., Abrahim, A., Cannavan, A., & Kelly, S. D. (2021). Differentiating Pakistani long-grain rice grown inside and outside the accepted Basmati Himalayan geographical region using a 'one-class' multi-element chemometric model. *Food Control*, 123, 107827. DOI: 10.1016/j.foodcont.2020.107827

Arion, O. V. (2024). Geographical indications and traditional products as the basis of enogastronomic tourism: Significance for the development of rural communities (on the example of Italy). *Journal of Geology Geography and Geoecology*, 33(1), 3–13. DOI: 10.15421/112401

Aronzon, S. M. (2020). Blockchain and geographical indications: a natural fit?. Journal of Intellectual Property Law & Practice.

Atanasova, I. (2019). Copyright infringement in digital environment. *Economics & Law*, 1(1), 13–22.

Ateljevic, J., & Page, S. (2017). *Tourism and entrepreneurship*. Routledge. DOI: 10.4324/9780080942728

Aulet, B. (2024). *Disciplined Entrepreneurship: 24 Steps to a Successful Startup, Expanded & Updated*. John Wiley & Sons.

Auralita, L. (2023). Unlocking the Power of Intellectual Property: Safeguarding Books Against Piracy. *Journal of Judicial Review*, 25(1), 1–16. DOI: 10.37253/jjr.v25i1.7743

Auttri, B., Chaitanya, K., Daida, S., & Jain, S. K. (2023). Digital Transformation in Customer Relationship Management: Enhancing Engagement and Loyalty. [EEL]. *European Economic Letters*, 13(3), 1140–1149.

Azmi, E., Che Rose, R. A., Awang, A., & Abas, A. (2023). Innovative and Competitive: A Systematic Literature Review on New Tourism Destinations and Products for Tourism Supply. *Sustainability 2023, Vol. 15, Page 1187, 15*(2), 1187. DOI: 10.3390/su15021187

Bagiastuti, N. K. (2023). Denpasar City Branding as Tourism Development Strategy: Law Branding Aspect Point of View. *International Journal of Social Science and Human Research*, 6(04), 2462–2469. DOI: 10.47191/ijsshr/v6-i4-60

Balaji, G. (2024, March 27). *Unconventional Trademarks in India: Protection Challenges & Prospects*. Depenning & Depenning. https://depenning.com/blog/unconventional-trademarks-evolution/

Baltierra, S. (2023, January). Virtual Reality and Augmented Reality Applied to E-Commerce: A Literature Review. In *Human-Computer Interaction: 8th Iberoamerican Workshop, HCI-COLLAB 2022, Havana, Cuba, October 13–15, 2022, Revised Selected Papers* (p. 201). Springer Nature.

Baral, K. C. (Ed.). (2023). *Cultural forms and practices in northeast India*. Springer Nature Singapore., DOI: 10.1007/978-981-19-9292-6

Barham, E. (2003). Translating terroir: The global challenge of French AOC labeling. *Journal of Rural Studies*, 19(1), 127–138. DOI: 10.1016/S0743-0167(02)00052-9

Barjolle, D., Paus, M., & Perret, A. (2009). Impacts of geographical indications - review of methods and empirical evidences. International Association of Agricultural Economists Conference, Beijing, China.

Bartoli, C., Bonetti, E., & Mattiacci, A. (2022a). Marketing geographical indication products in the digital age: A holistic perspective. *British Food Journal*, 124(9), 2857–2876. DOI: 10.1108/BFJ-03-2021-0241

Başaran, B. (2020). Perceptions, Attitudes and Behaviours of Consumers Towards Traditional Foods and Gastronomy Tourism: The Case of Rize. *Journal of Tourism and Gastronomy Studies*, 8(3), 1752–1769. DOI: 10.21325/jotags.2020.632

Basheer, S., Farooq, S., Hassan, V., Malik, Y. M., & Reshi, M. A. (2023). Augmented Reality and Virtual Reality in Cultural Heritage Tourism Enhancing Visitor Experiences. In Rawal, Y. S., Sinha, R., Mukherjee, S. K., & Batabyal, D. (Eds.), *Advances in Hospitality, Tourism, and the Services Industry* (pp. 13–34). IGI Global., DOI: 10.4018/978-1-6684-9957-3.ch002

Basile, G., & Cavallo, A. (2020). Rural Identity, Authenticity, and Sustainability in Italian Inner Areas. *Sustainability 2020, Vol. 12, Page 1272, 12*(3), 1272. DOI: 10.3390/su12031272

Bassey, B. (2015). Transforming the Nigeria tourism industry through tourism entrepreneurial development. *African Journal of Business Management*, 9(15), 569–580. DOI: 10.5897/AJBM2015.7844

Bendix, R. (1989). Tourism and Cultural Displays: Inventing Traditions for Whom? *Journal of American Folklore*, 102(404), 131–146. DOI: 10.2307/540676

Benson, T. J. (2019). Intellectual property rights in gastronomic tourism. In *The Routledge Handbook of Gastronomic Tourism* (pp. 499–505). Routledge. DOI: 10.4324/9781315147628-60

Berman, B., & Pollack, D. (2021). Strategies for the successful implementation of augmented reality. *Business Horizons*, 64(5), 621–630. DOI: 10.1016/j.bushor.2021.02.027

Berry, L. L. (2000). Cultivating Service Brand Equity. *Journal of the Academy of Marketing Science*, 28(1), 128–137. DOI: 10.1177/0092070300281012

Bhati, D. (2020). Agribusiness module of value added underutilized food products towards livelihood support of hills population (Doctoral dissertation).

Bhatt, V., Singh, P., Mishra, S., Bhartiya, S., & Tyagi, P. (2024). A Retrospective Analysis of Information Technology in Tourism Research. *African Journal of Hospitality, Tourism and Leisure*, 13(2), 410–420. DOI: 10.46222/ajhtl.19770720.523

Bienabe, E., Kirsten, J., & Bramley, C. (2013). *Developing geographical indications in the South*. Springer.

Birch, D., & Memery, J. (2020). Tourists, local food and the intention-behaviour gap. *Journal of Hospitality and Tourism Management*, 43, 53–61. DOI: 10.1016/j.jhtm.2020.02.006

Birdir, S. S., Dalgic, A., & Birdir, K. (2018). Destination marketing and destination image. In *The Routledge handbook of destination marketing* (pp. 71–81). Routledge. DOI: 10.4324/9781315101163-7

Biygautane, M., Clegg, S., & Al-Yahya, K. (2020). Institutional work and infrastructure public–private partnerships (PPPs): The roles of religious symbolic work and power in implementing PPP projects. *Accounting, Auditing & Accountability Journal*, 33(5), 1077–1112. DOI: 10.1108/AAAJ-04-2019-3982

Blain, C., Levy, S. E., & Ritchie, J. R. B. (2005). Destination Branding: Insights and Practices from Destination Management Organizations. *Journal of Travel Research*, 43(4), 328–338. DOI: 10.1177/0047287505274646

Blakeney, M. (2001). Proposals for the international regulation of geographical indications. *The Journal of World Intellectual Property*, 4(5), 629–652. DOI: 10.1111/j.1747-1796.2001.tb00131.x

Boateng, B. (2013). The Hand of the Ancestors: Time, Cultural Production, and Intellectual Property Law. *Law & Society Review*, 47(4), 943–973. https://www.jstor.org/stable/43670364. DOI: 10.1111/lasr.12053

Booth, G. (2015). Copyright Law and the Changing Economic Value of Popular Music in India. *Ethnomusicology*, 59(2), 262–287. DOI: 10.5406/ethnomusicology.59.2.0262

Boukas, N., & Ioannou, M. (2020). Co-creating visitor experiences in cultural heritage museums: The avenue towards sustainable tourism development. *International Journal of Tourism Policy*, 10(2), 101. DOI: 10.1504/IJTP.2020.110862

Boyd, S. (2002). Cultural and heritage tourism in Canada: Opportunities, principles and challenges. *Tourism and Hospitality Research*, 3(3), 211–233. https://www.jstor.org/stable/23747289. DOI: 10.1177/146735840200300303

Bramley, C., & Bienabe, E. (2013). Why do geographical indications matter? In Gangjee, D. (Ed.), *Research handbook on intellectual property and geographical indications* (pp. 15–30). Edward Elgar Publishing., DOI: 10.4337/9781783472608.00007

Bratspies, R. M. (2006). The New Discovery Doctrine: Some Thoughts on Property Rights and Traditional Knowledge. *American Indian Law Review*, 31(2), 315–340. DOI: 10.2307/20070790

Brooks, L., & Young, M. (2020). Sustainable human resource practices in the ecotourism industry. *International Journal of Hospitality Management*, 89, 102561. DOI: 10.1016/j.ijhm.2020.102561

Brown, T., & Green, M. (2020). IP management in eco-tourism: Innovations and challenges. *Sustainability*, 12(8), 3344. DOI: 10.3390/su12083344

Bunten, A. C. (2008). Sharing Culture or Selling Out? Developing the Commodified Persona in the Heritage Industry. *American Ethnologist*, 35(3), 380–395. DOI: 10.1111/j.1548-1425.2008.00041.x

Burns, P. (2022). *Entrepreneurship and small business*. Bloomsbury Publishing.

Burri, M. 2020. Cultural Heritage and Intellectual Property. Oxford University Press eBooks, pp.459–482. DOI: 10.1093/law/9780198859871.003.0020

Bu, Y., Parkinson, J., & Thaichon, P. (2021). Digital content marketing as a catalyst for e-WOM in food tourism. *Australasian Marketing Journal*, 29(2), 142–154. DOI: 10.1016/j.ausmj.2020.01.001

Bytes Care. 2024. Copyrights In Online Marketing // Bytescare. Available at: https://bytescare.com/copyrights-in-online-marketing(Accessed: 08 August 2024)

Bytescare 2024. What is Digital Copyright. Available at: https://bytescare.com/what-is-digital-copyright#:~:text=Digital%20copyright%20infringement%2C%20often%20termed,be%20infringed%20upon%20have%20grown. (Accessed: 19 August 2024)

Caboni, F., & Hagberg, J. (2019). Augmented reality in retailing: A review of features, applications and value. *International Journal of Retail & Distribution Management*, 47(11), 1125–1140. DOI: 10.1108/IJRDM-12-2018-0263

Calboli, I. (2018). Introduction. In Calboli, I., & Senftleben, M. (Eds.), *Oxford University Press eBooks* (pp. 1–10). Oxford University Press., DOI: 10.1093/oso/9780198826576.003.0001

Camilleri, M. A. (2018a). *Strategic perspectives in destination marketing*. IGI Global.

Camilleri, M. A. (2018b). *The branding of tourist destinations: Theoretical and empirical insights*. Emerald Publishing Limited. DOI: 10.1108/9781787693739

Camilleri, M. A. (2018c). *Travel marketing, tourism economics and the airline product: An introduction to theory and practice*. Springer International Publishing. DOI: 10.1007/978-3-319-49849-2

Camilleri, M. A. (2024). *Tourism planning and destination marketing*. Emerald Publishing Limited. DOI: 10.1108/9781804558881

Carayannis, E. (2020). *Encyclopedia of creativity, invention, innovation and entrepreneurship*. Springer International Publishing. DOI: 10.1007/978-3-319-15347-6

Carter, N., & Johnson, T. (2020). Human resources and intellectual property in the context of sustainable tourism. *Sustainability*, 12(21), 8956. DOI: 10.3390/su12218956

Carton, S. (2019). *What impact will immersive technologies such as augmented and virtual reality have on the retail sector?* (Doctoral dissertation, Dublin, National College of Ireland).

CCH Canadian v. Law Society of Upper Canada (2004) 236 DLR (4th) 395.

Čehić, A., Mesić, Ž., & Oplanić, M. (2020). Requirements for development of olive tourism: The case of Croatia. *Tourism and Hospitality Management*, 26(1), 1–14. DOI: 10.20867/thm.26.1.1

Cei, L., Defrancesco, E., & Stefani, G. (2018). From Geographical Indications to Rural Development: A Review of the economic effects of European Union policy. *Sustainability (Basel)*, 10(10), 3745. DOI: 10.3390/su10103745

Celebi, D., Pirnar, I., & Eris, E. D. (2020). Bibliometric analysis of social entrepreneurship in gastronomy tourism. Tourism. *Tourism (Zagreb)*, 68(1), 58–67. DOI: 10.37741/t.68.1.5

Cerdan, C., Vitrolles, D., Delfosse, C., Velloso, C. Q., Nabinger, C., & Silva, A. L. (2009). Penser la conservation des ressources bioculturelles sous l'angle de la valorisation de l'origine: La mise en place d'indications géographiques dans le Sud Brésil. *Autrepart (La Tour d'Aigues)*, 50, 153–166. DOI: 10.3917/autr.050.0153

Çetin, B. (2021). Gastronomy Tourism. TOURISM STUDIES AND SOCIAL SCIENCES, 16.

Chabot, Y., Lefevre, V., & Lefrancq, C. (2022, June 20). The paleoenvironment of Mahasthangarh (Bangladesh) during the Pre-Modern Period. DOI: 10.5194/icg2022-75

Chacón, G. E. (2020). Material Culture, Indigeneity, and Temporality: The Textile as Legal Subject. *Textual Cultures, 13*(2), 49–69. https://www.jstor.org/stable/26966965

Chakraborty, A., & Jain, V. (2022). Leveraging Digital Marketing and Integrated Marketing Communications for Brand Building in Emerging Markets. In Adeola, O., Hinson, R. E., & Sakkthivel, A. M. (Eds.), *Marketing Communications and Brand Development in Emerging Economies* (Vol. I). Palgrave Studies of Marketing in Emerging Economies. Palgrave Macmillan., DOI: 10.1007/978-3-030-88678-3_13

Chasomeris, M., Munapo, E., Khumalo, T., & Adeyeye, O. (2015). The South African tea industry: challenges and business strategies. *Environmental economics*, (6, Iss. 4 (contin.), 133-142.

Chauhan, S., Bansal, O., & Puriya, A. (2024). Innovating Urbanity: The Synergy of Smart Cities and Circular Economy in India. In Majumdar, S., Kandpal, V., & Anthopoulos, L. G. (Eds.), *Smart Cities* (pp. 249–278). Springer Nature Switzerland., DOI: 10.1007/978-3-031-59846-3_11

Chen, J., Jiang, L., Luo, J., Tian, L., Tian, Y., & Chen, G. (2022). Characteristics and Influencing Factors of Spatial Differentiation of Market Service Industries in Rural Areas around Metropolises—A Case Study of Wuhan City's New Urban Districts. *ISPRS International Journal of Geo-Information 2022, Vol. 11, Page 170, 11*(3), 170. DOI: 10.3390/ijgi11030170

Chen, C., & Arus, B. B. M. (2024). Chinese Cultural and Opera Stage Architectural Design for Urbanization Henan, China. *South Asian Journal of Social Sciences and Humanities*, 5(3), 114–134. DOI: 10.48165/sajssh.2024.5307

Chen, Y., & Lin, C. A. (2022). Consumer behavior in an augmented reality environment: Exploring the effects of flow via augmented realism and technology fluidity. *Telematics and Informatics*, 71, 101833. DOI: 10.1016/j.tele.2022.101833

Chirico, F., Criaco, G., Baù, M., Naldi, L., Gomez-Mejia, L., & Kotlar, J. (2020). To patent or not to patent: That is the question. Intellectual property protection in family firms. *Entrepreneurship Theory and Practice*, 44(2), 339–367. DOI: 10.1177/1042258718806251

Choi, H., & Sirakaya-Turk, E. (2005). Sustainability indicators for managing community tourism. *Tourism Management*, 26(3), 465–475. DOI: 10.1016/j.tourman.2003.12.003

Chung, D., Yang, S., & Marhold, K. (2024). Investigating the Relationship between Technological Entrepreneurship and National Innovativeness: Moderating Effects of Intellectual Property Protection and R&D Transfer Environment. *Entrepreneurship Research Journal*, 14(3), 1341–1371. DOI: 10.1515/erj-2020-0530

Clarion solicitors 2020. Intellectual Property Infringement on Social Media – A Growing Problem. Available at: https://www.clarionsolicitors.com/articles/intellectual-property-infringement-on-social-media-a-growing-problem (Accessed: 19 August 2024)

Cohen, E. (1988). Authenticity and commoditization in tourism. *Annals of Tourism Research*, 15(3), 371–386. DOI: 10.1016/0160-7383(88)90028-X

Coombe, R. J. (1998). Intellectual Property, Human Rights & Sovereignty: New Dilemmas in International Law Posed by the Recognition of Indigenous Knowledge and the Conservation of Biodiversity. *Indiana Journal of Global Legal Studies*, 6(1), 59–115.

Covalkchuck, G. C. & Medeiros, M. D. L. (2023). Geographical indication of Sao Matheus as a boost to gastronomic tourism. Tourism & heritage journal, 5, 37-55. DOI: .DOI: 10.1344/THJ.2023.5.3

Cozzolino, A., Corbo, L., & Aversa, P. (2021). Digital platform-based ecosystems: The evolution of collaboration and competition between incumbent producers and entrant platforms. *Journal of Business Research*, 126, 385–400. DOI: 10.1016/j.jbusres.2020.12.058

Crammond, R. (2024). Developing intellectual property management skills and the entrepreneurial university element: An educator perspective. *International Journal of Intellectual Property Management*, 14(4), 389–409. DOI: 10.1504/IJIPM.2024.139664

Crupi, A., Cesaroni, F., & Di Minin, A. (2021). Understanding the impact of intellectual capital on entrepreneurship: A literature review. *Journal of Intellectual Capital*, 22(3), 528–559. DOI: 10.1108/JIC-02-2020-0054

D'Souza, C., Taghian, M., Lamb, P., & Peretiatko, R. (2007). Green decisions: Demographics and consumer understanding of environmental labels. *International Journal of Consumer Studies*, 31(4), 371–376. DOI: 10.1111/j.1470-6431.2006.00567.x

Dabbous, M., Chachoua, L., Caban, A., & Toumi, M. (2020). Managed Entry Agreements: Policy Analysis From the European Perspective. *Value in Health*, 23(4), 425–433. DOI: 10.1016/j.jval.2019.12.008 PMID: 32327159

Dadashpour Moghaddam, M., Ahmadzadeh, H., & Valizadeh, R. (2022). A GIS-Based Assessment of Urban Tourism Potential with a Branding Approach Utilizing Hybrid Modeling. *Spatial Information Research*, 30(3), 399–416. DOI: 10.1007/s41324-022-00439-4

Dagne, T. W. (2010). Harnessing the development potential of geographical indications for traditional knowledge-based agricultural products. *Journal of Intellectual Property Law & Practice*, 5(6), 441–458. DOI: 10.1093/jiplp/jpq002

Dana, L. (2021). *World encyclopedia of entrepreneurship*. Edward Elgar Publishing. DOI: 10.4337/9781839104145

Dar, M. A., & Ojha, M. (2023). Destination imaging, compatibilities with intellectual property rights-based tourism industry. *The Journal of World Intellectual Property*, 26(2), 328–335. DOI: 10.1111/jwip.12268

Das, D., & Dileep, M. R. (2023). Geographical Indication and Tourism: A Study on the Awareness, Factors Influence, and the Scope of GI Tagging in Kerala as a Rural Tourism Development Tool. *International Journal of Hospitality and Tourism Systems*, 16(4), 25–34.

Das, K. (2006). International Protection of India's Geographical Indications with Special Reference to "Darjeeling" Tea. *The Journal of World Intellectual Property*, 9(5), 459–495. DOI: 10.1111/j.1422-2213.2006.00300.x

Davis, K., & Mendez, A. (2022). Trade secrets and sustainable practices in the tourism sector. *Journal of Business Research*, 142, 79–89. DOI: 10.1016/j.jbusres.2021.12.010

de Almeida, A. R., & Carls, S. (2021). The Criteria to Qualify a Geographical Term as Generic: Are We Moving from a European to a US Perspective? *IIC; International Review of Industrial Property and Copyright Law*, 52(4), 444–467. DOI: 10.1007/s40319-021-01045-x

De Carlo, M., & Dubini, P. (2010). Integrating Heritage Management and Tourism at Italian Cultural Destinations. *International Journal of Arts Management*, 12(2), 30–43.

De Mattos Fagundes, P., Padilha, A. C. M. H., Sluszz, T., & Padula, A. D. (2012). Geographical indication as a market orientation strategy: An analysis of producers of high-quality wines in Southern Brazil. *Journal of Database Marketing and Customer Strategy Management*, 19(3), 163–178. DOI: 10.1057/dbm.2012.18

Deb, S. K., Nafi, S. M., & Valeri, M. (2024). Promoting tourism business through digital marketing in the new normal era: A sustainable approach. *European Journal of Innovation Management*, 27(3), 775–799. DOI: 10.1108/EJIM-04-2022-0218

Defossez, D. A. L. (2017). Global regulation of international intellectual property through Agreement on Trade-Related Aspects of Intellectual Property Rights (TRIPS): The European Union and Brazil. Revista de Direito Setorial e Regulatório= Journal of Law and Regulation, 3(2), 131-160.

Delimatsis, P. (2021). A Partnership of Equals?'Deeper'Economic Integration Between the EU and Northern Africa. *European Foreign Affairs Review*, 26(4).

Delphine, M. V. (2008). From plant variety definition to geographical indication protection: A search for the link between Basmati rice and India/Pakistan. *The Journal of World Intellectual Property*, 11(4), 321–344. DOI: 10.1111/j.1747-1796.2008.00341.x

Derclaye, E., 2019. Assessing the Impact and Reception of the Court of Justice of the European Union case law on UK copyright law: What does the future hold?. Revue Internationale du Droit d'auteur, 2014(240).

Derek, M. (2021). Nature on a Plate: Linking Food and Tourism within the Ecosystem Services Framework. *Sustainability (Basel)*, 13(4), 1687. DOI: 10.3390/su13041687

Deshbhratar, S., Joshi, S., Alwaali, R. N., Saear, A. R., & Marhoon, H. A. (2023, September). Augmented reality of online and physical retailing: A study of applications and its value. In *AIP Conference Proceedings* (Vol. 2736, No. 1). AIP Publishing. DOI: 10.1063/5.0170917

Dewalska-Opitek, A., & Hofman-Kohlmeyer, M. (2021). Players As Prosumers-How Customer Engagement In Game Modding May Benefit Computer Game Market. Central European Business Review, 10(1).

Dharmawan, N. K. S., Kasih, D. P. D., Dewi, A. A. I. A. A., & Kurniawan, I. (2020). Trademark protection for small-medium enterprises in Bali: Strengthening Community-based tourism in the era of fourth industrial revolution. *J. Legal Ethical & Regul. Isses*, 23, 1.

Dias, Á. (2024). Tourism business startup: recognizing opportunities and barriers to entry. In *Handbook of Tourism Entrepreneurship* (pp. 188–200). Edward Elgar Publishing. DOI: 10.4337/9781803920023.00022

Dodson, M., & Barr, O. (2007). Breaking the Deadlock: Developing an Indigenous Response to Protecting Indigenous Traditional Knowledge. *Australian Indigenous Law Review*, 11(2), 19–32.

Dogan, B., & Gokovali, U. (2012). Geographical indications: The aspects of rural development and marketing through the traditional products. *Procedia: Social and Behavioral Sciences*, 62, 761–765. DOI: 10.1016/j.sbspro.2012.09.128

Dominas, K., Wesołowska, E., & Trocha, B. (Eds.). (2016). *Antiquity in Popular Literature and Culture* (1st ed.). Cambridge Scholars Publishing., https://www.cambridgescholars.com/resources/pdfs/978-1-4438-9024-3-sample.pdf

Dona, S. A., & Nelshani, S. (2023). Implementation of Export Business Strategy for Internationalization Entrepreneurial Startups to achieve Competitive Advantage in an Emerging Economy.: Evidence from Sri Lankan SMEs Textile and Tea Industry.

Dong, J. D., Peng, M., & Uddin, M. G. (2020). Mapping The Linguistic Landscape of the Cultural Heritage Sites and Tourist Spots in Bangladesh. *Randwick International of Education and Linguistics Science Journal*, 1(2), 226–241. DOI: 10.47175/rielsj.v1i2.89

Dosso, M., & Vezzani, A. (2020). Firm market valuation and intellectual property assets. *Industry and Innovation*, 27(7), 705–729. DOI: 10.1080/13662716.2019.1685374

Drahos, P. (2016). *A philosophy of intellectual property*. Routledge.

Dratler, J. (2023). *Licensing of intellectual property*. Law Journal Press.

Dratler, J.Jr, & McJohn, S. M. (2024). *Intellectual property law: Commercial, creative and industrial property*. Law Journal Press.

Duan, W., Khurshid, A., Khan, K., & Calin, A. C. (2024). Transforming industry: Investigating 4.0 technologies for sustainable product evolution in china through a novel fuzzy three-way decision-making process. *Technological Forecasting and Social Change*, 200, 123125. DOI: 10.1016/j.techfore.2023.123125

Dubey, A. (2020). An Analysis of the Challenges Faced by India in the Protection and Enforcement of Geographical Indication through the Case Study of Darjeeling Tea. *International Journal of Law Management & Humanities*, 3(6). https://heinonline.org/HOL/Page?handle=hein.journals/ijlmhs8&id=833&div=&collection=

Dutfield, G. (2017). *Intellectual property rights and the life science industries: A twentieth century history*. Routledge. DOI: 10.4324/9781315252131

Dutfield, G., & Suthersanen, U. (2019). Traditional knowledge and genetic resources: Observing legal protection through the lens of historical geography and human rights. *Washburn Law Journal*, 58, 399.

Dutta, P., Choi, T. M., Somani, S., & Butala, R. (2020). Blockchain technology in supply chain operations: Applications, challenges and research opportunities. Transportation research part e: Logistics and transportation review, 142, 102067.

Duxbury, N., Bakas, F. E., Vinagre de Castro, T., & Silva, S. (2021). Creative Tourism Development Models towards Sustainable and Regenerative Tourism. *Sustainability (Basel)*, 13(1), 2. DOI: 10.3390/su13010002

Dwivedi, Y. K., Pandey, N., Currie, W., & Micu, A. (2024). Leveraging ChatGPT and other Intellectual property(AI)-based applications in the hospitality and tourism industry: Practices, challenges and research agenda. *International Journal of Contemporary Hospitality Management*, 36(1), 1–12. DOI: 10.1108/IJCHM-05-2023-0686

Dwyer, L., & Kim, C. (2003). Destination competitiveness: Determinants and indicators. *Current Issues in Tourism*, 6(5), 369–414. DOI: 10.1080/13683500308667962

Eastern Book Company v. D. B. Modak (2008) (36) PTC 1 (SC).

Elrehail, H. (2020). Employee satisfaction, human resource management, and competitive advantage in tourism. *European Journal of Management and Business Economics*, 29(2), 23–36. DOI: 10.1108/EJMBE-01-2019-0001

Emrich, D. (1946). "Folk-Lore": William John Thoms. *California Folklore Quarterly*, 5(4), 355–374. DOI: 10.2307/1495929

Erjansola, A. M., Lipponen, J., Vehkalahti, K., Aula, H. M., & Pirttilä-Backman, A. M. (2021). From the brand logo to brand associations and the corporate identity: Visual and identity-based logo associations in a university merger. *Journal of Brand Management*, 28(3), 241–253. DOI: 10.1057/s41262-020-00223-5

Escudeiro, N., Escudeiro, P., Cunha, B., & Gouveia, M. C. (2023). Inclusive Cultural Heritage Tourism. In Abreu, A., Carvalho, J. V., Liberato, D., & Galdames, I. S. (Eds.), *Advances in Tourism, Technology and Systems* (Vol. 340, pp. 207–217). Springer Nature Singapore., DOI: 10.1007/978-981-19-9960-4_19

Eweje, G., Sajjad, A., Nath, S. D., & Kobayashi, K. (2021). Multi-stakeholder partnerships: A catalyst to achieve sustainable development goals. *Marketing Intelligence & Planning*, 39(2), 186–212. DOI: 10.1108/MIP-04-2020-0135

Fan, X., Jiang, X., & Deng, N. (2022). Immersive technology: A meta-analysis of augmented/virtual reality applications and their impact on tourism experience. *Tourism Management*, 91, 104534. DOI: 10.1016/j.tourman.2022.104534

Farronato, C., Fradkin, A., Larsen, B. J., & Brynjolfsson, E. (2024). Consumer Protection in an Online World: An Analysis of Occupational Licensing. *American Economic Journal. Applied Economics*, 16(3), 549–579. DOI: 10.1257/app.20210716

Febriany, T., Kurniawan, H., & Setiyawan, D. (2022). The Implementation of Intellectual Property Registration for Startups in the Industrial Revolution Era 4.0 in Pontianak. *Indonesia Law Reform Journal*, 2(3), 382–388. DOI: 10.22219/ilrej.v2i3.23309

Ferdian, M. (2021). Legal Protection of Geographical Indications for Local Handicrafts in Tourism Activities in Indonesia. *Advances in Social Science, Education and Humanities Research*, 605, 333–336.

Fernández-Zarza, M., Amaya-Corchuelo, S., Belletti, G., & Aguilar-Criado, E. (2021). Trust and Food Quality in the Valorisation of Geographical Indication Initiatives. *Sustainability (Basel)*, 2021(13), 3168. DOI: 10.3390/su13063168

Figueroa-Domecq, C., De Jong, A., & Williams, A. (2020). Gender, tourism & entrepreneurship: A critical review. *Annals of Tourism Research*, 84, 102980. DOI: 10.1016/j.annals.2020.102980

Figueroa-Domecq, C., Kimbu, A., de Jong, A., & Williams, A. (2023). Sustainability through the tourism entrepreneurship journey: A gender perspective. In *Gender and Tourism Sustainability* (pp. 107–130). Routledge. DOI: 10.4324/9781003329541-7

Firoj, K., & Mohammad, B. T. (2024). Measuring sustainability in the broadcasting media industry in Bangladesh. *I-Manager's. Journal of Management*, 18(3), 51. DOI: 10.26634/jmgt.18.3.20234

Folklore from India. (1916). Folklore from India. *Folklore*, 27(4), 418–419. https://www.jstor.org/stable/1255595. DOI: 10.1080/0015587X.1916.9718944

Forsyth, M. (2013). Protecting traditional knowledge and cultural heritage: Who, what, why, and where? *Indigenous Law Bulletin*, 8(8), 8–12.

Forsyth, P. (2013). Climate change and tourism: Policy and international perspectives. *Journal of Sustainable Tourism*, 21(1), 12–22. DOI: 10.1080/09669582.2012.695842

Friedmann, D. (2020). Grafting the Old and New World: Towards a Universal Trademark Register that Cancels Generic IGO Terms. In Wine Law and Policy (pp. 311-345). Brill Nijhoff.

Fusté-Forné, F. (2020). Savouring place: Cheese as a food tourism destination landmark. Journal of Place Management and Development.

Gaafar, H., & Al-Romeedy, B. (2024a). Bridging the Digital Divide: Unleashing the Power of Big Data Analytics for Touristic Destination Promotion. In *Marketing and Big Data Analytics in Tourism and Events* (pp. 17-37). IGI Global.

Gaafar, H., & Al-Romeedy, B. (2024b). Data Fusion for Destination Success: Exploring the Integration of MKIS and BDA in Marketing Touristic Destinations. In *Marketing and Big Data Analytics in Tourism and Events* (pp. 38-60). IGI Global.

Gan, R. (2020). "Pure Michigan" and "Napa Valley 100%": Is Protection of American Origin Wines as Geographic Indications on Fertile Ground? In Wine Law and Policy (pp. 392-414). Brill Nijhoff.

Gandhi, V. H. (2022). Intellectual Property Disputes and Resolutions. [JIPR]. *Journal of Intellectual Property Rights*, 26(1), 14–19. DOI: 10.56042/jipr.v26i1.39447

Gangjee, D. (2010). Non Conventional Trade Marks in India. *National Law School of India Review, 22*(1), 67–95. https://www.jstor.org/stable/44283714

George, A. S. (2023). Future Economic Implications of Artificial Intelligence. *Partners Universal International Research Journal*, 2(3), 20–39.

George, R. (2021). *Marketing tourism and hospitality: Concepts and cases*. Springer Nature. DOI: 10.1007/978-3-030-64111-5

Gervais, D. J. (2005). Traditional knowledge & intellectual property: A TRIPS-compatible approach. *Detroit College of Law at Michigan State University Law Review*, 2005(1), 137–166.

Ghamat, S., Pun, H., Critchley, G., & Hou, P. (2021). Using intellectual property agreements in the presence of supplier and third-party copycatting. *European Journal of Operational Research*, 291(2), 680–692. DOI: 10.1016/j.ejor.2020.09.041

Ghose, A., & Ali, S. M. A. (2023). Protection and preservation of traditional cultural expressions & traditional knowledge in handicraft trade: Advocating the need for a global cultural policy framework. *Revista de Direito Internacional*, 20(2). Advance online publication. DOI: 10.5102/rdi.v20i2.9109

Ghosh, S. (2020, March 31). Plagiarism! The curious case of Badshah's 'Genda Phool' and a Bengali folk singer in darkness! *The Times of India*. https://timesofindia.indiatimes.com/entertainment/bengali/music/plagiarism-the-curious-case-of-badshahs-genda-phool-and-a-bengali-folk-singer-in-darkness/articleshow/74914938.cms

Ghouri, A. M., Mani, V., Jiao, Z., Venkatesh, V. G., Shi, Y., & Kamble, S. S. (2021). An empirical study of real-time information-receiving using industry 4.0 technologies in downstream operations. *Technological Forecasting and Social Change*, 165, 120551. DOI: 10.1016/j.techfore.2020.120551

Giovannucci, D., Barham, E., & Pirog, R. (2010). Defining and marketing "local" foods: Geographical indications for US products. *The Journal of World Intellectual Property*, 13(2), 94–120. DOI: 10.1111/j.1747-1796.2009.00370.x

Goldstein, D. (2015). Vernacular Turns: Narrative, Local Knowledge, and the Changed Context of Folklore. *Journal of American Folklore*, 128(508), 125–145. DOI: 10.5406/jamerfolk.128.508.0125

Gov, 2024. The Data Protection Act. Available at: https://www.gov.uk/data-protection(Accessed: 05 August 2024)

GOV. 2023. Executive summary Online copyright infringement tracker survey (12th Wave). Available at: https://www.gov.uk/government/publications/online-copyright-infringement-tracker-survey-12th-wave/executive-summary-online-copyright-infringement-tracker-survey-12th-wave (Accessed: 21 August 2024)

Gowling, W. L. G. 2024. Copyright issues in advertising: what to consider? Available at: https://gowlingwlg.com/en/insights-resources/articles/2023/copyright-issues-in-advertising-what-to-consider(Accessed: 07 August 2024).

Gray, B., Purdy, J., & Ansari, S. (2022). Confronting Power Asymmetries in Partnerships to Address Grand Challenges. *Organization Theory*, 3(2). Advance online publication. DOI: 10.1177/26317877221098765

Greenfield, J., & Kumar, S. (2019). The interplay between intellectual property and sustainable development in tourism. *Tourism Management Perspectives*, 31, 212–220. DOI: 10.1016/j.tmp.2019.05.007

Gregorič, A., Rabbiosi, L., & Santangelo, G. D. (2021). Diaspora ownership and international technology licensing by emerging market firms. *Journal of International Business Studies*, 52(4), 671–691. DOI: 10.1057/s41267-020-00324-y

Gretzel, U., Fesenmaier, D. R., Formica, S., & O'Leary, J. T. (2006). Searching for the future: Challenges faced by destination marketing organizations. *Journal of Travel Research*, 45(2), 116–126. DOI: 10.1177/0047287506291598

Gretzel, U., & Jamal, T. (2009). Conceptualizing the creative tourist class: Technology, mobility, and tourism experiences. *Tourism Analysis*, 14(4), 471–481. DOI: 10.3727/108354209X12596287114219

Grimaldi, M., Greco, M., & Cricelli, L. (2021). A framework of intellectual property protection strategies and open innovation. *Journal of Business Research*, 123, 156–164. DOI: 10.1016/j.jbusres.2020.09.043

Grimm, M. S., & Wagner, R. (2022). Challenging the linearity assumption of intrabrand image confusion. *Journal of Marketing Analytics 2022 12:2, 12*(2), 355–374. DOI: 10.1057/s41270-022-00202-6

Gupta, R., Nair, K., Mishra, M., Ibrahim, B., & Bhardwaj, S. (2024). Adoption and impacts of generative artificial intelligence: Theoretical underpinnings and research agenda. *International Journal of Information Management Data Insights*, 4(1), 100232. DOI: 10.1016/j.jjimei.2024.100232

Gupta, V. (2024). An Empirical Evaluation of a Intellectual propertyTechnology Adoption Model from Entrepreneurs' Perspectives. *Systems*, 12(3), 103. DOI: 10.3390/systems12030103

Gursoy, D., & Cai, R. (2024). Artificial intelligence: An overview of research trends and future directions. *International Journal of Contemporary Hospitality Management.* Advance online publication. DOI: 10.1108/IJCHM-03-2024-0322

Habimana, J. (2024). Rural Development Strategies through Livestock Policy. *International Journal of Livestock Policy*, 3(1), 1–15. DOI: 10.47941/ijlp.1747

Hadelan, L.. (2021). Food geographical indication in enhancing agricultural and tourism performance. *Scientific Papers. Series Management, Economic, Engineering in Agriculture and Rural Development*, 21(1), 361–368.

Haigney, S., Lu, D., Gianordoli, G., & Syam, U. (2021, August 13). The Hidden Melodies of Subways Around the World. *The New York Times.* https://www.nytimes.com/interactive/2021/08/13/arts/subway-train-sounds.html

Hajra, V. (2015). Role of Indian Folk Culture in Promotion of Tourism in the Country. *Indian Journal of Research*, 4(2), 231–235. https://www.worldwidejournals.com/paripex/recent_issues_pdf/2015/February/February_2015_1425292942__76.pdf

Haleem, A., Javaid, M., Qadri, M. A., Singh, R. P., & Suman, R. (2022). Artificial Intelligence (AI) Applications for marketing: a literature-based Study. *International Journal of Intelligent Networks, 3*(3), 119–132. sciencedirect. DOI: 10.1016/j.ijin.2022.08.005

Halid, H., Ravesangar, K., Mahadzir, S. L., & Halim, S. N. A. (2024). Artificial Intelligence (AI) in Human Resource Management (HRM). In *Building the Future with Human Resource Management* (pp. 37–70). Springer International Publishing. DOI: 10.1007/978-3-031-52811-8_2

Hall, C. M. (2014). *Tourism and social marketing.* Routledge. DOI: 10.4324/9780203854259

Hanafiah, M. H., Asyraff, M. A., Ismail, M. N. I., & Sjukriana, J. (2024). Understanding the key drivers in using mobile payment (M-Payment) among Generation Z travellers. *Young Consumers*, 25(5), 645–664. DOI: 10.1108/YC-08-2023-1835

Hanna, S., Rowley, J., & Keegan, B. (2021). Place and destination branding: A review and conceptual mapping of the domain. *European Management Review*, 18(2), 105–117. DOI: 10.1111/emre.12433

Hazarika, A., & Rahmati, M. (2023). Towards an evolved immersive experience: Exploring 5G-and beyond-enabled ultra-low-latency communications for augmented and virtual reality. *Sensors (Basel)*, 23(7), 3682. DOI: 10.3390/s23073682 PMID: 37050742

Heracleous, L., & Wirtz, J. (2010). *The Globe: Singapore Airlines' Balancing Act*. Harvard Business Review. https://hbr.org/2010/07/the-globe-singapore-airlines-balancing-act

Hernández-Chea, R., Vimalnath, P., Bocken, N., Tietze, F., & Eppinger, E. (2020). Integrating intellectual property and sustainable business models: The SBM-IP canvas. *Sustainability (Basel)*, 12(21), 8871. DOI: 10.3390/su12218871

Herrera, A. (2013). Heritage Tourism, Identity and Development in Peru. *International Journal of Historical Archaeology*, 17(2), 275–295. DOI: 10.1007/s10761-013-0221-6

Hinchliffe, S., Bard, A., Chan, K. W., Adam, K., Bruce, A., Reyher, K., & Buller, H. (2024). Regulating antimicrobial resistance: Market intermediaries, poultry and the audit lock-in. *Agriculture and Human Values*, 41(2), 801–814. DOI: 10.1007/s10460-023-10525-4

Hjalager, A. M. (2020). Land-use conflicts in coastal tourism and the quest for governance innovations. *Land Use Policy*, 94, 104566. DOI: 10.1016/j.landusepol.2020.104566

Hodson, J. M. (2021). *Connecting Brand Identity and Consumer-Based Brand Equity for Tourism Destinations*. Springer Fachmedien Wiesbaden. DOI: 10.1007/978-3-658-33057-6

Ho, K. L. P., Quang, H. T., & Miles, M. P. (2022). Leveraging entrepreneurial marketing processes to ameliorate the liability of poorness: The case of smallholders and SMEs in developing economies. *Journal of Innovation & Knowledge*, 7(4), 100232. DOI: 10.1016/j.jik.2022.100232

Hollebeek, L. D., & Macky, K. (2019). Digital content marketing's role in fostering consumer engagement, trust, and value: Framework, fundamental propositions, and implications. *Journal of Interactive Marketing*, 45(1), 27–41. DOI: 10.1016/j.intmar.2018.07.003

Holter, M. G. (2024, January 30). Branding the City of Light's Signature Landmark. *Washington Post*. https://www.washingtonpost.com/archive/politics/2005/05/15/branding-the-city-of-lights-signature-landmark/139104a8-a81c-4e32-9dcd-c43899c928c9/

Hoppen, A., Brown, L., & Fyall, A. (2014). Literary tourism: Opportunities and challenges for the marketing and branding of destinations? *Journal of Destination Marketing & Management*, 3(1), 37–47. DOI: 10.1016/j.jdmm.2013.12.009

Horner, S., & Swarbrooke, J. (2020). *Consumer behaviour in tourism*. Routledge. DOI: 10.4324/9781003046721

Hosany, S., Ekinci, Y., & Uysal, M. (2006). Destination image and destination personality: An application of branding theories to tourism places. *Journal of Business Research*, 59(5), 638–642. DOI: 10.1016/j.jbusres.2006.01.001

Hossain, M., Saha, C., Saha, S., Islam, H. M. N., Ahmed, M., Ahmed, T., Sikder, A. H. F., & Billah, M. (2024). Is the Sundarbans of Bangladesh in a State of Pollution? *Open Journal of Forestry*, 14(01), 19–41. DOI: 10.4236/ojf.2024.141002

Housawi, A., Amoudi, A. Al, Alsaywid, B., Lytras, M., Moreba, Y. H. B., Abuznadah, W., & Alhaidar, S. A. (2020). Evaluation of Key Performance Indicators (KPIs) for Sustainable Postgraduate Medical Training: An Opportunity for Implementing an Innovative Approach to Advance the Quality of Training Programs at the Saudi Commission for Health Specialties (SCFHS). *Sustainability 2020, Vol. 12, Page 8030, 12*(19), 8030. DOI: 10.3390/su12198030

Huang, C. C. (2023). Empirical research on the sustainable development of ecotourism. *Sustainability*, 15(13), 10307. DOI: 10.3390/su151310307

Huang, C. C., & Zhang, S. (2023). Sustainable development of eco-tourism: Challenges and opportunities. *Tourism Management*, 87, 104280. DOI: 10.1016/j.tourman.2022.104280

Hua, Z., Song, H., & Zou, K. (2021). Research on Disney's Possible Expansion Strategy in Asian Market. *Proceedings of the 2021 3rd International Conference on Economic Management and Cultural Industry (ICEMCI 2021), 203*, 2618–2625. DOI: 10.2991/assehr.k.211209.426

Hudson, S. (2017). Marketing for tourism, hospitality & events: a global & digital approach.

Hudson, S. (2009). Tourism and hospitality marketing: A global perspective. *Sage (Atlanta, Ga.).*

Hudson, S., & Ritchie, J. R. B. (2009). Branding a memorable destination experience. The case of "Brand Canada.". *International Journal of Tourism Research*, 11(2), 217–228. DOI: 10.1002/jtr.720

Huynh, H. T. N., Trieu, H. D. X., Van Nguyen, P., Tran, T. G., & Lam, L. N. H. (2021). Explicating Brand Equity in the Information Technology Sector in Vietnam. *Administrative Sciences 2021, Vol. 11, Page 128, 11*(4), 128. DOI: 10.3390/admsci11040128

Ianioglo, A., & Rissanen, M. (2020). Global trends and tourism development in peripheral areas. *Scandinavian Journal of Hospitality and Tourism*, 20(5), 520–539. DOI: 10.1080/15022250.2020.1848620

Indulia, B. (2022, September 16). *A Perspective on Non-Conventional Trademarks and the Difficulties in Extending IP Protection to Them*. SCC Times. https://www.scconline.com/blog/post/2022/09/16/a-perspective-on-non-conventional-trademarks-and-the-difficulties-in-extending-ip-protection-to-them/

Institute of Inner St–dies v. Charlotte Anderson and Ors. (2011) CS(OS) 2252/2011 & I.A. No.14617/2011.

Interglobe 2023. Social Media and its impact on Travel. Available at: https://www.interglobe.com/social-media-and-its-impact-on-travel (Accessed: 22 August 2024)

Islam, M., Farjana, F., Nasrin, N., & Ahmed, M. S. (2023). The economic, social and environmental implications of heritage tourism: Evidence from Bangladesh. *SN Business & Economics*, 3(2), 42. DOI: 10.1007/s43546-022-00411-2

Islam, S. A. M. Z., & Al Sajib, S. M. S. (2021). Technology Supported Tourism: A Study on the Buddhist Vihara at Paharpur in Bangladesh. In Hassan, A. (Ed.), *Technology Application in the Tourism and Hospitality Industry of Bangladesh* (pp. 157–173). Springer Singapore., DOI: 10.1007/978-981-16-2434-6_10

Jaelani, A. K., Handayani, I. G. A. K. R. & Karjoko, L. (2020). Development of tourism based on geographic indication towards to welfare state. International journal of advanced science and technology, 29(3), 1227-1234.

Jaelani, A. K., Handayani, I. G. A. K. R., & Karjoko, L. (2020). Development of tourism based on geographic indication towards to welfare state. *International Journal of Advanced Science and Technology*, 29(3s), 1227–1234.

Jafari, J. (1996). Tourism and culture: an inquiry into paradoxes. In *Culture, Tourism Development: Crucial Issues for the XXIst Century*. UNESCO.

Jain, S. C. (1996). Problems in International Protection of Intellectual Property Rights. *Journal of International Marketing*, 4(1), 9–32. https://www.jstor.org/stable/25048632. DOI: 10.1177/1069031X9600400103

Jamieson, W. (1998). Cultural Heritage Tourism Planning and Development: Defining the Field and Its Challenges. *APT Bulletin: The Journal of Preservation Technology*, 29(3/4), 65–67. DOI: 10.2307/1504616

Jantapoon, K., & Saenchaiyathon, K. (2023). Supply chain strategy under VUCA world for Sustainable of the Tea Entrepreneur in Thailand. In *E3S Web of Conferences* (Vol. 440, p. 06006). EDP Sciences. DOI: 10.1051/e3sconf/202344006006

Jarma Arroyo, S. E., Hogan, V., Ahrent Wisdom, D., Moldenhauer, K. A., & Seo, H. S. (2020). Effect of geographical indication information on consumer acceptability of cooked aromatic rice. *Foods*, 9(12), 1843. DOI: 10.3390/foods9121843 PMID: 33322325

Jarvenpa, R. (1994). Commoditization versus Cultural Integration: Tourism and Image Building in the Klondike. *Arctic Anthropology*, 31(1), 26–46.

Johnsson, D. Z., & Tualima, H. Y. (2017). Cultural Heritage, Traditional Knowledge and Intellectual Property. In Xanthaki, A., Valkonen, S., Heinämäki, L., & Nuorgam, P. (Eds.), *Indigenous Peoples' Cultural Heritage: Rights, Debates, Challenges* (pp. 218–228). Brill. DOI: 10.1163/9789004342194_011

Jones, P., & Hillier, D. (2022). Intellectual property and eco-tourism: Balancing protection and accessibility. *Journal of Sustainable Tourism*, 30(6), 892–908. DOI: 10.1080/09669582.2021.1941123

Josefsson, J., & Aronsson, I. L. (2016). Heritage as life-values: A study of the cultural heritage concept. *Current Science*, 110(11), 2091–2098. DOI: 10.18520/cs/v110/i11/2091-2098

JugJugg Jeeyo. T-Series refutes Pakistani singer's claims over Nach Punjaban song, says 'legally acquired rights'. (2022, May 23). *Hindustan Times*. https://www.hindustantimes.com/entertainment/bollywood/jugjugg-jeeyo-t-series-refutes-pakistani-singer-s-claims-over-nach-punjaban-song-says-legally-acquired-rights-101653307639742.html

Kacprzak, A., & Hensel, P. (2023). Exploring online customer experience: A systematic literature review and research agenda. *International Journal of Consumer Studies*, 47(6), 2583–2608. DOI: 10.1111/ijcs.12966

Kalvet, T., Olesk, M., Tiits, M., & Raun, J. (2020). Innovative Tools for Tourism and Cultural Tourism Impact Assessment. *Sustainability 2020, Vol. 12, Page 7470, 12*(18), 7470. DOI: 10.3390/su12187470

Kamal, M., & Himel, A. S. (2023). Redefining Modern Marketing: An Analysis of AI and NLP's Influence on Consumer Engagement, Strategy, and Beyond. *Eigenpub Review of Science and Technology*, 7(1), 203–223.

Karim, K. M. R. (2022a). Opportunities and the Challenges of Tourism Industry in Bangladesh. In Jana, N. C., Singh, A., & Singh, R. B. (Eds.), *Livelihood Enhancement Through Agriculture, Tourism and Health* (pp. 223–236). Springer Nature Singapore., DOI: 10.1007/978-981-16-7310-8_11

Katt, F., & Meixner, O. (2020). A systematic review of drivers influencing consumer willingness to pay for organic food. *Trends in Food Science & Technology*, 100, 374–388. DOI: 10.1016/j.tifs.2020.04.029

Kaushal, V., & Yadav, R. (2023). Learning successful implementation of Chatbots in businesses from B2B customer experience perspective. *Concurrency and Computation*, 35(1), e7450. DOI: 10.1002/cpe.7450

Kaushik, N. (2013). Intellectual Property: Licensing and Franchising. SSRN *Electronic Journal*. https://doi.org/DOI: 10.2139/SSRN.2315960

Ketter, E. (2020). Millennial travel: tourism micro-trends of European Generation Y. Journal of Tourism Futures.

Khaokhrueamuang, A., & Chueamchaitrakun, P. (2019). Tea cultural commodification in sustainable tourism: perspectives from Thai and Japanese farmer exchange. *Special Issue of Rajabhat Chiang Mai Research Journal*, 104-117.

Khaokhrueamuang, A. (2020). International exchange in tea tourism: reconceptualizing Japanese green tourism for sustainable farming communities. In *Tourism Development in Japan* (pp. 140–159). Routledge. DOI: 10.4324/9780429273513-8

Kickul, J., & Lyons, T. (2020). *Understanding social entrepreneurship: The relentless pursuit of mission in an ever changing world*. Routledge. DOI: 10.4324/9780429270406

King, K. (2022). *AI Strategy for Sales and Marketing: Connecting Marketing, Sales and Customer Experience*. Kogan Page Publishers.

Klimas, P., Czernek-Marszałek, K., Wójcik, D., & Juszczyk, P. (2023). The Two-Sided Effect of the Sharing Economy and Its Impacts on Inter-organizational Co-operation in the Tourism Sector. *Contributions to Management Science*, 351–383. DOI: 10.1007/978-3-031-18134-4_17

Klink, R. R. (2000). Creating Brand Names With Meaning: The Use of Sound Symbolism. *Marketing Letters*, 11(1), 5–20. DOI: 10.1023/A:1008184423824

Knežević, Ž. (2017). Cultural heritage and tourism – an introduction. *Liburna*, 2(1). Advance online publication. DOI: 10.15291/lib.992

Kolb, B. (2020). *Entrepreneurship for the creative and cultural industries*. Routledge. DOI: 10.4324/9780367817046

Kozak, M., & Baloglu, S. (2010). *Managing and marketing tourist destinations: Strategies to gain a competitive edge* (Vol. 21). Routledge. DOI: 10.4324/9780203842300

Kozak, M., & Kozak, N. (2015). *Destination marketing: An international perspective*. Routledge. DOI: 10.4324/9781315720050

Kulindwa, Y. J. (2024). Community Involvement in Cultural Heritage Tourism: The Case of Ngorongoro Conservation Area, Tanzania. In Sigala, M., Fang, M., Yeark, A., Albrecht, J. N., & Vorobjovas-Pinta, O. (Eds.), *Case Based Research in Tourism, Travel, and Hospitality* (pp. 213–230). Springer Nature Singapore., DOI: 10.1007/978-981-97-1891-7_12

Kumar, S., Talukder, M. B., Kabir, F., & Kaiser, F. (2024). Challenges and Sustainability of Green Finance in the Tourism Industry: Evidence from Bangladesh. In Taneja, S., Kumar, P., Grima, S., Ozen, E., & Sood, K. (Eds.), (pp. 97–111). Advances in Finance, Accounting, and Economics. IGI Global., DOI: 10.4018/979-8-3693-1388-6.ch006

Kumar, S., Talukder, M. B., & Pego, A. (Eds.). (2024). *Utilizing Smart Technology and AI in Hybrid Tourism and Hospitality*. IGI Global., DOI: 10.4018/979-8-3693-1978-9

Kumar, V. R. (2018). The Influence of Sufism in Gaana Songs. *International Journal of Current Humanities and Social Science Researches*, 2(4), 22–26.

Kuruk, P. (2007). Cultural heritage, traditional knowledge, and indigenous rights: An analysis of the Convention for the Safeguarding of Intangible Cultural Heritage. *Macquarie Journal of International and Comparative Environmental Law*, 4(2), 1–20.

Kuruk, P. (2020). *Traditional Knowledge, Genetic Resources, Customary Law and Intellectual Property: A Global Primer*. Edward Elgar Publishing. DOI: 10.4337/9781785368486

Kurup, R., & Pradeep, N. A. (2020). NON-CONVENTIONAL TRADEMARKS IN INDIA: THE WHAT, THE WHY AND THE HOW. *Journal of Academic Innovation and Research in Intellectual Property Assets (E-JAIRIPA, 1*(01), 131–148. https://cnlu.ac.in/wp-content/uploads/2022/08/9-Rachna-R-Kurup-and-Nimita-Aksa-Pradeep.pdf

Kwon, O. (2020). A study on how startups approach sustainable development through intellectual property. *Sustainable Development (Bradford)*, 28(4), 613–625. DOI: 10.1002/sd.2012

Kyrylov, Y., Hranovska, V., Boiko, V., Kwilinski, A., & Boiko, L. (2020). International Tourism Development in the Context of Increasing Globalization Risks: On the Example of Ukraine's Integration into the Global Tourism Industry. *Journal of Risk and Financial Management 2020, Vol. 13, Page 303, 13*(12), 303. DOI: 10.3390/jrfm13120303

Labra, O., Castro, C., Wright, R. and Chamblas, I., 2020. Thematic analysis in social work: A case study. Global social work-cutting edge issues and critical reflections, 10(6), pp.1-20.

Laplane, A., & Mazzucato, M. (2020). Socializing the risks and rewards of public investments: Economic, policy, and legal issues. *Research Policy*, 49, 100008. DOI: 10.1016/j.repolx.2020.100008

Lauer-Schmaltz, M. W., Cash, P., Hansen, J. P., & Maier, A. (2024). Towards the Human Digital Twin: Definition and Design—A survey. *arXiv preprint arXiv:2402.07922*.

Lavoye, V., Tarkiainen, A., Sipilä, J., & Mero, J. (2023). More than skin-deep: The influence of presence dimensions on purchase intentions in augmented reality shopping. *Journal of Business Research*, 169, 114247. DOI: 10.1016/j.jbusres.2023.114247

Lavuri, R., & Akram, U. (2023). Role of virtual reality authentic experience on affective responses: Moderating role virtual reality attachment. *Journal of Ecotourism*, •••, 1–19.

Law School Policy Review. 2024. Need for a Digital Copyrights Act: Adjusting to the New Normal. Available at: https://lawschoolpolicyreview.com/2024/02/12/need-for-a-digital-copyrights-act-adjusting-to-the-new-normal/#(Accessed: 07 August 2024)

Leal Filho, W., Dibbern, T., Pimenta Dinis, M. A., Coggo Cristofoletti, E., Mbah, M. F., Mishra, A., Clarke, A., Samuel, N., Castillo Apraiz, J., Rimi Abubakar, I., & Aina, Y. A. (2024). The added value of partnerships in implementing the UN sustainable development goals. *Journal of Cleaner Production*, 438, 140794. DOI: 10.1016/j.jclepro.2024.140794

Lee, K., Nguyen, A. T., Nguyen, N. P., Nguyen, T. H., Tran, N., Nguyen, T. L., ... & Vu, T. T. (2024). Determinants of agritourism development in green tea farms of the northern mountains of Vietnam: A hybrid approach based on the combination of diffusion of Innovation (DOI) theory and PLS-SEM. *Multidisciplinary Science Journal, 6*(4).

Lee, R. (2021). The Effect of Supply Chain Management Strategy on Operational and Financial Performance. *Sustainability 2021, Vol. 13, Page 5138, 13*(9), 5138. DOI: 10.3390/su13095138

Lee, C. K., Ahmad, M. S., Petrick, J. F., Park, Y. N., Park, E., & Kang, C. W. (2020). The roles of cultural worldview and authenticity in tourists' decision-making process in a heritage tourism destination using a model of goal-directed behavior. *Journal of Destination Marketing & Management*, 18, 100500. DOI: 10.1016/j.jdmm.2020.100500

Lee, J. K., & Thompson, P. (2019). Intellectual property issues in eco-tourism: A global perspective. *Journal of Global Tourism Research*, 14(2), 131–148. DOI: 10.1080/21568316.2018.1502873

Leimgruber, W. (2010). Switzerland and the UNESCO Convention on Intangible Cultural Heritage. *Journal of Folklore Research*, 47(1–2), 161–196. DOI: 10.2979/jfr.2010.47.1-2.161

Lerner, J., & Leamon, A. (2023). *Venture capital, private equity, and the financing of entrepreneurship*. John Wiley & Sons.

Liu, C. H., & Jiang, J. F. (2020). Assessing the moderating roles of brand equity, intellectual capital and social capital in Chinese luxury hotels. *Journal of Hospitality and Tourism Management*, 43, 139–148. DOI: 10.1016/j.jhtm.2020.03.003

Liu, Y., & Chen, R. (2022). IP and eco-tourism: A review of recent developments and future directions. *Tourism Review International*, 25(1), 45–60. DOI: 10.3727/154427222X16572611591851

Lojo, A., Li, M., & Xu, H. (2020). Online tourism destination image: Components, information sources, and incongruence. *Journal of Travel & Tourism Marketing*, 37(4), 495–509. DOI: 10.1080/10548408.2020.1785370

Lombart, C., Millan, E., Normand, J. M., Verhulst, A., Labbé-Pinlon, B., & Moreau, G. (2020). Effects of physical, non-immersive virtual, and immersive virtual store environments on consumers' perceptions and purchase behavior. *Computers in Human Behavior*, 110, 106374. DOI: 10.1016/j.chb.2020.106374

Lotz, M. (2002). Colliding Worlds: Indigenous Rights, Traditional Knowledge, and Plant Intellectual Property. *Business & Professional Ethics Journal*, 21(3/4), 71–94. DOI: 10.5840/bpej2002213/416

Lu, L., Nguyen, R., Rahman, M. M., & Winfree, J. (2021). Demand Shocks and Supply Chain Resilience: An Agent Based Modelling Approach and Application to the Potato Supply Chain (No. w29166). National Bureau of Economic Research.

Lucier, G., & Parr, B. (2020). *Vegetable and pulses outlook*. United States Department of Agriculture. April.

Luekveerawattana, R. (2024). Enhancing innovation in cultural heritage tourism: Navigating external factors. *Cogent Social Sciences*, 10(1), 2301813. DOI: 10.1080/23311886.2024.2301813

Lukose, L. P. (2015). NON-TRADITIONAL TRADEMARKS: A CRITIQUE. *Journal of the Indian Law Institute*, 57(2), 197–215. https://www.jstor.org/stable/44782501

Luongo, S., Sepe, F., & Del Gaudio, G. (2023). Regional innovation systems in tourism: The role of collaboration and competition. *Journal of Open Innovation*, 9(4), 100148. DOI: 10.1016/j.joitmc.2023.100148

Lycett, M., Meechao, K., & Reppel, A. (2024). *Materializing Design Fictions for Metaverse Services.*

MacDonald, A., Clarke, A., & Huang, L. (2022). Multi-stakeholder Partnerships for Sustainability: Designing Decision-Making Processes for Partnership Capacity. *Business and the Ethical Implications of Technology*, 103–120. DOI: 10.1007/978-3-031-18794-0_7

Macmillan, F. (2020). *Intellectual and cultural property: between market and community*. Routledge. DOI: 10.4324/9780429425844

Maes, P. (2018). *Disruptive Selling: A New Strategic Approach to Sales, Marketing and Customer Service*. Kogan Page Publishers.

Majerčáková, D., & Greguš, M. (2021). The Analysis of the Investment Opportunities into the Wine. In *Eurasian Business and Economics Perspectives* (pp. 189–201). Springer. DOI: 10.1007/978-3-030-65147-3_13

Manuel, P. (1988). Popular Music in India: 1901-86. *Popular Music*, 7(2), 157–176. https://www.jstor.org/stable/853534. DOI: 10.1017/S0261143000002737

Mao, D. (2022). Geographical Collective Marks in the EU: Should They Be Redefined in the EU Trade Mark Law? Or Should They Be Incorporated into the GIs Regime? SSRN *Electronic Journal*. https://doi.org/DOI: 10.2139/SSRN.4289585

Marescotti, A., Quiñones-Ruiz, X. F., Edelmann, H., Belletti, G., Broscha, K., Altenbuchner, C., Penker, M., & Scaramuzzi, S. (2020). Are protected geographical indications evolving due to environmentally related justifications? An analysis of amendments in the fruit and vegetable sector in the European Union. *Sustainability (Basel)*, 12(9), 3571. DOI: 10.3390/su12093571

Marie-Vivien, D. (2020). Protection of Geographical Indications in ASEAN countries: Convergences and challenges to awakening sleeping Geographical Indications. *The Journal of World Intellectual Property*, 23(3–4), 328–349. DOI: 10.1111/jwip.12155

Marr, B. (2021). *Extended reality in practice: 100+ amazing ways virtual, augmented and mixed reality are changing business and Society*. John Wiley & Sons.

Martin, R., & Thomas, S. (2023). The challenges of IP in preserving cultural heritage within eco-tourism. *Cultural Heritage Management and Sustainable Development*, 12(1), 15–30. DOI: 10.1108/CHMSD-09-2022-0165

Mascarello, G., Pinto, A., Parise, N., Crovato, S., & Ravarotto, L. (2015). The perception of food quality. Profiling Italian consumers. *Appetite*, 89, 175–182. DOI: 10.1016/j.appet.2015.02.014 PMID: 25681654

Mashood, K., Kayani, H. U. R., Malik, A. A., & Tahir, A. (2023). ARTIFICIAL INTELLIGENCE RECENT TRENDS AND APPLICATIONS IN INDUSTRIES. *Pakistan Journal of Science*, 75(02). Advance online publication. DOI: 10.57041/pjs.v75i02.855

Masunah, J., Dyani, P., Gaffar, V., & Sari, M. (2022). Production of shadow puppet performances in building artistic entrepreneurship. *Journal of Sustainable Tourism and Entrepreneurship*, 3(2), 104–116.

Matulionyte, R., Paton, E., McIntyre, P., & Gleadhill, D. (2017). The system of book creation: Intellectual property and the self-publishing sector of the creative industries. *Creative Industries Journal*, 10(3), 191–210. DOI: 10.1080/17510694.2017.1393193

Matviichuk, L. Y., Lepkyi, M. I., Dashchuk, Y. Y., Sydoruk, S. V., & Mezentseva, I. V. (2023). Approach to formation of enogastronomic tourism based on the geographical indication system. *Journal of Geology Geography and Geoecology*, 31(4), 689–701. DOI: 10.15421/112265

McCabe, S. (2014). *The Routledge handbook of tourism marketing*. Routledge. DOI: 10.4324/9781315858265

MDPI. (2024). Assessment and empirical research on the suitability of eco-tourism in nature reserves. *Land (Basel)*, 13(4), 438. DOI: 10.3390/land13040438

Medium, 2024. 7 Essential Tools You Should Use to Protect Your Digital Content. Available at: https://medium.com/follower-booster-hub/7-essential-tools-you-should-use-to-protect-your-digital-content-10ca9a311363(Accessed: 06 August 2024)

Meißner, M., Pfeiffer, J., Peukert, C., Dietrich, H., & Pfeiffer, T. (2020). How virtual reality affects consumer choice. *Journal of Business Research*, 117, 219–231. DOI: 10.1016/j.jbusres.2020.06.004

Menggala, S. R., Vanhove, W., Muhammad, D. R. A., Rahman, A., Speelman, S., & Van Damme, P. (2021). The Effect of Geographical Indications (GIs) on the Koerintji Cinnamon Sales Price and Information of Origin. *Agronomy 2021, Vol. 11, Page 1410, 11*(7), 1410. DOI: 10.3390/agronomy11071410

Meng, L., Yan, F., Fang, Q., & Si, W. (2024). Research on the Educational Tourism Development of Intangible Cultural Heritage: Suitability, Spatial Pattern, and Obstacle Factor. *Sustainability (Basel)*, 16(11), 4647. DOI: 10.3390/su16114647

Merges, R. (2011). *Justifying intellectual property*. Harvard University Press. DOI: 10.4159/harvard.9780674061125

Meschnig, A., Decker-Lange, C., & Dubiel, A. (2023). Burning the candle at both ends: How to balance potential profitability and brand protection when licensing brands. *European Journal of Marketing*, 57(9), 2407–2431. DOI: 10.1108/EJM-01-2021-0016

Meyer, C., Gerlitz, L., & Klein, M. (2022). Creativity as a Key Constituent for Smart Specialization Strategies (S3), What Is in It for Peripheral Regions? Co-creating Sustainable and Resilient Tourism with Cultural and Creative Industries. *Sustainability 2022, Vol. 14, Page 3469, 14*(6), 3469. DOI: 10.3390/su14063469

Mgbeoji, I. (2001). Patents and Traditional Knowledge of the Uses of Plants: Is a Communal Patent Regime Part of the Solution to the Scourge of Bio Piracy? *Indiana Journal of Global Legal Studies*, 9(1), 163–186. https://www.jstor.org/stable/20643824

Michael Edwards. 2024. Copyright Compliance in Marketing and Advertising Campaigns. Available at: https://michaeledwards.uk/copyright-compliance-in-marketing-and-advertising-campaigns/#:(Accessed: 09 August 2024)

Miller, C., & Lopez, G. (2021). Securing sustainable tourism practices through intellectual property management. *Journal of Sustainable Development*, 14(3), 245–259. DOI: 10.5539/jsd.v14n3p245

Mingjing, Q. (2023). Barriers and opportunities for women in tea tourism: A qualitative examination of policy context in Yaoqu township, China. *Jurnalul Practicilor Comunitare Pozitive*, 23(3), 67–82.

Mishra, N. (2008). Registration of Non-Traditional Trademarks. *Journal of Intellectual Property Rights*, 13(1), 43–50. https://nopr.niscpr.res.in/bitstream/123456789/407/1/JIPR%2013(1)%20(2008)%2043-50.pdf

Mitric, J., Radulovic, I., Popovic, T., Scekic, Z., & Tinaj, S. (2024). AI and Computer Vision in Cultural Heritage Preservation. *2024 28th International Conference on Information Technology (IT)*, 1–4. DOI: 10.1109/IT61232.2024.10475738

Mogaji, E., Viglia, G., Srivastava, P., & Dwivedi, Y. K. (2024). Is it the end of the technology acceptance model in the era of generative artificial intelligence? *International Journal of Contemporary Hospitality Management*, 36(10), 3324–3339. DOI: 10.1108/IJCHM-08-2023-1271

Mohamed, Ů. (2024). *Integrating Digital Techniques/Technologies in Developing Egyptian Museums (Case Study: Alexandria Library Museums-Alexandria City).* Sohag Engineering Journal.

Mohammad, B. T., & Fahmida, K. (2023). Economic impact of river tourism: Evidence of Bangladesh. *I-Manager's. Journal of Management*, 18(2), 47. DOI: 10.26634/jmgt.18.2.20235

Mohammad, B. T., Mushfika, H., & Iva, R. D. (2024). Opportunities of tourism and hospitality education in bangladesh: Career perspectives. *I-Manager's. Journal of Management*, 18(3), 21. DOI: 10.26634/jmgt.18.3.20385

Mohanty, D. (2017, June 29). Odia folk song Rangabati controversy: District magistrate ends song and dance. *Hindustan Times*. https://www.hindustantimes.com/india-news/odia-folk-song-rangabati-controversy-district-magistrate-ends-song-and-dance/story-Kqw0YuqaAFDsPrfZDbOmgM.html

Montenyohl, E. (1996). Divergent Paths: On the Evolution of "Folklore" and "Folkloristics.". *Journal of Folklore Research*, 33(3), 232–235.

Morgan, N. J., Pritchard, A., & Piggott, R. (2003). Destination branding and the role of the stakeholders: The case of New Zealand. *Journal of Vacation Marketing*, 9(3), 285–299. DOI: 10.1177/135676670300900307

Morgan, N., Pritchard, A., & Pride, R. (2011). *Destination brands: Managing place reputation*. Routledge.

Morrison, A. M. (2013). *Marketing and managing tourism destinations*. Routledge. DOI: 10.4324/9780203081976

Motari, M., Nikiema, J. B., Kasilo, O. M., Kniazkov, S., Loua, A., Sougou, A., & Tumusiime, P. (2021). The role of intellectual property rights on access to medicines in the WHO African region: 25 years after the TRIPS agreement. *BMC Public Health*, 21(1), 1–19. DOI: 10.1186/s12889-021-10374-y PMID: 33706726

Moyle, C., Moyle, B., & Burgers, H. (2020). Entrepreneurial strategies and tourism industry growth. *Tourism Management Perspectives*, 35, 100708. DOI: 10.1016/j.tmp.2020.100708

Mtapuri, O., Giampiccoli, A., & Jugmohan, S. (2017). Marketing community-based tourism ventures: Pathways in a marketing route model. *Journal for New Generation Sciences*, 15(1), 385–401.

Munar, A. M., & Jacobsen, J. Kr. S. (2014). Motivations for sharing tourism experiences through social media. *Tourism Management, 43*(0261-5177), 46–54. DOI: 10.1016/j.tourman.2014.01.012

Nabi, R., & Salimullah, A. H. M. (2022). Promoting Catamaran Tourism in Bangladesh: The Challenges of Blue Economy. In Hassan, A. (Ed.), *Technology Application in Tourism Fairs, Festivals and Events in Asia* (pp. 181–208). Springer Singapore., DOI: 10.1007/978-981-16-8070-0_11

Naji, K. K., Gunduz, M., Alhenzab, F., Al-Hababi, H., & Al-Qahtani, A. (2024). A Systematic Review of the Digital Transformation of the Building Construction Industry. *IEEE Access : Practical Innovations, Open Solutions*, 12, 31461–31487. DOI: 10.1109/ACCESS.2024.3365934

Nast, C. (2019, August 2). *How a Hotel Gets Its Signature Scent.* Condé Nast Traveler. https://www.cntraveler.com/story/how-a-hotel-gets-its-signature-scent

Neck, H., Neck, C., & Murray, E. (2023). *Entrepreneurship: The practice and mindset.* Sage publications.

Neuwirth, R. J. (2023). Prohibited artificial intelligence practices in the proposed EU artificial intelligence act (AIA). *Computer Law & Security Report*, 48, 105798. DOI: 10.1016/j.clsr.2023.105798

Newall, V. J. (1987). The Adaptation of Folklore and Tradition (Folklorismus). *Folklore*, 98(2), 131–151. https://www.jstor.org/stable/1259975. DOI: 10.1080/0015587X.1987.9716408

Ngo, T., Hales, R., & Lohmann, G. (2019). Collaborative marketing for the sustainable development of community-based tourism enterprises: A reconciliation of diverse perspectives. *Current Issues in Tourism*, 22(18), 2266–2283. DOI: 10.1080/13683500.2018.1446919

Nithyaprakash, V., Niveathitha, S., & Shanmugapriya, V. (2021). *Indian Handloom Design Innovations and Interventions Through Sustenance Lens.* 221–249. DOI: 10.1007/978-981-16-5967-6_10

Nizam, D., & Tatari, M. F. (2022). Rural revitalization through territorial distinctiveness: The use of geographical indications in Turkey. *Journal of Rural Studies*, 93, 144–154. DOI: 10.1016/j.jrurstud.2020.07.002

Noaime, E. (2023). *Historic Syrian Cities in the Post-War Period: Balancing Cultural Preservation and Tourism Investment.* DOI: 10.20944/preprints202303.0457.v1

Nowreen, S., & Moran, S. (2022). Broadening Tourism and Cultivating Sustainability: Exploring Opportunities in Bangladesh. *Journal of Sustainable Development*, 16(1), 93. DOI: 10.5539/jsd.v16n1p93

Nurani, N., Nurjanah, R., & Prihantoro, I. (2021). Competence of Human Resources of Small and Medium Enterprises (MSMEs) of West Java through Intellectual Property Rights (IPR) Protection in the COVID-19 Pandemic Era. *Psychology and Education Journal*, 58(3), 251–264.

Okumu, O. S. (2016). The concept of intangible cultural heritage in Kenya. In Deisser, A.-M., & Njuguna, M. (Eds.), *Conservation of Natural and Cultural Heritage in Kenya: A Cross-Disciplinary Approach* (1st ed., pp. 45–58). UCL Press., DOI: 10.2307/j.ctt1gxxpc6.10

Oraman, Y. (2015). Türkiye'de coğrafi işaretli ürünler. *Balkan and Near Eastern Journal of Social Sciences*, 1(1), 76–85.

Otay Demir, F., Yavuz Görkem, Ş., & Rafferty, G. (2022). An inquiry on the potential of computational literary techniques towards successful destination branding and literary tourism. *Current Issues in Tourism*, 25(5), 764–778. DOI: 10.1080/13683500.2021.1887100

Owen, L., Udall, D., Franklin, A., & Kneafsey, M. (2020). Place-Based Pathways to Sustainability: Exploring Alignment between Geographical Indications and the Concept of Agroecology Territories in Wales. *Sustainability 2020, Vol. 12, Page 4890, 12*(12), 4890. DOI: 10.3390/su12124890

Özdemir, B. P. (2018). Branding a Millennia-old Turkish City: Case of Gaziantep. *Ankara Üniversitesi İlef Dergisi*, 5(2), 121–140.

Pacult, F. P. (2021). Buffalo, Barrels, & Bourbon: The Story of How Buffalo Trace Distillery Became The World's Most Awarded Distillery. John Wiley & Sons.

Page, S., & Connell, J. (2020). Tourism and entrepreneurship. In *Tourism* (pp. 262–279). Routledge. DOI: 10.4324/9781003005520-15

Palfrey, J. (2011). *Intellectual property strategy*. Mit Press. DOI: 10.7551/mitpress/9066.001.0001

Pamukçu, H., Saraç, Ö., Aytuğar, S., & Sandıkçı, M. (2021). The Effects of Local Food and Local Products with Geographical Indication on the Development of Tourism Gastronomy. *Sustainability (Basel)*, 13(12), 6692. DOI: 10.3390/su13126692

Pamuru, V., Khern-am-nuai, W., & Kannan, K. (2021). The impact of an augmented-reality game on local businesses: A study of Pokémon go on restaurants. *Information Systems Research*, 32(3), 950–966. DOI: 10.1287/isre.2021.1004

Panas, G., Thrasidi, N., Halkiopoulos, C., & Gkintoni, E. (2022). Consumer Behavior and Cognitive Factors in Relation to Gastronomic Tourism and Destination Marketing in Greece. *Springer Proceedings in Business and Economics*, 655–677. DOI: 10.1007/978-3-030-92491-1_40

Panda, B., & Joy, S. (2021). Intellectual property rights-based debt financing to startups: Need for a changing role of Indian banks. *Vikalpa*, 46(3), 143–152. DOI: 10.1177/02560909211041817

Panda, T. K., Kumar, A., Jakhar, S., Luthra, S., Garza-Reyes, J. A., Kazancoglu, I., & Nayak, S. S. (2020). Social and environmental sustainability model on consumers' altruism, green purchase intention, green brand loyalty and evangelism. *Journal of Cleaner Production*, 243, 118575. DOI: 10.1016/j.jclepro.2019.118575

Pande, K., & Shi, F. (2023). Managing visitor experience at religious heritage sites. *Journal of Destination Marketing & Management*, 29, 100800. DOI: 10.1016/j.jdmm.2023.100800

Pandey, N., & Dharni, K. (2014). *Intellectual property rights*. PHI Learning Pvt. Ltd.

Parida, V., & Jovanovic, M. (2022). Servitization in global markets: Role alignment in global service networks for advanced service provision. *R & D Management*, 52(3), 577–592. DOI: 10.1111/radm.12505

Parr, R. (2018). *Intellectual property: valuation, exploitation, and infringement damages*. John Wiley & Sons. DOI: 10.1002/9781119419235

Patel, R., & Wang, X. (2021). The impact of IP laws on the adoption of green technologies in tourism. *Environmental Science & Policy*, 115, 98–106. DOI: 10.1016/j.envsci.2020.09.001

Paulino, F. F., & Cruz, T. (2024). Cultural Heritage, Tourism and Sustainable Development. The Model of the Cultural Heritage Digital Media Lab. In Chica-Olmo, J., Vujičić, M., Castanho, R. A., Stankov, U., & Martinelli, E. (Eds.), *Sustainable Tourism, Culture and Heritage Promotion* (pp. 139–149). Springer Nature Switzerland., DOI: 10.1007/978-3-031-49536-6_15

Pavlidis, G., & Markantonatou, S. (2020). Gastronomic tourism in Greece and beyond: A thorough review. *International Journal of Gastronomy and Food Science*, 21, 100229. DOI: 10.1016/j.ijgfs.2020.100229 PMID: 32834883

Payandeh, E., Allahyari, M. S., Fontefrancesco, M. F., & Surujlale, J. (2020). Good vs. Fair and Clean: An Analysis of Slow Food Principles Toward Gastronomy Tourism in Northern Iran. *Journal of Culinary Science & Technology*, •••, 1–20.

Pazhuhan, M., & Shiri, N. (2020a). Regional tourism axes identification using GIS and TOPSIS model (Case study: Hormozgan Province, Iran). *Journal of Tourism Analysis*, 27(2), 119–141. DOI: 10.1108/JTA-06-2019-0024

Peng, K., Tao, X., Jiang, J., & Zhai, J. (2023). The Experience Design of Cultural Heritage Tourism in the Perspective of Gamification. In Marcus, A., Rosenzweig, E., & Soares, M. M. (Eds.), *Design, User Experience, and Usability* (Vol. 14034, pp. 127–146). Springer Nature Switzerland., DOI: 10.1007/978-3-031-35705-3_10

Perkins, R., Khoo-Lattimore, C., & Arcodia, C. (2021). Collaboration in marketing regional tourism destinations: Constructing a business cluster formation framework through participatory action research. *Journal of Hospitality and Tourism Management*, 46, 347–359. DOI: 10.1016/j.jhtm.2021.01.004

Peukert, C., Pfeiffer, J., Meißner, M., Pfeiffer, T., & Weinhardt, C. (2019). Shopping in virtual reality stores: The influence of immersion on system adoption. *Journal of Management Information Systems*, 36(3), 755–788. DOI: 10.1080/07421222.2019.1628889

Pietronudo, M. C., & Leone, D. (2022). The Power of Augmented Reality for Smart Environments: An Explorative Analysis of the Business Process Management. In *Machine Learning for Smart Environments/Cities: An IoT Approach* (pp. 73–91). Springer International Publishing. DOI: 10.1007/978-3-030-97516-6_4

Pike, S., & Page, S. J. (2014). Destination Marketing Organizations and destination marketing: A narrative analysis of the literature. *Tourism Management*, 41, 202–227. DOI: 10.1016/j.tourman.2013.09.009

Ploman, E. W., & Hamilton, L. C. (2024). *Copyright: Intellectual property in the information age*. Taylor & Francis. DOI: 10.4324/9781003519973

Plotkina, D., Dinsmore, J., & Racat, M. (2022). Improving service brand personality with augmented reality marketing. *Journal of Services Marketing*, 36(6), 781–799. DOI: 10.1108/JSM-12-2020-0519

Poorna, R. L., Mymoon, M., & Hariharan, A. (2014). Preservation and protection of traditional knowledge – diverse documentation initiatives across the globe. *Current Science*, 107(8), 1240–1246.

Popp, D. (2019). Environmental policy and innovation: A decade of research. *Journal of Environmental Economics and Management*, 48(2), 411–434. DOI: 10.1016/j.jeem.2019.02.006

Power, B., & Reid, G. (2021). The impact of intellectual property types on the performance of business start-ups in the United States. *International Small Business Journal*, 39(4), 372–400. DOI: 10.1177/0266242620967009

Pratheep, P. S. (2017). The Impact of tourism on Indian culture. *KnE Social Sciences*, 429–437. https://doi.org/DOI: 10.18502/kss.v1i3.765

Prebensen, N. K., Chen, J. S., & Uysal, M. S. (2018). *Creating experience value in tourism*. Cab International. DOI: 10.1079/9781786395030.0000

Prevolšek, D., Kukurin, Ž., & Golja, T. (2024). Collaborative Synergies for Elevated Destination Experiences: A Model of Cooperation between Hotel Companies, DMOs, and Local Stakeholders. *Organizacija*, 57(1), 20–38. DOI: 10.2478/orga-2024-0002

Prsformusic 2019. Piracy costs the UK economy £9bn annually. Available at: https://www.prsformusic.com/m-magazine/news/piracy-costs-uk-economy-9bn-annually (Accessed: 20 August 2024)

Punchihewa, N. S. (2020). Branding of Tourism-Related Products and Services for a Competitive Advantage in Sri Lanka: An Intellectual Property Perspective.

Punchihewa, N. S. (2020). Exploring the use of intellectual property tools to promote tourism industry in Sri Lanka: A legal perspective. [JMTR]. *Journal of Management and Tourism Research*, 3, 27–30.

Punchihewa, N. S. (2021). Branding of tourism-related products and services for a competitive advantage in Sri Lanka: An intellectual property perspective. *South Asian Journal of Tourism and Hospitality*, 1(1), 138–157. DOI: 10.4038/sajth.v1i1.31

Qi, F. (2023). Balancing Cultural Heritage Preservation and Cultural Industry Development: The Role and Challenges of Museums. *Highlights in Business. Economics and Management*, 21, 1071–1073. DOI: 10.54097/hbem.v21i.14961

Raghavan, S., & Pai, R. (2021). Changing Paradigm of Consumer Experience Through Martech–A Case Study on Indian Online Retail Industry. *International Journal of Case Studies in Business* [IJCSBE]. *IT and Education*, 5(1), 186–199.

Rahaman, H., Rashid, M. M., & Rahman, M. (2010). Heritage interpretation: Collective reconstruction of Sompur Mahavihara, Bangladesh. *2010 16th International Conference on Virtual Systems and Multimedia*, 163–170. DOI: 10.1109/VSMM.2010.5665990

Rahmah, M. (2018). The Protection of Geographical Indication for Agricultural Development: Challenges for ASEAN.

Rahman, K., Prayogo, E., Fiyana, B. S., & Ardianti, R. (2024). Cultural landscape management and environmental protection at plaosan temple. *Journal of Law and Sustainable Development*, 12(6), e03424. DOI: 10.55908/sdgs.v12i6.3424

Rahman, M., Tanchangya, T., Rahman, J., Aktar, M. A., & Majumder, S. C. (2024). Corporate social responsibility and green financing behavior in Bangladesh: Towards sustainable tourism. *Innovation and Green Development*, 3(3), 100133. DOI: 10.1016/j.igd.2024.100133

Rajamannar, R. (2021). *Quantum marketing: mastering the new marketing mindset for tomorrow's consumers*. HarperCollins Leadership.

Ramires, K. S., López, G. A., & Suárez, A. (2024). Revitalizing Colonial Architecture in Havana, Cuba: Balancing Preservation and Modernization. *Studies in Art and Architecture*, 3(1), 10–20. DOI: 10.56397/SAA.2024.03.02

Rangnekar, D. (2004). The socio-economics of geographical indications: A review of empirical evidence from Europe. *UNCTAD/ICTSD*. Retrieved from https://unctad.org/system/files/official-document/ictsd2004ipd9_en.pdf

Ranjan, P. (2021). Trade-Related Aspects of Intellectual Property Rights Waiver at the World Trade Organization: A BIT of a Challenge. Available at *SSRN*. DOI: 10.2139/ssrn.3888980

Ranking Articles. 2023. Navigating Copyright Issues in Content Creation. Available at: https://ranking-articles.com/navigating-copyright-issues/(Accessed: 06 August 2024)

Rasheed, S., Iqbal, M. M. J. I., & Sharmin, F. (2023). A Walk Through the History and Exploring the Conservation Project of Lalbagh Kella, an Incomplete Mughal Fort of Dhaka, Bangladesh. *American Journal of Interdisciplinary Research and Innovation*, 2(1), 42–53. DOI: 10.54536/ajiri.v2i1.1214

Rasmi, A. A., Phuoc, J. C., Othman, Z., & Azman, N. (2022). Geographical indication for gastronomy tourism: Maximising intellectual property value and branding. *Academy of Strategic Management Journal*, 21(2), 1–13.

Rasoolimanesh, S. M., & Jaafar, M. (2016). Community participation toward tourism development and conservation programs in rural world heritage sites. In Butowski, L. (Ed.), *Tourism-From Empirical Research Towards Practical Application*. InTech., DOI: 10.5772/62293

Rathee, R., & Rajain, P. (2022). *Destination marketing: creating memorable tourism experiences*. Apple Academic Press. DOI: 10.1201/9781003282501

Ratten, V., Costa, C., & Bogers, M. (2019). Artisan, cultural and tourism entrepreneurship. *International Journal of Entrepreneurial Behaviour & Research*, 25(4), 582–591. DOI: 10.1108/IJEBR-05-2018-0319

Redford, A. (2020). Property rights, entrepreneurship, and economic development. *The Review of Austrian Economics*, 33(1), 139–161. DOI: 10.1007/s11138-019-00485-6

Reindrawati, D. Y. (2023). Challenges of community participation in tourism planning in developing countries. *Cogent Social Sciences*, 9(1), 2164240. Advance online publication. DOI: 10.1080/23311886.2022.2164240

Rejeb, A., Rejeb, K., Simske, S., & Treiblmaier, H. (2021). Blockchain Technologies in Logistics and Supply Chain Management: A Bibliometric Review. *Logistics (Basel)*, 5(4), 72. DOI: 10.3390/logistics5040072

ResearchGate. (2019). Assessing the adoption of sustainability practices in the tourism industry: Insights from a developing country. *ResearchGate*. https://www.researchgate.net/publication/338684634_Assessing_the_adoption_of_sustainability_practices_in_tourism_industry_Insights_from_a_developing_country

ResearchGate. (2020). A study on eco-tourism and its sustainability in India. *ResearchGate*. https://www.researchgate.net/publication/344838581_A_STUDY_ON_ECO-TOURISM_AND_ITS_SUSTAINABILITY_IN_INDIA

Richards, D. G. (2020). *Intellectual property rights and global capitalism: The political economy of the TRIPS agreement*. Routledge. DOI: 10.4324/9781003063650

Richards, G. (1996). Production and consumption of European cultural tourism. *Annals of Tourism Research*, 23(2), 261–283. DOI: 10.1016/0160-7383(95)00063-1

Richards, G. (2021). Evolving research perspectives on food and gastronomic experiences in tourism. *International Journal of Contemporary Hospitality Management*, 33(3), 1037–1058. DOI: 10.1108/IJCHM-10-2020-1217

Richards, G., & Hall, D. (Eds.). (2003). *Tourism and sustainable community development*. Routledge., DOI: 10.4324/9780203218602

Rincon, G. A., Cézar, R. F., & Hernandez, C. F. 2020, March. Beliefs about mathematics and academic performance: A descriptive-correlational analysis. In Journal of Physics: Conference Series (Vol. 1514, No. 1, p. 012021). IOP Publishing. DOI: 10.1088/1742-6596/1514/1/012021

Ritchie, J. R. B., & Ritchie, R. J. B. (1998). The Branding of Tourism Destinations: Past Achievements and Future Challenges. *Proceedings of the 1998 Annual Congress of the International Association of Scientific Experts in Tourism, Destination Marketing: Scopes and Limitations*, Marrakech, Morocco, 89-116.

Roadbook 2024. How is influencer marketing transforming the tourism industry? Available at: https://roadbook.com/travel/influencer-marketing-social-media-tourism-industry-trend/ (Accessed: 21 August 2024)

Robin, B. (2016). *The Power of Digital Storytelling to Support Teaching and Learning*. https://files.eric.ed.gov/fulltext/EJ1125504.pdf

Rodriguez-Sanchez, I., Williams, A., & Brotons, M. (2019). The innovation journey of new-to-tourism entrepreneurs. *Current Issues in Tourism*, 22(8), 877–904. DOI: 10.1080/13683500.2017.1334763

Rongmei, P. R. (2022, November 24). Experience the best of traditional Rajasthan at Chokhi Dhani. *The Times of India*. https://timesofindia.indiatimes.com/travel/destinations/experience-the-best-of-traditional-rajasthan-at-chokhi-dhani/articleshow/95735982.cms

Rosas, R. (2020). A Comparative Study of Trademarks: USMCA (US-Mexico-Canada Agreement) and NAFTA (North American Free Trade Agreement). *BU Int'l LJ*, 38, 38.

Ruggiano, N., & Perry, T. E. (2019). Conducting secondary analysis of qualitative data: Should we, can we, and how? *Qualitative Social Work: Research and Practice*, 18(1), 81–97. DOI: 10.1177/1473325017700701 PMID: 30906228

Ruiz-Real, J. L., Uribe-Toril, J., & Gázquez-Abad, J. C. (2020). Destination branding: Opportunities and new challenges. *Journal of Destination Marketing & Management*, 17, 100453. DOI: 10.1016/j.jdmm.2020.100453

Sadowski, J. (2023). Total life insurance: Logics of anticipatory control and actuarial governance in insurance technology. *Social Studies of Science*, •••, 03063127231186437. PMID: 37427796

Said, B. (2024). Architectural Influence of the Islamic University Mosque on New Mosques in Constantine: A Comparative Study. *Journal of Islamic Architecture*, 8(1), 152–160. DOI: 10.18860/jia.v8i1.23040

Saint-Amour, P. (2011). *The copywrights: intellectual property and the literary imagination*. Cornell University Press.

Santos, B., Gonçalves, J., Martins, A. M., Pérez-Cano, M. T., Mosquera-Adell, E., Dimelli, D., Lagarias, A., & Almeida, P. G. (2021). GIS in Architectural Teaching and Research: Planning and Heritage. *Education Sciences 2021, Vol. 11, Page 307, 11*(6), 307. DOI: 10.3390/educsci11060307

Santulli, M. (2019). *The influence of augmented reality on consumers' online purchase intention: the Sephora Virtual Artist case* (Doctoral dissertation).

Saputro, T. A., Pujiyono, P., & Latifah, E. (2023). The Role of the Local Community in Geographic Indications based on Tourism Intellectual Property. *ICLSSE*, 2022. Advance online publication. DOI: 10.4108/eai.28-10-2022.2326401

Sardella, M., Belcher, G., Lungu, C., Ignoni, T., Camisa, M., Stenver, D. I., Porcelli, P., D'Antuono, M., Castiglione, N. G., Adams, A., Furlan, G., Grisoni, I., Hall, S., Boga, L., Mancini, V., Ciuca, M., Chonzi, D., Edwards, B., Mangoni, A. A., & Le Louet, H. (2021). Monitoring the manufacturing and quality of medicines: A fundamental task of pharmacovigilance. *Therapeutic Advances in Drug Safety*, 12. Advance online publication. DOI: 10.1177/20420986211038436 PMID: 34394910

Sarıbaş, Ö., & Demír, C. (2022). The Impact of Sensory Branding on Tourist Experience. *Journal of Tourism and Gastronomy Studies*, 10(4), 4. Advance online publication. DOI: 10.21325/jotags.2022.1118

Savickaite, S. (2024). *Using Virtual Reality to explore individual differences in perception due to neurodiversity* (Doctoral dissertation, University of Glasgow).

Sayeda, T., Shetu, S. A., & Rahman, M. S.-U. -. (2020). Policy Overview for Bangladesh Tourism. In M. S.-U.- Rahman & A. Hassan (Eds.), *Tourism Policy and Planning in Bangladesh* (pp. 3–17). Springer Singapore. DOI: 10.1007/978-981-15-7014-8_1

Schaeffer, E. (2017). *Industry X. 0: Realizing digital value in industrial sectors*. Kogan Page Publishers.

Scheyvens, R. (1999). Ecotourism and the empowerment of local communities. *Tourism Management*, 20(2), 245–249. DOI: 10.1016/S0261-5177(98)00069-7

Schipper, F., Tchoukarine, I., & Bechmann Pedersen, S. (2018). *The history of the European travel comission.* European Travel Commission.

Sedkaoui, S. (Ed.). (2018). *Big data analytics for entrepreneurial success.* IGI Global.

Semerádová, T., & Weinlich, P. (2022). The place of virtual reality in e-retail: Viable shopping environment or just a game. In *Moving businesses online and embracing e-commerce: Impact and opportunities caused by COVID-19* (pp. 92–117). IGI Global. DOI: 10.4018/978-1-7998-8294-7.ch005

Sengupta, A., & Cao, L. (2022). Augmented reality's perceived immersion effect on the customer shopping process: Decision-making quality and privacy concerns. *International Journal of Retail & Distribution Management*, 50(8/9), 1039–1061. DOI: 10.1108/IJRDM-10-2021-0522

Şentürk, B. (2011). Coğrafi işaretlerin ekonomik etkileri: Mikro ve makro açıdan bir değerlendirme [Master's thesis]. Muğla University.

Serrano, L., Sianes, A., & Ariza-Montes, A. (2020). Understanding the Implementation of Airbnb in Urban Contexts: Towards a Categorization of European Cities. *Land 2020, Vol. 9, Page 522, 9*(12), 522. DOI: 10.3390/land9120522

Seyitoğlu, F., & Ivanov, S. (2020). A conceptual framework of the service delivery system design for hospitality firms in the (post-) viral world: The role of service robots. International Journal of Hospitality Sottile, F., Massaglia, S., & Peano, C. (2020). Ecological and economic indicators for the evaluation of almond (Prunus dulcis L.) orchard renewal in sicily. *Agriculture*, 10(7), 301.

Shahid, S., Paul, J., Gilal, F. G., & Ansari, S. (2022). The role of sensory marketing and brand experience in building emotional attachment and brand loyalty in luxury retail stores. *Psychology and Marketing*, 39(7), 1398–1412. DOI: 10.1002/mar.21661

Sharma, A., & Singh, B. (2022). Measuring Impact of E-commerce on Small Scale Business: A Systematic Review. *Journal of Corporate Governance and International Business Law*, 5(1).

Sharma, E., & Sharma, S. (2021). Talent Management Challenges for Heritage Tourism and Rural Sustainability: A Case Study of Surajgarh Fort Heritage Hotel, India. In Srivastava, S. (Ed.), *Capacity Building Through Heritage Tourism* (1st ed., pp. 157–169). Apple Academic Press., DOI: 10.1201/9781003034391-8

Sheth, J. N., Sinha, M., & Shah, R. (2016). *Breakout strategies for emerging markets: Business and marketing tactics for achieving growth.* FT Press.

Siedlecki, S. L. (2020). Understanding descriptive research designs and methods. *Clinical Nurse Specialist CNS*, 34(1), 8–12. DOI: 10.1097/NUR.0000000000000493 PMID: 31789957

Silva, V., & Paul, N. (2021). Potential impact of earthquakes during the 2020 COVID-19 pandemic. *Earthquake Spectra*, 37(1), 73–94. DOI: 10.1177/8755293020950328

Simkhada, S., Kattel, R. R., Dhakal, S. C., & Koirala, A. (2020). Determinants of Organic Tea Cultivation and Selection of Efficient Marketing Channels by the Orthodox Tea Growers in Nepal. *Journal of the Institute of Agriculture and Animal Science*, •••, 31–40. DOI: 10.3126/jiaas.v36i1.48380

Singh, B. (2023). Blockchain Technology in Renovating Healthcare: Legal and Future Perspectives. In Revolutionizing Healthcare Through Artificial Intelligence and Internet of Things Applications (pp. 177-186). IGI Global.

Singha, R., & Singha, S. (2024). Building Capabilities and Workforce for Metaverse-Driven Retail Formats. In *Creator's Economy in Metaverse Platforms: Empowering Stakeholders Through Omnichannel Approach* (pp. 111-131). IGI Global. DOI: 10.4018/979-8-3693-3358-7.ch007

Singh, A., & Gupta, R. (2019). Intellectual property challenges in the sustainable tourism sector. *Journal of Tourism Research & Hospitality*, 8(4), 334–346. DOI: 10.35248/jtrh.2019.334

Singh, B. (2019). Profiling Public Healthcare: A Comparative Analysis Based on the Multidimensional Healthcare Management and Legal Approach. *Indian Journal of Health and Medical Law*, 2(2), 1–5.

Singh, B. (2022). COVID-19 Pandemic and Public Healthcare: Endless Downward Spiral or Solution via Rapid Legal and Health Services Implementation with Patient Monitoring Program. *Justice and Law Bulletin*, 1(1), 1–7.

Singh, B. (2022). Relevance of Agriculture-Nutrition Linkage for Human Healthcare: A Conceptual Legal Framework of Implication and Pathways. *Justice and Law Bulletin*, 1(1), 44–49.

Singh, B. (2022). Understanding Legal Frameworks Concerning Transgender Healthcare in the Age of Dynamism. *ELECTRONIC JOURNAL OF SOCIAL AND STRATEGIC STUDIES*, 3(1), 56–65. DOI: 10.47362/EJSSS.2022.3104

Singh, B. (2023). Federated Learning for Envision Future Trajectory Smart Transport System for Climate Preservation and Smart Green Planet: Insights into Global Governance and SDG-9 (Industry, Innovation and Infrastructure). *National Journal of Environmental Law*, 6(2), 6–17.

Singh, B. (2024). Legal Dynamics Lensing Metaverse Crafted for Videogame Industry and E-Sports: Phenomenological Exploration Catalyst Complexity and Future. *Journal of Intellectual Property Rights Law*, 7(1), 8–14.

Situmeang, T., & Murniarti, E. (2021). Asean Attitudes Toward Patent Protection of The Covid-19 Vaccine Versus Humanitarian Interests. Jurnal Hukum dan Peradilan, 10(2), 255-276.

Smith, A., & Jones, B. (2021). The role of IP in sustainable tourism: An empirical study. *Tourism Economics*, 27(3), 445–461. DOI: 10.1177/13548166211010582

Smith, M. K. (2003). *Issues in cultural tourism studies*. Routledge. DOI: 10.4324/9780203402825

Soliman, M., & Al Balushi, M. K. (2023). Unveiling destination evangelism through IPRtools. *ROBONOMICS: The Journal of the Automated Economy*, 4(54), 1.

Soltanifar, M., Hughes, M., & Göcke, L. (2021). *Digital entrepreneurship: Impact on business and society*. Springer Nature. DOI: 10.1007/978-3-030-53914-6

Solvoll, S., Alsos, G., & Bulanova, O. (2015). Tourism entrepreneurship–review and future directions. *Scandinavian Journal of Hospitality and Tourism, 15*(sup1), 120-137.

Sood, E., & Sharma, Y. (2024). Geographical Indicators as Tools of Economic Development. Https://Doi.Org/10.1177/00195561241248137. DOI: 10.1177/00195561241248137

Sorokina, E., Wang, Y., Fyall, A., Lugosi, P., Torres, E., & Jung, T. (2022). Constructing a smart destination framework: A destination marketing organization perspective. *Journal of Destination Marketing & Management*, 23, 100688. DOI: 10.1016/j.jdmm.2021.100688

Spinello, R. (2009). *A defense of intellectual property rights*. Edward Elgar Publishing. DOI: 10.4337/9781848449428

Springer, R. (2007). Folklore, Commercialism and Exploitation: Copyright in the Blues. *Popular Music*, 26(1), 33–45. https://www.jstor.org/stable/4500298. DOI: 10.1017/S0261143007001110

Sruthijith, K. K. (2010, November 16). Jodhpur: A faith in rhythms of Rajasthan. *The Economic Times*. https://economictimes.indiatimes.com/jodhpur-a-faith-in-rhythms-of-rajasthan/articleshow/6936423.cms?from=mdr

Steiner, C. 2024. INTELLECTUAL PROPERTY AND THE RIGHT TO CULTURE. Available at: https://www.wipo.int/edocs/mdocs/tk/en/wipo_unhchr_ip_pnl_98/wipo_unhchr_ip_pnl_98_2.pdf

Stein, M. B. (1987). Coming to Terms with the Past: The Depiction of "Volkskunde" in the Third Reich since 1945. *Journal of Folklore Research*, 24(2), 157–185.

Stim, R. (2024). *Patent, copyright & trademark: an intellectual property desk reference*. Nolo.

Stoianoff, N. P., & Wright, E. (2018). Fair Use and Traditional Cultural Expressions. In Corbett, S., & Lai, J. C. (Eds.), *Making Copyright Work for the Asian Pacific: Juxtaposing Harmonisation with Flexibility* (pp. 75–94). ANU Press. DOI: 10.22459/MCWAP.10.2018.03

Stokes, S. (2019). *Digital copyright: law and practice*. Bloomsbury publishing. DOI: 10.5040/9781509917327

Styvén, M. E., Mariani, M. M., & Strandberg, C. (2020). This is my hometown! The role of place attachment, congruity, and self-expressiveness on residents' intention to share a place brand message online. *Journal of Advertising*, 49(5), 540–556. DOI: 10.1080/00913367.2020.1810594

Süess, A. (2012). Feta and chablis-what's in a name?: systems of GI protection under the aspect of genericness (Master's thesis, University of Cape Town).

Suh, J., & MacPherson, A. (2007). The impact of geographical indication on the revitalisation of a regional economy: A case study of 'Boseong' green tea. *Area*, 39(4), 518–527. DOI: 10.1111/j.1475-4762.2007.00765.x

Supriatna, A. D., Tresnawati, D., Kurniadi, D., & Cahyana, R. (2021, March). Web-based geographic information system for mapping religious tourism object. [). IOP Publishing.]. *IOP Conference Series. Materials Science and Engineering*, 1098(3), 032071. DOI: 10.1088/1757-899X/1098/3/032071

Surono, S., Bastoni, B., Triutama, O. P., & Nisa, A. N. K. (2024). Intellectual Property Rights in Tourism Management in Cirebon. *Jurnal Toursci*, 1(4), 171–175. DOI: 10.62885/toursci.v1i4.203

Syahban, K. R., & Marsasi, E. G. (2024). Implementation of Integrated Marketing Communication Based on Purchase Intention in The Artisan Tea Marketing Program. *Jurnal Manajemen Bisnis, 11*(1), 01-13.

Syed, A. A., Gaol, F. L., Pradipto, Y. D., & Matsuo, T. (2021). Augmented and virtual reality in e-commerce—A survey. *ICIC Express Letters*, 15, 1227–1233.

Tajeddini, K., Ratten, V., & Denisa, M. (2017). Female tourism entrepreneurs in Bali, Indonesia. *Journal of Hospitality and Tourism Management*, 31, 52–58. DOI: 10.1016/j.jhtm.2016.10.004

Talukder, M. B., Kumar, S., Kaiser, F., & Mia, Md. N. (2024a). Pilgrimage Creative Tourism: A Gateway to Sustainable Development Goals in Bangladesh. In M. Hamdan, M. Anshari, N. Ahmad, & E. Ali (Eds.), *Advances in Public Policy and Administration* (pp. 285–300). IGI Global. DOI: 10.4018/979-8-3693-1742-6.ch016

Talukder, M. B., & Hossain, M. M. (2021). Prospects of Future Tourism in Bangladesh: An Evaluative Study. I-Manager's. *Journal of Management*, 15(4), 1–8. DOI: 10.26634/jmgt.15.4.17495

Tan, C. C., & Sitikarn, B. (2018). *Coffee-and-Tea based and Social Entrepreneurship-Oriented Community-based Tourism (CBT) in Northern Thailand: Contributing towards a Theory*. International Multidisciplinary Research Foundation.

Tembrevilla, G., Phillion, A., & Zeadin, M. (2024). Experiential learning in engineering education: A systematic literature review. *Journal of Engineering Education*, 113(1), 195–218. DOI: 10.1002/jee.20575

Thakkar, A. (2023, November 3). *What & Why Sensory Marketing is used to attract customers?* Infidigit. https://www.infidigit.com/blog/sensory-marketing/

Thakur, R. (2018). Cybersecurity and the digital transformation of the tourism industry: A review and research agenda. *Journal of Hospitality and Tourism Technology*, 9(3), 314–328. DOI: 10.1108/JHTT-10-2017-0106

Thaler, S. (2022, March 16). *The Northern Lights at NYC's Hudson Yards*. BizBash. https://www.bizbash.com/production-strategy/event-production-fabrication/article/22118556/the-northern-lights-at-nycs-hudson-yards

Thomas, S. (2021). Investigating interactive marketing technologies-adoption of augmented/virtual reality in the Indian context. *International Journal of Business Competition and Growth*, 7(3), 214–230. DOI: 10.1504/IJBCG.2021.116266

Tiberghien, G., Bremner, H., & Milne, S. (2017). Performance and visitors' perception of authenticity in eco-cultural tourism. *Tourism Geographies*, 19(2), 287–300. DOI: 10.1080/14616688.2017.1285958

Tien, N. H., Dung, H. T., & Tien, N. V. (2019). Branding building for Vietnam tourism industry reality and solutions. *International journal of research in marketing management and sales, 1*(2), 63-68.

Timothy, D. J., & Nyaupane, G. P. (2009). *Cultural heritage and tourism in the developing world: A regional perspective*. Routledge., DOI: 10.4324/9780203877753

Tomkowicz, R. (2013). *Intellectual Property Overlaps: Theory, Strategies, and Solutions*. Routledge. DOI: 10.4324/9780203804049

Török, Á., Jantyik, L., Maró, Z. M., & Moir, H. V. (2020). Understanding the real-world impact of geographical indications: A critical review of the empirical economic literature. *Sustainability (Basel)*, 12(22), 9434. DOI: 10.3390/su12229434

Tresiana, N., & Duadji, N. (2018). Social entrepreneur model for tourism development in Kiluan Bay. *MIMBAR, Jurnal Sosial dan Pembangunan, 34*(1), 83-92.

Turkish Patent Institute. (n.d.). Coğrafi işaretler. Retrieved from http://www.turkpatent.gov.tr

Turner, D., & Smith, L. (2022). Intellectual property protection for sustainable tourism initiatives. *Journal of Environmental Management*, 292, 112830. DOI: 10.1016/j.jenvman.2021.112830

Tussyadiah, I. P., & Wang, D. (2016). Tourism experience facilitation through mobile apps: A case study of MyTripApp. *Annals of Tourism Research*, 64, 139–152. DOI: 10.1016/j.annals.2016.03.008

Tzampazaki, M., Zografos, C., Vrochidou, E., & Papakostas, G. A. (2024). Machine Vision—Moving from Industry 4.0 to Industry 5.0. *Applied Sciences (Basel, Switzerland)*, 14(4), 1471. DOI: 10.3390/app14041471

U.S. Copyright Office. (2021). *Copyright basics*. Retrieved from https://www.copyright.gov/circs/circ01.pdf

Ubertazzi, B. (2022). *Intangible cultural heritage, sustainable development and intellectual property: international and European perspectives* (Vol. 18). Springer Nature. DOI: 10.1007/978-3-031-08104-0

United Nations World Tourism Organization. (2019). *Tourism and intellectual property rights: A guide for tourism stakeholders*. UNWTO., DOI: 10.18111/9789284421295

Upadhyaya, K. D. (1954). A General Survey of Folklore Activities in India. *Midwestern Folklore*, 4(4), 201–212.

Usakli, A., & Baloglu, S. (2011). Brand personality of tourist destinations: An application of self-congruity theory. *Tourism Management*, 32(1), 114–127. DOI: 10.1016/j.tourman.2010.06.006

USPTO. (2021). *What is a trademark?*Www.uspto.gov. https://www.uspto.gov/trademarks/basics/what-trademark#:~:text=A%20trademark%20can%20be%20any

Van Caenegem, W., Cleary, J. A., & Drahos, P. (2014). Pride and profit: Geographical indications as regional development tools in Australia. *Journal of Economic and Social Policy*, 16(1), 1–25.

Vandecandelaere, E., Arfini, F., Belletti, G., & Marescotti, A. (2009). *Linking people, places and products: A guide for promoting quality linked to geographical origin and sustainable geographical indications*. FAO. Retrieved from https://www.fao.org/3/i0500e/i0500e.pdf

Vandecandelaere, E., Teyssier, C., Barjolle, D., Fournier, S., Beucherie, O., & Jeanneaux, P. (2020). Strengthening sustainable food systems through geographical indications: Evidence from 9 worldwide case studies. Journal of Sustainability Research, 4(3). *Management*, 91, 102661.

Varela, L., Putnik, G., & Romero, F. (2024). Collaborative manufacturing and management contextualization in the Industry 4.0 based on a systematic literature review. *International Journal of Management Science and Engineering Management*, 19(1), 78–95. DOI: 10.1080/17509653.2023.2174200

Vargas-Sánchez, A., Fotiadis, A., Manuel Alcaraz, J., Castellanos-Verdugo, M., Manuel Hernández-Mogollón, J., Pierre Levy-Mangin, J., Manuel Berbel-Pineda, J., José Martínez-López, F., Riquel-Ligero, F., Miguel Rodríguez-Antón, J., Francesc Valls-Giménez, J., Abbate, T., Aguas, P., Jere Jakulin, T., Morvillo, A., Nigro, C., Allee, J., Chung-chi Wu, S., Jafari, J., & Sheldon, P. (2022). MACAO'S NON-GAMING ENTERTAINMENT, CULTURE AND CITY BRANDING. *ENLIGHTENING TOURISM. A PATHMAKING JOURNAL, 12*(1), 304–336. DOI: 10.33776/et.v12i1.5432

Vellas, F. (2016). *The international marketing of travel and tourism: A strategic approach*. Bloomsbury Publishing.

Venkatesh, D. N. (2021). *Winning with employees: Leveraging employee experience for a competitive edge*. SAGE Publishing India.

Vinaykarthik, B. C. (2022, October). Design of Artificial Intelligence (AI) based User Experience Websites for E-commerce Application and Future of Digital Marketing. In *2022 3rd International Conference on Smart Electronics and Communication (ICOSEC)* (pp. 1023-1029). IEEE.

Visković, N. R., & Komac, B. (2021). Gastronomy tourism: A brief introduction. *Acta Geographica Slovenica*, 61(1), 95–105.

Vuong, N. A., & Mai, T. T. (2023). Unveiling the Synergy: Exploring the Intersection of AI and NLP in Redefining Modern Marketing for Enhanced Consumer Engagement and Strategy Optimization. *Quarterly Journal of Emerging Technologies and Innovations*, 8(3), 103–118.

Wagner, A. and de Clippele, M.-S., 2023. Safeguarding Cultural Heritage in the Digital Era – A Critical Challenge. International Journal for the Semiotics of Law - Revue internationale de Sémiotique juridique, 36(5), pp.1915–1923. DOI: 10.1007/s11196-023-10040-z

Walia, S. K. (Ed.). (2020). *The routledge handbook of community-based tourism management: Concepts, issues & implications* (1st ed.). Routledge., DOI: 10.4324/9780429274664

Walker, M., & Nelson, P. (2023). IP protection and the green economy: Insights for eco-tourism. *Green Business Journal*, 5(2), 134–150. DOI: 10.1080/27683182.2023.2197887

Wanda George, E. (2010). Intangible cultural heritage, ownership, copyrights, and tourism. *International Journal of Culture, Tourism and Hospitality Research*, 4(4), 376–388. DOI: 10.1108/17506181011081541

Wang, J., Sun, Y., Zhang, L., Zhang, S., Feng, L., & Morrison, A. M. (2024). Effect of display methods on intentions to use virtual reality in museum tourism. *Journal of Travel Research*, 63(2), 314–334. DOI: 10.1177/00472875231164987

Wang, P. Q. (2024). Personalizing guest experience with IPRin the hotel industry: There's more to it than meets a Kiwi's eye. *Current Issues in Tourism*, •••, 1–18.

Wheeler, J. (2023). *The Digital-First Customer Experience: Seven Design Strategies from the World's Leading Brands*. Kogan Page Publishers.

Williams, A., Rodríguez Sánchez, I., & Škokić, V. (2021). Innovation, risk, and uncertainty: A study of tourism entrepreneurs. *Journal of Travel Research*, 60(2), 293–311. DOI: 10.1177/0047287519896012

Wind, Y. J., & Hays, C. F. (2016). *Beyond advertising: Creating value through all customer touchpoints*. John Wiley & Sons.

Wiśniewski, J. (2020). On the impossibility of intellectual property. *Quarterly Journal of Austrian Economics*, 23(1), 33–45. DOI: 10.35297/qjae.010051

Woodside, A. (1982). Positioning a Province Using Travel Research. *Journal of Travel Research*, 20(3), 2–6. DOI: 10.1177/004728758202000301

World Intellectual Property Organization, & World Tourism Organization. (2021). *Boosting tourism development through intellectual property.* World Intellectual Property Organization ; Madrid.

World Intellectual Property Organization. (2013). *Trademarks and sustainable development.* Retrieved from https://www.wipo.int/wipo_magazine/en/2013/04/article_0002.html

World Intellectual Property Organization. (2016). *Understanding patents.* Retrieved from https://www.wipo.int/patents/en/

World Intellectual Property Organization. (2017). *Intellectual property, traditional knowledge, and traditional cultural expressions.* Retrieved from https://www.wipo.int/tk/en/igc/

World Intellectual Property Organization. (2017). *Making a Mark: An Introduction to Trademarks for Small and Medium-Sized Enterprises.* Wipo.

World Intellectual Property Organization. (2019). *Geographical indications: An introduction.* Retrieved from https://www.wipo.int/publications/en/details.jsp?id=4222

World Intellectual Property Organization. (2020). *E-commerce and intellectual property.* Retrieved from https://www.wipo.int/ecommerce/en/

World Intellectual Property Organization. (2020). *Intellectual property and sustainable tourism development.* Retrieved from https://www.wipo.int/ip-development/en/agenda/

Xue, L. (2022). *Designing effective augmented reality platforms to enhance the consumer shopping experiences* (Doctoral dissertation, Loughborough University).

Yalin, G. (2021). An Overview of Gastronomy Tourism. TOURISM STUDIES AND SOCIAL SCIENCES, 134.

Yang, D. (2021). *Understanding and profiting from intellectual property in international business: Strategies across borders.* Springer Nature. DOI: 10.1007/978-3-030-54034-0

Yang, L. (2014). Ethnic tourism. In Jafari, J., & Xiao, H. (Eds.), *Encyclopedia of Tourism* (pp. 1–3). Springer International Publishing., DOI: 10.1007/978-3-319-01669-6_80-1

Yang, L., Kumar, R., Kaur, R., Babbar, A., Makhanshahi, G. S., Singh, A., Kumar, R., Bhowmik, A., & Alawadi, A. H. (2024). Exploring the role of computer vision in product design and development: A comprehensive review. [IJIDeM]. *International Journal on Interactive Design and Manufacturing*, 18(6), 1–48. DOI: 10.1007/s12008-024-01765-7

Yeganegi, S., Laplume, A., & Dass, P. (2021). The role of information availability: A longitudinal analysis of technology entrepreneurship. *Technological Forecasting and Social Change*, 170, 120910. DOI: 10.1016/j.techfore.2021.120910

Yen, D., Jang, J., Wei, L., Morgan, N., & Pritchard, A. (2023). Leveraging folklore and fantasy to promote small destinations: The case of Visit Wales. *Journal of Policy Research in Tourism, Leisure & Events*, 1–15. DOI: 10.1080/19407963.2023.2263860

Yıkmı, S. & Ünal, A. (2016). The importance of geographical indication in gastronomy tourism: Turkey. International Journal of Agricultural and Life Sciences- IJALS (2016), Volume 2(4) pp.73-79.

Yılmaz, G., & Tekeli, N. (2021). The Importance and Role of Digital Marketing in the Preference of Touristic Products in Turkey. *University of South Florida M3 Center Publishing, 18*(9781732127586). DOI: 10.5038/9781732127586

Yim, M. Y. C., & Park, S. Y. (2019). "I am not satisfied with my body, so I like augmented reality (AR)": Consumer responses to AR-based product presentations. *Journal of Business Research*, 100, 581–589. DOI: 10.1016/j.jbusres.2018.10.041

Yongxun, Z., & Lulu, H. (2021). Protecting Important Agricultural Heritage Systems (IAHS) by Industrial Integration Development (IID): Practices from China. *Journal of Resources and Ecology*, 12(4), 555–566. DOI: 10.5814/j.issn.1674-764x.2021.04.013

Zaki, H. O. (2022). The Impact Of Artificial Intelligence On Content Marketing. *Journal of Strategic Digital Transformation In Society*, 2(3).

Zappalaglio, A. (2021). Sui generis, bureaucratic and based on origin: a snapshot of the nature of EU Geographical Indications. In *Intellectual Property as a Complex Adaptive System*. Edward Elgar Publishing. DOI: 10.4337/9781800378384.00018

Zhang, J. (2020). A systematic review of the use of augmented reality (AR) and virtual reality (VR) in online retailing.

Zhang, Z. (2023). Digital Operational Strategies in The Post-Pandemic Era for Travel Companies: A Case Study of Ctrip. *Highlights in Business. Economics and Management*, 23, 521–525. DOI: 10.54097/h0w3ar97

Zhao, L., & Wang, Y. (2021). Protecting innovation and cultural heritage in eco-tourism: A legal perspective. *Legal Studies*, 41(4), 678–693. DOI: 10.1111/lest.12287

Zhao, R., Cao, Y., Zheng, X., & Wang, H. (2020). The innovation economy calls for proactive growth of intellectual property by various innovation carriers–A China case. *Global Transitions Proceedings*, 1(1), 23–31. DOI: 10.1016/j.gltp.2020.04.001

Zhao, X., Elahi, E., Wang, F., Xing, H., & Khalid, Z. (2024). Sustainable tourism development for traditional Chinese drama's intangible cultural heritage. *Heliyon*, 10(3), e25483. DOI: 10.1016/j.heliyon.2024.e25483 PMID: 38333833

Zhao, X., & Stiles, D. R. (2024). Stuck in Limbo: How sensemaking discrepancy over strategy-related performance leads to disjointed collaboration in an international joint venture. *Asia Pacific Journal of Management*, 41(2), 903–945. DOI: 10.1007/s10490-023-09877-6

Zhu, W., Owen, C. B., Li, H., & Lee, J. H. (2024). Personalized in-store e-commerce with the promopad: An augmented reality shopping assistant. *Electronic Journal for E-commerce Tools and Applications*, 1(3), 1–19.

About the Contributors

Ahmad Albattat, is an Associate Professor In Graduate School of Management, Post Graduate Centre, Management and Science University, Shah Alam, Selangor, Malaysia. He is a visiting Professor and external examiner in Medan Academy of Tourism (Akpar Medan). He holds a doctoral degree in Hospitality Management "Disaster and Emergency Planning and Preparedness" from University Sains Malaysia (USM). He worked as an Assistant Professor, Ammon Applied University College, Amman, Jordan. Senior Lecturer and research coordinator in School of Hospitality & Creative Arts, Management and Science University, Shah Alam, Selangor, Malaysia, and Researcher at Sustainable Tourism Research Cluster (STRC), Pulau Pinang, Malaysia. He was working for the Jordanian hospitality industry for 17 years. He has participated and presented research papers in a number of academic conferences held in Malaysia, Taiwan, Thailand, Indonesia, Sri Lanka, and Jordan. He is an active member of Scientific and Editorial Review Board on Hospitality management, hotel, tourism, events, emergency planning, disaster management, human resource for Journal of Tourism Management, Journal of Hospitality Marketing & Management (JHMM), Current Issues in Tourism (CIT), Asia-Pacific Journal of Innovation in Hospitality and Tourism (APJIHT), International Journal of Economics and Management (IJEAM), AlmaTourism, Journal of Tourism, Culture and Territorial Development, International Journal of Tourism and Sustainable Community Development. His latest works have been published in the refereed international journals, conference proceedings, books and book chapters.

Azman, N. is a lecturer in Faculties of Business Management and Professional Studies, Management and Science University, Shah Alam, Selangor, Malaysia. She holds a doctoral degree in Business Management "Consumer behavioural intention in healthy food product" from Management and Science University (MSU).. With the strong 7 years industrial experience, her particular specialization is digital marketing, big data, management, human resource, consumer behavior and marketing. She also receives Certified Marketing Professional from American Industrial Certification Institute for completing marketing professional courses. She has participated and presented research papers in several International academic conferences. International academic conferences.

Marco Valeri is Associate Professor of Organizational Behavior, Faculty of Economics, Niccolo' Cusano University, Italy. He is Lecture in Applied Organizational Behaviour, Xenophon College, UK. He is Visiting Professor at University of Information Science and Technology (UIST) St. Paul The Apostle, Macedonia. He is Adjunct Professor at Faculty of Social Sciences and Leisure Management, School of Hospitality, Tourism and Events, Taylor University, Malaysia. He is Adjunct Professor at Faculty of Economics, Lovely Professional University (LPU), Phagwara, India. He is Associate Researcher in Strategy, Magellan Research Center, School of Management, Iaelyon Business School, Jean Monet University, France. He is Honorary Associate Professor, University of Pannonia, Hungary. Ranked #7 worldwide the most productive family economics scholars according to the ranking published by Texas State University. Heâs teaching and consultancy fields include strategic management, leadership development, cross-cultural management, international hospitality management. He is member of several Editorial Boards of international tourism journals, reviewer and editor of several handbooks on entrepreneurship, tourism and hospitality management (Emerald Publishing, Springer Publishing, Routledge Publishing, Edward Publishing and IGI Global Publishing).

Zunirah Mohd Talib, currently is an academic scholar at Management and Science University (MSU) and still teaching mainly in Operation Management, Total Quality Management and Industrial management. She has been working with MSU (Management & Science University) since 2015 and become the Head of the Department of Business management and law from Oct 2015 until Dec 2019. Later in Jan 2020, she became the Dean of Faculty Business Management and Professional Studies and currently, she is a Professor at the Graduate School of Management, Post Graduate School. Before starting her career in lecturing, she became a researcher at the University of Science Malaysia (USM) and decided to involve in teaching more seriously. With experiences, she would like to share and extend her knowledge in Operation management, especially in Halal operation management, Total Quality Management and Industrial management area. She has been working with SONY Corporation, in Prai, Penang Malaysia known as SONY EMCS & SONY AUDIO from 1991 to 2002 in New System & Production Control Department and also in Human Resource Department. She also has experience working in local companies such as Infoseni Sdn Bhd, Penang and GLC Government Link Companies such as SilTerra Malaysia Sdn Bhd in Kulim, Kedah before starting her Ph.D. in Operation/ Technology Management at the School of Management at University Science Malaysia (USM). She enrolled in PhD research on Halal Orientation Strategy in 2009 and graduated in 2014. Her research mainly focuses on production and operation including Halal food companies, logistics, entrepreneurship, in Malaysia. Her first publication in 2010 appeared through Medwell Journals in the Pakistan Journal of Social Sciences, titled Conceptualizations on the Dimensions for Halal Orientation for Food Manufacturers: A Study in the Context of Malaysia, which has about 103 citations. Her experiences in the industry for 15 years exposed her a lot in hands-on activities in the production, training and management aspects. She obtained her first degree in Agricultural & Bio-System Technology (specializing in crop production and water management) from the University of Arizona, Tucson, USA in 1991 and her MBA in 2004 from at Northern University of Malaysia (UUM)

Pankaj Kr. Tyagi is an accomplished academician, researcher, and consultant. He is presently working as Professor at Chandigarh University, Mohali, India. Dr. Tyagi is an alumnus of Hemwati Nandan Bahuguna Garhwal University (Central University) and Kurukshetra University. He has over 2 decades of experience in the industry, teaching, training, consultancy, and expertise in destination management, travel process and disruptive technologies. He has published over 40 research papers in international journals indexed in the quality database and authored/edited 15 books with premium publications Like IGI-GLOBAL, Emerald Publications, CRC, Apple Academic Press and many more. He is a reviewer for many international tourism, management, and technology journals. His area of expertise is Travel Technologies, Sustainable Development Goals, Disruptive Technologies, Community Based Tourism, Meaningful Tourism, Hospitality Operations, Events and Festivals, Digital Innovation in Service Sector etc.

Nur Amalina binti Abdul Ghani holds a Bachelor of Laws (LL.B) and a Master of Laws (LL.M) in Banking Law from the International Islamic University Malaysia, and a PhD in Islamic Banking from the University of Bolton. With over a decade of experience, she has served as a legal assistant, legal partner, and senior lecturer.

S. M. Aamir Ali is presently Assistant Professor at Symbiosis Law School Pune, Symbiosis International (Deemed University), Pune. He is currently pursuing his PhD from West Bengal National University of Juridical Sciences (WBNUJS), Kolkata, and has completed his LL.M from National Law School of India University (NLSIU), Bengaluru, with a specialization in Human Rights Law. Mr Ali has been teaching across specializations in Constitutional Law, Human Rights and Criminal Law at UG and PG levels since 2019.

|NILESH ARORA - Contributing Author|Professor & Director, University School of Business, Chandigarh University, Gharuan.

Shuvasree Banerjee from Hyderabad, India presently working as a Sr.Tourism and Management Lecturer in a reputed hotel management institution placed globally for the past 6 years. I am also having a total experience of 9 yrs in the academic field. I have done my graduation in BBA in (Tourism & Hospitality) from Burdwan University, Burdwan, West Bengal. Following my PGDM in Travel & Tourism from IITTM, Bhubaneswar, under Ministry of Tourism, Govt. of India. Following with my further MBA in (Tourism & Hospitality) from Jawaharlal Nehru Technological University, Hyderabad, India. Presently pursuing last yr of my Phd in (Tourism & Hospitality) from Chandigarh University, Mohali, Chandigarh, India under the guidance of Professor Dr. Pankaj Kumar Tyagi.

Iylia Dayana Mohamed Izwan is a lecturer of Accounting at Faculty of Business Management and Professional Studies, Management and Science University (MSU). She holds Master from University Teknologi MARA and Association of Chartered Certified Accountants from Sunway College. She joined MSU since 2011. With over 10 years of experience in academia, Iylia has taught courses undergraduate, covering topics as Corporate Governance and Financial Reporting. Her research areas are accounting, corporate governance and ESG. She had published in few scholarly journals such as Asia-Pacific Management Accounting Journal and International Journal of Business and Applied Social Science.

Vipin Nadda I am currently serving as Senior Lecturer and Programme Manager (Tourism, hospitality, and Events) with University of Sunderland in London. A science graduate with MBA (Marketing), MTA (Tourism) and PhD (Tourism Management), I have more than twenty years of experience in academics and Industry. As an active researcher, I have authored and edited eight books, published more than thirty research articles, presented papers in various international conferences and published scores of book chapters. As an experienced academician, I have been Lecturing a variety of courses ranging from Sustainable tourism development, Service Marketing, International business environment to Service quality, International Tourism and Hospitality Management in the UK as well as overseas which echo my research interests as well. I am co-editor in chief for International Journal of Entrepreneurship, Management, Innovation and Development and have organised many international conferences

P.R.L. Rajavenkatesan is working as Professor of Law at VIT School of Law. He is an expert in the area of IPRs and Environmental Laws. At present, he is guiding four PhD candidates in VIT School of Law and one candidate has already been awarded PhD under his guidance. He is an external member of Doctoral Committee in other Institutions. He authored 12 books and published around 87 research papers. He has also received six research awards from VIT University. He is also active at the international level with paper presentations in conferences organised in the USA, Japan and Nepal.

Shalieza Binti Razali worked for nearly 20 years in the corporate sector before becoming a Senior Lecturer at Management and Science University (Malaysia). With her 20 years of experience in marketing, branding, and strategic communication as well as her background in corporate partnerships and international higher education, Dr. Shalieza guarantees success through cross-organizational collaboration and brand building. Dr. Shalieza is inspired to write and publish on Higher Education Internationalization, and she has completed a thesis titled The Impact of Franchise Programmes through Education Export to Malaysia's Private Higher Education Institutions. Her remarkable publishing ability, which began with corporate communication marketing collateral such as bulletins, news write-ups, annual reports, brochures, and others, aroused her interest in publication. Her extensive experience in Sales, Marketing, and Branding has led to work with Malaysian private companies and even government link companies, in addition to her exceptional experience working directly with the United Kingdom at the University of Hertfordshire.

Bassam Samir Al-Romeedy: Al-Romeedy is a motivated Associate Professor at the faculty of tourism and hotels, University of Sadat City - Egypt, and an Accredited external auditor at the National Authority for Quality Assurance of Education and Accreditation – Egypt. I also work as a market research consultant and statistical analyst. Dr. Al-Romeedy has published in premier peer-reviewed journals including Tourism Review, Journal of Tourism and Technology, Journal of Vacation Marketing, Journal of Human Resources in Hospitality & Tourism, Corporate Social Responsibility and Environmental Management, and others.

Karun Sanjaya is an Assistant Professor at Symbiosis Law School, Nagpur and a Research Scholar at VIT School of Law, Vellore Institute of Technology, Chennai, India. He specializes in the area of Intellectual Property Laws. He is a recipient of many awards including the prestigious Justice V.R. Krishna Iyer Memorial Merit Awards in the year 2019 and 2022. He has published over fifty research items and is a keen researcher in diverse areas of law including Intellectual Property Laws.

Rajeev Semwal, an accomplished academician, holds the position of Assistant Professor and Head of the Department at Amity Institute of Travel and Tourism, situated within the vibrant campus of Amity University in Greater Noida. His academic journey is marked by a Ph.D. and UGC Net in tourism, coupled with credentials including MTM, PGDTTM, B.A. (TTM), and a diploma in building design. Over the past 12 years, Dr. Semwal has made notable contributions to the industry, from community-based tourism to adventure marketing. At the Greater Noida campus, he passionately imparts knowledge, specializing in cultural heritage tourism, adventure tourism, sustainable tourism development, and strategic tourism marketing, shaping the future leaders of the tourism industry.

|Rajeev Semwal - Contributing Author|Dr. Rajeev Semwal, an accomplished academician, holds the position of Assistant Professor and Head of the Department at Amity Institute of Travel and Tourism, situated within the vibrant campus of Amity University in Greater Noida. His academic journey is marked by a Ph.D. and UGC Net in tourism, coupled with credentials including MTM, PGDTTM, B.A. (TTM), and a diploma in building design. Over the past 12 years, Dr. Semwal has made notable contributions to the industry, from community-based tourism to adventure marketing. At the Greater Noida campus, he passionately imparts knowledge, specializing in cultural heritage tourism, adventure tourism, sustainable tourism development, and strategic tourism marketing, shaping the future leaders of the tourism industry.

Amrik Singh is working as Professor in the School of Hotel Management and Tourism at Lovely Professional University, Punjab, India. He obtained his Ph.D. degree in Hotel Management from Kurukshetra University, Kurukshetra. He started his academic career at Lovely Professional University, Punjab, India in the year 2007. He has published more than 40 research papers in UGC and peer-reviewed and Scopus/Web of Science) journals. He has published 12 patents and 01 patent has been granted in the inter-disciplinary domain. Dr. Amrik Singh participated and acted as a resource person in various national and international conferences, seminars, research workshops, and industry talks. His area of research interest is accommodation management, ergonomics, green practices, human resource management in hospitality, waste management, AR VR in hospitality, etc. He is currently guiding 8Ph.D. scholars and 2 Ph.D. scholars have been awarded Ph.D.

Bhupinder Singh working as Professor at Sharda University, India. Also, Honorary Professor in University of South Wales UK and Santo Tomas University Tunja, Colombia. His areas of publications as Smart Healthcare, Medicines, fuzzy logics, artificial intelligence, robotics, machine learning, deep learning, federated learning, IoT, PV Glasses, metaverse and many more. He has 3 books, 139 paper publications, 163 paper presentations in international/national conferences and seminars, participated in more than 40 workshops/FDP's/QIP's, 25 courses from international universities of repute, organized more than 59 events with international and national academicians and industry people's, editor-in-chief and co-editor in journals, developed new courses. He has given talks at international universities, resource person in international conferences such as in Nanyang Technological University Singapore, Tashkent State University of Law Uzbekistan; KIMEP University Kazakhstan, All'ah meh Tabatabi University Iran, the Iranian Association of International Criminal law, Iran and Hague Center for International Law and Investment, The Netherlands, Northumbria University Newcastle UK,

Mohammad Badruddoza Talukder is an Associate Professor, College of Tourism and Hospitality Management, IUBAT - International University of Business Agriculture and Technology, Dhaka-1230, Bangladesh. He holds PhD in Hotel Management from Lovely Professional University, India. He has been teaching various courses in the Department of Tourism and Hospitality at various universities in Bangladesh since 2008. His research areas include tourism management, hotel management, hospitality management, food & beverage management, and accommodation management, where he has published research papers in well-known journals in Bangladesh and abroad. Mr. Talukder is one of the executive members of the Tourism Educators Association of Bangladesh. He has led training and consulting for a wide range of hospitality organizations in Bangladesh. He just became an honorary facilitator at the Bangladesh Tourism Board's Bangabandhu international tourism and hospitality training institution.

Priyanka Tyagi is a Tourism & Hospitality Skill Council (India) Certified Master Trainer & Assessor. She is also associated as Lead Assessor and Trainer with Management & Entrepreneurship and Professional Skill Council (India). She has earned Master of Tourism Administration degree from Hemwati Nandan Bahuguna Garhwal Central University, India, Master of Business Administration Degree from Maharishi Dayanand University, India and M.Phil from Madurai Kamaraj University, India. She has 14 years of experience in the industry, academics & skill-based vocational training. Ms Priyanka has published many research papers in international peer-reviewed journals and edited 4 books. She has expertise in product development, resources management, human resources practice and cultural tourism.

Index

N

R

S

T

V

www.ingramcontent.com/pod-product-compliance
Lightning Source LLC
LaVergne TN
LVHW080605300926
849162LV00005B/1049
9798369341711